CoMe aS YoU aRE

THE STORY OF NIRVANA

MicHAeL AZerRAd

MAIN STREET BOOKS

doUbLEdAY

NeW yORk

lOnDoN

ToROnTO

SydNeY

aUCklAnD

COmE
aS YOu
ARe

A MAIN STREET BOOK

PUBLISHED BY DOUBLEDAY
a division of Bantam Doubleday Dell Publishing Group, Inc.
1540 Broadway, New York, New York 10036

MAIN STREET BOOKS, DOUBLEDAY, and the portrayal of
a building with a tree are trademarks of Doubleday, a division of
Bantam Doubleday Dell Publishing Group, Inc.

Book design by Marysarah Quinn

Library of Congress Cataloging-in-Publication Data

Azerrad, Michael
    Come as you are: the story of Nirvana / Michael Azerrad. — 1 st ed.
        p.   cm.
    "A Main Street book" — T.p. verso.
1. Nirvana (Musical group)   2. Rock musicians—United States—
Biography   I. Title.
ML421.N57A9   1993
782.42166'092'2—dc20
[B}   93-19821
                                              CIP
                                              MN

Lyrics to songs by Nirvana courtesy of Hal Leonard Publishing Corporation.
Lyrics to "Damaged II" by Greg Ginn courtesy SST Records.
Lyrics to "Left of Centre" courtesy of Sloan.
"The Motorcycle Song" by Arlo Guthrie © 1967, 1969 by Appleseed Music Inc.
All Rights Reserved. Used by Permission.
All photographs by Michael Lavine by permission of Outline Press.
All photographs by Kristin Callahan by permission of London Features.

ISBN 0-385-47199-8

Printed in the United States of America

October 1993

First Edition

10 9 8 7 6 5 4 3 2 1

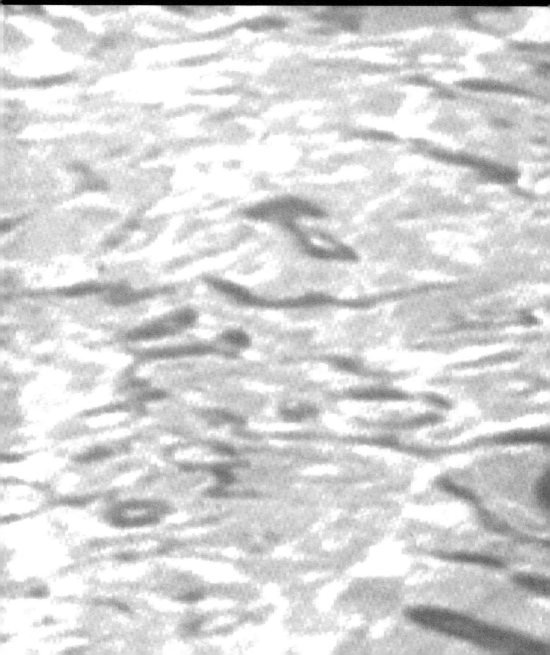

FoR JuLie

AcKNowLedgmEnTs

My deepest thanks to the following people for their assistance
and their encouragement.

Kurt & Courtney
Chris & Shelli
Dave
Chad Channing
John Silva, Bethann Buddenbaum, and Michael Meisel
Susie Tennant & Chris Swenson
Randy Wagers
Mark Kates, Rochelle Fox, Luke Wood, Dennis Dennehy, and
Chrissy Shannon at Geffen
Charles Peterson
Tracy Marander
Neil Ross
Bruce Tracy
Scott Moyers
Sarah Lazin and Laura Nolan
Ms. Burnyce Channing
Wendy O'Connor
Marysarah Quinn
Kerry Fried
Amy Finnerty
Nils Bernstein
Mark Doctrow
Beth Cohen
Matt Sweeney

No thanks to: *Lunatic Fringe* (high score: 29,715, level 40)

C>O>N>T E<N<T<S

It's April 9, 1993, at the Cow Palace in San Francisco. Eleven thousand people—grunge kids, jocks, metalheads, mainstreamers, punks, little kids with their parents, hippie-types—have come from as far away as Los Angeles and Seattle to see Nirvana's first American show in seven months, a benefit for Bosnian rape victims. Besides a seven-week club tour in late 1991, the closest most American fans had come to seeing the band in concert was their appearance on "Saturday Night Live" over a year before. So much has happened in the meantime: drug rumors, breakup rumors, lawsuits, and about five million more copies of the *Nevermind* album sold worldwide. And much *hasn't* happened—a U.S. arena tour, a new album. It's a crucial show.

The band walks out on stage. Kurt Cobain, sporting an aqua cardigan, an inside-out Captain America T-shirt and decomposing blue jeans, gives a nervous little wave to the crowd. He's dyed his hair blond for the occasion; a mop of it obscures his eyes and indeed the entire top half of his face.

From the opening chords of "Rape Me," the band plays with explosive force, salvos of sound catapulting off the stage and into the crowd—"Breed," "Blew," "Sliver," "Milk It," "Heart Shaped Box." Toward the end, they play "The Hit" and even though Kurt mangles the opening chords, the moshers on the floor go berserk. As matches and lighters are held aloft during "Lithium," everyone in this cavernous barn is reminded of exactly why they love Nirvana.

Although Chris Novoselic and Kurt are at least thirty feet apart, they move and react to each other as if they are much closer; the communication is effortless. Midway through the set, Kurt calls over to Chris, "I feel great! I could play another hour!" And they do, packing twenty-four songs in an hour and a half, including eight songs from the upcoming album. The crowd applauds the new stuff enthusiastically, especially the ferocious assault on "Scentless Apprentice" and the majestic "All Apologies," which dissolves in a haze of mantra-chant and feedback.

Eddie Vedder from Pearl Jam watches from the side of the stage; not far away is the Melvins' Dale Crover. Frances Bean Cobain is upstairs in her dad's dressing room with her nanny; Courtney comes down just in time to dodge a plastic bottle of mineral water that Kurt has thrown without looking. She waves at him sarcastically.

At the end of the set, Kurt, Chris, and Dave Grohl disappear behind the drum riser and pass around a cigarette as they discuss what songs to play, then return for a seven-song, half-hour encore climaxing with "Endless, Nameless," the mystery track that closes *Nevermind*. As the band accelerates the song's main riff, it becomes a trance. Kurt walks across the top of his amp stack. It's not that high off the ground, but he's riveting anyway, like a potential suicide walking along the ledge of a building. The music speeds up even more. The guitars are squalling, Chris has unstrapped his bass and is waving it in front of his amp; Dave Grohl flails with precise abandon. As the music peaks, Kurt falls hard onto the drum set and drums and cymbal stands fall outward, like a carnivorous flower opening up and swallowing its prey. Show over.

People ask each other if he's all right. It's not showmanship. If it were, they'd put down padding first. Maybe it's a geek stunt, like the kid in grade school who would make his nose bleed and smear the blood on his face so the bully would leave him alone, a case of "I'll hurt myself before you can" from a guy who opened the set with a song called "Rape Me." Perhaps it's an homage to two of Kurt's favorite stuntmen, Evel Knievel and Iggy Pop. Or is it that he's so jazzed up from the music that he's impervious to all physical harm, like a psyched-up swami who can walk across hot coals? Judging by the audience, all agog and aglow, that last explanation seems to fit the best.

Afterward, the entire entourage celebrates the triumphant gig in the courtyard of the trendy Phoenix motel—except for Kurt and Courtney, who have retired to a fancy hotel across town. The Phoenix, Courtney says, holds some bad memories for them. And besides, the bath towels are too small. Even without them, the place has turned into a little Nirvana village. Dave and his mother and sister are there, Chris and Shelli are there, so is smiling Ernie Bailey the guitar tech and his wife Brenda, tour manager Alex Macleod, lighting designer Suzanne Sasic, folks from Gold Mountain Management, Mark Kates from Geffen/DGC, even members of Seattle's Love Battery who happen to be in town. Chris goes down to the grocery store and gets a couple of armloads of beer and the party lasts into the wee hours of the morning.

The next day, Chris makes a pilgrimage to the fabled Beat landmark, the City Lights Bookstore. He goes outside to a cash machine, where a homeless man announces, "Good news, people! We are pleased to accept twenty-dollar bills for Easter!" Chris gives him one.

The Cow Palace show was a victory. It seemed like a confirmation that a punk rock band that hit the mainstream jackpot wasn't a fluke after all. That victory had repercussions for the band, all the bands like them, and maybe even the culture at large. As Sonic Youth's Kim Gordon said recently, "When a band like Nirvana comes out of the underground, it really expresses something that's going on in the culture and it's not a commodity."

What was going on in the culture was reflected not only in the sound of the music, but just as importantly, how it became popular. The punk rock phenomenon started practically the moment Johnny Ramone first put pick to string, inspiring a decade and a half's worth of hard work by countless bands, independent record labels, radio stations, magazines and fanzines, and small record stores that struggled to create some sort of alternative to the bland, condescending corporate rock which was being foisted on the public by the cynical major labels, the impersonal arenas, the mega-sized record stores, the lowest-common-denominator radio stations and the star-struck national rock magazines.

Galvanized by the punk rock revolution, the music underground formed a worldwide network, a shadow music industry. It grew and grew until not even the best efforts of the baby boomer-controlled music industry could hold it back. R.E.M. was the first explosion, Jane's Addiction came later, and then came the Big Bang: *Nevermind* has sold over eight million copies worldwide to date. It defied the best efforts of the likes of Michael Jackson, U2, and Guns n' Roses, and hit #1 on the Billboard album chart.

After this, everything was either pre- or post-Nirvana. Radio and press started taking the "alternative" thing seriously. Suddenly, record labels were rethinking their strategy. Instead of heavily promoted lightweight pop that would sell well at first and never be heard from again, they decided to start signing acts with long-term potential. And they were promoting them from a more grass-roots level, instead of throwing money at them until they started selling. This was an imitation of the way Nirvana broke—a small core group of grass-roots media and music fans whose valuable word of mouth expanded the group's base little by little at first, and then by leaps and bounds. Minimum hype, just good music.

The investigative zeal required in order to make one's way through the morass of independent music was in effect a rebuke of herd consumerism. It was a pesky development for the major labels, who had come to depend on promotional dollars to make the public see their way. Independent music required independent thinking, all the way from the artists who made the music to the entrepreneurs who sold it, to the people who bought it. It's a lot harder to track down that new Calamity Jane single than it is to pick up the latest C+C Music Factory CD.

In 1990, not one rock album hit the #1 spot, prompting some industry pundits to prophesy the end of rock. The audience for the music had been systematically fragmented by radio programmers looking for the perfect demographic, and it appeared unlikely that rock fans could unite around one record in large enough numbers to put it at the top of the charts. And while rock degenerated into a blow-dried, highly processed *faux* rebellion, genres such as country and rap more directly addressed the mood and concerns of the masses. Although several other rock albums hit #1 in 1991,

Nevermind united an audience that had never been united before—the twentysomethings.

Tired of having old fogies such as Genesis and Eric Clapton or artificial creations such as Paula Abdul and Milli Vanilli rammed down their throats, the twentysomethings wanted a music of their own. Something that expressed the feelings *they* felt. A staggering number are children of divorce. They had the certain knowledge that they were the first American generation to have little hope of doing better than their parents, the generation that would suffer for the fiscal excesses of the Reagan eighties, that spent their entire sexual prime in the shadow of AIDS, that spent their childhoods having nightmares about nuclear war. They felt powerless to rescue an embattled environment and spent most of their lives with either Reagan or Bush in the White House, enduring a repressive sexual and cultural climate. And they felt helpless and inarticulate in the face of it all.

Throughout the eighties, many musicians were protesting various political and social inequities, but most of them were boomers like Don Henley, Bruce Springsteen, and Sting. And many fans saw this protest for what it essentially was: posturing, bandwagon-jumping, self-righteous self-promotion. Exactly why *did* Duran Duran appear on Live Aid, anyway? Kurt Cobain's reaction to bad times was as direct as can be, and a hell of a lot more honest. He screamed.

It's a mistake to call Kurt Cobain a spokesman for a generation, though. Bob Dylan was a spokesman for a generation. Kurt Cobain isn't supplying any answers and he's barely even asking the questions. He makes an anguished wail, reveling in negative ecstasy. And if that is the sound of teen spirit these days, so be it.

The songs on *Nevermind* might have been about alienation and apathy, but alienation and apathy about things that didn't mean much anyway. By contrast, the band has expressed strong feelings about feminism, racism, censorship, and especially homophobia. And any hint of passivity was blown away by the awesome force of the music (particularly Dave Grohl's explosive drumming) and the undeniable craft of the songwriting. This was passionate music that didn't pretend. Getting into Nirvana was empowering for a generation that had no power.

The early lives of the band members echo that of their generation. All three come from broken homes. All three (and even their previous drummer) led painfully alienated childhoods; two are high school dropouts.

Although they're considered part of the "Seattle sound," they're not a Seattle band—Kurt Cobain and Chris Novoselic come from the isolated coastal logging town of Aberdeen, Washington. The band came of age there and in nearby Olympia, home of K Records and the "naive pop" band Beat Happening, both major philosophical, if not musical, influences on Nirvana. When Kurt talks about punk rock, he doesn't mean green hair and safety-pinned nostrils. He means the do-it-yourself, be-yourself, low-tech ethos of K, Touch & Go, SST, and other fiercely indie labels. It's an effort to reclaim music from the corporate realm and bring it back to the people, to make it electronic folk music.

The members of Nirvana clearly weren't corporate employees (they've visited their label's L.A. headquarters exactly once)—the band carefully defined themselves as being outside an idealized generic mainstream as concocted by Madison Avenue, television executives, the major record labels, and Hollywood. To use a now co-opted term, Nirvana presented an alternative. When eight million people said they felt the same way, the mainstream was redefined.

Many bands in the charts made good enough music, but it was merely entertainment. This music had *resonance*. It wasn't slick, it wasn't calculated. It was exhilarating, frightening, beautiful, vicious, vague, and exultant. And not only did it rock, but you could hum along to it.

Fame was not something the band wanted or was equipped to deal with. It was a surprise. It was embarrassing to them. It was too much too soon. Chris and Dave took it hard enough, but Kurt took it harder. They lay low for much of 1992, and by the early spring of the following year, Kurt, Chris, and Dave could look back on everything that had happened with 20/20 hindsight.

Dave told his side of the story at the Laundry Room, the modest Seattle recording studio he co-owns with his old friend and drum tech Barrett Jones. Sitting on the floor amid instruments, amps, and cables, he wore a K Records button on his button-down shirt and wolfed down a toxic meal from the nearby 7-Eleven. Dave is articulate, poised well beyond his twenty-four years. He is extremely self-possessed; he harbors no delusions of grandeur, nor will he sell himself short. "He's the most well-adjusted boy I know," Kurt is fond of saying.

Dave is the least visible of the three—after all, he's not six foot seven like Chris and he's not the frontman like Kurt. Like Chris, he goes to shows in Seattle all the time, and can be found standing in the crowd just like everyone else. He's in an ideal position and he knows it—he's in one of the most successful rock bands on the planet, yet he can go out on the town for the evening and count the number of people who even recognize him on one hand.

"Chris has a heart of gold," says a family friend. "He is a good soul." Chris speaks slowly, cautiously, and although he's not a book-learned intellectual type, he's a genius of horse sense, always ready with plain-spoken perceptions that cut through the bullshit. A self-described "news junkie," he is deeply concerned and deeply knowledgeable about the situation in what was once Yugoslavia, where his family comes from.

He and his gracious and levelheaded wife Shelli own a modest house in Seattle's quiet, suburban University District. It's a communal sort of place—his sister Diana lives with them, as does tour manager Alex Macleod, a bright, pony-tailed Scot so loyal he'd probably step in front of a bullet for any member of the band. Chris's brother Robert stops by all the time. Early in March, Sonic Youth's Kim Gordon and Thurston Moore stay there while they're in town to finish up a world tour. Gordon, Moore, and Mudhoney's Mark Arm stop by after a day of buying records, one of which is an old Benny Goodman 78. As "Royal Garden Blues" emerges from the crackles and hisses of his old Victrola, Chris jokes to Moore, "Yeah, man, low-fi. This is what our new record sounds like!"

A huge jukebox dominates the living room, which is decorated with funky old thrift shop furniture, but mostly everyone—including the cats Einstein and Doris—hangs out in the kitchen. The refrigerator is stocked with organic this and preservative-free that. Recycled paper is used wherever possible. A vintage late fifties dry bar and three pinball machines—Kiss, the Addams Family, and Evel Knievel—are down in the basement, where Chris threw a party the night before the band left to record *In Utero*. Old friends like Matt Lukin from Mudhoney, Tad Doyle from TAD, and Dee Plakas from L7, new friends like Eddie Vedder, folks from Nirvana's extended family like Ernie Bailey and Geffen/DGC A&R (Artists and Repertoire) man Gary Gersh all partied into the wee hours. Shelli whipped up some vegetarian hors d'oeuvres.

Chris lives low to the ground, spends his money wisely. This is hardly a high-living rock star—the door falls off his aged tape deck.

***

After a quick preliminary interview just before Christmas of 1992, the first round of more than twenty-five hours of interviews with Kurt took place in early February. They began very late at night, after Kurt would return from rehearsals for *In Utero*, lasting until four or five in the morning. In the midst of moving into a temporary home in Seattle, Kurt padded around his and Courtney's hotel suite in mismatched pajamas, chain smoking as he peppered his story with a supremely dry and sarcastic wit. Once, he strapped on a virtual reality machine—something between a Walkman and a private psychedelic light show—that he was experimenting with to control his chronic stomach pain. Various settings supposedly stimulate memory, creativity, energy, and relaxation.

For internationally famous celebrities, Kurt and Courtney live a pretty no-frills lifestyle. There are no minders, no beefy bodyguards around them. Kurt takes a taxi around town, stops in the McDonald's for a burger, wearing a ridiculous Elmer Fudd hat pulled down on his head for a disguise. A visitor to their hotel room one night walked into the hotel, took the elevator to their floor, and walked right through their open door to find Kurt and Courtney in their pajamas and nestling together on the bed, watching a trashy Leif Garrett TV movie in the dark. "Oh hi," Courtney said, not even startled.

Kurt appears frail, rail-thin. He speaks in a sort of deadpan sing-song, abraded by too many cigarettes into a low growl. It makes him seem sad and spent, as if he's just finished a crying jag, but that's just the way he is. "Everyone thinks of me as this emotional wreck, this total negative black star—*all the time*," Kurt says. "They're always asking 'What's the matter?' And there's nothing wrong with me at all. I'm not feeling blue at all. It got to the point where I had to look at myself and figure out what people are seeing. I thought maybe I should shave my eyebrows. That might help."

Although Kurt's charisma is almost palpable, he is profoundly low-key. It helps to mentally amplify his every reaction: a distracted "hmph" translates into "Wow!"; a quick chuckle is a guffaw; a dirty look is murder.

As in photographs, his face takes on many different aspects. Sometimes he looks like an angelic boy, sometimes like a dissipated wastrel, sometimes like the guy who fixes your transmission. And sometimes, in certain lights, he even looks eerily like Axl Rose. His pale complexion is lightly veiled by scruffy stubble. An angry red patch on his scalp shows through the trademark unwashed hair, which is strawberry blond for the time being. He usually wears pajamas and is perpetually unkempt. Although the time of day has very little to do with his schedule, he always wears a watch bearing the likeness of Tom Peterson, the owner of a chain of appliance stores in Oregon.

Kurt's eyes are so extremely blue that they give his face a perpetually startled expression. In his pajamas, he gives the impression of a shell-shocked young private padding around a veteran's home. But he doesn't miss a trick.

By early March, after the recording of the band's new album, *In Utero*, Kurt, Courtney and their baby Frances moved into a largish rented house overlooking Lake Washington. At the kitchen table, Kurt would play at disemboweling a plastic anatomical model, chainsmoking the whole time. "I like the idea that you can take them all apart and just see the guts," he said. "Organs fascinate me. They work. And a lot of times they fuck up, but it's hard to believe that a person can put something as poisonous as alcohol or drugs in their system and the mechanics can take it—for a while. It's amazing they take them at all."

The place is sparsely furnished—there's beige wall-to-wall carpeting and nothing on the walls—but this is just temporary. They'll be moving to a remodeled house in a small town a few dozen miles out of Seattle later this year, and they're looking for a *pied à terre* on Seattle's hip Capitol Hill. Upstairs is the bedroom, the baby's room, and Kurt's painting room, where an easel holds a portrait of a withered, forlorn creature with skeletal arms and lifeless black eyes. In the downstairs bathroom sits an MTV Award for Best New Artist, the little silver astronaut keeping a close watch over the toilet. Frances's nanny, Jackie, has a room down in the basement. In the dining room off the kitchen, a model-car track is set up.

One room of the house is designated "the mess room." The floor is covered with old letters, notes, work tapes, records, photographs, and posters dating back to the earliest days of Kurt's musical life. Against one wall is Courtney's Buddhist chanting shrine, which she doesn't use much anymore, probably because she can't get to it through the clutter. A brown paper bag has tipped over, disgorging a score or so of plastic Colonel Sanders and Pillsbury Doughboy dolls.

Guitars are everywhere, even in the bathroom. A sonorous old Martin sits in the living room alongside a more modest instrument painted red and covered with appliqués of flowers.

Seven-month-old Frances Bean Cobain is a beautiful baby with her father's piercing blue eyes and her mother's jaw line. Although her parents seem to dote on her for the benefit of the visitor, they are clearly loving. Kurt seems a little more graceful with children than Courtney, but both do a fine job of making the usual goo-goo noises for the obvious amusement of the baby.

By all accounts, Frances did wonders for Kurt. "He looks at Frances all the time and he says, 'That's the way I used to be! That's the way I used to be!'" Courtney says. "You can't change a person, but my goal in life is to make him that happy again. But it's hard because he's always dissatisfied with stuff."

One night, Courtney quietly strums an acoustic guitar into a boom box in the living room upstairs while down in the garage next to their used Volvo, Kurt bangs on a dilapidated drum set left over from some long-forgotten tour. The garage is filled with boxes and boxes of papers, artwork, guitar guts, and years of thrift shop purchases. Two boxes are crammed with transparent plastic men, women, and even horses. Close by are an amplifier, a bass guitar, and the one thing in the house that could conceivably be called an indulgence—a Space Invaders-type video game that Kurt picked up for a couple of hundred bucks. He records high scores on it with initials like "COK" and "POO" and "FUK."

Our conversations were extremely frank. Kurt has a simple explanation for his candor. "I'm caught," he says, referring to his widely-publicized problems with heroin, "so I may as well fess up to it and try to put it in a little bit more perspective. Everyone thinks I've been a junkie for years. I was a junkie for a really small amount of time."

Furthermore, he's not worried about exploding the band's—or his own—formidable myth. Quite the opposite. "I never intended to have some kind of a mystery about us," he said to me once. "It's just that I didn't have anything to say in the beginning. Now that it's gone on long enough, there's a story, in a way. Still, every night after you leave, I think, 'God, my life is so fucking boring compared to so many people that I know.'"

Kurt is eager to set the record straight. There have been so many rumors about him, his wife, and even his infant daughter that he figures the best way he can cut his losses is just to tell exactly what happened. His tales are sometimes self-serving, full of rationalization and self-contradiction, but even his distortions are revealing about his life, his art, and the connections between the two.

CHAPTER 1

Aberdeen, Washington (pop. 16,660), is one hundred and eight long miles southwest of Seattle, way out on the remote Washington coast. Seattle has a lot of rain, but Aberdeen has more—up to seven feet a year—casting a constant, dreary pall over the town. Far from the nearest freeway, nothing comes in and rarely does anything come out.

Art and culture are best left to the snooty types over in Seattle—among the "fascinating activities" listed in a brochure from the Grays Harbor County Chamber of Commerce are bowling, chain-saw competitions, and video arcades.

A GREASY-HAIRED LITTLE REBELLIOUS KID

Route 12 into Aberdeen is bordered by an endless succession of trailer parks; beyond them are hundreds of thousands of acres of timberland, often marred by vast stubbly scars where the loggers have been clear-cutting. Coming in from the east, the first thing a visitor sees of Aberdeen is the sprawling, ugly Weyerhauser lumberyard fronting the Wishkah River, where the limbless carcasses of once-proud trees lie stacked like massacre victims. Surveying the scene from the other side of the river is a long strip of plastic fast food joints.

Logging dominates the town; or rather, it once did. Business has been falling off for years and layoffs are turning Aberdeen into a ghost town. These days, the streets downtown are slowly filling with empty or boarded-up storefronts. The only places that are doing good business are taverns like the Silver Dollar and the aptly named Pourhouse, as well as the local pawnshop, which overflows with guns, chain saws, and electric guitars. The suicide rate of Grays Harbor County is one of the highest in the nation; alcoholism is rampant and crack came to town years ago.

People hate the spotted owl—recipes for cooking the endangered creature pop up on local bumper stickers—even though decentralization of the timber industry, rising labor costs, and automation are really what's putting people out of work. One of the biggest mills in town used to employ scores of workers and now it has five: four men and a laser-guided computerized cutting machine.

One of the biggest growth industries in the county is the cultivation of marijuana and psychedelic mushrooms, which people grow in order to supplement their meager or nonexistent incomes.

Things didn't used to be so rough. Aberdeen was once a bustling seaport where sailors stopped off for rest, food, and some rented female companionship. Fact is, the town was once one big whorehouse, centered on the notorious Hume Street (which the town fathers renamed State Street in the fifties to try to bury the memories). Later, the town became a railroad terminus and the home of dozens of sawmills and logging operations. Aberdeen teemed with single young men making plenty of money in the wood industry and prostitution thrived, with as many as fifty bordellos ("women's boardinghouses," they were called) in the downtown area at one point. Prostitution lasted as long as the late fifties, when a police crackdown finally put an end to it. Some say Aberdeen's unsavory past gives its residents an inferiority complex.

This is where Kurt Donald Cobain was born on February 20, 1967, to Wendy Cobain, a homemaker, and her husband Donald, a mechanic at the Chevron station in town. The young family started out in a rental house in nearby Hoquiam, then moved to Aberdeen when Kurt was six months old.

Kurt grew up not knowing where his family name came from. His maternal grandfather is German, but that's all he knew. Only recently did he discover that his father's side of the family is full-blooded Irish, and that Cobain is a corruption of the name Coburn.

Although the Cobains were of humble means, life started out very well for their golden-haired son. "My mom was always physically affectionate with me," says Kurt. "We always kissed good-bye and hugged. It was really cool. I'm surprised to find out that so many families aren't that way. Those were pretty blissful times."

Kurt's sister Kim was born three years after he was, but Kurt and his mother had already established a tight bond. "There's nothing like your first-born—nothing," says Wendy, now remarried and still living in the same house in Aberdeen with her husband and eight-year-old daughter. "No child even comes close to that. I was totaled out on him. My every waking hour was for him."

Kurt was obviously a bright child. "I remember calling my mother," Wendy recalls, "and telling her it kind of scared me because he had perceptions like I've never seen a small child have."

Kurt just before his second birthday.

Kurt had started showing an interest in music when he was two, which was not surprising since his mother's side of the family was very musical—Wendy's brother Chuck played in a rock and roll band, her sister Mary played guitar, and everyone in the family had some sort of musical talent. At Christmas, they would all sing or act out skits.

Wendy's uncle changed his name from Delbert Fradenburg to Dale Arden, moved to California to become an operatic balladeer, and cut a few records in the late forties and early fifties. He became friends with actor Brian Keith (who later starred in the sixties sitcom "Family Affair") and Jay Silverheels, who played Tonto in the "Lone Ranger" TV series. So, as Wendy jokes, "this celebrity thing is nothing new to the family."

Aunt Mary gave Kurt Beatles and Monkees records when he was seven or so. She would invite Kurt over to her house to watch her band practice. A country musician who had actually recorded a single, Mary had played in bar bands around Aberdeen for years, sometimes appeared solo at the Riviera steak house, and once placed second on a local TV talent contest called "You Can Be a Star."

Mary tried to teach Kurt how to play guitar, but he didn't have the patience—in fact, it was hard to get him to sit still for anything. He had been diagnosed as hyperactive.

Like many kids of his generation, Kurt had been given the drug Ritalin, a form of speed, which counteracts hyperactivity. It kept him up until four in the morning. Sedatives made him fall asleep in school. Finally, they tried subtracting sugar and the infamous Red Dye #2 from his diet, and it worked. It was hard for a hyperactive kid to stay away from sugar because, as Wendy puts it, "They are, like, addicted to it."

But not being able to have a candy bar hardly dampened Kurt's spirits. "He got up every day with such joy that there was another day to be had," says Wendy. "He was so enthusiastic. He would come running out of his bedroom so excited that there was another day ahead of him and he couldn't wait to find out what it was going to bring him."

"I was an extremely happy child," says Kurt. "I was constantly screaming and singing. I didn't know when to quit. I'd eventually get beaten up by kids because I'd get so excited about wanting to play. I took play very seriously. I was just really happy."

The first kid of his generation, Kurt had seven aunts and uncles on his mother's side alone who would argue over who got to baby-sit for him. Used to being the center of attention, he entertained anybody who wanted to watch. "He was so dramatic," says Wendy. "He'd throw himself down on the floor at the store for this old man because this old man would just love to have Kurt sing for him." One of Kurt's favorite records was *Alice's Restaurant* by Arlo Guthrie. Often, he'd sing Guthrie's "Motorcycle Song." "I don't want a pickle/ I just want to ride on my motorcycle/ And I don't want to die!"

His aunt Mary gave him a bass drum when he was seven. Kurt would strap it on and walk around the neighborhood wearing a hunting hat and his dad's tennis shoes, beating the drum and singing Beatles songs like "Hey Jude" and "Revolution."

Kurt didn't like it when men looked at Wendy, a very attractive woman with blond hair and pretty blue eyes. Don never seemed to care, but Kurt always got angry and jealous—"Mommy, that man's looking at you!" he'd say. Once, he even told off a policeman.

Even at age three, Kurt didn't much like policemen. When he'd spot one, he'd sing a little song. "Corn on the cops, corn on the cops! The cops are coming! They're going to kill you!" "Every time I saw a cop I'd start singing that at them and pointing at them and telling them that they were evil," says Kurt, grinning. "I had this massive thing about cops. I didn't like them at all." When he was a couple of years older, Kurt would fill 7-Up cans full of pebbles and heave them at police cars, although he never actually hit one.

That was also about the time that Kurt somehow learned how to extend his middle finger in the time-honored manner. While his mother drove around town doing errands, he'd sit in the backseat of the car and flip the bird to everyone they passed by.

By the time Kurt was in second grade, everybody had noticed how well he could draw. "After a while," says Wendy, "it kind of got crammed down his throat. Every present was a paintbrush or an easel. We kind of almost killed it for him."

Everybody thought Kurt's drawings and paintings were great. Except for him. "He would never be happy about his art," says Wendy. "He would never be satisfied with it, like typical artists are." One day around Halloween Kurt came home with a copy of the school paper. It had a drawing Kurt had done on the cover, an honor usually reserved for kids who were at least fifth-graders. Kurt was really mad about it when he came home, because he didn't think his picture was that great. "His attitude toward adults changed because of that," says Wendy. "Everybody was telling him how much they loved his art and he was never satisfied with it."

Up until third grade, Kurt wanted to be a rock star—he'd play Beatles records and mime along with his little plastic guitar. Then, for a long time, he wanted to be a stuntman. "I liked to play outside, catch snakes, jump my bicycle off the roof," he recalls. "Evel Knievel was my only idol." Once, he took all the bedding and pillows out of the house, put it on the deck, and jumped onto it from the roof; another time, he took a piece of metal, duct-taped it to his chest, and put a bunch of firecrackers on it and lit them.

Sometimes Kurt would visit Uncle Chuck, Wendy's brother, who played in a band. Chuck had built speakers for his basement studio that were so big he couldn't get them out of the room. He'd put Kurt downstairs, give him a microphone, and roll some tape. Wendy still has a tape he made when he was four or so. Kurt sings and then, when he thinks no one's listening, he starts saying dirty words. "Poo-doo," he says. "*Poo-doo!*"

Don and Wendy got Kurt a little Mickey Mouse drum set. "I kind of pushed drums on him because *I* wanted to be a drummer," Wendy admits. "But my mother thought that was *so* unfeminine, so she never let me play." Kurt didn't need to be pushed—as soon as he could sit up and hold things, he had been banging on pots and pans. He thrashed his Mickey Mouse drum set every day after school until it was broken.

Although it wasn't in the best section of Aberdeen—in fact, the neighborhood is quite run down—the Cobain home was always the nicest on the block. Don kept it in tip-top shape, installing the wall-to-wall carpeting, the fake-brick fireplace, the imitation-wood paneling. "It was white trash posing as middle class," Kurt says of his upbringing.

Wendy came from a family that was hardly well-to-do, but her mother always made sure that her children looked like they had a lot more than they did. Wendy was the same way. Every morning, she would diligently feather Kurt's hair for that Shaun Cassidy look, make sure he brushed his teeth, and dress him in the nicest clothes they could afford, and he would trudge off to school in his waf-flestomper hiking boots. She even made Kurt wear a sweater that he was allergic to, because it looked good on him. "Both my kids were probably the best-dressed kids in Aberdeen," says Wendy. "I made sure of that."

Wendy tried to keep her kids away from what she calls "certain friends from certain kinds of backgrounds that lived in certain situations." Kurt says she basically told him to stay away from poor kids. "My mom thought that I was better than those kids, so I picked on them every once in a while—the scummy kids, the dirty kids," says Kurt. "I just remember there were a couple of kids that stunk like pee all the time and I would bully them around and get in fights with them. By fourth grade I realized that these kids are probably cooler than the higher class children, more down to earth, down to the dirt." Later on, Kurt's unwashed hair, ever-present stubble, and tattered wardrobe would become world-famous trademarks.

Kurt started taking drum lessons in third grade. "Ever since I can remember, since I was a little kid," says Kurt, "I wanted to be Ringo Starr. But I wanted to be John Lennon playing drums." Kurt played in the school band in grade school, though he never learned how to read music—he'd just wait for the kid in the first chair to learn the song and then copy what he was doing.

By the Christmas of 1974, when he was seven, Kurt got the idea that his mom thought he was a problem child. "The only thing I really wanted that year was a five-dollar Starsky and Hutch gun," Kurt says. "I got a lump of coal instead."

Kurt says he was ambidextrous, but his father tried to force him to use his right hand, fearing Kurt would have problems later in life as a lefty. He became a lefty anyway.

For most of his life, Kurt has been plagued by one health problem or another. Besides his hyperactivity, he's always suffered from chronic bronchitis. In eighth grade, Kurt was diagnosed with a minor case of scoliosis, or curvature of the spine. As time went by, the weight of his guitar actually made the curvature worse. If he had been right-handed, he says, it would have corrected the problem.

In 1975, when Kurt was eight, his parents divorced. Wendy says she divorced Don because he simply wasn't around very much—he was always off playing basketball or baseball, coaching teams or referees. In retrospect, she wonders if she ever really loved him. Don bitterly opposed the divorce. Both Wendy and Don admit the kids were later used in a war between their parents.

Kurt took the divorce and its aftermath very hard. "It just destroyed his life," says Wendy. "He changed completely. I think he was ashamed. And he became very inward—he just held everything. He became real shy.

"I think he's *still* suffering," she adds.

Instead of the sunny, outgoing kid Kurt once was, "He became real sullen," Wendy says, "kind of mad and always frowning and ridiculing." On the wall in his bedroom, Kurt wrote, "I hate Mom, I hate Dad, Dad hates Mom, Mom hates Dad, it simply makes you want to be sad." A few feet over he drew caricatures of Wendy and Don along with the words "Dad sucks" and "Mom sucks." Below he drew a brain with a big question mark over it. The drawings are still there to this day, along with some nifty Led Zeppelin and Iron Maiden logos that he drew (he denies he made them, but sisters don't lie).

Kurt was like a lot of kids of his generation—in fact, everyone who has ever been in Nirvana (but one) has come from a broken home. The divorce rate skyrocketed in the mid-seventies, more than doubling in ten years. The children of these broken marriages didn't have a world war or a Depression to contend with. They just didn't have a family. Consequently, their battles were private.

Kurt says it was a like a light went out in him, a light he's been trying to recapture ever since. "I just remember all of a sudden not being the same person, feeling like I wasn't worthy anymore," he says. "I didn't feel like I deserved to be hanging out with other kids, because they had parents and I didn't anymore, I guess."

"I was just pissed off at my parents for not being able to deal with their problems," he continues. "Throughout most of my childhood, after the divorce, I was kind of ashamed of my parents."

But Kurt had begun to feel like an outsider even before the divorce. "I didn't have anything in common with my dad especially," says Kurt. "He wanted me to be in sports and I didn't like sports and I was artistic and he just didn't appreciate that type of thing, so I just always felt ashamed. I just couldn't understand how I was a product of my parents because they weren't artistic and I was. I liked music and they didn't. Subconsciously, maybe I thought I was adopted—ever since that episode of the 'Partridge Family' when Danny thought he was adopted. I really related to that."

Kurt's creativity and intelligence—and the early realization that he was an artist—compounded the problem. "Until I was about ten or eleven, I didn't realize that I was different from the other kids at school," he says. "I started to realize that I was more interested in drawing and listening to music, more so than the other kids. It just slowly grew on me and I started to realize that. So by the time I was twelve I was fully withdrawn." Convinced he'd never find anyone like himself, he simply stopped trying to make friends.

"This town—if he would have been anywhere else he would have been fine," says Wendy. "But this town is just exactly like Peyton Place. Everybody is watching everyone and judging and they have their little slots they like everyone to stay in and he didn't."

Kurt lived with his mother for a year after the divorce. But he didn't like her new boyfriend, whom he calls a "a mean huge wife-beater." At first, Wendy attributed Kurt's dislike of her boyfriend to mere jealousy. Five years later, she realized her boyfriend was "a little nuts"—a paranoid schizophrenic, in fact. Kurt was extremely unhappy and would take out his anger on everyone from Wendy to his baby-sitters, whom he would usually lock out of the house. Wendy couldn't control him anymore, so she sent him to live with Don at his trailer home in Montesano, an even smaller logging community about twenty miles east of Aberdeen.

Don's place wasn't a mobile home, but a prefabricated house that is towed in sections behind a truck to a trailer park and assembled. "It wasn't one of the more luxurious ones—the double-wide ones that the *rich* white trash got to live in," Kurt says.

At first it was great. Don bought Kurt a minibike and they did things together like go to the beach for the weekend or go camping.

"He had everything," says Don. "He had it made. He had the run of the whole house, he had a motorcycle, he got to do whatever *he* wanted to do, we were always doing stuff. But then when two other kids and a new mother comes in..."

Don Cobain.

Don once offhandedly told Kurt that he'd never get married again. He soon remarried in February of 1978. His new wife brought along her two kids, and they all moved into a proper house in Montesano. Kurt didn't get along with his new family at all, especially his new stepmom. "Still, to this day, I can't think of a faker person," he says. "She's one of the most nicest people," Don protests. "Treated him perfect, tried stuff, she got him jobs and tried to cope with everything but it was just screwing up the whole family, just the way he was acting and things that he was doing—and not doing."

Kurt skipped school and refused to do household chores. Don says he didn't even show up for the table-bussing job he arranged for him. He began picking on his younger stepbrother and didn't like his stepsister much, either—even though she was four years younger than Kurt, she was assigned to baby-sit for him when their parents went out.

Then he noticed that his dad started to buy lots of toys for his stepsister and brother. While he skulked around in his basement room, they would go out to the mall and come back with a Starhorse or a Tonka truck.

"I tried to do everything to make him feel wanted, to be part of the family and everything," says Don, who maintains he got legal custody of Kurt just to make him feel more a part of the family. "But he just didn't want to be there and wanted to be with his mom and she didn't want him. And then here she is the goody-goody and I'm the big bad guy."

But there may be more to it than that. "I'm emotional at times, but other times I'm not and I just don't know how to express myself," Don admits. "Sometimes my smart-ass stuff hurts people's feelings. I'm not trying to hurt somebody's feelings but I don't know I'm doing it, I guess." Maybe something like that happened with Kurt. "Maybe," says Don. "Definitely."

Oddly, Don seems to have genuine amnesia about his years with Kurt. Although he comes across as a sweet and simple man these days, the strain of the divorce may have brought out a darker side. "Did I rule with a strong arm?" he says. "Okay, my wife says I do. I do probably blow up before I think. And I hurt people's feelings. And I get over it, I forget about it and nobody else does. Yeah, my dad, he beat me with a belt and stuff, give me a black eye and stuff, but I don't know, I spanked him with a belt, yes."

"Everything that Kurt did was a reflection on Don," says Wendy. "If he was bad at a baseball game, he would be just infuriated after that game to the point where he'd just humiliate Kurt. He would never allow Kurt to be a little kid. He wanted him to be a little adult and be perfectly behaved, never do anything wrong. He would knuckle-rap Kurt and call him a dummy. He'd just get irritated really quickly and—whack, over the head. My mom says she remembers a time when he actually threw Kurt clear across the room when he was like six." Don says he doesn't remember any of this.

"It's called 'denial,'" Wendy replies.

After the divorce, Don had begun working at Mayer Brothers, a logging company, as a tallyman. "Basically," says Kurt, "he just walked around all day and counted logs.

"His idea of a father-and-son day out would be to take me out to work on Saturdays and Sundays," Kurt continues. "I would sit in his office while he went and counted logs. It's really a quite exciting weekend." In his dad's office, Kurt would draw pictures and make prank phone calls. Sometimes he'd go out into the warehouse and play on top of the stacks of two-by-fours. After all that excitement, he would get into his dad's van and listen to Queen's *News of the World* over and over again on the eight-track. Sometimes he'd listen so long that he'd drain the battery and they'd have to find someone to jump-start the engine.

Don used to run around with the jock crowd in high school, but he never excelled in sports, perhaps because he was small for his age. Don's father expected a lot from him, but he just couldn't compete. Some believe that's why Don pushed Kurt into sports.

Don got Kurt to join the junior high wrestling team. Kurt hated the grueling practices and worse yet, having to hang out with jocks.

"I hated it—every second of it," says Kurt. "I just fucking hated it." He'd come home in the evening from practice, "and there'd be this disgusting, shriveled-up, dry meal that my stepmom had cooked with a lot of love and preparation and it had been sitting there since dinnertime and the oven on low heat and everything was totally dried up and awful. She was the worst cook."

Nevertheless, Kurt says he did pretty well at wrestling, basically because he could vent his anger on the mat. But on the day of a big championship match, Kurt decided to get back at his dad. He and his opponent walked onto the mat and got in position while Don sat in the bleachers, rooting for his son. "I was down on my hands and knees and I looked up at my dad and smiled and I waited for the whistle to blow," says Kurt, "just staring straight into his face and then I just instantly clammed up—I put my arms together and let the guy pin me. You should have seen the look on his face. He actually walked out halfway through the match because I did it like four times in a row." Don doesn't remember that episode either, but Kurt says the incident resulted in one of the times he had to move out of the house and live with an aunt and uncle.

Don also took Kurt hunting once, but once they got to the woods, Kurt refused to go with the hunting party. He spent the whole day, from dawn to dusk, in the truck. "Now that I look back on it," Kurt says, "I know I had the sense that killing animals is wrong, especially for sport. I didn't understand that at the time. I just knew that I didn't want to be there."

Meanwhile, Kurt began to discover other kinds of rock music besides just the Beatles and the Monkees. Don had begun to develop a pretty serious record collection after someone talked him into joining the Columbia House record and tape club. Every month, records by bands like Aerosmith, Led Zeppelin, Black Sabbath, and Kiss would come in the mail. Don never got around to opening them, but after a few months, Kurt did.

Kurt had begun hanging out with a bunch of guys who sported pukka shells and feathered hair and Kiss T-shirts. "They were way older than me—they must have been in junior high," says Kurt. "They were smoking pot and I just thought they were cooler than my geeky fourth-grade friends who watched 'Happy Days.' I just let them come over to my house and eat my food, just to have friends." These stoner guys soon noticed Don's awesome record collection and urged Kurt to play the records. "After they turned me on to that music," says Kurt, "I started turning into a little stoner kid."

"He never came out and said anything, even in his early years, about what was really bothering him or what he wanted," says Don. "He's like me—don't say anything and maybe it'll disappear or something. And don't explain. You just bottle it all up and it all comes out at one time."

"He got married and after that I was one of the last things of importance on his list," Kurt says. "He just gave up because he was convinced that my mom had brainwashed me. That's a real pathetic weak thing to base your son's existence on."

"I don't really think of my dad as a macho jerk," Kurt says. "He isn't half as extreme as a lot of fathers I've seen." So exactly what is Kurt's beef with his father? "I don't even know," he confesses. "I wish I could remember more. I never felt like I really had a father. I've never had a father figure who I could share things with."

Ultimately, Don couldn't deal with his son either, so Kurt was shuffled through the family, eventually living with three different sets of aunts and uncles, as well as his grandparents on his father's side. He moved at least two times a year between Montesano and Aberdeen, switching high schools as well.

Wendy knew she should take Kurt back, but she had been going through her own traumas—she had finally gotten rid of the paranoid schizophrenic, who had mentally and physically abused her, even putting her in the emergency room at one point. She had since lost her job and asked her brother Chuck, the musician, to take care of Kurt.

For Kurt's fourteenth birthday, Chuck told Kurt he could either have a bicycle or a guitar. Kurt took the guitar, a secondhand electric that barely played, and a beat-up little ten-watt amp. "I don't think it was even a Harmony," Kurt says of the guitar. "I think it was a Sears." He dropped the drums and took guitar lessons for a week or so, just long enough to learn how to play AC/DC's "Back in Black." "That's pretty much the 'Louie, Louie' chords," says Kurt, "and that's all you need to know." After that, he started writing his own songs. His guitar teacher, Warren Mason (who played in a band with Chuck), remembers Kurt as "a quiet, little nice kid." Kurt vehemently denies it, but Mason says he really wanted to learn how to play "Stairway to Heaven."

Kurt found Aberdeen intimidating. Compared to Montesano, Aberdeen was like the big city. "I just thought these kids were a higher class of people and I wasn't quite worthy of being in their group," he says.

In class, he'd read S. E. Hinton books like *Rumblefish* and *The*

Outsiders and avoided speaking to anybody. He says he didn't make a single friend that year. Instead, he'd come home every day and play guitar until it was time for bed. He already knew how to play "Back in Black" and he figured out a few more covers—the Cars' "My Best Friend's Girl," "Louie, Louie," and Queen's "Another One Bites the Dust."

Early in 1980, when Kurt was twelve, he and his friend Brendan had seen the B-52's on "Saturday Night Live." They got bitten by the new wave bug and Brendan got his parents to buy him some checkered Vans. Kurt's dad couldn't afford that, so Kurt just drew a checkerboard pattern on his regular sneakers.

Somewhere around the summer before tenth grade, Kurt began following the exploits of the Sex Pistols in *Creem* magazine. The idea of punk rock fascinated him. Unfortunately, the record store in Aberdeen didn't stock any punk rock records, so he didn't know what it sounded like. Alone in his room, he played what he *thought* it sounded like—"three chords and a lot of screaming," says Kurt. Not so far off the mark, as it turned out.

A few years later, he finally tracked down a "punk" record, the Clash's sprawling, eclectic three-album set, *Sandinista*, and was disappointed when it didn't sound like what he thought punk should sound like.

Kurt describes his early music as "really raunchy riff-rock." "It was like Led Zeppelin but it was raunchy and I was trying to make it as aggressive and mean as I could," he says. "I was thinking, 'What would punk rock really be like? What is it? How nasty is it?' And I would try to play as nasty as I could. Turn my little ten-watt amplifier up as loud as it could go. I just didn't have any idea what I was doing.

"It was definitely a good release," says Kurt. "I thought of it as a job. It was my mission. I knew I had to practice. As soon as I got my guitar, I just became so obsessed with it.

"I had this feeling all the time—I always knew I was doing something that was special," says Kurt. "I knew it was better, even though I couldn't prove it at the time. I knew I had something to offer and I knew eventually I would have the opportunity to show people that I could write good songs—that I could contribute something musically to rock and roll."

Kurt was desperate to take the next logical step and form a band. "I wanted to see what it was like to write a song and see what it sounded like with all the instruments at once," Kurt says. "I just wanted that. At least to practice. That's all I wanted." It would be four years before he would find a band, but it wasn't for lack of trying.

In school, he met two kids named Scott and Andy who played bass and guitar and jammed out in an abandoned meat locker way out in the woods. Kurt went out there and played one day and the three decided to form a band. Kurt agreed to leave his guitar out there because after all, he was going to come back the very next day and rehearse again. But Scott and Andy kept putting off practice and days turned into weeks, weeks into months. Kurt couldn't get his instrument back because he didn't have a car, and his mom wouldn't drive him. He made do with a right-handed guitar owned by a kid whose mother had died and was staying at the Cobains' house. "He was just this stoner guy who was really stump dumb," says Kurt. "I liked him because he was a real depressed person." Eventually, Kurt got a friend to drive him out to the woods where his guitar was and they found it in pieces—just a neck and some electronic guts. Kurt painstakingly made a new body in wood shop, only to find that he didn't know the correct proportions to make it stay in tune.

"When I was a lot younger, around seven years old, I thought for sure I could be a rock star," says Kurt. "There was no problem because I was so hyperactive and the world was in my hands—I could do anything. I knew I could be the president if I wanted to, but that was a stupid idea—I'd rather be a rock star. I didn't have any doubt. I was really into the Beatles and I didn't understand my environment, what was lying ahead, what kind of alienation I would feel as a teenager.

"I thought of Aberdeen as any other city in America," Kurt continues. "I thought they were all the same—everyone just got along and there wasn't nearly as much violence as there actually was and it would be really easy. I thought the United States was about as big as my backyard, so it would be no problem to drive all over the place and play in a rock band and be on the cover of magazines and stuff.

"But then when I started becoming this manic depressive at nine years old, I didn't look at it that way. It seemed so unrealistic."

By tenth grade, Kurt had abandoned all fantasies of fame. "I was so self-conscious at that time," he says. "I had such a small amount of esteem that I couldn't even think of actually becoming a rock star, never mind dealing with what they would expect a rock star to be. I couldn't imagine being on television or doing interviews or anything like that. Stuff like that didn't even seep into my mind at the time."

Kurt's father had made him join the Babe Ruth league baseball team. Basically, Kurt just warmed the bench, and whenever he was called to bat, he'd strike out on purpose, just so he wouldn't have to get into the game. On the bench, he hung out with a guy named Matt Lukin and they talked about Kiss and Cheap Trick. The two had met before in electronics class at Montesano High. Lukin remembers Kurt as "this greasy-haired little rebellious kid."

Lukin played bass in a local band called the Melvins, whom Kurt had actually seen rehearse one night the summer before ninth grade. Kurt's friend Brendan knew someone who knew the drummer for the Melvins and they wangled an invitation to the Melvins' practice, which was then an attic in someone's house. The Melvins had not gone punk yet, and were playing Hendrix and Who covers.

It was the first time Kurt had seen a real rock band up close and he was terrifically excited. "I'd been drinking wine all night and I was really drunk and obnoxious and I remember complimenting them about a million times," says Kurt. "I was so excited to see people my age in a band. It was so great. I was thinking, 'Wow, those guys are so lucky.'" Disgusted with this fawning little squirt, they kicked Kurt out. Still drunk, he fell down the attic ladder as he left.

In art class at Montesano High that year, Kurt again met Melvins leader Buzz Osborne, a stocky, wild-looking kid a couple of years his senior. At the time, Osborne was a big Who fan, but soon moved into punk rock. He had a photo book on the Sex Pistols, which he let Kurt borrow. Kurt was riveted. It was the first time he had gotten to see punk rock other than those precious few spreads in *Creem*. "This was the Sex Pistols in all their wildness," says Kurt, "and I got to read about them and everything. It was really cool." Soon he was drawing the Sex Pistols logo on his desk in every class and all over his Pee-Chee folder. Then he began telling anyone who would listen that he was going to start a punk rock band and that it was going to be really popular, still not having any idea what punk rock sounded like.

"He struck me as a freak," says Kurt of Osborne. "Someone who I definitely wanted to get to know." Kurt envied Osborne because he had a punk rock band that actually played sometimes in Seattle and Olympia. "And that's all I ever really wanted to do at that point," says Kurt. "I didn't have any high expectations for my music at all. I just wanted to have the chance to play in front of some people in Seattle. The thought of being in a band that was successful enough to actually go on tour was too much to ask for at that time."

The Melvins also included original drummer Mike Dillard, who was later replaced by Dale Crover. In their first punk phase, they played faster-than-light hardcore. Then, when everyone began doing the same, they played as slow as they possibly could, just to piss everybody off. And to *really* piss them off, they injected heavy metal into the mix. With 1987's seminal *Gluey Porch Treatments* album, the Melvins would become one of the founding fathers of what eventually became known as "grunge"—a new, mutant form of punk rock that absorbed heavy metal as well as proletarian seventies hard rock bands such as Kiss and Aerosmith. Their sound revolutionized the Seattle music scene, which had previously been dominated by art-rock bands.

The Melvins had already played in Seattle when Kurt first saw them, and by 1985, had appeared on the protean *Deep Six* collection along with the U-Men, Soundgarden, Green River, Malfunkshun, and Skin Yard. Except for the art-rock U-Men, all mixed varying amounts of punk, seventies-style hard rock, and proletarian heavy metal into a crude but effective musical mongrel.

Kurt would sometimes help the Melvins haul their equipment to Seattle for gigs. Aberdeen didn't have much of a musical history—although half of platinum-selling speed-metalers Metal Church hailed from the town—and a band that played in Seattle was big news.

Kurt was very unhappy about getting shuttled from relative to relative. In May of 1984, Wendy had married Pat O'Connor, a longshoreman. Pat was drinking heavily then and Wendy had her hands full with that—she didn't feel she could also deal with Kurt, but Kurt eventually convinced her to have him back. "It took months of being on the phone crying every night, trying to talk her into letting me live with her," says Kurt.

Pat went out one night and didn't come back until seven in the morning, drunk and, as Wendy puts it, "reeking of a girl." She was furious, but she still went to work at the department store. Then a couple of townies walked through the store just to taunt her. "Hey, where was Pat last night?" they cackled. Wendy got so mad that she went out and got drunk with a friend, then came home and exploded at Pat. In front of both the kids, she grabbed one of his many guns out of the closet and threatened to shoot him—but she couldn't figure out how to load the gun. Then she took all his guns—shotguns, pistols, rifles, antique guns—and dragged them down the alley, with Kim hauling a big bag of bullets, to the Wishkah River and dumped them in.

Kurt was watching from his bedroom window. Later that day, he paid a couple of kids to fish as many guns as they could find out of the river and then sold them. Kurt bought his first amplifier with the proceeds. Then he drove the guy who sold the amp to him to his pot dealer's place and the guy spent all the money on pot.

Kurt played his guitar very loud. The neighbors complained. Wendy marked up the ceiling with her broom handle. Kurt loved it when the family left to go shopping or something, because that meant he could crank. "We'd come home hoping we had windows left," says Wendy. Kurt tried to get his friends to play with him, but no one had any musical talent. He'd be very bossy and direct in his criticism. He knew exactly what he wanted.

Nobody knew he was also *singing* up there in his room. "One day," says Wendy, "Pat and I heard him. He was singing real low. He did *not* want us to hear it. We put our ears to the door and we both looked at each other, wrinkled up our noses, and said, 'Better stick to the guitar.'"

Nirvana at the Crocodile. (© Charles Peterson)

CHAPTER TWO

Around this time, Kurt first noticed Chris Novoselic at Aberdeen High. "I remember thinking he was definitely somebody I wanted to meet," says Kurt. "But we never connected." The two didn't have any classes together—Kurt occasionally saw Chris at pep assemblies, where he would sometimes participate in little skits, only to sabotage them by doing things like spontaneously singing "The Star-Spangled Banner."

"He was a hilarious person who obviously had a different sense of humor," says Kurt. "Everyone was just laughing *at* him but I was laughing *with* him, because he was basically making fools out of everybody else. He was just a really clever, funny, loud-mouth person. He was taller than anybody in school. He was *huge*. It was too bad I never got to hang out with him, because I really needed a friend during high school."

WE WERE JUST CONCERNED
WITH FUCKING AROUND

Kurt felt like an outcast, but even outcasts can find other outcasts to hang out with. Except, apparently, in Aberdeen. "I wanted to fit in somewhere, but not with the average kid, not with the popular kids at school," says Kurt. "I wanted to fit in with the geeks, but the geeks were *sub*-geeks in Aberdeen. They weren't the average geek. They weren't the type of kid who would listen to Devo. They were just usually deformed."

Kurt says there were only two other guys in school that he even *thought* about being friends with. Both were at least cool enough to be into Oingo Boingo, the manic new wave band from Los Angeles. "But they were just such geeks—total idiots," Kurt says. "They were the kind of guys who would paint their faces at football games."

High school was a teenage wasteland for Kurt, composed of three castes: the social types, the math nerds, and the stoners. The girls at Aberdeen High had noticed Kurt's dimples and blue eyes, and decided that he was cute. "They kind of liked me," says Kurt, "but I just didn't like any of those girls because they were just stupid." And because girls liked Kurt, their jock boyfriends tried to buddy up to him, but Kurt blew them off, too.

Kurt considered hanging out with the nerdy kids who were into computers and chess, but they didn't like music.

That left the stoners. "Although I hated them," he says, "they were at least into rock and roll." So Kurt donned the typical stoner jacket—the jean jacket with the fleece lining which still finds favor among today's wasted youth—and began hanging out at the traditional stoner hangout, the smoker's shed. Kurt hardly said a word to anybody; he was so quiet that occasionally, someone would ask him if he was a narc.

Kurt had fallen out of touch with the Melvins after his move back to Aberdeen. But then he met a fellow music fan named Dale Crover at the smoker's shed. Chris also knew Crover because Crover used to jam with Chris's younger brother Robert. When the Melvins needed a drummer, Chris suggested Crover, who got the gig. And since Kurt knew Crover, he began hanging out with the Melvins again.

The Melvins began practicing in an extra room at Crover's parents' house. Anywhere the Melvins rehearsed quickly turned into a seemingly permanent haven for a group of Aberdeen stoners dubbed "the cling-ons," and Crover's place was no different. Clad in bell-bottom jeans and quilted pullover jackets with zippered pockets so they could keep their pot safe, "these guys were just the most classic cartoon types of stoner metalhead kids that you could imagine," Kurt recalls. "They were so hilarious—zits, no teeth, reeking of pot."

For the cling-ons, hanging out at the Melvins' practice space was just about the only source of excitement there was. "All there was to do in Aberdeen was drink beer, smoke pot, and worship Satan," quips Crover. "There's nothing there. We watched a lot of TV."

The practice space itself was festooned with posters of Kiss, Motley Crue, and Ted Nugent, pages torn out of *Circus* magazine, and pictures of naked women with different faces pasted on them (a similar image would one day resurface on a Nirvana T-shirt). Visitors would go up the stairs of the back porch of the house, through a tiny room, and then into the rehearsal room. Buzz didn't like many people around at practice, so the cling-ons contented themselves with hanging out on the back porch while the Melvins rehearsed. The band's daily practice usually lasted three or more hours, but only because they had to stop playing every twenty minutes or so while one of the members transacted some business with the cling-ons.

Kurt auditioned to become a Melvin, but it didn't work out. "I totally botched it," Kurt says. "I was so nervous that I forgot all the songs. I literally couldn't play a note. I just stood there with my guitar and played feedback with a blushed face."

It was just as well, because Kurt was already writing and recording his own material. Matt Lukin recalls a tape Kurt made of his own songs, just guitar and vocals. "They were just some really cool songs," recalls Lukin, "especially for somebody in Aberdeen who played guitar at that point that was our age—most guys just wanted to play Judas Priest. We found it kind of odd that some kid was writing his own songs and would rather play that than Motley Crue."

And then Buzz Osborne introduced Kurt Cobain to punk rock. Osborne made a few compilation tapes, mostly Southern California bands such as Black Flag, Flipper, and MDC. The first song on the first tape was Black Flag's "Damaged II," an all-out attack of abrasive guitars and shambling but assaultive drums, brimming with buzzsaw rancor. "Damaged by you, damaged by me/ I'm confused, I'm confused/ Don't want to be confused" screamed singer Henry Rollins.

Kurt was floored. "It was like listening to something from a different planet," he says. "It took me a few days to accept it." By the end of the week, though, he was a certified, self-proclaimed punk rocker. "I sensed," says Kurt, "that it was speaking more clearly and more realistically than the average rock and roll lyric."

Soon after that, in August of 1984, Kurt, Lukin, Osborne, and others drove up to Seattle to see Black Flag play the Mountaineer Club during the *Slip It In* tour. In order to raise enough money for a ticket, Kurt sold his record collection—which at that time consisted of albums by bands such as Journey, Foreigner, and Pat Benatar—for twelve dollars. "It was really great," says Kurt of the show. "I was instantly converted."

"Becoming a punk rocker fed into my low self-esteem because it helped me realize that I don't need to become a rock star—I don't *want* to become a rock star," Kurt says. "So I was fighting this thin line—I was always on the left or right side of not caring and not wanting to and not being able to, yet kind of wanting to at the same time. Still wanting to prove myself to people. It's kind of confusing. I'm so glad that I got into punk rock at the time I did because it gave me these few years that I needed to grow up and put my values in perspective and realize what kind of person I am.

"I'm just really glad I was able to find punk rock," Kurt says. "It was really a godsend."

Osborne also showed him a way to deal with his environment. "He just had a really awesome attitude toward the average redneck," says Kurt. "I was really inspired by his attitude. It was 'Fuck with them as much as you can get away with.' We would go to jock parties and follow the big muscle men around and spit on their backs. And write dirty sayings on the walls of their houses and take the eggs out of the refrigerator and put them in the host's bed. Just try to get away with as much damage as we could."

Eventually, Kurt met a guy named Jesse Reed, who "was the only nice friend that I could find in Aberdeen." Besides a handsome kid named Myer Loftin.

Kurt met Loftin in art class and the two hit it off after discovering they were into the same music—everything from stuff like AC/DC, Aerosmith, and Led Zeppelin to punk rock. To Loftin, Kurt "looked like your average blue-jeans-and-nice-neat-haircut, kind of straight-laced kid." It really surprised him that Kurt was a musician. "He was kind of mild-mannered and quiet," says Loftin. "Very nice, very sincere." They became good friends.

What Kurt didn't know at first was that Loftin was gay. Loftin mentioned it to Kurt soon after they started hanging out. "He said, 'Well, that's okay, you're still my friend, I still love you, it's no problem,'" says Loftin. "And we hugged."

Loftin would sometimes stay over at Kurt's house and Wendy, a "cool mom," let them "party" in the house as long as they didn't drive anywhere until the next morning. Once, Wendy came home drunk and caught them smoking pot. In a futile attempt to psyche Kurt out of smoking pot, she ate his stash and got terribly stoned and sick afterward. On less eventful nights, they'd hang out in Kurt's room and Kurt would teach Loftin Led Zeppelin licks on the guitar.

But hanging out with an openly gay friend was a little more risky than Kurt had anticipated. Soon, says Kurt, "I started to realize that people were looking at me even more peculiarly than usual." He started to get harassed. It always seemed to happen in P.E. class. After everybody got dressed, somebody would inevitably call Kurt a faggot and push him up against a locker. "They felt threatened because they were naked and I was supposedly gay," says Kurt. "So they either better cover up their penises or punch me. Or both."

Life in high school just got harder for Kurt. Often, jocks would chase him on the way home from school. Sometimes they caught him. "Every day after school," says Kurt, "this one kid would hold me down in the snow and sit on my head."

"After that," says Kurt, "I started being proud of the fact that I was gay even though I wasn't. I really enjoyed the conflict. It was pretty exciting, because I almost found my identity. I was a *special* geek. I wasn't quite the punk rocker I was looking for, but at least it was better than being the *average* geek."

But the social pressures eventually became too strong and one day, Kurt walked up to Loftin, visibly upset, and told him that he couldn't hang around with him anymore. He was just getting too much abuse for being the friend of a "faggot." Loftin understood completely, and they parted ways.

Kurt had started smoking pot in ninth grade and got high every day until senior year, when he at least waited until nightfall. "I was getting so paranoid from it that I couldn't be as neurotic as I already naturally was and have it intensified by pot," Kurt says.

He did badly in school and began skipping classes in eleventh grade; moving around so much between schools was only part of the problem. "The biggest reason I flunked out of certain classes was because I hated the teachers so much," says Kurt. "There was this one guy who was a religious fanatic, an apocalyptic racist. He taught social sciences and he would do nothing but waste our time by incorporating Revelations into history. He was part of the mid-eighties Cold War scare—the Russians are coming, one of the crusaders for that Reagan mentality. Son of a bitch. I wanted to kill him every day. I used to fantasize how I'd kill him in front of the class. Because the rest of the class were completely buying it hook, line, and sinker. Totally swallowing this garbage. I couldn't believe so many people were just taking it."

Kurt was rebelling at home, too. "He didn't want to be part of the family but he wanted to live in the family house," says Wendy. "He complained about everything I asked him to do, which was very minimal." Meanwhile, Wendy acknowledges that her patience with Kurt wore thin because she was also angry at Pat for his drinking. She often transferred some of her anger to her kids.

For a few months, Kurt went out with "a stoner girl," a very pretty young woman named Jackie. According to Kurt, "she was basically using me until her boyfriend got out of jail."

One night, Kurt sneaked Jackie up to his room. Kurt was psyched—he was about to lose his virginity. They had just gotten their clothes off when Wendy suddenly burst into the room, flicked on the lights, and hissed, "Get that *slut* out of here!" Kurt ran away to a friend's house and stayed until his friend's mother called up and said, "Wendy, I think your son's living at my house."

Kurt stopped smoking pot "in an attempt to try to turn my life around." Then Kurt's stepmother called up and asked Kurt to live there again. Right away, Don said that if Kurt were to stay there, he'd have to stop doing music and start doing something constructive with his life. He somehow persuaded Kurt to pawn his guitar, then got him to take the Navy entrance exam. Kurt got a very high score and an excited local recruiter came by the house two nights in a row. But on the second night, right on the brink of signing up, Kurt went downstairs to his basement room, found some pot, smoked it, came back upstairs and said "No thanks," then packed up his stuff and left. He'd been there only a week. He wouldn't see his father again for another eight years.

To this day, Don collects all the magazine articles on Kurt that he can find. He's got a big scrapbook and a cupboard full of memorabilia. "Everything I know about Kurt," says Don Cobain, "I've read in newspapers and magazines. I got to know him that way."

Wendy sent Kurt off to live with his buddy Jesse Reed, whose parents were born-again Christians.

Kurt was broke and told a local drug dealer that he would sell him his guitar and left it at his house on good faith. After a week Kurt changed his mind, but the dealer kept the guitar anyway and Kurt went without it for months until he and Reed snatched it back.

Kurt wasn't quite the ideal house guest at the Reeds'. "I was a bad influence on Jesse," Kurt says. "I smoked pot and I didn't like to go to school." Once, Kurt spent a long phone conversation insulting Mrs. Reed, then hung up the phone only to realize she had been listening in on an extension. The final straw came one day when Kurt, locked out of the house, did the only logical thing and kicked in the door. Kurt says that Reed's father hit the roof and told him, "Kurt, we've tried really hard to turn you into a good citizen but it's just not going to work. You're a lost cause. So I'd appreciate it if you packed up your stuff and left." Mrs. Reed explained to Wendy that "Kurt was leading Jesse down the wrong road."

A special remedial program for school didn't work out. Six months before graduation, Kurt realized he had almost two years of credits to make up. Mr. Hunter, his art teacher, had entered him in some college scholarship competitions and Kurt had won two, but he still decided to drop out in May of 1985, just a few weeks short of what should have been his graduation.

Kurt had decided to make music his life's work, but Wendy felt he was wasting his time. "I told him he better get his life going," says Wendy. "If you're not going to finish school, you better get a job and get your life going, because you're not going to stay here mooching off of us."

But Kurt did continue to mooch off his mom and one day, she laid down the law. "I told him 'If this doesn't get better, if you don't get a job, you're going to be *out*,'" says Wendy. "'You're going to come home one day and you're going to find your stuff in a box.'" Sure enough, Kurt came home from hanging out at the Melvins' practice space one day to find all his belongings packed in cardboard boxes stacked on the dining room floor. "I played the 'tough love' thing," says Wendy. "That was when 'tough love' was first coming into being and I thought 'Well, I'm going to try this on him.'"

Using some of Don's child support money as a deposit, Kurt moved into an apartment in Aberdeen with Jesse Reed, paying his rent with money he earned working at a restaurant at one of the resorts on the Washington coast. He tried to enlist Reed to play with him. They would talk about guitars all the time when they first met, and Reed's dad used to play in a surf band that had actually put out some singles. When Reed mentioned that he had just got a bass guitar, Kurt got very excited. "We started playing together one night and it turns out he's one of the most musically retarded people I've ever met," says Kurt, the disappointment still plain in his voice. "He couldn't even play 'Louie, Louie.'"

Soon, Kurt got a job as a janitor back at Aberdeen High, spending most of his days scraping gum off the bottoms of desks. It was the last place on earth he wanted to be. One day, he smuggled home a sample case of shaving cream and decorated a doll with it so it looked like something out of *The Exorcist*, with the green, slimy goo hanging out of its mouth. He hung the doll by its neck in the window that overlooked the sidewalk, just to freak out the rednecks.

"I had the apartment decorated in typical punk rock fashion with baby dolls hanging by their necks with blood all over them," says Kurt. "There was beer and puke and blood all over the carpet, garbage stacked up for months. I never did do the dishes. Jesse and I cooked food for about a week and then put all our greasy hamburger dishes in the sink and filled it up full of water and it sat there for the entire five months I was there." People would party at Kurt's place all the time and the bash would invariably peak with an all-out shaving cream war.

While hanging out at the Melvins' practice space, Chris Novoselic and Kurt had struck up a friendship. Chris mentioned that he played guitar and they would hang out and listen to music, drink, and make little movies with Chris's super-8 camera. Sometimes Chris's girl-friend Shelli would come over to the apartment and party, too. They were outcasts and weirdos, but at least they were outcasts and weirdos together. "We all had so much in common," Shelli recalls. "It was like us against everybody else. It was great to have our own circle and we were really close-knit and nothing bugged us. If one person would do something, we wouldn't hold grudges and we were less jaded and more accepting of other things. It was really fun."

After three months, Jesse Reed moved out to join the Navy.

One day, Kurt was acid tripping with a friend who had come over to Kurt's place on a scooter. When the friend went downstairs to get something from his scooter, Kurt's redneck neighbor began beating up his friend because he had parked the scooter on his property. Kurt heard the commotion and dashed downstairs as his friend ran away. The neighbor settled for Kurt instead, eventually pushing Kurt into his apartment and punching and manhandling him for two hours like a cat playing with a mouse.

Eventually he stopped punching Kurt and sat down to rest. Then he looked around the room and noticed the mutilated Barbie dolls and the paintings of the three-headed babies and the graffiti and the garbage. And a flicker of fear and confusion crossed his face. "He started asking me questions," says Kurt. "Why did I do all that stuff to my room?" He started to shove Kurt around again and Kurt screamed until the landlady hollered upstairs that she was going to call the police. The bully ran away. Eventually the police came, but they advised Kurt not to antagonize his neighbor by pressing charges.

Kurt got his revenge. For a month afterward, his friends would come over and pound on the neighbor's walls and scream obscenities and death threats while the bully cowered in his apartment. Kurt says he left little presents on his doorstep, like a six-pack of beer with acid in it or a painting of a redneck hanging from a tree.

Kurt stayed on for a couple of months after Reed left. At first he could sweet-talk the landlady into letting him pay his rent late, but she began to notice the condition of the apartment. Kurt's friends would write all over the walls in the stairway. The apartment itself was a shambles.

Kurt couldn't keep up with the rent and eventually moved out in the late fall of 1985, owing several months' rent. Unemployed and virtually penniless, he passed the time that winter by hanging out in the library reading books and writing poetry. At the end of the day, he'd buy a six-pack of beer and bring it over to a friend's house, where they would drink and eventually Kurt would crash on the couch. Other times, he'd sleep in a cardboard box on Dale Crover's porch, Chris and Shelli's van, or sneak back into his mother's house while she was at work and crawl up into the attic or sleep on the deck of the house overnight. And sometimes he'd sleep under the North Aberdeen Bridge, which crosses the Wishkah River near Wendy's house.

As a single male, Kurt qualified for forty dollars' worth of food stamps a month, but he rarely bought food with them. Instead, he and his friends would fan out around town and buy Jolly Rancher penny candies with the food stamps and use the change to buy a case of beer. The operation was an entire day's work.

He was rather proud of himself for being able to survive without having to have a job or a home. His only worries were being able to steal food, catch fish from the river, and get food stamps. And bum the occasional macaroni and cheese from his friends. "I was just living out the Aberdeen fantasy version of being a punk rocker," says Kurt. "It was really easy. It was nothing compared to what most kids are subjected to after they run away to the big city. There was no threat of danger, ever." Kurt would have moved to Seattle, but he was too intimidated by the big city to do it alone—he'd barely been out of the Aberdeen-Montesano area—and nobody else in Aberdeen was brave enough to make the move.

Sometimes he'd stop by Wendy's house and she'd make him lunch. "For my guilt over letting Kurt go and live with his dad," says Wendy, "I have always pampered Kurt. He would come to visit— 'You want some lunch?' Fix, fix, fix. Because I was guilty, I was feeling horribly guilty."

Wendy became pregnant and was feeling depressed about what had become of Kurt. "I've really screwed up my first kid, so what am I doing having another one?" she remembers thinking to herself.

"And he came home at one point when I was very pregnant and I was crying about it," she says. "He asked me what was the matter and I told him I felt so awful having one in the oven and one out on the streets and he just knelt down and put his arms around me and said he was doing fine and not to worry about him and that he was going to do just fine."

That winter, Kurt got together with Dale Crover on bass and Greg Hokanson on drums and began rehearsing some of his material. Once, the trio, which Kurt dubbed Fecal Matter, opened for the Melvins at the Spot Tavern, a beach bar in Moclips, a remote little town on the Washington coast. After a while, they ditched Hokanson, whom they didn't like much anyway. The two began rehearsing intensively in preparation for recording a demo tape. With Matt Lukin behind the wheel of the trusty blue Impala, they set out for the Seattle home of Kurt's aunt Mary, the musician, who had a four-track tape recorder.

Mary was taken aback by the aggressiveness of Kurt's vocals. "She didn't have any idea that I was such an angry person," says Kurt. He recorded the guitars directly into the tape machine, a classic low-budget punk rock technique that he used again years later on *Nevermind*'s "Territorial Pissings." They recorded seven tracks with titles like "Sound of Dentage," "Bambi Slaughter" and "Laminated Effect," which sounds like a cross between *Nevermind*'s "Stay Away" and the MTV theme, as well as a slowed-down, instrumental version of "Downer," which would later appear on the *Bleach* album. The Fecal Matter tape contained some of the ingredients that would distinguish Kurt's later music—mainly the ultra-heavy riffing sparked by an ear for the hook, but it also had thrashworthy tempos and a gnarled sense of song structure as reminiscent of the Melvins as it is of Metallica. There were not yet any strong melodies to speak of and Kurt's vocals range from a gruff bark to a blood-curdling howl.

Later, Kurt rehearsed the Fecal Matter songs for a while with Buzz Osborne on bass and former Melvins drummer Mike Dillard, but then Dillard lost interest and the project evaporated completely when, as Osborne remembers it, "Kurt got disgusted with it because I wouldn't buy a bass system and so he said that I wasn't dedicated enough."

Kurt had met a hardcore partier named Steve Shillinger at Aberdeen High, where his father Lamont was (and still is) an English teacher. Shillinger had first noticed Kurt because he had written "Motorhead" on his Pee-Chee folder. Shillinger remembers tapes

Kurt would make of his music—"really cheesy heavy metal songs," as he recalls—with titles like "Suicide Samurai." The first time Shillinger and Kurt made plans to hang out together—at a Metal Church concert—Shillinger ditched him because "there wasn't enough booze to go around and I didn't know him that well."

Shillinger's friends had worn out their welcome with his parents, so when Kurt needed a place to stay, he befriended Shillinger's brother Eric. The Shillingers had five sons and one daughter, so another mouth to feed wasn't a big deal. Kurt wound up staying there for about eight months, beginning late that winter of 1985, and faithfully did his chores just like everyone else.

Eric also played guitar, and Steve Shillinger swears that Eric and Kurt would plug their guitars into the family stereo and play a particularly tasty section of Iron Maiden's "Rhyme of the Ancient Mariner." Both Eric and Kurt totally deny this, but as Shillinger says, "People often deny their past."

The Shillingers had taken in several "strays" over the years, and usually a day or two later, a concerned parent would call the house and ask whether the kid was there. Not this time. "We didn't hear word one from Kurt's mom the whole time he was there," says Lamont Shillinger.

That summer, Kurt intensified his long career as a graffitist. He'd been a vandal ever since he started getting drunk in seventh grade, but this summer's work was, as Kurt says, "the focused statement." He'd play the Bad Brains' *Rock for Light* album over and over by day, then drink and eat acid by night throughout that summer. He, Osborne, Steve Shillinger, and others started with marker pens, prowling the alleys behind the main streets of Aberdeen, writing provocative things like "ABORT CHRIST" and "GOD IS GAY" or spray painting "QUEER" on four-by-four pickups (preferably with rifle rack) to annoy the rednecks. Other times they wrote deliberate nonsense like "AMPUTATE ACROBATS" or "BOAT AKK," just to baffle people.

One night they noticed a huge, ornate Pink Floyd mural which someone had painstakingly painted in one of the alleys. Its minutes were numbered. "We were freshly punk," Shillinger explains. "And we had spray paint."

Kurt had silver spray paint and Shillinger had black, and right over the "Pink," Shillinger wrote "Black"; over the "Floyd," Kurt wrote "Flag." "We had hippies who just wanted to kick our fuckin' asses the whole rest of the summer," says Shillinger, still gleeful. "We were like hunted underground figures."

Kurt was out on a graffiti raid with Osborne and Chris, who had just spray-painted the words "HOMO SEX RULES" on the side of a bank wall when a police car appeared out of nowhere and caught Kurt in its headlights. Chris and Osborne ran away and hid in a garbage dumpster, but Kurt was hauled in to the police station and took the rap. A police report detailed the contents of his pockets: one guitar pick, one key, one can of beer, one mood ring, and one cassette by the militant punk band Millions of Dead Cops. He got a $180 fine and a thirty-day suspended sentence.

Vandalism wasn't anything new to Kurt. While he was still in high school, he and his friends would find an abandoned house, or one that was in the midst of being vacated, break in and destroy everything in sight. Kurt had always wanted to rent one particular house that stood in a field because it was a perfect band rehearsal pad but the owners repeatedly refused to let him rent the place, always renting it to somebody else. Late one night, Kurt was walking home from a party with a friend and they noticed the house was vacant again. They broke in and went berserk, throwing the appliances around the house, taking care to break every single window and smashing everything else to bits with a weight set. "I got my revenge," says Kurt.

Eventually, he took a job as a maintenance man at the YMCA about a block away from the Shillingers' house, mostly so he could afford some musical equipment, should he suddenly find a band. In the morning, he'd walk over to work, check in with his boss, then go back over to the house and sit around and watch TV and drink until quitting time. Sometimes he'd have to clean off the graffiti that he himself had written the night before. A little later, Kurt got the only regular job he's ever really loved—as a swimming instructor for kids age three through seven.

Kurt's first live performance was with Dale Crover on bass drum, snare and cymbal, Buzz Osborne on bass, and Kurt essentially rapping his poetry over improvised heavy rock at GESCCO Hall, a barnlike performance space in Olympia associated with Evergreen State College. The trio was originally called Brown Towel, but a misspelling on the poster made it Brown Cow. Kurt was extremely nervous. "I had to get drunk," he says. "I got totally wasted on wine."

Attendance was sparse and the reaction was lackluster, but two people in the audience—Olympia scenester Slim Moon and his buddy Dylan Carlson, a self-made intellectual who played guitar in several bands around town—were blown away. The two knew Kurt as a member of the Melvins entourage, but now he was something more. "That's when our perception of Kurt changed from the dweeby trench coat new waver that hung out with the Melvins," says Slim Moon, "to realizing, 'Wait, this guy has talent.'" Carlson, now one half of the ultra-heavy guitar noise duo Earth, walked up to Kurt afterward and told him the show was one of the best things he'd ever seen. They began bumping into each other at cool shows in Olympia and soon became fast friends, as they are to this day.

Meanwhile, Kurt had begun to hang out with a drug dealer named Grunt (not his real name). "He was this total drug fiend stoner," says Kurt. "He was like the overlord king of drugs." Grunt was a despicable person, but people hung out with him because he could get practically any drug. No one knew it at the time, but he got his wares by burglarizing pharmacies along with his lover, sidekick, and whipping boy. Grunt began bringing Kurt handfuls of Percodans, an opiate-derived painkiller, each in their little foil and plastic pouches, charging him only a dollar a day. Kurt liked Percodans because they made him feel "relaxed." "It just felt like the best euphoric state that I'd ever been in," he says. "It was just like sleeping. It was as close to sleep as I could get without actually having to sleep."

Kurt was so naive about drugs that he didn't know Percodan was addictive and got hooked without even realizing it. He eventually took up to ten Percodans a day and was "getting real itchy." After about two months, Grunt's supply ran out, and Kurt had to go cold turkey. "It wasn't that bad," he says. "I had diarrhea and I sweated in Eric's bed for a couple of days."

One night that summer, Grunt and Kurt did heroin together. Grunt shot Kurt up. "It was really scary," says Kurt. "I always wanted to do it—I always knew that I would." He's not exactly sure why he was so sure he'd eventually do it. "I don't know," says Kurt. "I just knew."

Besides, by then he'd done just about every drug except PCP ("I'd always heard about people freaking out and jumping off of buildings after they did it"). Heroin was the final frontier. Another attraction was the decadent, outlaw glamour the drug had acquired through its association with rockers such as Keith Richards and Iggy Pop. "Iggy Pop, he was my total idol," says Kurt. "I just wanted to try it because I knew that I liked opiates. It was such a scarce thing to find heroin in Aberdeen that I just thought I would try it." Kurt knew there was no chance of getting hooked on the drug because it was impossible to get a steady supply in Aberdeen.

Heroin's illusion of euphoria may also have had something to do with it. Euphoria of any kind was in short supply in Kurt's life. Beginning in high school, he had become so angry at his surroundings that he developed nervous tics like popping his knuckles, scratching his face, and flipping his hair compulsively. His eye twitched. He thought he might be becoming schizophrenic.

"It was a mixture of hating people so much because they didn't live up to my expectations and just being so fed up with being around the same kind of idiot all the time," he says. "It was obvious in my face and how I reacted toward people that I couldn't stand them. I had this personal vendetta toward them because they were so macho and manly and stupid. I started to become aware of this—that people were noticing that I had this hatred toward a lot of people."

Kurt was convinced that everyone knew he felt this way, which only made him feel more neurotic. He grew more and more paranoid because he was sure everyone knew he could freak out at any time. "They thought I was the kid who was most likely to succeed—to bring an AK-47 to the school and blow everybody away," Kurt says. "I just had this air about me that I would eventually explode one day. People eventually just stayed away from me."

Opiates like Percodan gave Kurt a sense of relief; on opiates, he didn't hate people so much. "I had a little bit of affection for them or at least could see past the superficiality of their personality and think of them as a real person," he says. "Maybe they had a fucked-up childhood or maybe it's their environment that's making them this way. It relieved some of the animosity that I had toward people. I needed to do that because I was tired of hating people so much and being so judgmental toward everyone. It just allowed me to have a few days of peace of mind."

Meanwhile, although Kurt and Eric had started off as friends, their friendship had begun to disintegrate, perhaps because of a musical rivalry. The antagonism built and built until one night, eight months after Kurt arrived at the Shillingers', when Kurt, Eric, and Steve Shillinger came home from three different parties, all quite drunk. Steve says it was over a frozen pizza pie, while Kurt thinks it was because he wanted to sleep and Eric wanted to watch TV, but for some reason a fight broke out between Kurt and Eric. Kurt declared a cigarette break and then the fight resumed in the backyard. "There was actual blood on the wall," says Steve. "I don't want to get involved in who won the fight—all I'll say is, it was a very bloody and terrible battle."

Kurt beat a hasty exit after it was all over. The next day, he paid Steve Shillinger ten dollars to put his stuff into garbage bags and take it to Dale Crover's house. Kurt stayed at Buzz Osborne's house for a few days, then briefly moved back in with Wendy.

Mr. Shillinger asked Kurt to come back, but he refused and went back to the bridge, where every once in a while he'd catch fish and eat them until one day someone told them they were poisonous. Other times, he slept in the apartment above Chris's mom's beauty parlor.

He'd have to wake up by seven in the morning so he could get out of there before she came to work.

In the fall of 1986, Kurt got Wendy to put down money on 1000½ East Second Street in Aberdeen, a decrepit little shack a few hundred yards from her house. It rented for only a hundred dollars a month, perhaps because the porch was falling off the front of the house. "It was the bottom of houses," Kurt recalls, but at least it was his. It had two small bedrooms and two small living rooms. His housemate was Melvins bassist Matt Lukin, who was also a trained carpenter. Lukin had to do a lot of work on the house before it was even livable.

As usual, hygiene was not a priority. If you drank a beer, you could just throw the can on the floor. And with all the partying going on at the shack, the floor was covered with festive detritus. They didn't have a fridge, so they kept all the food in an unplugged old icebox out on the back porch. They cooked in a toaster oven. Wendy stopped by occasionally with care packages of food.

One day Kurt bought about half a dozen turtles and put them in a bathtub in the middle of the living room; a terrarium attached to the tub took up most of the rest of the room. For irrigation, carpenter Lukin drilled a hole in the floor and drained the smelly hamburger meat-and-turtle-poop-fouled water into the floor underneath the house. But the foundation was so rotten that water would rise up into the floorboards. "It was, needless to say, a very smelly, very odorous place," says Kurt.

Kurt felt a special attraction to turtles. "There's a fascination with them I really can't describe," he says. "Turtles basically have this 'fuck you' attitude—'I'm stuck in the tank, I'm miserable, I hate you, and I'm *not* going to perform for you.'"

Then there are those protective shells. "Actually those shells really aren't that helpful," Kurt says. "It's part of their spine and it's real sensitive—if you knock on the shell it hurts them, so it really isn't the protective covering that everyone thinks it is. If they fall on their back, it'll split open and they'll die. It's like having your spine on your outside."

Kurt got a job at the Polynesian Hotel in Ocean Shores, a coastal resort about twenty miles from Aberdeen, as a janitor, fireplace cleaner, and "maintenance butt-boy." Once again, he didn't exactly strive to be an ideal worker. Instead of cleaning or fixing things in the hotel rooms, he'd just walk into an unoccupied room, turn on the TV, and take a nap.

Kurt was always on the lookout for a cheap new high. "Back then, none of us had any money so you don't want to spend a bunch of money on coke and stuff," recalls Lukin. "There was a lot of people who got into cough syrup to get high. I remember this guy I went to high school with who ate handfuls of aspirin and got high off of that."

At the time, a lot of kids in Aberdeen were doing acid, not to mention the powerful local marijuana, inexplicably nicknamed "affy bud." Lukin, Jesse Reed, Kurt, and a few other stoners were sitting around one night bemoaning the fact that they were tired of all the usual highs. Then Reed remembered all those cans of shaving cream that Kurt had hung on to ever since they shared an apartment together. The shaving cream came with a little rubber stopper on the bottom of the can where the propellant was pumped in. Inhaling the propellant produced a buzz not unlike that of nitrous oxide. The manufacturers of the shaving cream have since altered the stopper on the can to discourage such abuse.

The problem was, a lot of it would escape, so Reed showed them how to tape a toilet paper roll onto the bottom, poke a hole in the side, and insert a screwdriver in it to pry the gasket loose, then inhale it like a bong. They all ran down to the 7-Eleven and each bought more shaving cream. There was a brief panic when they found the gas lowered their voices—but not permanently—and the high was decent. "We were all yelling at Kurt that he shouldn't have wasted all that shaving cream on decorating the doll that summer," says Lukin. "We could have been getting high off it!"

And then in the wee hours of one winter morning, Kurt came to Wendy's house. "Mom," Kurt called up to her, his voice weak with fear, "I've lost my hand. I've burnt my hand and it's just gone." He burst into tears. Kurt had been making french fries, his staple food, and severely burned his hand on the hot grease. "It was horrible," she says. "It was burned clear down—it was the most sickening thing I ever saw and I had to bandage it twice a day and peel off the—it was horrible."

Kurt had already been to the hospital, where a doctor had bandaged it up and told Kurt he'd never play guitar again. But then Wendy took him to a specialist she knew from working at the Grays Harbor College nursing program. Now, you can't even see a scar.

While he recuperated, Kurt stayed home and tried to play guitar. Without any income from work, he was forced to live on little else but rice for several months. Every once in a while he'd splurge on a frozen Salisbury steak. "I was starving to death, living in this pigsty," Kurt says, "not being able to pay guitar, with the threat of the landlady calling me up every day reminding me that I owed her money. It was just a real sketchy scene." Kurt didn't know where he was going to live pretty soon.

Kurt badly wanted to form a band with Chris, but Chris didn't seem interested. "I kept always making it obvious that I wanted someone to play with in a band," says Kurt, "but still Chris never wanted to." Kurt even lent Chris his amplifier for a week and a half to try to butter him up. But Chris didn't respond to Kurt's overtures and even made Kurt come to his house to retrieve his own amp. "It sounded really nice," says Chris, "but I decided to give it back to him."

Kurt would slide Chris a copy of the Fecal Matter tape now and then as a not-so-subtle hint, but Chris never said a word about it. Then, a whole year after the demo had been recorded and three years after they first met, Chris told Kurt, "I finally listened to that tape you made. It's pretty good. We should start a band."

Kurt had a guitar and a Peavey amp. Chris used to have an amp, but he had to give it to Matt Lukin in return for bailing him out of jail after a scuffle with some rednecks in the parking lot of the Aberdeen 7-Eleven. For a P.A., they used another guitar amp and a cheap microphone with the diaphragm taped to it—it was a wreck, but it worked. There was an empty apartment above Mrs. Novoselic's beauty shop and they'd play there for hours, with Chris on bass and Kurt on guitar and someone named Bob McFadden whom Chris recalls only as "some jock guy" who happened to own a drum set. Unfortunately, the place soon became a hangout just like the Melvins' practice space and Chris eventually had to post a sign which read "This is not a big crash pad. So just get out of here because we want to rehearse."

The underground scene was so small in Aberdeen that even Cure fans with their trendy quiffs and goth clothes would hang around the practice space. Chris and Shelli called them the Haircut 100 Club. "We weren't tight with them because they were more concerned with the fashion aspect of it," says Shelli. "We were just concerned with fucking around."

The band worked up a little material but for some reason, the project eventually fell apart after about a month and all three went their separate ways. Chris and Shelli went to Arizona to look for work.

Kurt didn't like the guys who would hang out at the shack. They tended to be underage drinkers who used the house as a place to get trashed. Lukin's work as a cabinet maker was far from steady, so more often than not he and his drinking buddies would be up until all hours, while Kurt had to get up to go to work at the resort. After five months, Lukin realized he should move out.

Dylan Carlson mentioned that he was unemployed, so Kurt told him about these great jobs they could get laying carpet in a hotel out at Ocean Shores. Carlson was going to take Lukin's room at the shack, but he stayed only two weeks because the carpet-laying job never panned out. They went out to Ocean Shores early one morning to find that the boss was so drunk that he couldn't get off the floor to unlock the door. When they went out there a second time, the door was unlocked, but the boss had passed out in front of it, blocking the way. Carlson gave up, but Kurt tried a third time. He got in, but the boss went out to a bar and got falling-down drunk. The great carpet-laying job never materialized.

Kurt had been going more and more frequently to Olympia, about fifty miles east of Aberdeen, with the Melvins. The state capital, Olympia, is the home of Evergreen State College, a haven for bohemians and misfits of all stripes and a hotbed of adventurous independent music. Kurt went there most weekends to check out bands. Olympia was a small town but it had national indie scene connections that extended from Evergreen's KAOS radio station, *Op* magazine (which has since metamorphosed into *Option* magazine), fanzine publisher Bruce Pavitt, and Calvin Johnson's K Records.

The youth culture there wasn't into hard rock, but instead favored a kind of naive music, pigeonholed as "love rock," made by the likes of Jad Fair and the group Beat Happening, led by Calvin Johnson. Johnson dominated the scene and inspired a legion of clones—whom Kurt calls "the Calvinists"—who talked and dressed just like him, aspiring to an innocent child-like state.

It was a whole community of geeks—they were even dismissed by punk rockers. The Calvinists didn't take drugs—at least they said they didn't—and wore their hair short. Everyone played in each other's band, everyone slept with one another. They had their own coffee shop, their own record store, and, practically speaking, KAOS had become their own radio station. "They started up their own little planet," says Kurt.

They also had their own record label. Along with Candace Peterson, Johnson ran K Records, a small but well-connected indie label which also distributed like-minded foreign bands such as Young Marble Giants, Kleenex, and the Vaselines.

Kurt didn't completely buy the K ethos. He liked to wear his hair long and he liked to take drugs. But he did like the music and its message. "It opened up new doors to music that I'd never heard before," Kurt says. "It made me realize that for years I hadn't looked back on my childhood. I tried to forget about it. I'd just forgotten about it. It made me look back on my childhood and have fond memories of it. It was just a nice reminder of innocence." "To try to remind me to stay a child," Kurt got a tattoo of the K logo, a "K" inside a simple shield, on his left forearm.

Kurt remained at the shack for another two months after Lukin left, owing the landlady back rent.

In the meantime, Kurt started seeing a young woman named Tracy Marander. She wasn't like any of the other girls he knew. She had a zebra-stripe coat and her hair was dyed fire-engine red and she lived in Olympia. Tracy liked to party and had her share of eccentricities, but she was also a placid, nurturing soul. After a few weeks, she became Kurt's first serious girlfriend.

Tracy and Kurt had met a year or so before, in front of the Gorilla Gardens, a barnlike all-ages punk club (now defunct) in the Chinatown section of Seattle. They met through their mutual friend Buzz Osborne. She and her boyfriend were sitting in their car drinking beer and talking to Buzz and Kurt, who were also drinking beer. The meeting was cut short when Tracy noticed a couple of cops heading their way and took off in the car, leaving Kurt and Buzz behind to get busted.

Tracy thought Kurt was nice, if a little young-looking. He was skinny and had short hair. "I was struck by how blue his eyes were," she recalls. "I'd never seen eyes that blue before."

After befriending Chris and Shelli, she became a cling-on and met Kurt again a year later while they hung out at Buzz Osborne's parents' house one day watching Buzz and Chris drink Mad Dog. After Kurt left, Buzz informed her that Kurt was the guy who made the really cool Kiss mural on the side of the Melvins' tour van—known as the Mel-Van—using Magic Markers. Every time a pen ran out, he'd go into the Shop-Rite in Montesano and steal another one. "I thought that was kind of cool," says Tracy.

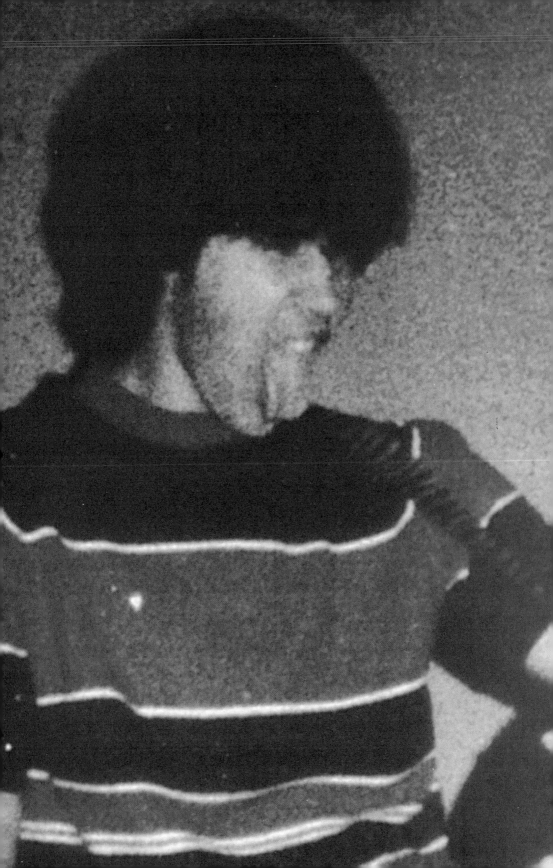

CHAPTER THREE

Krist Anthony Novoselic was born on May 16, 1965, in Compton, California. His parents, Krist and Maria, were Croatian immigrants; Mr. Novoselic (the name means "new settler" in Croatian) moved to the United States in 1963, his wife-to-be the following year. They set up house in Gardena, California, and Mr. Novoselic got a job driving a truck for Sparklets drinking water.

After moving around to a series of apartments with Chris and his younger brother Robert, they got a modest house and then another, nicer one in 1973 when Chris's sister Diana was born.

THAT'S MY BROTHER CHRIS. HE LISTENS TO PUNK ROCK.

Although busing had been instituted in California, in Gardena kids of different races didn't mix—except for one group. "There was the one scene with all of us who were in bonehead math," says Novoselic. "We were totally integrated. Whoever didn't really fit in all bonded together and there was no racial thing. So integration did work.

"Robert and I were kind of big boys and we used to get into trouble," says Chris of his preteen years. "Slash tires, stuff like that. My dad would just have to whip us, because that's all he knew how to do. We were scared of him. But it wasn't like he was an abuser—I don't think he abused us at all. It's not like he would slap us for *anything*. It was action and reaction.

"Like Robert, he got glasses and the first day he got his glasses, he busted 'em," Chris continues. "That's just Robert. We'd just do shit like that. Go throw rocks at houses, throw rocks at cars. There was a time when vandalism was really cool. We really got into vandalism. Throwing eggs…"

Chris says he and his brother straightened out by the time the family moved to Aberdeen in 1979, when Chris was fourteen. Property values in Southern California were getting too high for the Novoselic family and they could get a nice house for a little money in Aberdeen. Besides, there were lots of other Croatian families in the area. Mr. Novoselic got a job as a machinist at one of the town's many lumber mills.

After sunny California, Chris didn't like Aberdeen at all. "It's got everything against it," he says. "It's cloudy and rainy, there's mud in the streets from all the trucks. The buildings are all kind of dirty. It's like an East German town or something. Everything is so damp down there that the wood just gets kind of soft and things fall apart."

Like Kurt, Chris had a hard time at school because he didn't fit in. The California stereotype held true—things really were mellower there. "I was perplexed by the weird, twisted social scene they had in Aberdeen," says Novoselic. "It just seemed like people were a lot more uptight and judgmental."

Aberdonians wore leather tennis shoes and elephant flares, while Chris sported deck shoes and straight-leg Levi's. You were a geek if you wore straight-leg pants. "Three years later," says Chris, "everybody was wearing straight-leg pants. And I suffered for nothing."

And he was very tall—he was six foot seven by the time he graduated from high school. His parents were hoping he'd become a basketball player but his height only made Chris awkward. "I was just weird and maladjusted more than anything else," Chris says. "I was really depressed when I came up to Aberdeen. I couldn't get along with anybody. I'd go home and sleep all afternoon and listen to music by myself. I couldn't get along with those kids. They were assholes. They treated me really badly. I didn't understand. They just weren't cool."

Chris was into bands like Led Zeppelin, Devo, Black Sabbath, and Aerosmith while his peers were into Top Forty, perhaps because that was all the local radio station played. They'd play Top Forty radio on the school bus and Chris was forced to endure the sound of Kenny Rogers warbling "Coward of the County." Over and over again.

Luckily, geography smiled on Chris Novoselic. His family's house was on Think of Me Hill, the tallest hill in Aberdeen (named because at the turn of the century there was a big sign on the hill overlooking the town that advertised Think of Me tobacco), so he got excellent radio reception—on clear days, he could get Portland, Oregon. He'd lie in his room depressed and listen to the hip Seattle rock stations on his clock radio for hours.

By June of 1980, Chris's parents got so worried about his depression that they sent him to live with relatives in Croatia. Chris had picked up Croatian "around the house," and is still fluent in it. He loved living there—he made lots of friends and the schools were excellent. He even heard something there called "punk rock," and discovered the Sex Pistols, the Ramones, and even some Yugoslavian punk bands. It didn't make too much of a dent, however. "It was just music to me," Chris recalls. "It didn't really mean anything to me—it was just music that I liked." After a year, his parents called him back home.

"I was just in a weird limbo," Chris says. He began drinking and smoking pot heavily. "I've always been a big drinker," says Chris. "When I drink, I just don't stop. I like to drink because you're in some weird cartoon land where anything goes. Your vision is blurry and nothing and everything makes sense. It's crazy. It's a different reality and a different world of consciousness."

Chris became well known on the party circuit. "You'd go to parties and people would be like 'Hey, Novie!'" says Matt Lukin. "They always knew him as the big wacky guy because he was always doing weird things. They just thought he was kind of weird. He'd go to parties and jump around."

He had some people to hang out with, but he was hard pressed to call them friends. "I hung out with them because I had nowhere else to go," says Chris. "It was kind of odd and uncomfortable." He finally got a job at the local Taco Bell and threw himself into work, working every night and not socializing, just saving money. By senior year of high school, he had bought a car, some stereo speakers, and a guitar. He took some lessons along with his brother Robert and told his teacher, Warren Mason—the same guy who taught Kurt—that he really wanted to play the blues. He quit after a few months and then woodshedded intensively in his bedroom, patiently working out the licks to old B. B. King records with his brother.

Then he met Buzz Osborne.

Chris worked at the Taco Bell with a fellow named Bill Hull, whose principal claim to fame was that he had been expelled from Aberdeen High for planting a pipe bomb in the greenhouse. When Hull got transferred to Montesano High, he met Buzz and Matt Lukin. One day, Buzz and Matt visited Hull at the Taco Bell. "And there was this big tall doofy guy back there singing along to the Christmas carols they're playing on the Muzak," Lukin recalls. Chris mentioned that he played guitar and later Osborne called up and invited him to hang out in Montesano.

They talked politics and Osborne turned him on to some cool music—blazing music from the Vibrators, Sex Pistols, Flipper, Black Flag, Circle Jerks. "It was like wow, *punk rock*," says Novoselic, marveling still. "I just totally disavowed all this stupid metal—Ozzy Osbourne, Judas Priest, Def Leppard, it was just shit, I just could not listen to it anymore. It was crap, it had lost its appeal for me. Sammy Hagar, Iron Maiden, I just didn't like it. I was still into Zeppelin and Aerosmith and stuff." Chris had gone through a prog-rock phase—Yes, Emerson, Lake and Palmer, and their ilk—but, in his favorite phrase, "it never yanked my crank."

Like Kurt, Chris had a delayed reaction to punk rock. "It didn't really grab me right away because it sounded really live," says Chris. "It took about a week into it and it finally grabbed me. I was listening to *Generic Flipper* and the record moved me. It was like, Art. This is *Art*. It was so *substantial*. People pay credence to *Led Zeppelin IV* or the White Album and this was the same thing. So that turned my life around."

He began reading punk fanzines such as *Maximumrocknroll*, discovered political hardcore bands like MDC, and read about everything from anarchism to animal rights. Then he discovered bands such as the Butthole Surfers, Minor Threat, and Hüsker Dü. He and a bunch of friends would pile into Matt Lukin's mammoth blue Impala and drive up to Seattle to see punk rock shows—two hours up, two hours back. Awed by the big city, they kept to themselves.

Around this time, Chris's brother Robert brought his friend Kurt Cobain over to the Novoselic house. When Kurt asked about the racket emanating from the upstairs stereo, Robert replied, "Oh, that's my brother Chris. He listens to punk rock." Kurt thought that was very cool and filed the information away.

Chris graduated from high school in 1983. Soon after, his parents divorced. It was a rough enough time as it was, but he also had some plastic surgery done on his face—doctors cut a small section of bone out of Chris's jaw and moved some teeth forward to correct a severe underbite ("I looked like Jay Leno," he says).

Lukin remembers stopping by with Osborne on the day of the operation. They rang the doorbell over and over again, but nobody answered. Then they tossed some pebbles at Chris's window. "Just as we were ready to give up," says Lukin, "the window slides open and he had this huge head, it was totally swollen up—he almost looked like a little fat oriental baby. It was like an elephant man coming up to the window." Chris was mad because they'd woken him up from his anesthetized sleep. His jaws were tightly wired shut, yet he still managed to communicate something to his friends. "You fuckers!" he cried.

Chris's jaw was wired shut for six weeks. He still went out to parties, except he had to carry a pair of wire cutters with him in case he threw up or something got caught in his throat. "He'd go out and get all fucked up," Lukin recalls, "and he'd be puking and it would be draining through his wires. He said he never did have to cut them, but all the food was like milkshakes anyway, no solid food. Still, it was somewhat reckless of him."

"Then the swelling went down," says Chris, "and I had a new face."

One day during his senior year in high school, he had been walking behind two junior girls in the hall who were raving about the album *Never Mind the Bollocks, Here's the Sex Pistols*. "Yeah, they're really great!" he piped up. Shelli remembered him as a "class clown-type guy, always joking." They talked a little and made friends.

Shelli was also friendly with Kurt and remembers him as a "smart-ass" who would delight in riling the redneck who sat next to him in art class. Kurt's mom boarded a friend of Kurt's for a while and Shelli knew his sister, who was old enough to buy beer. She'd go over to Kurt's house sometimes to find him and his friends getting very stoned and grooving to Led Zeppelin.

Shelli dropped out her senior year and took a job at McDonald's and got her own hundred-dollar-a-month apartment on Market Street, across from the fire department. On her way to work, she would walk past the Foster Painting company where Chris worked and she would talk to him. She got his phone number and started calling him up. They had a lot in common—Shelli had been an odd-ball in school, too—and by March 1985, they had started hanging out as friends at Shelli's apartment, listening to punk rock records and going to shows. Soon they started going out.

Chris and Osborne briefly had a band with original Melvins drummer Mike Dillard, with Chris on guitar and Osborne on bass. Chris played a punked-up version of "Sunshine of Your Love" with members of the Melvins as the opening act of a Melvins/Metal Church bill at the D&R Theater in Aberdeen. Chris became the lead singer for the Stiff Woodies, the Melvins satellite project whose revolving door lineup featured, at various times, Osborne, Crover, Lukin, a fellow named Gary Cole, and others, including drummer Kurt Cobain ("We sounded just like the Butthole Surfers," Kurt claims). Chris was a flamboyant frontman, recalls Dale Crover. "He wore this big long purple fringe vest and he'd do all these big high kicks," says Crover. "It was hilarious." The Stiff Woodies played a few parties before going the way of all satellite projects, probably because Chris's vocal talents were at roughly the same level as his cameo at the beginning of *Nevermind*'s "Territorial Pissings."

Chris played bass in another Melvins satellite project, a Mentors cover band. His stage name was Phil Atio.

He had been laid off from his painting job by then and was collecting fifty-five dollars a week unemployment. He usually slept in all morning and then hung out at the Melvins' practice space, where the band rehearsed every afternoon. Gradually, Chris moved in with Shelli. Chris didn't hang out with the cling-ons at the Melvins' practice space so much after that, preferring to spend most of his time with his girlfriend.

They didn't have a TV or a phone and they got everything from thrift stores. They had tie-dye curtains and listened to Cream and early Rolling Stones records. "It was one of the greatest times of our lives," says Shelli. "Everything was so new. Everything was so bright for us. It was the first time we'd been away from our parents and the world was ours. It was really cool."

Chris and Shelli moved to a larger but more decrepit house in Aberdeen in December. It was a drafty place, especially in the damp Northwestern winter—you could actually see sunlight streaming through the cracks in the walls.

Noting that the Melvins were awarded the princely sum of eighty dollars for a night's work, Chris and Kurt started a Creedence Clearwater Revival cover band aptly named the Sellouts. They figured CCR was country-rock and therefore would go over well in rural Aberdeen. The band was Kurt on drums, Chris on guitar, and a fellow named Steve Newman on bass (Newman later lost his fingers in a woodcutting accident). They practiced at Chris and Shelli's house, but it only got as far as five or six rehearsals. They broke up after Kurt and Newman got into a big fight one day at Chris and Shelli's. They were sitting around drinking when Newman tried to attack Kurt with a vacuum cleaner. Kurt grabbed a two-by-four and brained his much larger opponent.

Although they had left high school behind, they still hadn't escaped Aberdeen and their provincial peers. "It was your basic nowhere town and these people considered it the center of the universe," says Matt Lukin. "There were these bigwigs that were popular in high school who belonged to these little cliques and it kind of carried over out of high school because everybody still hung out. Small-town mentality—real narrow-minded people who looked at something they weren't used to as something bad."

"Kurt was really a victim," says Shelli. "People wanted to beat him up. He was different from them. He wasn't a redneck and he liked his own music and people are afraid of that in a small town—you're different and you're the freak. We got all kinds of shit in Aberdeen. Chris was talking about socialism at a party once and these guys were talking about slitting his throat, these rednecks because they thought he was a Communist. It was a scary atmosphere, especially back in 1985."

In March of 1986, Chris and Shelli moved to Phoenix, Arizona, in search of work. But they soon tired of the stifling, relentless heat and all those Republicans and moved back to the hundred-dollar-a-month apartment. They stayed there for six months before moving to an apartment in nearby Hoquiam (Quinault Indian for "hungry for wood") above a garage.

They became vegetarians. Chris got turned on to the idea by a friend from work named Dwight Covey, a hip older guy who had built a cabin for himself out in the woods and used no electricity or running water. Chris quit eating red meat, then gradually dropped poultry and fish. "I was just looking for a better way to live, I guess," he says. "I started thinking about all the cows slaughtered. It just seemed like a really good thing to do."

CHAPTER FOUR

Later that winter of 1987, Chris and Kurt found a new drummer—mustachioed Aaron Burckhard, who lived down the street from Kurt. A stoner, Burckhard was one of the cling-ons and would occasionally get to sit behind Dale Crover's drum set and play. "He's a very upbeat, happy person," says Kurt. "Loud but not so obnoxious to the point where you hate his guts or anything. And he's a magnet for trouble." Burckhard was a bit of a rascal-about-town and had been in a car which a friend drove through the front window of the Shop-Rite in Aberdeen, causing fifteen thousand dollars' worth of damage. Not long afterward, his face made the front page of the Aberdeen *Daily World* when another car he was in flipped over a median strip and burst into flames, killing the driver.

Burckhard had his drawbacks, but he was the only person in Aberdeen Kurt and Chris knew who played drums, so he was in. He had a steady job at the Burger King in town, but somehow couldn't find the money for a proper drum set, so they scrounged up a set using a few drums that Burckhard had, bits of Dale Crover's banged-up old Sears kit, and even a sheet music stand to hold up one of the cymbals.

After Chris's parents got divorced, Maria Novoselic had moved into the apartment above her beauty shop, so the fledgling band rehearsed at Kurt's little house. Kurt now had a little Fender Champ and Chris had a PMS brand amp and a clunky old Hohner bass he had borrowed from Greg Hokanson. They started rehearsing in earnest, taking inspiration from the hardworking Melvins.

At first, Kurt sang in an English accent. "When I first heard American punk rock," he says, "it didn't sound punk rock enough to me because the accent was missing." They learned most of the Fecal Matter tape at first, but then started writing new material almost immediately. Within three months they had about a dozen new songs.

At the time, Chris was big into beads, incense, and psychedelic rock from the sixties—"a full-blown hippie," says Kurt. Chris was raving about a record he had found by Shocking Blue, the Dutch band best known for the classic 1970 pop hit "Venus." Kurt didn't like the album, but just to humor Chris, he agreed to cover one of its songs, a pseudo-trippy wad of bubblegum called "Love Buzz." Kurt rocked it up considerably, dispensing with all but the first verse, essentially because he was too lazy to figure out the rest of the words.

Early on, some friction developed between Burckhard and the rest of the band. Burckhard was more into mainstream metal than what he calls "the punk shit" and didn't quite grasp Kurt's music, which recalled arty, dissonant bands such as early Gang of Four, Scratch Acid, and the Butthole Surfers. "I was listening more to the mainstream and Kurt was into the underground scene," says Burckhard. "But I dug their music." Looking back on it, it was an early indication of the broad-based appeal Kurt's music would have—heavily influenced by punk and underground rock, it somehow translated into the mainstream.

It was a constant battle to try to get Burckhard to practice. He lived with a divorced mother of two who was six years older than he was. She was on welfare, and when the check came in at the first of the month, she and Burckhard would go out and whoop it up—along with all the other unemployed folks in Aberdeen. "The first is wild around this town," says Burckhard.

"When the welfare check came in," says Kurt, "it was impossible to get him to practice."

In the beginning, even Chris found it difficult to match Kurt's zeal—he'd sometimes miss practice or claim he had something else to do, perhaps because Chris's mother, a proud woman who had started her own successful business, didn't like Kurt very much. "Fuck, she hated my guts," says Kurt. "She called me trash. She hated me. I always heard her talking to Chris, saying he should find other friends, always putting him down and calling him a loser, calling all his friends losers."

Kurt brought Chris home a few times. Wendy remembers Chris would accidentally bang his head over and over again on the cross-beams in the house. "Oh don't worry," he'd say matter-of-factly, "that happens all the time." Chris was so shy that he would do anything to avoid Wendy, an admitted "yakker."

Burckhard recalls that Kurt's torn jeans and bohemian attitude set him apart from the usual Aberdeen stoner. "It was just the way he carried himself about—like he didn't give a shit," says Burckhard. "He didn't care what other people thought about him."

Kurt was unstoppable. "I wanted to put out a record or play some shows, instead of having it fall apart like everything else for the past six years," says Kurt. "We would play the set and then I would just start playing the songs again right away without even looking up to see if those guys wanted to play them again. I'd just whip them into shape."

Eventually, Kurt's zeal won Chris over and the two became so driven that even one bad practice would get them deeply upset. "We'd get really mad," says Kurt. "We took it very seriously." They soon set their sights on getting a gig. "We just had to play a show," says Kurt. "God, if we could just play a show, it would be so great."

At last, they got a gig—a party in Olympia. They loaded up Chris's VW bug with equipment and rode to the gig all keyed up and excited—their first show! But they arrived to find that the party had already been shut down by the police, so they simply turned around and made the hour's drive all the way back to Aberdeen.

Their first real gig was a house party in nearby Raymond, a town even more isolated than Aberdeen, opening for a metal band featuring Aberdeen's then-reigning guitar hero ("this guy knew *all* the Eddie Van Halen licks," says Chris, still semi-impressed). Burckhard recalls the hosts were "these higher-class yuppie people and they had a caseful of Michelob—good beer—and Chris ended up jumping through the window, running around to the front door and repeatedly doing it. He had this fake vampire blood and he just basically made a fool out of himself, but it was fun."

"We had everyone so scared of us that they were in the kitchen hiding from us," says Kurt. "We had the run of the entire living room and the rest of the house." Just to shock the bourgeoisie, Shelli and Tracy started making out; Kurt would jump on a table mid-solo and they would caress his legs. "Of course, by the end of the evening, most of the girls at the party had talked their boyfriends into wanting to beat us up," says Kurt. "They didn't beat us up, but they let us know we weren't welcome. 'It's time to pack up and leave now, boys.'"

Most people were confused because the band didn't play many covers. "They didn't know what to think," says Chris, who remembers that an adventurous few walked up to the band after the set and raved. "Who knows what happened to the people who thought it was cool," he adds, shaking his head in pity.

By then, their repertoire included originals like "Hairspray Queen," "Spank Thru," "Anorexorcist," "Raunchola" ("That was really raunchy," Chris explains), "Aero Zeppelin," "Beeswax," and "Floyd the Barber," as well as covers such as "Love Buzz," "White Lace and Strange" by the obscure sixties band Thunder and Roses, Flipper's epic "Sex Bomb," and Cher's "Gypsies, Tramps, and Thieves" with Chris on lead vocals.

Soon they played their first big gig—closing night of GESCCO Hall in Olympia. They took out the backseat of Chris's Volkswagen bug again and polished off a gallon bottle of wine on the drive up from

Skid Row's debut at GESCCO Hall. (Tracy Marander)

Aberdeen. There were perhaps ten people at the show, but they all tore down the yards of arty plastic sheeting on the walls and rolled it around them as the band played. It was a good beginning.

Then the band got a show at the Community World Theater, a converted porno theater in Tacoma. Tracy was a friend of the proprietor, Jim May, and helped get them the gig. May charged only a couple of bucks at the door and didn't mind if underaged kids drank beer. Bands with names like the Dicks and Jack Shit played the Community, as well as the Melvins and touring punk bands such as the Circle Jerks.

The band didn't have a name yet and May wanted a name to put on the marquee, so Kurt came up with the name Skid Row (the term had originated in Seattle). None of their friends expected much from the band, but a bunch went to see the show. And sur-

Kurt at an early show at the Community World Theater. Yes, those are satin trousers. (Tracy Marander)

prise—the band was good—they had real songs and Kurt could really sing. And they were not above a little showmanship—for a while, Kurt would put on a pair of outrageous silversparkle platform shoes during "Love Buzz," jump five feet in the air and land in a split. Skid Row soon amassed its own group of "clingons."

In April of 1987, the band played a radio show on KAOS, the station at Evergreen State College in Olympia. Kurt had made friends in Olympia from going to Melvins shows there, and one of them was a KAOS DJ. Their recorded appearance—a live midnight show—became the band's first demo. They did remarkably full-blown versions of "Love Buzz," "Floyd the Barber," "Downer," "Mexican Seafood," "Spank Thru," "Hairspray Queen," and three other songs that even Kurt doesn't remember the names of. Burckhard turned out to be a solid, hard hitter in the John Bonham vein—sort of the hard rock ancestral conscience of the band (interestingly, a Bonham maniac would one day become their best drummer). Kurt sings in a few voices—including a desperate death-metal growl and a strangulated cat-in-heat scream—that sound

Chris doing his best Gene Simmons imitation at the Community World Theater, spring 1987. (Tracy Marander)

nothing like he does today.

Later, they went through various names, including Ted Ed Fred, Bliss ("I was on acid one night," Kurt explains), Throat Oyster, Pen Cap Chew, and Windowpane. And finally, the band settled on Nirvana, a Hindu and Buddhist concept which Webster's defines as "the extinction of desire, passion, illusion and the empirical self and attainment of rest, truth and unchanging being." That idea of heaven—a place, as David Byrne once put it, "where nothing ever happens"—sounds a lot like the way Kurt felt when he did heroin, but he says that wasn't the idea. "I wanted a name that was kind of beautiful or nice and pretty instead of a mean, raunchy punk rock name like the Angry Samoans," says Kurt. "I wanted to have something different." These days, Kurt isn't so crazy about the name anymore. "It's too esoteric and serious," he says. And later on, he'd have to pay another band fifty thousand dollars for a name he didn't even care for that much.

Kurt hadn't paid rent on the little shack for several months and was being evicted. Tracy asked if he'd like to move into her place in Olympia, and Kurt agreed. It was convenient because Chris and Shelli had decided to move to Tacoma and it was a lot easier to keep the band together if Kurt moved, too. Tacoma was out of the question for Kurt, being, as he describes it, "a more violent Aberdeen." Besides, Olympia was a cool college town.

In the fall of 1987, Kurt moved into Tracy's tiny studio apartment at 114 North Pear Street in Olympia (a "shoe box," according to Kurt), which they rented for 137 dollars a month, including electricity, hot water, and garbage pickup. They stayed there a little over a year, then moved to a small one-bedroom in the same building.

Kurt had escaped from Aberdeen. Tracy remembers that shortly after Kurt moved in with her, he told her that while she was away at work, he had had a meal of cream cheese and crab, and that he felt very cultured sitting in Olympia on a real hardwood floor eating such fancy food.

For about a month that summer, Chris and Shelli lived there during the week, too, to avoid the two-hour commute to their jobs, meaning that four people were now crammed into the little studio apartment. Shelli and Tracy both worked the graveyard shift at the Boeing cafeteria, while Chris worked in Tacoma making six dollars an hour as an industrial painter. Kurt would sleep at night and hang out at the house by day. Chris and Shelli would go back to their place in Hoquiam on the weekends.

The four spent lots of time together, partying or just hanging out at the apartment watching TV or going out tripping. "The acid wasn't what the Beatles took," Chris recalls. "It was more speedy, dirty acid... We'd just go wild, raging all night long."

Kurt describes the apartment as "a curiosity shop." Tracy would take Kurt thrift shopping every weekend and come back with carloads of kitsch. "You couldn't even move in that place," he says. The apartment was completely decorated with thrift purchases, including a huge Aerosmith poster on the living room wall and a bunch of transparent plastic anatomical models. The walls were lined with Kurt's paintings, cutouts from the *Weekly World News* and the *National Enquirer,* and strangely adulterated religious pictures. Always lurking around was one of Kurt's most prized possessions—Chim-Chim, his plastic monkey.

There were animals everywhere—three

Chris and Shelli fall off the veggie wagon at their Tacoma home in the fall of 1990.
(© Ian T. Tilton)

cats, two rabbits, some pet rats, and a bunch of turtles. It was as "odorous" as the shack back in Aberdeen. "Rat piss hell" is Kurt's succinct description. By chance, an Olympia punk rock scenester by the name of Bruce Pavitt stopped by one day and one of the pet rats bit him on the finger ("He screamed like a woman," Tracy says with a giggle). Pavitt would go on to found Sub Pop Records, Nirvana's first label.

As usual, Kurt stayed indoors, sometimes not venturing outside for weeks at a time, indulging in what he calls his "little art world fantasy." He didn't particularly take advantage of Olympia's cultural scene, but it was nice to know it was there. And he didn't have to worry about having to deal with doltish stoners and rednecks. He let his hair grow long and concentrated on his art.

Kurt began collecting and making dolls. It was the start of a long obsession that continues still. He found a type of clay that turned all sorts of strange colors when it was baked and he made dolls out of it —like the doll on the cover of *Incesticide*, but much more intricate and bizarre. He'd find baby dolls, cover them with clay and bake them in the oven until they looked like ancient artifacts. He also collected antique baby dolls, especially eerily lifelike ones.

Once, when Kurt was working at the resort hotel, he had gone into a room where a gynecologist was staying and lifted a book full of pictures of diseased vaginas. He cut them out and combined them into a collage with pictures of pieces of meat and an illustration of Kiss and put it on the refrigerator door.

Kurt went through a brief death rock phase (Black Sabbath—*not* Bauhaus) and started constructing nativity scenes full of decayed bodies, skeletons, and demons.

He'd make psychedelic tapes that strung together Christian records, political speeches, commercials, and music that was slowed down or speeded up. He made collages, but mostly, he painted. His paintings had lots of weird distended figures or fetuses set in thorny landscapes. It's hard not to look at those paintings as autobiographical—helpless children set adrift in hostile worlds.

Kurt also sculpted. "He would make these incredibly beautiful, intricate sculptures out of weird shit he'd buy at thrift stores," says Slim Moon. "Little invisible man things and figurines. It would be this weird mixture of pop culture artifacts that you'd get from thrift stores, mixed up with actual clay sculpture of these tortured figures. He'd make a huge four-foot by four-foot diorama or he'd make it inside an aquarium and he'd spend weeks on it and anybody who came over would be totally amazed at what a great sculptor he was.

We used to try to talk him into getting a show at the Smithfield [cafe] and he'd say no and he'd tear it all down. You'd go over the next day and it would be all gone and he'd be starting on a new one."

Necessity is the mother of invention, which is how Kurt came up with one of his favorite decorations. "I have this weird magnetic attraction to flies," says Kurt. "Or flies attract to me, actually. I'd wake up in the morning and these flies would keep me awake for hours, buzzing and bouncing off my face. They'd just attack me and this has happened over and over again in my life." Kurt hung up dozens and dozens of fly strips all over the apartment and they soon collected all kinds of dead insects.

Kurt insists that his income from the band paid the meager rent, but occasionally, Tracy would ask him to get a job and Kurt would offer to move out and live in his car, which was enough to keep her from asking again for a while. It seemed as if Tracy was as much Kurt's patron as she was his lover.

Kurt insists he was pulling his weight, partly because of something unusual that was happening in Seattle. For a few years before Nirvana arrived, antimaterialistic Seattle punk bands had allowed themselves to be fleeced by the local clubs. But by this time, Seattle musicians had informally united and made it known that they wouldn't play for peanuts anymore. The emerging Seattle record label Sub Pop played a big part in making sure that a lot of their artists got paid well for live gigs. Kurt remembers playing an early show at the Vogue to three hundred people and the band pulling in six hundred dollars, a lot of money even now.

But in order to save up enough money to record a proper demo tape, that fall he took a job at a janitorial company for four bucks an hour. He would ride around town in a cramped van with two "co-workers from hell," as Kurt puts it, "worse than your typical brain-dead Aberdonian." Typically, his workmates would down a couple of sixes each in the course of a night's work while they called Kurt a fag and jostled him around the van. Several of their clients were doctors and dentists, and they would show Kurt how to steal pills and inhale nitrous oxide without anyone finding out.

Dylan Carlson and Slim Moon eventually moved in next door. Since Kurt worked at night and Carlson was unemployed, they hung out a lot, sharing their disdain for the Calvinists ("I think Kurt and I were the only ones not throwing a yo-yo that summer," cracks Carlson). They'd hang up strings of tacky lamps from the fifties (another thrift store purchase) and have barbecues in the backyard. Sometimes Chris would come over and they'd inevitably break out a bottle of red wine and start to act up. The police showed up one time after the three attacked an abandoned Cadillac with some lawn chairs.

Still, Kurt was basically a recluse, and remained so for virtually the entire four years he lived in Olympia. "He was like a hermit in a cave," says Slim Moon. "That was the way we perceived him—the mad hermit who would sit there and play his guitar for twelve hours a day and never leave his house except to go on tour."

Although Kurt was hardly outgoing, he was rather popular around town. He'd go to parties and sit down somewhere and just smile quietly. To most of the Olympia scenesters, he was a blank slate who was whatever they wanted him to be. They liked Kurt, but they really couldn't figure out why, and that mystery seemed to suffuse his music as well.

After a while, Kurt was awarded his own janitorial route, but he was far from a model worker. He'd go off in the van to the first building on his route, throw away a few papers here and there, and then go home and nap. Toward the end of his shift, he'd go to a few more places and do the same slipshod job. After eight months of that, he was fired.

Kurt admits he's always been lazy, but he says his dismal employment record doesn't stem from mere lassitude. "I've always had this terrible relationship with co-workers," he says. "I just cannot get along with average people. They just get on my nerves so bad, I just cannot ignore them at all. I have to confront them and tell them that I hate their guts."

Still, Kurt had learned *something* from his workmates: how to steal drugs. His favorites—when he could get them—were codeine and Vicodin, an opiate-derived painkiller. He smoked pot and did heroin again a few times. He tried cocaine and speed but didn't like them. "I felt too confident and too sure of myself," he says. "Just too sociable."

Around this time, he first experienced a terrible, piercing pain in his stomach. "It's burning, nauseous, like the worst stomach flu you can imagine," Kurt says. "You can feel it throbbing like you have a heart in your stomach and it just hurts really bad. I can just feel it being all raw and red. It mostly just hurts when I eat. About halfway through a meal and once it gets up to a certain area, right where it's inflamed and red, once it starts hitting there it starts hurting because the food sits on it and it burns. It's probably one of the worst pains I've ever felt." The condition has dominated Kurt's life—and baffled even the most distinguished specialists—ever since.

Meanwhile, Aaron Burckhard kept promising to get a new pair of

Aaron Burckhard. (Photo courtesy Aaron Burckhard)

drums, but never did and had trouble showing up for practice, preferring instead to go out partying with his buddies. "They wanted to practice every night," says Burckhard. "*Every* night. I'm like, give me a break. I didn't show up a couple of times and they got kind of pissed off." For Burckhard, the band was just for fun—"We're not going to make no money off it or anything, you know?"

There may have been some basic incompatibility, too. Although Burckhard now says he's a punk rock fan, he wasn't as committed to it as Kurt and Chris were. "I'm not that much into that kind of scene," Burckhard admits, "where your hair is all different colors and whatnot."

By now, Chris and Shelli were in Tacoma and Kurt was in Olympia, but Burckhard didn't move—his girlfriend was staying in Aberdeen and he himself had hopes of becoming a full manager at the Burger King. Ironically, his cousin married the daughter of the owner of the franchise, and Burckhard never got past production manager. They temporarily lost touch with Burckhard.

During this time Kurt and Chris decided to practice with Dale Crover with the intention of recording a demo. It was a way of keeping the band alive. They practiced with Crover three weekends in a row, then went up to Reciprocal Recording in Seattle and recorded a demo on January 23, 1988. "After the demo tape was recorded," Kurt recalls, "we realized that it was actually good music and there was something special about it so we took it a lot more seriously."

Kurt says he happened to choose the most happening studio in Seattle simply by comparison shopping in the *Seattle Rocket*, a free music paper that remains the house organ of the Seattle scene. It was one of the cheapest studios in town, which is why it was the hottest studio in town. But others insist that Kurt chose Reciprocal because that was where his favorite new record, the *Screaming Life* EP by Soundgarden, had been recorded for the fledgling Seattle indie label, Sub Pop. "Kurt really wanted to record there because he really liked the sound of the Soundgarden record," says Crover, who set up the studio time. "He was really into it that summer, I remember." Kurt strenuously denies this. At any rate, they were scheduled to work with another engineer, but at the last minute Jack Endino stepped in, probably because he wanted to work with Crover, who was already known as an excellent drummer.

Endino, a former Navy engineer, had already become the godfather of the Seattle scene. By recording (he never "produced"—that wasn't punk rock) countless bands for very little money, he fostered the growing scene and made Sub Pop a viable financial proposition. Endino's easygoing, avuncular personal style and rip-roaring sound made him a favorite with the young, raw bands from the area. He founded Reciprocal Recording, a studio in the Ballard section of Seattle, with Chris Hanszek, who had also produced the *Deep Six* compilation.

Reciprocal was as casual as a band practice room—the paint peeled off the particle-board walls, there were cigarette burns all over every horizontal surface, and it didn't matter a bit if you spilled your beer on the carpet. There are few bands in Seattle who haven't seen the inside of Reciprocal (or its latest incarnation, Word of Mouth).

Chris's friend Dwight Covey drove the band and their equipment up to Seattle in his beat-up Chevy camper, complete with working wood stove.

After Chris laid down his parts, he decided to party with Dwight and Dwight's son, Guy. "He had this two-paper bomber with all bud and we smoked it in the bathroom," says Chris. "I got so stoned that I had to go outside." They sat in the camper and lit the fire while Kurt did his vocals.

The band recorded and mixed ten songs in six hours (Endino charged them for only five). All the tracks were basically cut live, and in one or two takes. Kurt did all the vocals in one take. By three in the afternoon, they had finished all the recording. "Floyd the Barber," "Paper Cuts," and "Downer" all wound up on *Bleach*. Two others

School
Love Buzz
Floyd the barber
Mr moustache
Paper Cuts
Mexican Seafood
Spank Thru
Aeroslepperin
Sifting
Hairspray Queen
Big cheese

BLEW

Blandest - Downer - Run Rabbit Run - immigrant song -
en Cap Chew - Vendetagainst - Bad moon Rising -

An early set list. Note the Led Zeppelin and
Creedence Clearwater Revival covers on the
reserve list.

have never been released: "If You Must" and "Pen Cap Chew," which had a fade ending because the tape ran out. A version of "Spank Thru" was later rere-corded with Chad Channing on drums and released on *Sub Pop 200*. The remaining four tunes— "Beeswax," "Mexican Seafood," "Hairspray Queen," and "Aero Zeppelin" —can be found on *Incesticide*. Chris had been laid off, so Kurt paid the $152.44 for the recording with money he made as a janitor.

Crover had arranged a show for them that night in Tacoma at the Community World Thea-ter. They didn't have a band name again, so Crover suggested Ted Ed Fred, his nickname for Greg Hokanson's mom's boyfriend at the time. Chris finally came down from the effects of the two-paper bomber just before show time.

Kurt was really happy with the demo. Tracy remembers him sit-ting in her car holding on to the finished tape, with a huge smile on his face. Endino liked the tape, too, so he made a mix for himself that night and gave a cassette to Jonathan Poneman, who had just released the Soundgarden EP on Sub Pop, which had been founded by his partner, Bruce Pavitt, a few months earlier. There weren't that many Seattle bands that Poneman, a former club booker, didn't already know about, but like Endino says, "These guys were from *Aberdeen*."

Poneman was looking for more bands to fill out Sub Pop's roster, so he asked Endino if he'd heard anything good lately. Endino replied, "Well, there was this one guy who came in—I don't really know *what* to make of it, to tell you the truth. This guy's got a really amazing voice, he came in with Dale Crover. I don't know what to make of it, but his voice has a lot of power. And he looks a lot like an auto mechanic."

Poneman loved the tape. "I was just thoroughly blown away by the guy's voice," he says. "It wasn't like I was listening to any one song that was blowing me away, but at the time, the songs were kind of secondary to the whole feel. The band obviously had a lot of raw power. I just remember hearing that tape and going, 'Oh my God.'"

Poneman excitedly brought the demo in to Muzak, the background music company, where just about anybody who was anybody in the Seattle scene worked at menial jobs like cleaning tape cartridge boxes or duplicating tapes. Green River's Mark Arm (now of Mudhoney), Room Nine's Ron Rudzitis (now of Love Battery), Tad Doyle (an Idaho transplant who would soon lead the band TAD), Chris Pugh of Swallow, Grant Eckman from the Walkabouts, and Bruce Pavitt all worked at Muzak, making it a place where ideas and opinions about rock and roll were developed and discussed. "If anyone wants to get rich," Poneman announced, "this band is looking for a drummer."

But the jukebox jury didn't like it. The music relied too heavily on tortured, complex arrangements for the Muzak bunch, who were getting into more straight-ahead rock such as early Wipers, Cosmic Psychos, and the Stooges. But the guy did have a great voice. On the other hand, the Muzak crowd might not have liked it no matter what. "Everybody wanted their closest friends to be the biggest stars," says Pavitt, "and [Nirvana] was from out of town so people were hedging their bets a little bit." Poneman remembers Mark Arm saying the tape sounded like Skin Yard, "but not as good." "Basically people were pretty much focused on their clique," says Pavitt, "and the music that was coming out of that clique."

Pavitt thought it was too "rock"—too much heavy metal and not enough underground. Poneman and Pavitt caught a show at the Central Tavern—eight on a Sunday night—that was sparsely attended, even though hundreds of people now claim to have been there. The band was rough but some of the material was very good. Pavitt agreed the band had potential. Poneman remembers Kurt threw up backstage before the show.

"I wasn't completely swept over by the band," Pavitt admits. "I did not see an interesting musical angle with Nirvana." But Poneman loved the music, and Pavitt, a former journalist, began looking for a hook with which to sell the band to the music press—small indie labels depend on the media to do their promotion for them. Then Pavitt hit on something.

"The more I spent time thinking about who they were and what was going on in Seattle," says Pavitt, "it really started to fit in with this Tad thing—the butcher from Idaho—the whole real genuine working class—I hate to use the phrase 'white trash'—something not contrived that had a more grassroots or populist feel." Up until then (and to a large extent ever since), independent music was dominated by the East Coast circuit of tip sheets, fanzines, radio stations, and clubs. Instead of the pointy-headed college/art school cabal, "We were trying to work with people who were intelligent and creative but weren't necessarily in college," says Pavitt. "And the more I got to know Kurt, they really seemed to fit that picture as well as Tad."

When Kurt first moved in with Tracy in Olympia, he complained that he was shunned in Seattle because he wasn't part of a clique. A year later, he didn't want to go to shows because so many people wanted to talk to him. They had all heard the demo tape. Endino would make tapes for his friends, who would make copies for their friends.

Kurt dubbed off a bunch of cassettes and sent them to every indie label he could think of, including SST in

Tracy Marander, February 1989.
(© 1993 by Alice Wheeler)

Lawndale, California, and San Francisco's Alternative Tentacles. But the label he really wanted to be on was Chicago's Touch & Go—home of some of Kurt's favorite bands: Scratch Acid, Big Black, and the Butthole Surfers. He sent about twenty copies to the label, always accompanied by letters and "little gifts," which ranged from little toys and handfuls of confetti to a used condom filled with plastic ants or a piece of paper encrusted with boogers (a stunt which sounds suspiciously similar to what Big Black did with their *Lungs* EP). No one, especially Touch & Go, called back.

He didn't send a tape to Sub Pop because he barely knew it existed. Not a moment too soon, Poneman called Kurt to tell him he liked the tape. Kurt figured Poneman was cool because he was associated with Soundgarden, his favorite band at the time. They arranged a meeting at the Café Roma on Broadway in Seattle.

Kurt arrived first with Tracy. Tracy was vaguely suspicious and wary of the whole thing—she didn't like the way Poneman kept his hands jammed in the pockets of his long trench coat, or the way he kept nervously sweeping his eyes around the room. "It looked like the police were after him," she recalls.

Poneman remembers Kurt as being "very timid, very respectful" and "a very nice, gentle guy." Chris, who came in soon after Kurt and Tracy, was a different story. Chris was nervous about the meeting and had polished off a few Olde English forty-ouncers on the way up to Seattle. By the time they arrived, he was quite drunk and was swigging from yet another forty-ouncer that he kept under the café table. Throughout the meeting, he would glare at Poneman and insult him, burping loudly and occasionally turning around to bellow at the other customers—"What the fuck are you people looking at? Hey! *Hey!*" Kurt remembers it as "one of the funniest things I've ever seen."

Poneman did his best to ignore Chris, and somehow managed to convey the idea that he wanted to put out a Nirvana single in the near future.

Early 1988 was a fallow period for the Seattle scene. Key bands such as the Melvins, Green River, and Feast were either on hiatus or had broken up. Bands such as Tad, Mudhoney, and Mother Love Bone were just getting started. And so was Sub Pop Records.

Sub Pop began as a fanzine written by Bruce Pavitt, a Chicago transplant who studied punk rock at the free-thinking Evergreen State College in Olympia. Pavitt soon began making tape compilations which highlighted regional music scenes in the United States and eventually spotlighted Seattle in his first vinyl release, *Sub Pop 100*.

In 1987, he released *Dry as a Bone* by Green River, a Seattle band that dared mix the antithetical sounds of metal and punk (the band later splintered into Mudhoney and Pearl Jam). Their mutual friend Kim Thayil of Soundgarden introduced Pavitt to Jonathan Poneman, a radio DJ and promoter of rock shows in Seattle. They released Soundgarden's *Screaming Life* LP in 1988.

Canny, articulate, and blessed with good ears, Pavitt and Poneman had a flair for self-promotion, and having closely studied the successes and failures of previous indie labels, rapidly established both the Seattle scene in general and Sub Pop in particular as the coolest thing in indie rock. There were other labels in town, including Popllama (who had the Young Fresh Fellows), but Sub Pop had the promotional moxie. On most of the front covers, Pavitt's friend Michael Lavine took arty, polished studio photographs that created the impression that the label had shelled out big bucks for a fancy photographer. And on the inside and back covers, Charles Peterson created Sub Pop's defining images—grainy, blurry black-and-white shots that often featured more of the audience than the band. Peterson would fearlessly wade deep into the mosh pit, capturing all the violent motion—all sweat, hair, and bare male chests.

An interesting new band like Nirvana was big news. Kurt's guitar style was jagged, yet had an undeniable metal streak. The riffs were clever. The fact that they could sound so good in so little time amazed Endino, who'd recorded many bands already. Even back then, Kurt was setting his melodies in an unusual way against the rhythms and chord changes. Instead of simply following the guitars, he invented almost contrapuntal melody lines. But what put the band over the top were Kurt's vocals—somehow, he was able to scream *on pitch*, as well as sing in a very accessible and attractive way.

They had crappy equipment and terrible-sounding amps. For a long time, they had to put a two-by-four under Chris's bass cabinet because he was missing a wheel (the problem was remedied only recently).

By that point—early 1988—Crover had left to move to San Francisco with Osborne, but not before recommending Dave Foster from Aberdeen to be his replacement. Foster played bass with Crover in a Melvins satellite band, but was also a fine drummer. Kurt and Chris knew they didn't want Foster in the band permanently—with his souped-up pickup truck and his mustache, Foster was too mainstream, too macho for Kurt and Chris. Still, they played him the Crover demo and Foster seemed to like it.

"They taught me a lot as far as playing," says Foster, who had studied jazz drums in high school. "They just said forget all that shit and just hit 'em hard. That and cutting the size of my drum set in half. When I got in that band, I had a twelve-piece set, and when I got out, I had a six-piece."

They rehearsed in the front room of Chris and Shelli's new house on Pearl Avenue in Tacoma, near the Tacoma Zoo.

The first party they played was packed with Greeners and hippies and punkers. Kurt was wearing his usual cut-off denim jacket with his plastic monkey Chim-Chim glued to the shoulder and a cut-out section of a Woolworth's tapestry of the Last Supper on the back, while Foster was dressed in his usual Aberdeen metal dude clothes. During their set, a punker grabbed the microphone and said, "Gosh, drummers from Aberdeen are sure weird looking!"

Dave Foster,
Kurt, and Chris.
(© 1993 by Rich Hansen)

"I felt out of place," says Foster, "but I was into what they were doing. I loved to play their music."

Poneman got them their first show in Seattle in early 1988 at the Vogue. It was Sub Pop Sunday. Charles Peterson, a key Seattle tastemaker, recalls there were about twenty people there, even though KCMU was playing "Floyd the Barber" regularly. Still, there was a buzz on the band, which reportedly sounded a lot like Blue Cheer. People like Mark Arm were there, scrutinizing this much-ballyhooed new band from the sticks. Kurt later commented that he thought they should have held up scorecards after every song.

The band played sloppily and the malfunctioning P.A. didn't help matters. Peterson, for one, was not impressed with the band's nearly nonexistent stage presence. "They were not particularly engaging," agrees Poneman. And the songs sounded too much like the Melvins. Peterson took Poneman aside and said, "Jonathan, are you *sure* you want to sign these guys?"

"We totally sucked," says Kurt. "We fucked it up."

Foster lasted only a few months. "He was a really straight guy but I think we really intimidated him because we were just weird," says Chris. "He'd just never seen anything like us before. We were just total counterculture people."

"I think *they* were the ones who were uncomfortable, being around what they thought was probably a redneck or something, I don't know. When all my friends came around, I think that made them uncomfortable. Because they weren't the type of people they hung out with," says Foster. "Everybody's got their own little clique, I guess."

"He also had a problem," says Chris. "He had to go to anger counseling. He'd get in fights and beat the hell out of people. One time we saw him and he was with this friend in his trick truck and the guy spat on his truck and he kicked the guy in the head."

Dave Foster's particular last straw came up when he found out his girlfriend was cheating on him. So he did the manly thing and went out and beat the hell out of the guy she was cheating with. Unfortunately for Foster, his victim happened to be the son of the mayor of nearby Cosmopolis. Foster got a one-year sentence but wound up serving two weeks in jail and getting his license revoked, which meant that he couldn't get up from Aberdeen to Tacoma to rehearse with Kurt and Chris.

Once he got out of jail, Foster would call Kurt, asking when he could come up and start practicing again. Kurt said they were writing new material and would get back to him. What he didn't say was they'd been rehearsing with Aaron Burckhard again, using Foster's drums.

But Burckhard's days in the band were numbered, too. One night after practice, Kurt and Burckhard were drinking at Burckhard's father's trailer home in Spanaway. Burckhard told Kurt he was going to get some more beer and borrowed Kurt's car. But instead of going to the package store, Burckhard hit the taverns instead. After two hours of drinking with his buddies, he left to go back to the trailer and was pulled over on a DWI charge by a black policeman who happened to be named Springsteen. Burckhard started drunkenly calling out "Hey, Bruce! What's up, Bruce!" and just generally giving the cop "a rash of shit." Officer Springsteen threw the book at him. Kurt's car got impounded.

Since Burckhard's trailer didn't have a phone, Chris got the call to get Burckhard out of jail. Chris says Burckhard had called the cop a "fucking nigger," which is really why he got the book thrown at him. "It was just really embarrassing for me to go get him," he says.

"I might have said a few things," Burckhard admits, "but I have the right to remain silent."

Kurt says he called Burckhard the next day and asked him to come to practice. Burckhard said he was too hung over to play and Kurt simply hung up the phone. Burckhard was out of the band for good.

"I loved playing with them guys," says Burckhard. "But I was young and stupid and kind of got carried away, you know?"

If Burckhard hadn't gone to the taverns that night, he might be a millionaire right now. "Yeah," he says. "But it's like playing the Lotto—you can get five numbers and not the sixth and you're like, 'God, one more number!' I don't regret a thing. I'll be like—what's that guy from the Beatles?'"

Nowadays, the Pete Best of Nirvana collects unemployment checks, having been laid off from his job insulating houses. He also plays in a speed-metal band called Attica, which boasts tunes such as "Fuck Blister" and "Drunken Hell Thrash." Burckhard recently spent three days in jail because he didn't pay a fine for driving while his license was revoked—apparently, he never did get his license back after that fateful DWI with Officer Springsteen.

Foster still thought he was in the band. Then one day early that summer, he picked up a copy of the *Seattle Rocket* to see if there were any good shows coming up. It said that Nirvana was playing a place in Seattle called Squid Row that very night. Foster called Kurt's house, and Tracy gave him some story. Then he called Chris's and his roommate accidentally spilled the beans. They had another drummer.

"I was so fuckin' pissed," says Foster. "It was just like if you caught your girlfriend in bed with someone else." Recall what happened last time Foster felt like that.

Foster was upset for a long time, particularly when he heard that Nirvana had opened for the Butthole Surfers. "Now that that other shit's happened it's even worse," Foster says. But he's philosophical about it. "They did what they thought best, I guess," he says. "I do wish things were different—all I ever wanted to do was play drums for a living."

"He was such a mainstream type of guy," says Chris. "I think we really intimidated him. We'd make him nervous and his beats would be off." "I wasn't uncomfortable at all," says Foster. "It seemed like *they* were the ones who were uncomfortable. It didn't bother me a bit."

"And he came from a stable family," Chris half jokes.

The drummer at Squid Row that night was Chad Channing, a small, pixieish fellow who sounds a little bit like Elroy from "The Jetsons." "He's an elf," says Kurt. "He should be in the Keebler factory. He's also one of the nicest people I've ever met." Channing lived on Bainbridge Island, an affluent suburb a ferry ride away from Seattle, across Puget Sound. Like Kurt, Chad had also been hyperactive and been given Ritalin. And like Kurt and Chris, his parents were separated, although not divorced.

Chad Channing was born on January 31, 1967, in Santa Rosa, California, to Burnyce and Wayne Channing. Wayne was a radio disc jockey and was forever moving to different jobs all over the country, from California to Minnesota to Hawaii to Alaska to Idaho and back. "Our motto was 'Move every six months,'" says Chad. "So whatever friends I made, wherever I went, I knew they were just temporary. Everything was just temporary. So that was kind of weird. You don't really hang out with many people because why make a friend if you're not going to be around—you're just going to be gone."

Chad had hoped to be a soccer player but when he was thirteen he shattered his thigh bone in a freak gym accident. It took almost seven years of rehabilitation and surgery for him to fully recover. In the meantime, he discovered music and picked up the drums, guitar, and a few other instruments.

Like Kurt, Chad dropped out of high school during his senior year. He'd lost so much schooling from being in the hospital that he would have had to go through months of summer school and night school to get his diploma. He wanted to be a musician and didn't see the sense of it. When he met Kurt and Chris, he was a sauté cook at a seafood restaurant on Bainbridge Island. By night, he partied with his friends, smoking pot, drinking, and doing the potent local acid, which many swear has fried the brains of an entire generation of Bainbridge Islanders.

When Chad first heard of Kurt and Chris's band, they were called Bliss. Bliss shared a show with Chad's band Tick-Dolly-Row (a sailor's term for "down and out") which featured lead singer Ben Shepherd, who went on to play guitar in Soundgarden. Kurt and Chris noticed Chad's North drum kit—which was made of fiberglass and had unique, flared shells. "They noticed my North kit," says Chad. "It was kind of loud and that's what they hit on there. I remember Kurt telling me a long time ago when they were first checking us out, 'God, man, I wish we could get that guy! Look at those drums! Those are the weirdest things I've ever fuckin' seen!'"

Kurt and Chris briefly considered asking Tad Doyle to be their drummer, then took out an ad in the *Rocket*: "Heavy, light punk rock band: Aerosmith, Led Zeppelin, Black Sabbath, Black Flag, Scratch Acid, Butthole Surfers. Seeks drummer." Kurt got a bunch of lackluster responses, but in the meantime, their mutual friend Damon Romero introduced Kurt and Chris to Chad at Malfunkshun's farewell show at the Community World Theater. They talked for a bit and agreed to jam soon at Chris's house. Chad liked the band, but he wasn't sure. Then he saw the band play a show at Evergreen and they talked some more and agreed to jam again. "I just kept on coming over and jamming," says Chad. "They never actually said, 'Okay, you're in.'"

Kurt and Chris built a rehearsal studio in Chris's basement from old mattresses, carpet they got at the Goodwill store, egg cartons that Shelli and Tracy brought home from work, and scrap wood they pinched from construction sites. It was still pretty loud and the neighbors would complain, so they couldn't practice late. One day Chris and Shelli's pet rabbit got out of its cage and chewed through the extension cord that ran down to the basement. The band had to suspend rehearsals for a week until they could get up enough money for a new cord.

After making Chad strip down his mammoth kit just like Dave Foster did, they rehearsed material from the Crover tape as well as new material such as "Big Cheese" and "School." They wrote as a band, with Kurt playing a riff and the other two joining in. They began rehearsing at least two or three times a week and a batch of new songs came together very quickly.

In early May, they played their first show with Chad at the Vogue. Chris sported enormous mutton chop sideburns, while Chad and Kurt's hair hung in long greasy curtains over their eyes. Poneman got them a gig at the Central Tavern in Seattle on a

Kenichewa
Dear _____.
NIRVANA is a three piece from the outskirts of Seattle WA.
Kurdt-Guitar/voice and Chris-bass have struggled with too many undedicated drummers for the past 3 years, performing under such names as: Bliss, Throat Oyster, Pen Cap Chew, Ted ed Fred ETC.. for the last 9 months we have had the pleasure to take Chad-drums under our wings and develop what we are now and always will be NIRVANA.
3 regularly broadcasted carts on K.C.M.U. (Seattle College Radio also KAOS olympia)
Played with: Leaving Trains, Whipping Boy, Hells Kitchen, Treacherous Jaywalkers & countless local acts.
Looking for: EP or LP   We have about 15 songs recorded on 8 tracks at Reciprocal studios in Seattle.
Willing to compromise on material (some of this shit is pretty old.)   Tour any-time forever | hopefully the music will speak for itself.
Please Reply   THANK YOU   Area code (206)
352-0992 114 N PEAR olympia WA. 98506

Saturday afternoon at some benefit show. Nobody was in the club at their scheduled six o'clock set time, so they just packed up their gear and drove back to Tacoma. They soon played another show at the Central, opening for Chemistry Set and Leaving Trains. Not many people were there, either.

The first article ever written about the band, by Dawn Anderson, editor of the free Seattle music paper *Backlash*, noted that the band seemed nervous when playing live. In the piece, Kurt confided, "Our biggest fear at the beginning was that people might think we were a Melvins rip-off," but Anderson bravely ventured that "with enough practice, Nirvana could become... *better than the Melvins!*"

The Seattle scene was really starting to bloom around then, with

NIRVANA

Floyd the barber
Spank Thru
Mexican Seafood
Big cheese
Love Buzz   Plenty
Beans   more
Paper cuts   of this
                 Heavy
                 RockStuff

Cracker   Mellow
Seed   4 track
SAD   shit
Montage
of
Heck
(206)
352-0992
Kurdt

NIRVANA

bands such as Skin Yard, the Fluid, Blood Circus, Swallow, TAD and Mudhoney playing the Vogue, the Underground, the Central, the Alamo. Mother Love Bone was gearing up, but the guys in Soundgarden were then the kings of the scene—miraculously, they had just gotten signed to A&M, a full-fledged major label.

On June 11, 1988, only a month or two after Chad joined, they did the main session for their first single, "Love Buzz."

"Love Buzz"—a cover tune, after all—may not have been Kurt's first choice for the band's first single, but he eventually came around. It was an accessible, easy-to-listen-to pop song that had become a live favorite of both the crowd and Kurt, who got to run around the stage during the song's extended guitar solo section. They liked the idea of recording a new track instead of rerecording something off the Crover demo. Besides, Kurt had started getting into primitive-sounding, garage-influenced bands like the Sonics, a legendary Northwest band from the early sixties, and Mudhoney, and had begun to abandon the Byzantine arrangements he had favored on the Crover demo. Even though he didn't write it, "Love Buzz," a stripped-down pop song, fit perfectly with the direction Kurt wanted to go.

Around this time, Kurt hand-wrote a bio of the band, presumably aimed at prospective record labels, with a few facts distorted to make the band seem a little more established than it really was. "NIRVANA is a three piece from the outskirts of Seattle WA. Kurdt—guitar/voice and Chris—bass have struggled with too many undedicated drummers for the past 3 years [sic]...For the last 9 [sic] months we have had the pleasure to take Chad—drums under our wings and develop what we are now and always will be NIRVANA.

"Willing to compromise on material (some of this shit is pretty old)," the bio concluded. "Tour any time forever. Hopefully the music will speak for itself."

Realizing that Sub Pop favored straight-ahead rock in the Stooges/Aerosmith vein, they recorded what little material they had that fit that style, instead of the more bizarre Scratch Acid–type songs they had been playing. Kurt regrets the decision now. "I wish we'd have put 'Hairspray Queen' or something," he says. "But the idea of going into the studio again, instead of using what we had on the demo already, was enough of a challenge."

Everybody was very excited about putting out their first record. Still, a pattern was already emerging. "For me, recording always went weird," says Chad. "I was there, I did my job, and that was it. I didn't really have any say about how this or that should sound. I might as well have gone up there, did my thing, and then gone out and get a candy bar or something. I'd bang on the drums, get the drum sound down and stuff like that, and then I'd just kick back and wait until they got the bass and guitar sounds and we'd do the song and that was kind of it. The rest of the time, I'd spend listening to see what they did with it. Kurt and Chris were like 'Let's do this and let's do that.' I would have had things to say, but I don't know, it just didn't feel right or something like that. I really had nothing to say or do."

Sub Pop didn't sign its bands to contracts back then. It wasn't done. Poneman simply told Nirvana that he liked that Shocking Blue cover they did, and would they like to do a single? At first, they held out to do their own song, but eventually relented. They recorded for five hours and ended up with several finished songs, including "Love Buzz," "Big Cheese," another stab at "Spank Thru," and "Blandest." It was Chad's first session. He wasn't hitting very hard then, but he'd come around.

"Blandest" was going to be the flipside. The song is indeed not nearly as remarkable as what made it to the single, but the track does feature a fairly embarrassing Robert Plant–like falsetto wail toward the end by Kurt. As Endino recalls, the song's title seemed all too fitting, so he convinced Kurt to use "Big Cheese." They returned for more work on June 30 and mixed it all on July 16. Poneman didn't like the vocals on the first mix, so Kurt rerecorded them, although Endino says even he was hard pressed to hear the difference.

Kurt remembers feeling that "Love Buzz" was sounding too lightweight. They blamed Chad, whom they felt was not as good or as hard-hitting a drummer as Dale Crover. "We just couldn't get a good sound out of it," says Kurt. "It sounded really clean and just didn't

have any low end. I think it's the wimpiest recording we've ever done."

The intro to "Love Buzz," a forty-five-second sound collage Kurt made from various children's records, was trimmed at Pavitt's request down to ten seconds. It appears only on the original seven-inch single. "They were just constantly having control right away," says Kurt. "Doing exactly what a major label would do and claiming to be such an independent label."

In September, Shelli broke up with Chris. The strain of Shelli's working the graveyard shift at the Boeing cafeteria and Chris's playing with the band got to be too much. She had just turned twenty-one and had never been alone. They decided to live separately. They broke up but saw each other often. They missed each other and were depressed.

As avid students of the indie-rock game, Pavitt and Poneman knew that American artists from Jimi Hendrix to Blondie had established a buzz in the U.K. before anyone in their native country noticed them. So they took the huge financial gamble of flying in a music journalist, *Melody Maker*'s Everett True, all the way from England to check out a few Sub Pop bands. True raved about the Seattle scene in a series of articles, and soon U.S. press and labels were foaming at the mouth, too.

Mudhoney's *Superfuzz Bigmuff* EP stayed on the U.K. indie charts for a year, almost unheard of for an American release. Three months later, ultra-influential Radio One DJ John Peel raved about the *Sub Pop 200* box set and basically said it was a testament to regional music not seen since Detroit's Motown label conquered the world in the mid-sixties.

The Brits went ga-ga over the Seattle scene. "The reason they picked it up was there was a regional identity and flavor to what we were doing," says Bruce Pavitt. "The history of rock music is broken down that way—it comes down to labels or scenes. We understood that from the beginning. Look at the cast of characters—that's how you create a soap opera that people come back into. So all of a sudden, people knew who Mark Arm was, Kurt, Tad, me, and Jon, Jack Endino, Peterson. We tried to introduce in our own way, these celebrities. Like our singles, the only thing that would be on the back was 'Recorded by Jack Endino' and 'Photo by Charles Peterson.' And after you get ten singles like that, with no information other than that, you're going, *'Who's Charles Peterson? Who's Jack Endino?'*"

On September 27, Nirvana and Endino mixed "Spank Thru" for the *Sub Pop 200* compilation. A seminal sonic document, the collection also featured tracks by Soundgarden, TAD, Mudhoney, Beat

Happening, and Screaming Trees. The tracks could easily have fit onto two LP's, but Pavitt and Poneman, who always said yes to another excess, decided to release it as a three-EP set with an extensive sixteen-page booklet of photos by Charles Peterson, limited to five thousand copies.

Meanwhile, Kurt and Poneman exchanged countless phone calls, trying to hash out the particulars of the single. So much time elapsed between the time that Poneman agreed to do a single and when it actually came out that Kurt and Chris began to become very suspicious of the deal. Kurt would call and ask about the single and Poneman would promise the record would come out soon. Five months later, Pavitt called up wondering if Sub Pop could borrow two hundred dollars to press the single. Kurt hung up on him and sent out another batch of demo tapes to the various labels. The single came out soon afterward, in November of 1988.

An early Sub Pop catalogue touted the "Love Buzz"/"Big Cheese" single as "Heavy pop sludge from these untamed Olympia drop-ins." It was the first Sub Pop Single of the Month, a clever scheme in which Sub Pop commanded exhorbitant prices for limited edition singles for which subscribers paid in advance—"We're ripping you off big time," the Sub Pop catalogue boasted. Only one thousand hand-numbered copies of the "Love Buzz" single were made. "We were really burned about that," Chris recalls. "We put a single out and nobody can buy it."

Actually, pressing only one thousand copies was a very canny move—like many other of Sub Pop's limited releases, the single sold out quickly, making the record an instant collector's item (it now fetches up to fifty dollars). "It was very effective promotion for the group," says Pavitt. "I do not regret that at all." Word of mouth on the single traveled far and wide.

And significantly, it had won over even the doubting Thomases in the Muzak posse. Pavitt knew something was up when Charles Peterson told him he played the single over and over at his party.

Except for Kurt's songwriting, "Love Buzz" had all the elements of classic Nirvana already in place: the mix of passivity and aggression in the way the song went from an almost hypnotic revelry to screaming, all-out frenzy; the sludgy, pounding drums; the grunged-up pop; and the Scream. With its slow, lurching rhythms and dire, barked vocals, "Big Cheese" showed a heavy Melvins influence. The song's title character is none other than Jonathan Poneman. "I was expressing all the pressures that I felt from him at the time because he was being so judgmental about what we were recording," says Kurt. Although not his finest songwriting hour, the lyrics were typi-

The cover of the "Love Buzz" / "Big Cheese" single.

cal of Kurt's gift for taking a situation specific to him and turning it into a universal—who hasn't felt resentment at being ordered around by someone else?

During a visit to Seattle, Kurt heard that the hip community radio station KCMU was playing their single. As he and Tracy were driving back to Olympia from Seattle, they listened to the station for "Love Buzz," but it never appeared. Kurt made Tracy stop the car at a telephone booth, where he called the station and requested the song. They couldn't drive any further or they'd lose the signal, so they waited twenty minutes until they played the single. Kurt was excited.

"It was amazing," says Kurt. "I never thought that I'd get to that point. I just thought I'd be in a band and maybe make a demo, but for them to play it on the radio was just too much to ask for at that time. It was really great. It was instant success and fame beyond my wildest dreams. More than I ever wanted. But once I got a taste of it, I really thought it was cool and I thought I would definitely like to hear my future recordings on the radio. And be able to pay my rent with this band, it would be really great. It made us step up mentally to another level where it was a reality that we could actually live off of this. I didn't think anywhere past ever being able to afford more than a hundred-dollar apartment. That was going to be the rest of my life—to be in a band and tour and play clubs and hear my songs on the radio once in a while. That was about it. I didn't think of ever looking forward to anything more than that."

Around that time, the so-called alternative rock scene was undergoing one of its periodic sea-changes. Although they wouldn't have been caught dead admitting it even a year before, people were now quietly admitting that yes, seventies dinosaurs like Aerosmith and Led Zeppelin and Kiss and Alice Cooper really did rock. But it wasn't like punk rock never happened, either. A new tide of musicians began synthesizing the hard rock they were raised on in the seventies and the American indie punk rock they had embraced in the eighties.

Some of the dogmatic barriers within the indie rock scene were falling—for a minute. Between the time of recording the demo and *Bleach*, Kurt and Chris were going through a crisis of musical identity. The demo had boasted overt Butthole Surfers and Scratch Acid sounds, yet they were also into cock-rock, as demonstrated by songs like "Aero Zeppelin." "There were a lot of real confused messages going on in our brains," says Kurt. "We just didn't know what we wanted to do at all. We just didn't have our own sound at all. Like everyone else, we were just coming to grips with admitting that we liked all different kinds of music. To be a punk rocker and if you were at a Black Flag show and you said you liked R.E.M. ... You just couldn't do it."

CHAPTER FIVE

Nirvana began practicing intensively in preparation for an album, even though Sub Pop, as was their custom for new bands, merely wanted an EP. The rehearsal place had moved from Chris's basement to the space above Maria's Hair Design. Chris's mom didn't close shop until eight in the evening, so practices started then, lasting into the wee hours of the morning, often breaking for Chinese food around midnight. Chad would travel all the way from Bainbridge Island, picking up Chris in Tacoma and then Kurt in Olympia. This went on for two or three weeks. "We'd practice for hours and then we'd go on some trip," says Chris. "One day we went out to the beach and walked around and one night we went out to this water tower." Sometimes they'd just drive around in Chris's van and listen to Celtic Frost and the Smithereens.

Nirvana's first photo session, summer 1989. (© 1993 by Alice Wheeler)

On December 21, 1989, about a week and a half before recording, they played a show at the Hoquiam Eagles Lodge. Chris played in his underpants and Kurt painted his neck red.

Shortly before he and Shelli broke up, Chris had quit his job in order to devote more time to the band. He had four hundred dollars saved up and blew it all in two weeks. "I'd go to parties and buy four cases of beer and just give out beer," says Chris. "Once, I gave out a case of beer in two minutes. Next thing I knew, I was broke."

"I was in bumland," says Chris of his bachelor days. "It was awesome." He moved back in with his mom in Aberdeen and it snowed for two weeks while Chris hung around the house and read *One Day in the Life of Ivan Denisovich*. "I felt like I was in a gulag," he says.

Nirvana wanted to record, but Sub Pop, like most indie labels, was having cash flow problems, thanks in part to the exorbitant costs of the cover art for the *Rehab Doll* EP by Green River, who were by then defunct. They went ahead and booked sessions for an album anyway. They began work on *Bleach* on December 24, 1988, and did five hours of basic tracks.

On the twenty-eighth, they played a release party for *Sub Pop 200* at the Underground. Legendary Seattle poet Steven Jesse Bernstein introduced them as "the band with the freeze-dried vocals." The next day, they did another five tracks, then more work on January 24, 1989. When all was said and done, Endino billed them for a total of thirty hours. On the way to recording, Kurt would sit in the front passenger seat, rest a piece of paper on the dashboard, and hastily finish writing down the lyrics to the songs they were about to record.

Chad had been in the band six months and they'd been playing a lot. Chad was a more straight-ahead drummer than Dale Crover and the tunes were correspondingly straightforward. They attempted "Floyd the Barber" and "Paper Cuts" again, but they didn't match the Dale Crover versions, so they remixed the Crover tapes and put them on the album. The as yet untitled album was sequenced and edited, but Bruce Pavitt ordered the album completely resequenced. The album was delayed a couple of months, but Sub Pop finally borrowed some money to get it out.

Kurt was very particular about his singing, and would get very angry if he couldn't make the sounds he wanted to make. "He'd start smacking his chest and stuff," says Chad. "Not into it."

If the mixes on *Bleach* sound a little strange, there may be a very good reason. "We were all sick by then," Chris remembers, "and we had this codeine syrup from the Pierce County Health Department. So we were drinking a lot of that for our sickness but we were really on codeine and we were mixing the record and getting really into it."

The album cost $606.17 to record. No one in the band had that kind of money, so a fellow named Jason Everman put up the cash.

Dylan Carlson had introduced him to Kurt, and it soon turned out that Jason had known Chad since they were in fifth grade. The two had even played in several bands together in high school. Jason had spent the past few summers as a commercial fisherman in Alaska and had piled up a lot of money, so lending his old friend six hundred dollars was no big deal—besides, he had heard the Crover demo and knew that the band was destined for bigger things.

He began hanging out with the band.

Kurt didn't have much experience with playing guitar and singing (and remembering the words) at the same time—he'd only been playing in a band for a year and a half, after all. And all of a sudden, they had a tour to do. So one day Kurt mentioned to Jason that they were thinking about getting a second guitar player to thicken up the sound. "We basically were ready to take anybody if they could play good guitar," says Kurt. Jason mentioned that he played, auditioned once, and that was it. "He seemed like a nice enough guy," says Kurt. "And he had long Sub Pop hair." And besides, like Kurt, Chris, and

Meet the Nirvanas: Kurt, Jason Everman, Chad, and Chris (© Ian T. Tilton)

Chad, Jason came from a broken home. He had even lived in Aberdeen for a while as a kid.

Although Jason is credited as a guitarist on *Bleach*, he didn't play on it. "We just wanted to make him feel more at home in the band," says Chris.

His first gig with Nirvana was a drunken dorm party at Evergreen State College. With another guitar player on stage, Kurt didn't have to try as hard; consequently, he became a much better player. Soundman Craig Montgomery recalls that he'd turn Kurt's guitar up much higher than Jason's. Early on, they began to realize what they had gotten into with Jason. Although Jason said he'd been into punk rock for years, Kurt's inspection of his record collection revealed, to his horror, little more than speed metal records.

Chris found a rehearsal space in Seattle, but they didn't have a place to live in town, so often they'd buy some forty-ouncers and drink in the van until they fell asleep.

In February of 1989, after the album was completed, they did a quick two-week West Coast tour. By leaps and bounds, the band was gaining confidence as a live act. Bruce Pavitt remembers Mudhoney guitarist Steve Turner coming back after his band played with Nirvana in San Jose and raving that "Kurt Cobain played guitar standing on his head!"

They weathered a devastating flu, visiting the Haight-Ashbury

A sketch of the band by Kurt, with Chad's North drums very much on display.

Free Clinic in San Francisco. While riding in their van around San Francisco, the band and Poneman and Pavitt noticed there was a major anti-AIDS campaign going on in town, with signs all over the city urging drug users to "bleach your works," meaning to clean needles with bleach to kill the AIDS virus. There was even a guy dressed up as a bleach bottle walking around downtown handing out bottles of bleach. "We were contemplating how bleach could become the most valuable substance on earth," says Pavitt. And so *Bleach* became the title of Nirvana's as yet unreleased first album.

A cover piece in the March 18, 1989, *Melody Maker* on the Seattle scene featured a brief blurb on Nirvana. "Basically, this is the real thing," it began. "No rock star contrivance, no intellectual perspective, no master plan for world domination. You're talking about four guys in their early twenties from rural Washington who wanna rock,

S.F.

Letter from Chad to his mother from the quickie West Coast tour.

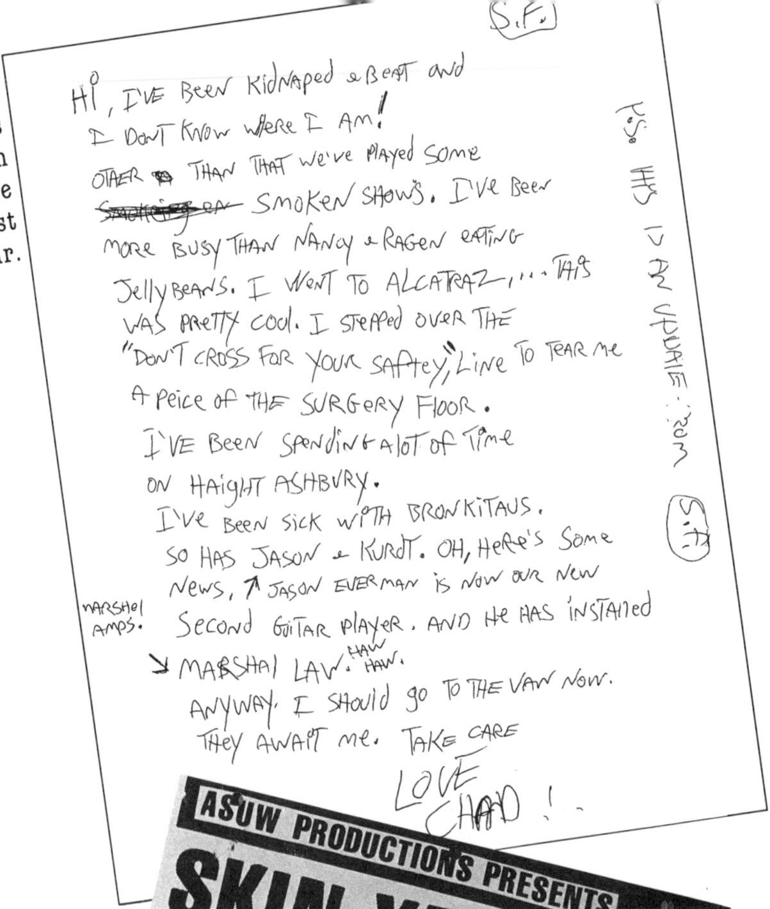

HI, I'VE BEEN KIDNAPED & BEAT AND I DON'T KNOW WHERE I AM! OTHER ~~THA BEA~~ THAN THAT WE'VE PLAYED SOME ~~SMOKING BEA~~ SMOKEN SHOWS. I'VE BEEN MORE BUSY THAN NANCY & RAGEN EATING JELLYBEANS. I WENT TO ALCATRAZ,.... THIS WAS PRETTY COOL. I STEPPED OVER THE "DON'T CROSS FOR YOUR SAFTEY" LINE TO TEAR ME A PEICE OF THE SURGERY FLOOR.

I'VE BEEN SPENDING A LOT OF TIME ON HAIGHT ASHBURY.
I'VE BEEN SICK WITH BRONKITAUS. SO HAS JASON & KURDT. OH, HERE'S SOME NEWS, ↗ JASON EVERMAN IS NOW OUR NEW SECOND GUITAR PLAYER. AND HE HAS INSTALED

MARSHOL AMPS.

↘ MARSHAL LAW. HAW. HAW.
ANYWAY, I SHOULD GO TO THE VAN NOW. THEY AWAIT ME. TAKE CARE
LOVE CHAD !

P.S. HE'S IN AN UPDATE...ROOM

S.F.

ASUW PRODUCTIONS PRESENTS

SKIN YARD
GIRL TROUBLE
THE FLUID
NIRVANA

ALL AGES

SAT FEBRUARY 25 8:30 PM

FOUR MORE BANDS
FOUR MORE BUCKS
(WITH CURRENT STUDENT ID)

HUB EAST BALLROOM
$4.00/UW Student
$6.00 General

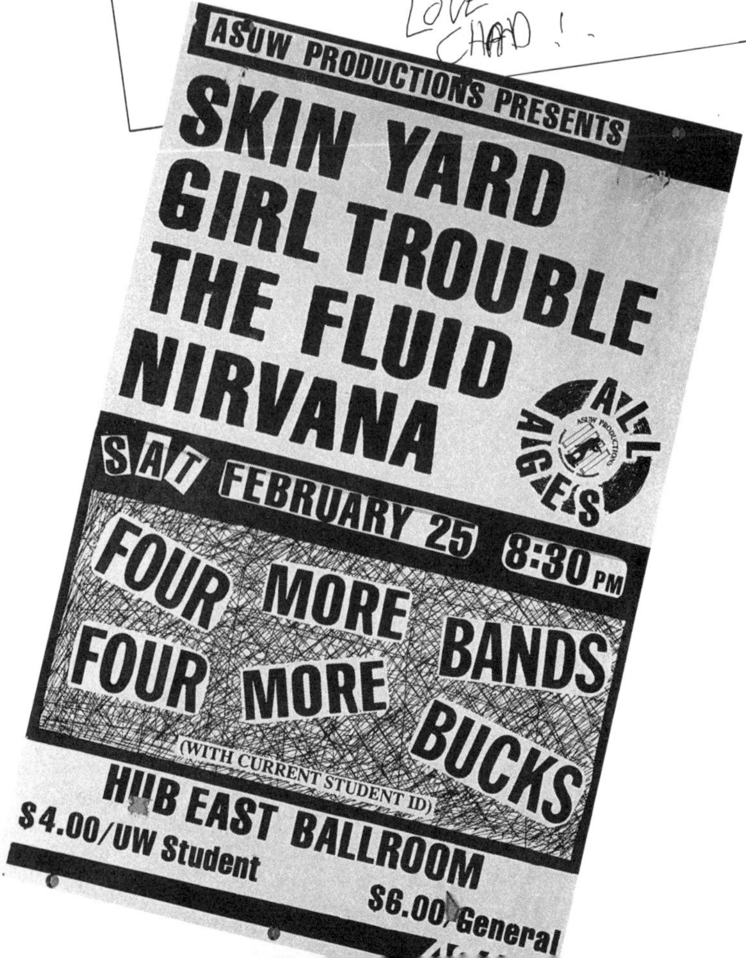

True grunge. Kurt at the HUB. (Both photographs © Charles Peterson)

Chris and Kurt at the HUB. (© Charles Peterson)

Chris puts his back into it at the HUB. Note
Jason's Soundgarden T-shirt. (© Charles Peterson)

who if they weren't doing this, they would be working in a supermarket or lumber yard, or fixing cars." It was a positive little piece, but you could cut the condescension with a knife.

The band came back from their tour and played a lot of area gigs—the Vogue, the HUB Ballroom at the University of Washington, and the Annex Theater, where the crowd paid Kurt the ultimate compliment by passing him over their heads during "Blew." Jonathan Poneman remembers that event as a milestone—only the ultra-cool Mark Arm had enjoyed that honor before.

They played a gig at a community center in Ellensburg, a deadbeat cowtown in rural Washington. In the audience was Steve Fisk, who had already made a name for himself as producer of Soundgarden, Beat Happening, and the first four records by the Screaming Trees.

"I hated them," says Fisk. "The P.A. system was set up really bad by this jock guy from Yakima. Kurt had broken a string and was really upset and stood in the corner trying to change his guitar string. They were just clowning off and they were all nervous—except for Chris—and they were playing *Ellensburg*. Even when it was obvious that Kurt wasn't playing his guitar they kept playing. Jason started moving his hair, but it wasn't in time with the music at all. I'm sorry—I've seen Black Flag and you move your hair in time with the music or you don't move it at all." Fisk walked out during the first song.

Bleach came out in June of 1989. Kurt disavows any personal relevance in the lyrics of the album. "Not much thought went into them at all," he says self-deprecatingly. "It's pretty obvious." But in truth, many of the songs tell a lot about Kurt and various incidents and situations in his life.

The night before the sessions, the band stayed over at Jason Everman's house in Seattle. Kurt still hadn't written lyrics for most of the songs on the album. "I didn't care about lyrics at all at that time," he says. "I didn't have any appreciation for them. I'd never thought of a song because of its lyrics at that point." But he had to sing *something*, so he sat down and wrote into the wee hours.

One of the remarkable things about *Bleach* is that the songs often have only one verse, which is repeated two, three, or more times ("School" has only fifteen words). It's barely noticeable because of Kurt's wide range of vocal styles and phrasings, and the hugely catchy riffs which constitute the songs. Kurt chalks up his laconic lyric style to short-term memory loss. "I decided to write songs that I would easily remember the lyrics to so I wouldn't fuck them up during the live show," he says.

"Swap Meet" comes straight from Aberdeen. A phenomenon of struggling rural America, swap meets take place in drive-ins or parking lots. People come from miles around to sell baked goods, handicrafts, bric-a-brac and whatever else they can salvage from the darkest recesses of their garages and attics. Some sell their belongings so they can make the rent, others become full-time swap meet merchants. According to Kurt, the latter is usually "a white trash entrepreneur who can't look further than selling junk because they *live* in junk. They're surrounded by it and their whole mentality is based on junk—grease and dirt and poverty."

"Mr. Moustache" would help set a trend in alternative rock—the title is found nowhere in the song. "I've never had any reason to name any of my songs," Kurt says. "That's the only difference between alternative bands and cock-rock bands. Alternative rock bands name their songs with titles that don't have anything to do with the song or the chorus."

"In high school," explains Matt Lukin, "having a mustache was

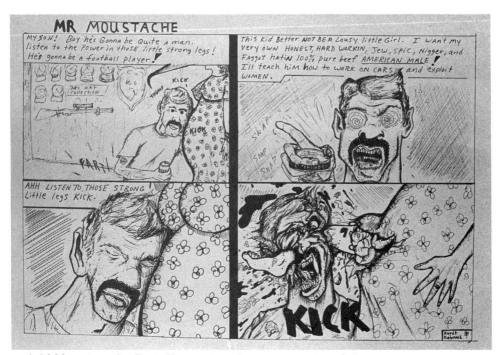

A 1988 cartoon by Kurt illustrating the true meaning of the term "Mr. Moustache."

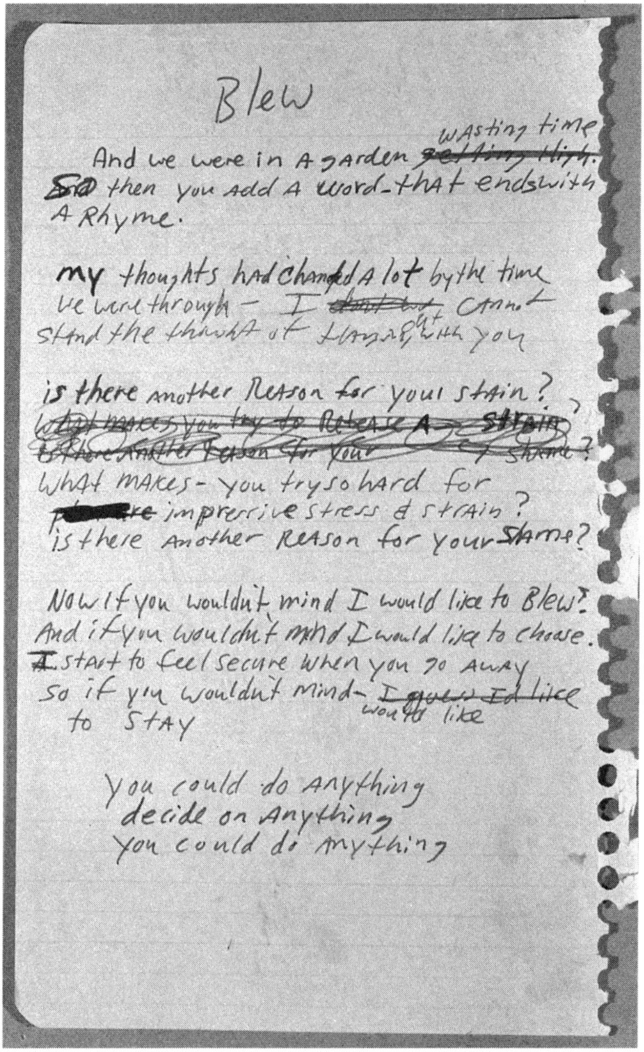

Blew

And we were in A garden ~~getting high~~ wasting time
~~So~~ then you add a word that ends with
A Rhyme.

my thoughts had changed A lot by the time
we were through — I ~~~~ cannot
stand the thought of Hanging with you

is there another Reason for your stain?
~~What makes you try to Release A strain?~~
~~Is there Another Reason for Your shame?~~
What makes - you try so hard for
~~~~ impressive stress & strain?
is there Another Reason for your shame?

Now if you wouldn't mind I would like to Blew?
And if you wouldn't mind I would like to choose.
~~I~~ start to feel secure when you go Away
So if you wouldn't mind — ~~I guess I'd like~~ would like
to stay

you could do Anything
decide on Anything
you could do Anything

considered a real metal thing to do. Kids who are like eighteen have a real soft peach-fuzz mustache. That was the metal stoner dude mustache. They'd have the jean jacket with the fake wool lining and a mustache and long hair, feathered and maybe an earring and usually they'd have pot for sale. You'd say, 'He's got a mustache' and you'd know exactly what kind of guy he was."

The mustache also symbolized the macho man that Kurt detested so much. But the song, with its refrain of "Yes, I eat cow/ I am not proud," is a swipe at self-righteous vegetarians ("poop as hard as rock"), who could be found in Olympia in abundant quantities. Of course, Chris was also a vegetarian, but the song is aimed more at the stridently politically correct types in Olympia, the kind who would walk up to a bare-chested guy and ask him to put his shirt back on in solidarity with women. This kind of thing put Kurt's sarcasm in high gear. "Fill me in on your new vision," he snarls in the opening verse. "Help me trust your mighty wisdom."

For "Blew," Kurt tuned down to what's called a "drop-D" tuning, but before recording the song, the band didn't realize they were already in that tuning and went down a whole step lower than they meant to, which explains the track's extraordinarily heavy sound. The leaden, distorted guitars ride a drunken rhythm just this side of plodding, producing a different kind of tension. The thick, gray tone of the track suits perfectly the theme of entrapment and control—"If you wouldn't care I would like to leave/ If you wouldn't mind I would like to breathe."

The genesis of "About a Girl" began when Tracy asked Kurt why he didn't write a song about her. So he did. The line "I can't see you every night for free" refers to the fact that Tracy was by then threatening to kick Kurt out of the house if he didn't get a job. The song was indicative of the pop direction that Kurt wanted to go in. It's an anomaly on the record and indeed in the entire Sub Pop scene—no one had written anything so unabashedly melodious and Beatlesque for the label yet (Kurt had also written "Polly" by then, but it fit the Sub Pop format even less).

As the night wore on, Kurt began to make his lyrics simpler and simpler.

Initially, Kurt and Chris disliked the tight-knit, incestuous Seattle scene; at first glance it resembled the exclusive cliques which they had despised in high school. "I just found Seattle so incestuously small and cliquey and everyone knew one another and they just seemed so stuck up and they'd seen it all," says Kurt. He had finally escaped abysmal Aberdeen and arrived in the promised land of Seattle, only to find the same situation all over again. No wonder the refrain of "School," "You're in high school again," sounds so desperate.

When Kurt came up with the basic riff for the song, it sounded so much like a typical Sub Pop grunge-rock riff to them that they considered calling the song "The Seattle Scene." But given Kurt's gift for taking a specific situation and making it universal, it got the broader tag of "School." "We wrote it about Sub Pop," says Kurt. "If we could have thrown in Soundgarden's name, we would have." Still, it's like one of those late seventies "disco sucks" songs that nevertheless used a disco beat. "It was a joke at first," says Kurt, "and then it turned out to be a really good song."

"Negative Creep" is a first-person narrative from an antisocial person—"I'm a negative creep and I'm stoned," goes the chanted chorus—the kind that hangs out on the smoker's porch, scowling and sporting long greasy hair and black T-shirts touting dubious metal bands. According to Kurt, that person is himself. "I just thought of myself as a negative person" is his simple explanation. Kurt caught some flak from the Seattle music community for the line "Daddy's little girl ain't a girl no more" because it was dangerously close to Mudhoney's "Sweet Young Thing Ain't Sweet No More." Kurt claims it was merely a subconscious theft.

By the end, it was very late and Kurt was getting burned out. He wrote "Scoff" and "Sifting" at this point. In "Scoff," Kurt listlessly wails "In my eyes, I'm not lazy" "In your eyes, I'm not worth it." It's a little bit of a stretch, but lines like that may be addressed to either Don or Wendy, who didn't consider Kurt's musical aspirations particularly worthwhile. With its mentions of teachers and preachers, "Sifting" seems to take on authority figures of all stripes, but as far as what it's about—it's anyone's guess, including Kurt's.

Two tracks (three on the CD version of *Bleach*) were taken straight from the Crover demo. With its slow, lurching beat, roared vocals, and ponderous chord progression, the eerie "Paper Cuts" is probably the most Melvins-influenced of all the tracks on the album. Part of the lyrics are based on a true story about an Aberdeen family who kept their children locked up in a room with the windows painted over, opening the door only to feed them—or remove the pile of newspapers they used for a latrine. Kurt actually knew one of the kids—he was his old dealer Grunt's sidekick.

But the song is also apparently quite autobiographical—Kurt can only be describing his alienation from Wendy when he sings, "The lady whom I feel a maternal love for/ cannot look me in the eyes/ but I see hers and they are blue/ and they cock and twitch and masturbate." Although it's quite a melodramatic comparison, Kurt seems to be making an analogy between the neglect the imprisoned children endured and the neglect he suffered from Wendy. "And very later I have learned to accept some friends of ridicule," he sings in the last verse, which seems to describe the outcasts he eventually befriended in Olympia. "Nirvana," Kurt moans five times on the chorus.

"Floyd the Barber" is another Melvins-styled number from the Crover demo. Floyd the Barber, of course, is a character from the early sixties sitcom "The Andy Griffith Show." It's not hard to divine the claustrophobic provincial theme. "It's just a small town gone bad," says Kurt. "Everyone turns into a mass murderer and they're all in cahoots with one another." But it's more than that—it's a

Freudian castration nightmare, as the narrator is tied to a barber's chair and cut with a razor. "I was shaved/ I was shamed," Kurt wails. Andy, Barney, Aunt Bee, and Opie all join in on the slashing.

"Downer" was included on the CD version of the album and also came from the Crover tape. It was an old song that Kurt wrote after being politicized by some of the more socially oriented punk rock bands. "I was trying to be Mr. Political Punk Rock Black Flag Guy," says Kurt. "I really didn't know what I was talking about. I was just throwing together words."

The album didn't sound as big and heavy as the band had hoped. It has a strangely claustrophobic, almost implosive feel that apparently unintentionally fits the general cast of the lyrics. Kurt is the first to point out that the album is one-dimensional—mostly slow, leaden, with not much melody. "We purposely made that record one-dimensional, more 'rock' than it should have been," he says.

Kurt purposely suppressed both his more melodic tendencies and his more arty, "new wave" streak because he knew the Sub Pop crowd wouldn't accept either. He figured Nirvana would have to make a grungy Sub Pop–style record to mobilize a fan base before he could get to do what he really wanted to do. "There was this pressure from Sub Pop and the scene to play 'rock music,'" says Kurt. "Strip it down and make it sound like Aerosmith. We knew that that was the thing to do. We had been doing it and we started doing that stuff on our own and now that it's a popular thing, we might as well cash in on it and become popular that way, because eventually we'll be able to do anything. We wanted to try to please people at first, to see what would happen."

Kurt had written a Vaselines-influenced song called "Beans," based on the Jack Kerouac book *The Dharma Bums*. "Beans, beans, beans/ Jackie ate some beans/ And he was happy and naked in the woods" went the chorus. He wanted to put it on the upcoming album, but Poneman didn't. "He thought it was stupid," says Kurt, who adds that the band wanted to be more diverse and experimental on their debut album, yet met with heavy resistance from Sub Pop, both stated and unstated. Since the band had no contract, they just didn't know how much they could ignore Poneman's wishes and still get to put their record out.

"Beans" was part of a four-song demo of "weird, quirky songs" that the band wanted to include on the record. Says Kurt, "[Poneman] thought we were retarded."

Ironically, the restrictions of the Sub Pop sound helped the band find its musical identity. Nirvana's new wave sound—Scratch Acid, Butthole Surfers, and the like—was derivative. It wasn't until they acknowledged the fact that they had grown up on Aerosmith and Black Sabbath that their music found its voice. "We just found ourselves reestablishing our songwriting within a couple of months," says Kurt. "It really was a great learning experience because that's really more where my roots are at anyhow—in rock, rather than the weird quirky new wave stuff that we were trying to do." This took a lot of nerve, especially in a climate where even the Sex Pistols were considered an oldies band.

Fessing up to liking working man's hard rock was an act of uncommon honesty in a world where arty poses were the norm, but it was something that needed to be said. When punk rock first erupted, it was necessary to play punk rock and only punk rock—that was the point. Once punk had made that point, it was ripe for assimilation, like any other source music.

Kurt saw only one hitch. "At that point I didn't think we had a unique sound," he says. "I didn't think we were really original enough to pull it off."

Bleach certainly has it moments, but there's no question that Kurt's songwriting is mired in grunge. That attracted a slightly different audience from the one the band expected—a relatively mainstream hard rock audience—a problem which dogs them to this day. "We were never that alternative," Chris says in retrospect. "*Bleach*, all the hair on the front of that record and all those fuckin' rock riff songs—people always knew we had a pretty accessible appeal. We were just basically a rock band."

Like many Seattle bands, Nirvana sported a serious Black Sabbath streak. Kurt dug Black Sabbath, but he dug the pop side as much as the heavy side. Sabbath classics like "Paranoid" and "Looking for Today" have a catchy verse-chorus structure; they even have bridges. "I remember years ago asking Eric Shillinger, 'How successful do you think a band could be if they mixed really heavy Black Sabbath with the Beatles? What could you do with that?'" says Kurt. "I wanted to be totally Led Zeppelin in a way and then be totally extreme punk rock and then do real wimpy pop songs." He'd have to wait four years to do that.

Kurt first heard the Pixies' classic 1988 *Surfer Rosa* album after recording *Bleach*. An amalgam of blood-curdling screams, grinding guitars, and nascent but clearly discernible pop-style melodies, it sounded exactly like what he had been wanting to do, but had been too intimidated to attempt. Up until then, it just wasn't cool to play pop music if you were a punk rock band. "I heard songs off of *Surfer Rosa* that I'd written but threw out because I was too afraid to play them for anybody," he says. The Pixies' popularity both in the U.K. and on American college radio helped give Kurt the encouragement to follow his instincts.

Bruce Pavitt and the band haggled for weeks over the cover shot. The band wanted a photo Tracy had taken of them

Photos for the proposed **Bleach** cover taken backstage after a February 1989 show at the HUB Ballroom. "We looked like mutants," Kurt says. (© 1993 by Alice Wheeler)

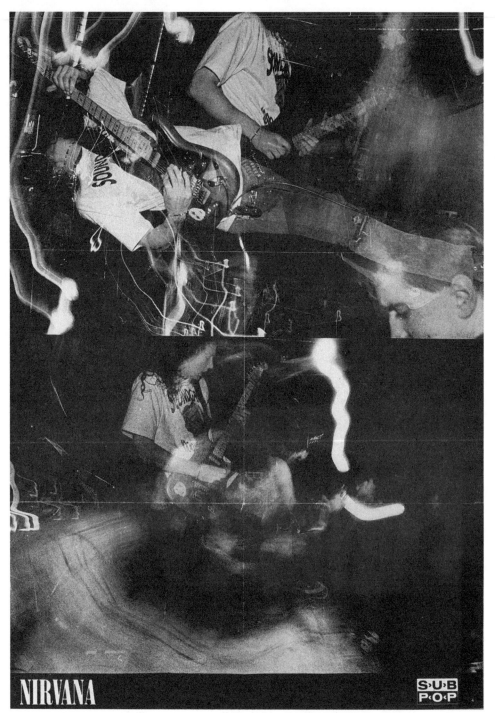

A limited edition poster included in early LP copies of **Bleach.**

at a show at Reko/Muse, a tiny club/art gallery in Olympia. It had been a very eventful night. Ben Shepherd induced the audience to do the Worm, a punk "dance" in which the participants roll around on the floor, trying to knock over everyone else. At that same gig, Chris threw his bass up in the air and it came straight down on Chad's head. "I was sitting there," says Chad, "and boom, it sent me right to the floor immediately. I don't remember anything. I came out of it and I was like, 'Whoah, everything's gettin' all radical.'"

It was also a big night for Chris and Shelli. All the time they had been apart, Shelli missed Chris terribly. She realized she loved him. Chris had gotten a new girlfriend, but he still couldn't keep Shelli off his mind. So when Shelli heard that Chris's girlfriend had just gone to college in Montana, she swooped right in. She called him up and asked what he was doing, and he said they were playing a show that night and to come on over. They got back together after the show and moved in together for good.

Pavitt, Sub Pop's image czar, wanted a series of intimate, unflattering shots that photographer Alice Wheeler had taken of the individual band members backstage under fluorescent lights after a show. Pavitt liked the shots because they fit with Sub Pop's populist theories. "You could really see the acne and the stubble and it was so *real*," says Pavitt. "These guys were *ugly*—this was the most un-L.A. look you could come up with. I really wanted to use these photos to dramatize the fact that these people are *real*."

"We looked like mutants," says Kurt.

"But to me that was part of the story," Pavitt replies. "If you look at it in context, everything was Spandex and hairspray and we were trying to create something that was the polar opposite to that, something that we felt people could relate to. The major labels were going the exact opposite way. To me, that's folk music—when you have common folk making music."

For the back cover, Pavitt wanted a photo that Charles Peterson had taken of Jason with his hair swinging in textbook Sub Pop style. Kurt didn't like that idea, so a compromise was reached, with the Jason shot featured on a limited edition poster which was included in the first two thousand copies of *Bleach* to be produced after the initial run of one thousand white vinyl pressings.

The shot on the inside of the CD version of Kurt splayed all over Chad's drum set was taken at the L.A. club Raji's in February of 1990. The shot was part of a sequence that also yielded the photo on the back of the "Sliver" single. *Bleach* also marked the debut of the Nirvana logo—set in Bodoni Extra Bold Condensed type. Because the typesetter was so rushed, the spacing was not graphically cor-

> Greetings,
>
> NIRVANA is A three piece spawned from the bowels of a Redneck logger town called Aberdeen WA. and the hippie Commune from Bainbridge Island. Only together for 7 months Kurdt–Guitar/vocals – Chris–bass & chad–Drums have Acquired a single on Sub Pop Records (& Song in Sub Pop 200 comp.) A Demo, success & fame & A following of millions. Selling their bottled Sweat & locks of hair have proven to be the largest money maker so far, but future: dolls, peechees, lunch boxes & bed sheets Are in the works. AN LP is due this April from the wonderful offices of Sub Pop world headquarters. talent Agents bruce PAvitt (alias Henry Mancini) And Jonathan Poneman (alias fred flintstone) have "treated the boys good" & we hope to work on more projects with them in the future.
>
> NIRVANA sounds like blacksabbath – playing the KNACK, Black flag, led Zeppelin, & the stooges, with A pinch of bay City Rollers. their musical influences Are: H.R. Puffnstuff, Marine Boy, Divorces, DRugs, Sound effects Records, the Beatles, Young marble Giants, slayer, leadbelly, IGGY.
>
> NIRVANA sees the underground music seen As becoming, stagnant And more Accessible towards commercial MAJOR LAbel interests. Does NIRVANA want to change this? No WAY! we want to CASH IN & suck butt up to the big wigs in hopes that we too can get high & fuck WAX figure-hot babes, who will be required to have A certified Aids test 2 weeks prior to the day of handing out back stage passes. Soon we will need chick spray Repellant. Soon we will be coming to your town & Asking if we can stay At your house & use your store. Soon we will do encores of GloriA & louie Louie At benefit concerts with All our celebrity friends.
>
> We Realize that there was once A 60's band called NIRVANA but don't get us confused with them because they totally Suck Big fucking DICK.
>
> 114 N pear olympia wy 98506
>
> Good Bye (206) 352-0992

Kurt's original draft of Nirvana's Sub Pop bio.

rect—there are large gaps on either side of the "V", for instance, that never did get fixed.

The credits on *Bleach* listed "Kurdt Kobain" on vocals and guitar, the first of several variations that Kurt made on his name. "I think I wanted to be anonymous at first," he explains. "I was really thinking about changing my name for the *Nevermind* record. But then I just decided to spell it the right way. I just wanted it to be confusing. I wish I would have done the same thing that Black Francis did. He's changed his name so many times that nobody really knows who he is. I wish nobody ever knew what my real name was. So I could some day be a normal citizen again. I have no real reason. I

From a publicity photo session with Charles Peterson. (© Charles Peterson)

just didn't bother with spelling it correctly. I didn't care. I wanted people to spell it differently all the time."

A Sub Pop bio at the time listed the band's influences as "H. R. Puffnstuff, Speed Racer, divorces, drugs, sound effects records, the Beatles, rednecks, hard rock, punk rock, Leadbelly, Slayer and of course, the Stooges."

"Nirvana sees the underground scene as becoming stagnant and more accessible to big league capitalist pig major record labels," the bio continued. "But does Nirvana fell [sic] a moral duty to fight this cancerous evil? NO WAY! We want to cash in and suck up to the big wigs in hopes that we too can GET HIGH AND FUCK. GET HIGH AND FUCK. GET HIGH AND FUCK."

On June 9, Nirvana played "Lamefest '89" at the Moore Theater, opening for TAD and Mudhoney. It was a landmark event—local bands had never packed such a large place before. The Seattle scene was starting to explode. The reviewer for *Backlash* bemoaned the bad sound treatment Nirvana received, because "the band utilizes a lot of melody within their grunge." "As for their performance—totally intense," the review continued. "Hair explosions, prat falls, jumps, body writhing and a trash-a-thon finale that left instruments and bodies strewn about the stage."

In an article in the University of Washington newspaper, Kurt said the band's music had a "gloomy, vengeful element based on hatred." The piece added that Kurt's outlook had improved of late, leading to what Kurt called "a gay pop song phase that will eventually die," although there would probably be more such tunes on the next album. "I'd like to live off the band," Kurt added. "I can't handle work."

They did a session at Evergreen State College which yielded an early version of "Dive" and a cover of Kiss's "Do You Love Me," which wound up on a tribute album, on the Seattle indie label C/Z Records, called *Hard to Believe*.

Around this time, Nirvana decided that they needed a contract with Sub Pop. They wanted to make sure they would get accurate and timely accounting statements. "We thought if we signed a contract," says Kurt, "we'd be able to hold it up against them in the future if we wanted to get out of their contract." Ironically, the contract eventually had the opposite effect.

As it happened, Sub Pop had been thinking along the same lines, and Poneman had been reading *This Business of Music* for tips on a standard contract for all of the label's roster (only Soundgarden had signed one at that point). Poneman had not yet drafted anything when one summer night, Pavitt had thrown a "wild disco party" for the visiting Babes in Toyland. As Pavitt recalls, the party got a little out of hand so he booted everybody out and they all went next door, where the Babes were staying. Meanwhile, an inebriated Chris Novoselic walked up to Pavitt's house, banged on the window, hollered, "You fuckers, we want a contract!" and fell backward into some bushes. He got up to leave and by sheer coincidence, bumped into Pavitt, who was going back to his house. "I often wonder," says Pavitt, "what if I had stayed next door one more minute."

They talked for about forty-five minutes or so, after which Pavitt called Poneman and told him Nirvana wanted a contract. Poneman stayed up all night typing a document. Legally speaking, it was a blunt instrument, but it would serve the label in good stead soon enough. Soon, Kurt, Chris, Chad, and Jason were up at Sub Pop's offices signing the contract, making them the first band to sign an extended contract with the label. "I remember thinking, 'This could be important,'" says Pavitt.

At first, the album didn't make a seismic impact on the indie scene or even on Sub Pop, for that matter. "*Bleach* sounded really good, but all [our] stuff sounded really good to me," says Poneman. "I was caught up with a lot of stuff we were putting out," adds Pavitt. "We were putting out a lot of really good records."

But then people started buying it. "We put out *Bleach*," says Pavitt, "and gosh, it just kept selling. Never ever in the history of our company have I seen a record just sell and sell and sell. They did tour, but a lot of bands tour. The word of mouth was there. There was something special there."

After *Bleach* was released in June of 1989, they went on their first U.S. tour, "a total hungry punk rock tour," says Chris, of twenty-six dates, starting June 22 at the Covered Wagon in San Francisco. This was the inaugural run of their trusty white Dodge van, soon nicknamed "The Van." Through three U.S. tours and seventy thousand miles, it never did break down. When it got too hot to drive, they'd pull into a parking garage and just hang out in the van until sundown.

Kurt, Chris, Chad, and Jason were their own road managers—they decided where they'd stay, when they'd leave. Of course, the accommodations weren't that great—most of the time, they'd end up sleeping outside or in the van, and if they were lucky, some fan gave them a floor to sleep on. A few dates into the tour, they were deep in the heart of Texas. They parked near a national park, which Chris recalls was essentially a swamp. A sign near their parking spot read "Caution: alligators," so they dug up a baseball bat and some two-by-fours that were kicking around the back of the van and kept them close by in case of reptilian attack. But eventually, they got hungry and decided to eat some of their canned soup. So they doused the bat and the two-by-fours in motor oil, set them on fire, and cooked the soup over the flames.

They were excited about being on tour and going to places like New Mexico, Illinois, and Pennsylvania and playing to new faces. They played the very lowest tier of the underground circuit, mostly bars; the band got a free case of beer and never more than one hundred dollars a night. "Every time we played a show," says Chad, "it seemed like we got just enough money to put gas in the tank and food in our stomach to make it to the next friggin' gig." Despite the marathon drives, the low pay, and often sparse audiences, morale was high. And attendance started to pick up halfway through the

One way of solving the height problem. (© Charles Peterson)

tour, when college radio began playing *Bleach* tracks like "School," "About a Girl" or "Blew." By the time they got out to the Midwest, they almost felt famous.

They started to win fans with their live show, too. "There was always people who came up afterward and said 'Wow, I thought you guys were pretty cool,'" says Chad, "but it's not like people got completely out of hand. There were some people who got like that, but they were drunk."

Chris was in charge of getting paid and keeping the books. It was a lot simpler then. "We'd go to a record store and we'd all buy these records," says Chris. "Maybe I could buy six records, Kurt would buy four records, Chad would buy three, and that was fine. It was 'All together, brothers.' And at the end of the tour, whoever got dropped off first, we'd count out all the money—a third for you, a third for you..."

Not that Chris would just fritter away the band's money. In fact, he became such a tightwad that he wouldn't let anyone turn on the air conditioning in the van—even in Texas in July—because it used up too much fuel.

Back home in Washington, Kurt and Chris often went a separate way from Chad socially—Chad stuck with his hippyish Bainbridge Island crowd—but being on tour was different. "When we were in that van, it was way closer," Chad says. "It wasn't like us against each other, it was like us against whatever's outside of the van."

Inside the van, they'd listen to a tuneful but twisted Scottish band called the Vaselines, as well as everything from the teenaged English pop band Tallulah Gosh to the aged headbangers in Motorhead. And they'd listen to the Beatles. Chris and Kurt made compilation tapes. Shelli had even made some, too.

Chris was hitting the bottle pretty hard. "He'd get pretty crazy, trashing things and stuff," Chad recalls. "When he'd first get wasted, he'd be all, 'Everybody's great! I love everybody!' and then the next moment he's telling everybody, 'You don't know anything about love! You just don't care! You don't understand!' And he'd pick up a chair and maybe toss it a half mile. Then he'd wake up and he'd say to me, 'Don't talk to me, Mr. Sunshine, I don't want to deal with you.' He'd always wake up looking and feeling like shit all the time."

Kurt was more amused than disturbed by Chris's drinking. "It never seemed like a big deal to me at all," he says. "Everyone gets drunk and he didn't get drunk every single night, it was just every *other* night. When he drinks, he drinks to the point of oblivion—he turns into literally a retard. He can't speak, all he can do is gesture and knock things over. I just never thought of it as a problem, although I'm probably more sympathetic to it now, over the last few years. But I've known so many people that drink that it seems like an ordinary thing."

At a tour stop in Minneapolis, the band stayed with Babes in Toyland drummer Lori Barbero, a famed hostess of indie bands who were traveling through the Twin Cities. Apparently, Chris thought Barbero had shot him a look and he hollered "Quit yer gawkin'!" flailed his arms, and fell backward into a cabinet full of plates, which all went crashing to the floor.

"He never meant any harm or anything," says Chad. "If he was in his right mind, he never would have done some of the shit he did. I think drinking brought out some things that he didn't think about

Poster from Nirvana's first U.S. tour.

much or things he'd like to say to people that he wouldn't when he wasn't wasted."

Pressed for specific incidents, Chad replies, "It's all blurring together now. When I think about it, I just see him wasted, and then something getting broken."

© Charles Peterson

Kurt would do some pretty weird stuff himself. In Chicago he bought a large crucifix at a garage sale. Out on the road, he'd roll down the window of the van, stick out the crucifix at some unsuspecting victim and snap his picture just to get the expression on his face. Yes, life on the road was pretty good. "We were totally poor," says Kurt, "but, God, we were seeing the United States for the first time. And we were in a band and we were making enough money to survive. It was awesome. It was just great. And if Jason wasn't such a prick, it would have been even better."

Chris had noticed Jason's dissatisfaction early in the tour and mentioned it to Chad and Kurt. "We tried to talk to him about it and he wouldn't talk," says Chris. "He got totally introverted."

Chris and Kurt would often go for long strolls and talk. During a stroll around Lake Mendota in Madison, Wisconsin, Chris asked, "Do you think the band is kind of weird ever since Jason joined? It's not the same band anymore." The band was looking and sounding more "rock," as Bruce Pavitt would say. They blamed it on Jason. Jason's stage style was more show-biz than the rest of the band—he

Kurt and Chris at the Halloween party at Evergreen. (Tracy Marander)

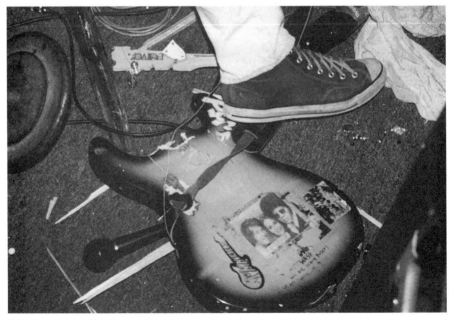

The first time Kurt smashed his guitar: during a Halloween party at Evergeen State College, October 30, 1988. (Tracy Marander)

posed, swinging his hair in the classic Sub Pop style, doing a rockist rooster strut around his side of the stage. "He was like a peacock on amphetamines," says Kurt. "He was so posey I couldn't believe it. It was embarrassing. It was so contrived and *sexual*. It was gross."

Actually, Jason's incompatibility had been plain from the start. "It was weird because he didn't even want to rehearse any new numbers," says Chris. "He'd go through the set but he didn't want to jam or anything. He'd set his guitar down." (Jason denies this, saying that since the band was so far-flung, they only rehearsed a handful of times before touring and that jamming was out of the question since their time was completely occupied by learning songs that Kurt had already written.)

"We just kind of noticed that yeah, Jason's kind of weird," says Chris, who also sensed a rockist tendency in Jason early on. "The first day we practiced, he brought these girls over, to kind of hang out. That kind of tells you something."

Neither Kurt nor Chris hung out with Jason much socially, and their alienation was only magnified by the rigors of the road. "Things started getting weird," says Chris. "And then *he* started getting weird." The band played a great show at the Sonic Temple in Pittsburgh, so great that Kurt smashed one of his favorite guitars, a sunburst Fender Mustang. Jason got really mad about that. "We said, 'What? It's rock and roll!'" says Chris, who concedes that "we were broke and he was kind of financing the show."

The band had begun trashing their instruments a few months before. If it was a bad show, they'd get angry and smash everything up. If it was a really good show, they'd smash out of pure glee. There were few merely average shows, so equipment got smashed often.

It all started on October 30, 1988, at a show at a dorm of Evergreen State College. "It just *started*," says Chris. "It was fun. It seemed like you couldn't end a show without doing something spectacular or sensational. No matter how good you played, it seemed like you didn't give it enough. So if you smashed all the gear and had this big gala ending, we could say, 'There, we did it.' We couldn't just walk off the stage."

On tour, they'd find cheap guitars at pawnshops—sometimes fans would just give them a guitar or in a pinch Jonathan Poneman would Fed Ex one out to them—and string them left-handed and smash them that night. "It was fun, and if you were doing a shitty show, it kind of made it spectacular," says Chris. "Then it became addictive."

***

Chris had recently scrawled the phrase NIRVANA:FUDGE PACKIN, CRACK SMOKIN, SATAN WORSHIPIN MOTHER-FUCKERS on a wall and was so pleased with the slogan that he told Kurt about it. Kurt put it on the back of a T-shirt design he had been working on. On the front was a reproduction of an engraving of one of the circles of Hell from Dante's *Inferno*, a book Kurt had discovered during his days passing the time in the Aberdeen library. Jason had all the T-shirts printed up, paid for them, and then sold them after every show. They quickly became a staple of indie-rock fashion. Jason probably made a mint.

They were supposed to go up into Canada, but made it only as far as New York City, where they played a lousy show on the eighteenth of July during the New Music Seminar at the Pyramid Club in the East Village. It was Jason's last show with Nirvana. "I don't think Jason really took the pressure of being on tour and being cooped up with us very well," says Chris. "I don't think he was happy with our band because he kind of wanted us to be more rock and we were more punk."

"We started making it toward New York and that's when Jason started getting really quiet," Chris continues. "He wouldn't even talk to us anymore. That's when we first met Anton Brookes, our publicist in the U.K. He was like, 'Who's this Jason? Why is he so quiet?' The Mudhoney guys were in New York: 'Why is this Jason so quiet?' We played this show at Maxwell's [in nearby Hoboken, New Jersey]. It was a good show. Still, Jason was quiet. We spent about four days in New York. The New Music Seminar. We watched Sonic Youth and Mudhoney and Laughing Hyenas at the Ritz. Jason went to see the speed metal band Prong at CBGB's. You know what I mean? That said a lot."

"That's when Chad and I and Kurt got really together," says Chris. "We bonded. We'd go out to eat together, all three, and pitch in for the meal with band money. Without Jason. He would not hang around with us."

They stayed a few days at the Alphabet City apartment of Janet Billig, a factotum at Caroline Records who knew Pavitt and Poneman, and like Babes in Toyland's Lori Barbero in Minneapolis, made her apartment a way station for needy bands coming through town. One night, Chris and Kurt went down to the street and bought some cocaine. The two of them drank some booze and snorted the coke off Billig's toilet seat. And they decided they were going home and that Jason was out of the band. "We were happy," says Chris. "It was a relief."

© Charles Peterson

"So we went up to him, 'Jason, what's wrong? Is there a problem?' He'd say 'No, no. Nothing. I'm over it.' We're like, 'What's *it*? Why is there a problem?'"

Kurt wouldn't confront Jason about it. "He was never in your face," says Chad. "Things would pile up for him underneath and finally it would be 'Man, I can't take this anymore.' When we were dealing with Jason, because we were all wondering what was up with him, Kurt was always silent about it. Then out of the blue he'd say, 'Man, I can't take this anymore.' It was like, 'Whoah, Kurt's going to say something!' I think it's because he's afraid of talking to the person. He doesn't want to bum them out. He doesn't want to be the one to say, 'This isn't working out and you're out of the band.' He hates that kind of confrontation. He doesn't want to be the executioner or the mean guy."

"I always felt kind of peripheral," says Jason. "I don't remember ever being asked for input on songs in that band, which is ultimately why I left." Kurt does concede that Jason may also have taken exception to Kurt's alcohol-fueled "volatile personality" at the time. Kurt also thinks Jason mistook the metallic ring of *Bleach* for the band's true direction instead of the compromise that it was. Even Jason acknowledges that he preferred ponderous songs like "Paper Cuts," "Sifting," and "Big Long Now" to the more melodic material Kurt was getting into. Jason never was afraid to declare that he liked metal. "That was always kind of a burr in Kurt and Chris's side because it wasn't exactly cool," Jason says. "But if there's a band with a cool song and a cool guitar riff I'd listen to it."

Jason, who was also a songwriter, wanted to have more input into the music. "I probably wanted to do things that were not simple enough for them, ideas that were *mine* as opposed to Kurt's," says Jason. "There wasn't a tremendous musical difference—maybe it was just a control thing.

"Basically, anybody besides Kurt or Chris is kind of disposable," Jason continues. "At the end of the day, Kurt could get in front of any bass player and any drummer and play his songs and it's not going to sound that much different."

They abruptly canceled the remaining seven shows of the tour—mostly Midwest dates—and drove home to Washington in fifty hours, not stopping for anything except to get gas, eat a doughnut, or go to the bathroom. The whole time, nobody said a word. Nobody even told Jason that he was out of the band. Jason claims he actually quit. "No, we were just too maladjusted to tell him to his face," Chris says. "We just didn't want to hurt anyone's feelings and that just compounded the problem. I think we're better at it now, more direct, more mature than back then."

"If I would have been in the band when they got huge, I'm sure I would have took my money and said, 'See ya later!'" says Jason. "I would have done whatever I wanted to do. I'd bail and just do whatever."

"Artistically, I think it was totally the right thing for me to do," says Jason of his departure from the band. "Economically, maybe not." Two weeks later, Jason got a call from Chris Cornell of Soundgarden, asking him to play bass in the band. He lasted a few months before being replaced by Ben Shepherd and now plays guitar in Mindfunk, a band on Megaforce Records. He says he has no hard feelings about his exit from Nirvana. "Each band is a weird, twisted family," Jason says. "I think I was more the retarded stepchild twice removed."

The band never did repay Jason the six hundred dollars he lent them for *Bleach*. "Mental damages," claims Kurt.

Kurt had become obsessed with the great Leadbelly, the black folk troubadour of the thirties and forties whose enduring musical legacy includes "Rock Island Line," "Midnight Special," and "Good Night, Irene." Kurt had gotten into Leadbelly after reading an article by William Burroughs which said something like "To hell with modern-day rock & roll. If you want to hear *real* passion, listen to Leadbelly." Kurt's next-door neighbor, Slim Moon, happened to have *Leadbelly's Last Sessions* and played it for Kurt. He was completely taken. Then he started buying all the Leadbelly records he could find. "It's so raw and sincere," he says. "It's something that I hold really sacred to me. Leadbelly is one of the most important things in my life. I'm totally obsessed with him."

He went out and bought every Leadbelly record he could find, learned how to play his music, and even decorated an entire wall of the apartment with Leadbelly pictures. It's easy to see Kurt's attraction to the blues—an exorcism of psychic pain—but it's also easy to see why he was especially attracted to Leadbelly, whose work transcended any category, an elegant songwriter who crafted sturdy but melodic music that synthesized several different genres, whose passionate music spoke volumes about the human experience. From Leadbelly and the blues, Kurt got the idea of using recognizable imagery to produce an original, almost mystical, vision.

Kurt had befriended Mark Lanegan, whose band, the Screaming Trees, played in Olympia often. In August 1989, Kurt and Lanegan decided to collaborate on some songs for Lanegan's solo album. Unfortunately Kurt couldn't write very well with someone else—he kept worrying that he would come up with something that he'd want to use for Nirvana instead—so they decided to record some songs by Leadbelly with Chris on bass and Screaming Trees' Mark Pickerel on drums.

The group wound up recording but two Leadbelly songs. "Where Did You Sleep Last Night?" wound up on Lanegan's magnificent solo album, *The Winding Sheet*. Kurt sang Leadbelly's "Ain't It a Shame." Both songs were to make up a single, but that fell through and "Ain't It a Shame" was never released. Jonathan Poneman calls it "one of Kurt's greatest vocal performances."

Eventually, the four turned into an informal blues band. Pickerel wanted to call it the Jury; Kurt wanted to call it Lithium. Poneman had big plans for an album, but somehow it never happened. Kurt concentrated on guitar, leaving Lanegan to do most of the vocals. Dylan Carlson remembers their best song was "Grey Goose," which they did in a heavy, dirge-blues style. "It was almost like watching one of the great English blues rock bands getting its feet," says Carlson. "It was pretty incredible." Kurt says he'd like to try a blues band again sometime.

Nirvana rehearsed and played a few shows in Seattle that summer as their following began to swell—strictly by word of mouth, since Sub Pop had long ago ceased directly promoting the album. They regularly sold out the Vogue and went on a two-week Midwest tour starting in late September to make up the dates they had missed by coming home prematurely with Jason. Along for the ride was roadie Ben Shepherd, who had been in a couple of bands (Mind Circus and Tick Dolly Row) with Chad.

Nirvana was thinking about getting Shepherd in the band, but once word got around that they were thinking about a new second guitarist, members of Screaming Trees, TAD, and Mudhoney all strenuously advised them to stay a three-piece—another guitarist just cluttered up the sound. "I still kind of regret that because I like that guy a lot—he would have added to the band, definitely," Kurt says of Shepherd. "He was kind of crazy sometimes, but that's okay—I'd rather have that than some moody metalhead." Shepherd later replaced Jason in Soundgarden.

The bigger the city, the bigger the crowd. The best show was at the Blind Pig in Ann Arbor, Michigan. "Everybody was totally into it," says Chad. "They were raging and it was great." It's still one of the band's favorite places to play. In Ann Arbor, they also interviewed comedian Bobcat Goldthwaite on a radio show. All Kurt had to do was mention Sylvester Stallone and Goldthwaite went on a half-hour riff about why the man who played Rambo fled to Switzerland to avoid the Vietnam War draft.

In Minneapolis, right at the start of the tour, Kurt had collapsed from stomach pain. Chris was frightened. "His stomach—God, he had nothing to throw up and he was still throwing up," he says. "His stomach hurt so bad. Took him to the hospital and they could do nothing for him."

Once they got back from the tour, Chris and Shelli decided to get married and the band began preparing to record material for an EP.

CHAPTER SIX

The band recorded the *Blew* EP in late summer of 1989 at the relatively upscale Music Source on Seattle's Capitol Hill, a twenty-four-track studio that specialized in ad jingles and movie soundtrack work. The producer was Steve Fisk. Despite that show in Ellensburg with Jason's out-of-sync hair, Fisk changed his mind about Nirvana after Bruce Pavitt sent him a copy of *Bleach*. "It was obvious," says Fisk, "that it was a very good band."

The band arrived with their instruments in tatters. Fisk recalls Chad and his mammoth North kit. "The smallest guy in the band had the biggest, stupidest drum set in the Northwest," says Fisk. "The kick drum was held together by miles and miles of duct tape because the bass had been used as a hatchet to chop the kick drum in half." The *Blew* sessions were the last appearance, recorded or otherwise, of Chad's North drums.

THESE GUYS ARE GOING TO BE BIGGER THAN THE BEATLES!

The rest of the band's equipment was in sad shape, too. Chris's bass had done a lot of aerial work, and had obviously suffered a few too many crash landings. The pickups were nearly shot and one of his two speakers was almost completely destroyed; the other one *was* completely destroyed. They spent a lot of time trying to get everything to sound good, tripling up the guitars. (Kurt was unsatisfied with the recording and later tried to rerecord some of the tracks with their soundman, Craig Montgomery, but they didn't turn out well, either.) "They wanted a Top 40 drum sound," says Fisk. "They were saying that out loud. They knew they were not doing a Top 40 song, but they really liked the idea of having the snare completely jacked up."

They recorded "Even in His Youth," the unreleased "Token Eastern Song," an electric version of "Polly" that went unfinished, "Stain," and "Been a Son." Only the last two made it onto the EP, which also included the title track and "Love Buzz," both culled from *Bleach*.

The instantly catchy two-minute wonder "Been a Son" describes the plight of a girl whose parents would have preferred a boy. "She should have died when she was born," Kurt sings, his vocal draped in most un-Sub Pop-like harmonies ("Total Lennon harmonies, right out of *Rubber Soul*," raves Fisk). Grunge, pop, and feelings of inferiority also merge on "Stain." Self-hatred never sounded so catchy— it's easy to miss the fact that the song is simply the same verse repeated three times. Although a different, peppier version of "Been

Backstage pass from TAD/Nirvana European tour.

TAD and Nirvana. That's Tad Doyle to Chris's right. (© Ian T. Tilton)

A Son" (minus Chris's tasty bass solo) wound up on *Incesticide*, the version of "Stain" hails from the Fisk sessions.

The hypnotic "Token Eastern Song" was a reaction to numerous critical observations that the band often favored Eastern modes, as in "Love Buzz." The back cover shot of the EP, a strangely desolate shot of a doctor's examination table, was taken by Tracy in her gynecologist's office shortly after an examination.

Then came the European tour with TAD. The two bands left Seattle for the first gig, in Newcastle, England, on October 20, 1989. Eleven guys—including the gigantic, three-hundred-pound-plus Tad Doyle and all six feet and seven inches of Chris—were crammed into a teeny Fiat van. At first, it was all laughter and smiles, but then little things began to get on people's nerves—some of the guys on the bus smoked, and they weren't always considerate of the guys who didn't. A kind of delirium swept through the van. One of the guys bought some dirty magazines on Hamburg's notorious Reeperbahn. One was a coprophiliac's magazine which got passed around the bus. "Shit on me!" the guy would bellow over and over, collapsing in laughter. But for Kurt and a few others, the joke got old real fast.

They played thirty-six shows in forty-two days. Nobody was eating very well and the pace was grueling. It was hard to sleep sitting up in the fiendishly uncomfortable seats. Nirvana was frustrated by their perennially cruddy equipment, hobbled further by the fact that they were smashing it to bits every night and then repairing it on the bus the next day. To make matters worse, the tour manager usually insisted on going straight to the venue when they arrived in town, meaning that the bands couldn't catch some sleep in their hotel room while awaiting their turn to do soundcheck. Instead, they waited around in the club for hours—cold, hungry, and tired—while the P.A. system was constructed.

And Doyle had chronic stomach problems. At least once a day, he would have to get the driver to stop on the highway while he got out to throw up. Everyone on the bus would watch and do their own imitations of Doyle's hurling style. "He was definitely the puke machine," Chad recalls. "A never-ending vomitron."

Although he didn't smoke hash like most of the other guys on the bus, Kurt got very withdrawn and would react to bad situations either by drinking or retreating behind a wall of sleep. "I used to really enjoy sleep because I could just get away from pain that way," Kurt says. "I used to sleep constantly. On tour, every time we got in the van, I'd fall asleep. Every time we got to a club and we were waiting for soundcheck, we would sleep. Either I'd go back to the hotel and sleep or stay at the club and sleep until right before we went on stage so I didn't have to be in reality."

Chris was constantly drunk and/or stoned, while Chad, Chris claims, "was kind of out of his mind. He was talking in weird voices and stuff." For his part, Chad says he's *always* talked to himself— once, a waitress in the restaurant where he worked caught him in the walk-in refrigerator talking to a lemon. And he insists that of all the people on the tour, he had the best time—his nomadic childhood was perfect training for touring.

The band was unprepared for the adulation they received in Europe. Although the U.K. press raved about Nirvana, the band had no idea that they had so many fans over there—they simply weren't getting any sales reports from their U.K. label. Virtually every show was sold out; the venues were packed, there were lines around the block.

"That was a crazy tour," says Chris with some understatement. During the first gig, Chris slammed his new bass on the stage out of frustration with a malfunctioning amp. The neck snapped off and went right through one of the speakers in Kurt's rented Twin Reverb amp. It went downhill from there.

They played Berlin the day after the wall came down. Kurt smashed his guitar six songs into the set and walked off. "I'm kind of glad he did," says Chris. "I was really, really, really stoned."

Kurt sent Tracy lots of postcards. There was one where he sketched a picture of a typical Italian toilet. "There was no water," Tracy says, "so there's just a toilet with a big stinky pile of shit." Another time he wrote "I love you" over and over again on a postcard and signed his name.

The way Poneman sees it, that tour was the beginning of the end of both bands' relationships with Sub Pop (TAD eventually signed to WEA-distributed Mechanic Records in 1992). In the midst of one of their (in)famous promotional schmooze tours, Poneman and Pavitt turned up at a show in Rome toward the end of the tour. In retrospect, Poneman realized the message that their arrival sent. "There's TAD and Nirvana riding around in this crummy little van," says Poneman, "and here come the moguls flying in to Rome. We thought that we were lending emotional support, but from their perspective, I can see them thinking, 'These arrogant sons of bitches... We don't have any money, we're barely eating, we're riding around in this cramped van, we've got this fat lead singer who's throwing up all over the place, and you've got a crazy drunk bass player, and here come the moguls.'"

Not coincidentally, the Rome show was the nadir of the tour. The P.A. was terrible and so was the rented gear. Disgusted with the sound, the bad food, the cramped bus, the low pay, and the frenetic schedule, Kurt smashed his guitar four or five songs into the set ("Spank Thru"), walked off stage, and climbed onto a speaker stack. "He had a nervous breakdown onstage," says Pavitt. "He was just going to jump off. The bouncers were freaking out and everybody was just begging him to come down. And he was 'No, no, I'm just going to dive.' He had really reached his limit... People literally saw a guy wig out in front of them who could break his neck if he didn't get it together."

When the P.A. stack started to sway, Kurt clambered through the rafters, screaming at the audience the whole way until he reached the balcony, where he threatened to throw down a chair until someone took it away from him. He wound up backstage, where someone from the venue was arguing with their tour manager over whether Kurt had broken some microphones. Kurt grabbed both mikes, flung them to the ground, and began stomping on them. "*Now* they're broken," he said, and walked away. Then he told everyone in the entourage that he was quitting and he was going home, then put his hood over his head and burst into tears. Poneman took him out for some air.

"I was walking around the club with him," Poneman recalls, "and he was saying, 'I just want to go home, I don't want to play for these people, these people are fucking idiots, they're stupid, they expect me to go up there and perform like a trained animal. I don't respect them. I want to be with my girlfriend and I want to quit music. This is not what I'm about.'" Poneman assured him that the next time the band came to Europe, conditions would be far better.

According to Kurt, the first words out of Poneman's mouth were, "Well, now that you're quitting Nirvana, we'd still be interested in you as a solo artist."

Chris and Chad also quit the band for a moment, but they all reconsidered and played the final two weeks of the tour.

The next day, they took a train to Switzerland and while Kurt was asleep, his shoes, his wallet, and most importantly, his passport were all stolen. "I don't think I have ever seen another human being look as absolutely miserable as Kurt Cobain did at that moment," says Poneman. He somehow got into Switzerland and got a new passport at the American Embassy. Then they went to a music store in Geneva and Poneman bought Kurt a new guitar.

And then Kurt got so sick that they had to cancel a show. "He just needed some time off," says Chris. "I had a crutch—I had booze and hash, but he was straight." Chad, meanwhile, exhibited an almost Buddha-like serenity. No one could tell whether he was some sort of spiritual savant or just oblivious.

Nirvana and TAD met up with the Mudhoney tour for the final gig on December 3 at the Astoria in London, dubbed the Lame Festival. Nirvana had one lousy guitar left, and it kept cutting out throughout the set and Kurt had to keep stopping to fix it. "Nirvana's set was pretty fucked up," says Mudhoney drummer Danny Peters. Chris was so angry that he swung his bass by the strap around his head; eventually, the strap snapped; the guitar flew straight at Danny Peters's head and he only barely managed to bat it out of the way.

"It stunk," is Chris's review of the show. "On a scale of one to ten, that was a zero." The *Melody Maker* reviewer at the concert that night agreed. "It all falls apart when the lanky, rubberlegged, frog-like bassist starts making a jerk of himself," went the review. "He'll *have* to go.

"As yet, I'm unmoved," the review concluded.

Others remember the show far more fondly. Bruce Pavitt rates the show as one of the best Nirvana has ever done, while Jonathan Poneman insists, "To this day, it's one of the proudest moments in my life." Journalist Keith Cameron, then with the now defunct U.K. music weekly *Sounds* recalls it this way: "It was one of these things

HEAVIER THAN HEAVEN R'N'R FROM SEATTLE

Tad

NIRVANA

Sa 25 Nov. 21h

CAVEAU'S FRI-SON FRIBOURG FRI-SON

where the hall is maybe half full when they started, but by the time they finished, everyone in the hall was listening and getting into this band," he says. "I just ran down the front and freaked out. It was the most amazing band I'd ever seen.

"What impressed me," Cameron continues, "was the complete and utter tension that existed between the three people on stage. They *thrived* upon it. It was uncomfortable watching them sometimes. It was exhilarating and it was exciting because that was the nature of the music but there was also an almost palpable sense of danger, that this whole thing could just fall apart any second but it wasn't. And it was maintained throughout the set—there was never any relaxation from the first note to the last."

At the end of the set, Kurt threw his guitar at Chris, who then smashed it with his bass as if he were hitting a baseball. Kurt's guitar completely disintegrated. "You see bands smash their equipment and it's not a revelation," says Cameron, "but somehow with them, I'd never seen it done with any purpose before. It seemed the perfect way to end that show. You sort of wondered whether Kurt meant to hit Chris with his guitar or was that how they planned it. You got the impression that it wasn't planned at all. That was what was so good about it—you got the impression that they were learning this for the first time and they were as much in the dark as anyone, but it was just perfect."

During their visit to London, Nirvana did a session for Radio One DJ John Peel including "Love Buzz," "About a Girl," "Polly," and "Spank Thru."

The British press had really started rolling in by this time, and the articles fed on the idea that the band came from rural, white-trash America. "They're a little bit gross and a little bit awesome," went one profile. "What else would you be if you grew up in the backwoods redneck helltown of Aberdeen..." Sub Pop played it up for all it was worth. "You've got the three-hundred-pound butcher hanging out with Kurt the trailer-trash kid and you've got the moguls—we'd be posing in suits and ties—adding a little theater," says Bruce Pavitt. "People got caught up in it."

Kurt didn't like getting painted as some sort of idiot savant yokel one bit. "To be thought of as this stump-dumb rocker dude from Aberdeen who just blindly found his way up to Seattle and this hip label," says Kurt, "it just felt degrading to be thought of as someone like that when that was something I was fighting against all my life.

"They were totally manipulating people in trying to put this package together," says Kurt of Pavitt and Poneman. "They've gotten so much credit for being these geniuses, these masterminds behind this whole thing when it really had nothing to do with them. It really didn't. It had more to do with Charles Peterson's fuzzy pictures than it did with their attempts at making sure we appeared stupid in interviews. I always resented them for that."

And Kurt found Pavitt's professed populism far more condescending than brilliant. "It was just obvious that he thought of himself as an educated white upper-middle-class punk rocker who knows everything and I'm just this idiot from Aberdeen," Kurt says. "That was always something that we sensed and we totally resented him for it." They felt similarly about Poneman, too.

To be fair, Pavitt and Poneman *had* seized on a bright idea—that art and culture didn't have to be developed and transmitted solely from the media centers of New York and Los Angeles. The indie labels had proved that people in places like Minneapolis and Chicago and Seattle had just as much to say as any New York City media creature. For Poneman and Pavitt, finding someone from a place like Aberdeen who made valid art was like hitting the jackpot. "They thrived on that," Kurt says. "They were excited about it. They'd found these redneck kids from a coastal town that they could exploit, or at least use their image to their benefit. They didn't really want to find out if we were smarter than they wanted us to be, because that would ruin everything."

Kurt might gripe a lot about Sub Pop, but he'll gladly acknowledge the crucial role the label, and Jonathan Poneman in particular, played in their career. "Jonathan was really, really supportive of us from the very beginning," Kurt says. "He wanted us to rule the world."

After the tour, Kurt and Chad went home, while Chris and Shelli flew to what was still called Yugoslavia to see Chris's father.

Chris and Shelli got married soon after they got back home to Tacoma, on December 30, 1989. The ceremony, which was conducted by a woman Shelli knew from work, took place in the couple's Tacoma apartment. It was a small apartment and it was packed. Besides Chris's mom and Shelli's mother and stepfather, there were Kurt and Tracy, Dan Peters, most of the guys from TAD, old friends and some neighbors. Matt Lukin was Chris's best man. "They got married," says Lukin, "and then everybody got drunk." The reception was distinguished by an inebriated three-way wrestling match between Chris, Kurt Danielson, and Tad.

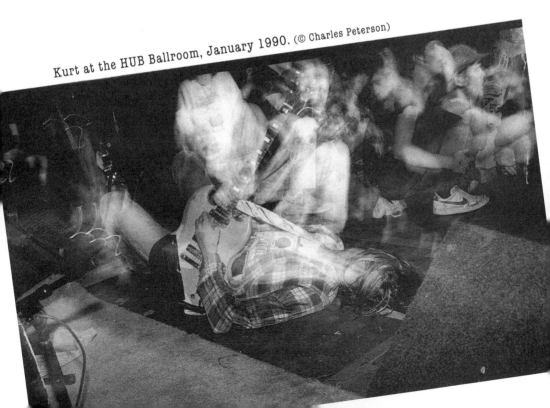

Kurt at the HUB Ballroom, January 1990. (© Charles Peterson)

Kurt at Raji's in Los Angeles, February 1990. (© Charles Peterson)

After a brief California tour and some local gigs, the band went out on a U.S. tour, Chad's last. They each picked up Pixelvision toy video cameras and shot movies in the van to pass the time. They hired a U-Haul trailer—"It was a total advancement in touring technology," says Chris—and put a loveseat in the back. It was a big step for the band—now they had the whole van to themselves. They also had a T-shirt that reproduced John Lennon and Yoko Ono's infamous nude *Two Virgins* album cover, except sticking Bruce Pavitt and Jonathan Poneman's faces on the bodies. They headlined at clubs with a few hundred capacity, making a few hundred dollars a night.

They played all the same clubs they used to play, except now they had a tour manager, a roadie, and soundman Craig Montgomery working for them full time. At first, the easygoing Montgomery was a little rattled by all the guitar smashing, but soon came to understand what it was all about. "That's part of the fun of Nirvana, is the unpredictability," he says. "If they didn't have that anger at some times, they wouldn't have that beauty at other times."

By this time, people in important places were beginning to buzz about Nirvana. Indie world demi-gods Sonic Youth had seen the band on the Jason tour and had become big fans and ardent boosters in the

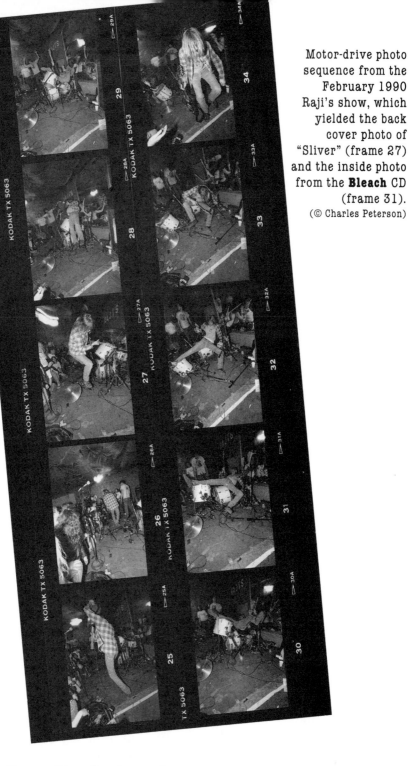

Motor-drive photo sequence from the February 1990 Raji's show, which yielded the back cover photo of "Sliver" (frame 27) and the inside photo from the **Bleach** CD (frame 31).
(© Charles Peterson)

press. Bassist Kim Gordon and guitarist Thurston Moore showed up at a gig in New York at the Pyramid Club, along with Geffen A&R (Artist and Repertoire) man Gary Gersh. Besides them, no one in the audience liked the band, except for Iggy Pop, who had been brought to the gig by photographer Michael Lavine. Pop hooted and hollered words of encouragement throughout the set, even though the band played miserably. In penance for the gig, Chris shaved his head in the cheap Jersey City motel the band was staying in, but not before they had started shooting a video for "In Bloom," which can be found on the Sub Pop compilation entitled *Sub Pop Video Network Program One.* In some scenes, Chris has hair and in some, he doesn't. So much for continuity.

On April 27, Tracy's birthday, Kurt called her from Amherst, Massachusetts, to tell her that he didn't want to live together, but that he still wanted them to be boyfriend and girlfriend. Tracy knew something like that was coming. "Near the end, we started fighting more and more," she says. "He wanted me to be artistic and I didn't have the time to be artistic. I was driving an hour to work and an hour back from work. I was supporting him and he wasn't doing any housework. He'd say 'Just leave it' and I'd say 'I can't leave it. I can leave it for a week or a few days and then I can't stand it anymore. I have to clean it because you won't do it.'"

A few days later in Florida, they met a kid who wanted to be on Sub Pop, and who let them spend the night at his dad's luxury condo. That night they did a lot of acid and drank a lot of Tom Collins drinks. Among other unspeakably strange and bizarre acts, Chris fried mayonnaise in a pan. The next morning, he found himself walking around the driveway stark naked, bald, and yelling "Cast away your possessions like I have! You're not worth anything!" Kurt hustled him back into the house, got him dressed, and they scrammed out of there before their still-unconscious host discovered all the damage they'd done.

Although Sub Pop didn't promote *Bleach* as heavily as other albums out at the time, it was a steady seller. It was promoted for two months and then, despite Kurt's request that the label stay on top of the record, Sub Pop went on to new projects. The label's relatively low-powered distribution and publicity were beginning to be a problem—their records were hard to find.

"It's the typical story of showing up at gigs and ten to twenty kids coming up to the stage and saying we can't find your record anywhere," Kurt says. "It got real tiring. We didn't do any interviews. We felt we deserved a little bit more than what we were getting. I would have been comfortable playing to a thousand people. That was basically our goal—to get up to that size of a club, to be one of the most

Kurt sees the light in an early Michael Lavine portrait. (© Michael Lavine)

popular alternative rock bands, like Sonic Youth." Kurt estimates they did about three interviews while they were on the label.

And Sub Pop was on the verge of going under. A distribution venture crashed and burned due to mismanagement, Poneman and Pavitt's high-rolling promotional style was draining the company dry, band members were raiding the stockroom and walking off with armloads of vinyl; the label was releasing a record a week while trying to keep too many bands on the road, and now that major labels were offering major label-sized advances to Seattle bands, Sub Pop felt compelled to try to match them. Sub Pop nearly went bankrupt. By the summer of 1990, they were bouncing hundred-dollar checks and owed money to everyone in town. "They hit rock bottom," Chris recalls. "It was just such a mess. They tried really hard to pay us because they really appreciated us and that's cool but it was just too much of a burden."

And further draining the label's coffers were Sub Pop's alleged legal negotiations (neither Pavitt nor Poneman will comment on them to this day) for distribution deals with Columbia Records and Hollywood Records. At one point, Nirvana met with Sub Pop's attorney, who tried to convince them that it was a good arrangement, but the way Kurt and Chris saw it, it simply made more sense for them to choose their own label, instead of someone else choosing it for them. "We decided to cut out the middleman," says Kurt.

No indie label could afford to buy Nirvana out of their Sub Pop contract, and besides, Sonic Youth and Dinosaur Jr, both bands of impeccable artistry and credibility, had recently signed to majors, so they began looking for a major label deal. When Poneman and Pavitt found out, they were deeply anguished. "I can think of very few things that have happened in my life that have hurt my feelings more," says Pavitt. "It really fucked with my head for a while."

Pavitt says he and Poneman only found out about the group's plans through the grapevine. "It was so obvious," Kurt replies. "We wouldn't return their phone calls for weeks and weeks at a time. Every time I talked to Jonathan, I feel that I made it clear that there was definitely an uncertainty in our relationship. I just don't understand how you're expected to come right out and tell someone something like that. I suppose it's the more adult thing to do, to tell someone that you don't want to have anything to do with them anymore. It's a really hard thing to do. I've always quit my jobs without any notice. I just quit one day and not show up."

Kurt admired Pavitt because he had an uncanny instinct for ferreting out great new underground music. Bearing albums by Daniel Johnston and the Shags as propitiatory offerings, Pavitt went down to Kurt's apartment in Olympia to try to talk him into a new, stronger contract. "For the first time, Bruce actually seemed like a human being to me," says Kurt. "Every other time I'd see Bruce, our conversation was always real limited and we never got to talk to each other on a human level. I also felt some kind of resentment because why all of a sudden, at that point, did he decide to treat me like a person instead of this casualty every time I came into his office?"

They spoke for five tense hours—"There were just beads of sweat on my forehead and everything," recalls Pavitt—and Kurt couldn't quite bring himself to tell Pavitt that he was sure he didn't want to be on Sub Pop anymore. A few days later, Chris gave Sub Pop the definitive word. They were leaving.

"I felt really bad," says Kurt. "I felt guilty because I wanted to be on their label still because I knew that these are people who share similar thoughts. I kind of felt like the enemy at the time. But still, there was nothing that [Pavitt] was going to do that would change my mind. They were just too risky."

By August, Soundgarden manager Susan Silver had also introduced them to lawyer Alan Mintz of the powerful Ziffren, Brittenham

& Branca firm. Mintz had already engineered outstanding deals for Jane's Addiction and Faith No More. The wining and dining began. Charisma, Slash, and Capitol all wanted the band badly. MCA flew the band down to L.A. and flew a rep up to Seattle. Island A&R man Steve Pross had already been chasing Nirvana, but the band was thoroughly uninterested in Island.

The labels were all excited about a tape the band had recorded in early April of 1990 at Smart Studios in Madison, Wisconsin, the home base of veteran underground producer Butch Vig, an immensely nice man who had become highly regarded for his fierce-sounding but economical production work on albums by Killdozer, the Laughing Hyenas, the Fluid, and Smashing Pumpkins and who had produced records for labels like Touch & Go, Mammoth, Twin/Tone, and Amphetamine Reptile. He'd also produced TAD's excellent *8 Way Santa* album for Sub Pop. Vig started with more pop records but adapted brilliantly to the mid-eighties indie boom with its abrasive sounds and tight recording budgets. Jonathan Poneman had hyped Vig on Nirvana by saying, "These guys are going to be bigger than the Beatles!"

Kurt was very quiet and let Chris do most of the talking. Chris made it clear that the band wanted to sound very heavy. Vig began to sense a tension between Kurt and Chad, who couldn't quite do what Kurt wanted him to.

They had spent a week recording seven songs for what was supposed to be their second Sub Pop album, but which became, in effect, the demo tape they shopped to the major labels. The arrangements are virtually identical to the *Nevermind* versions—in fact, the version of "Polly" is the one that appears on *Nevermind*, although remixed. "Breed" was then called "Imodium" (after the antidiarrhea medicine Tad had used on the European tour); "Stay Away" was originally titled "Pay to Play" and featured slightly different lyrics, spectacular feedback, and a screaming kamikaze coda. Also recorded at Smart were "In Bloom," "Dive," and "Lithium," which begins with Kurt playing the same rickety acoustic guitar that features on "Polly" and fades rather than stops. They also made another attempt at the elusive "Sappy," a highly catchy tune about romantic entrapment.

Vig was the perfect producer for the project. He could get nasty sounds, but he was also a self-described "pop geek." In the indie scene, music as melodic and downright catchy as this was anathema. Almost by definition, underground music wasn't supposed to be easy to like. The songs on the Smart sessions were a bold step, as bold and experimental as any noisy angst-fest—perhaps a lot more so. "I think of them as pop songs," Kurt told one U.K. magazine. "There aren't songs as wild and heavy as 'Paper Cuts' or 'Sifting' on the new record. That's just too boring. I'd rather have a good hook."

Both the songwriting and the recording weren't as rushed as *Bleach* had been, so Kurt had a lot of time to hone and polish the songs. "I had finally gotten to the point where I was mixing pop music and the heavy side of us in the right formula," says Kurt. "It was working really well, mostly because of the reports from our friends and other bands. Everyone was saying that it was really good. I could tell that it was definitely more advanced than *Bleach*."

But Kurt and Chris were growing more and more unhappy with Chad's drumming. This time, Kurt had the time to make sure that Chad played the parts that he had taught him—during the low-budget *Bleach* sessions, Chad would change his parts and there was no time to argue or do another take.

"I was really hoping to participate more and become part of what was going on," says Chad, "at least to have a say in how my own drums sounded. I wanted to get more involved in the band and feel like I was actually doing something. I was still happy dealing with the album, but I wanted to be more a part of it. It was then that I realized that it really is Kurt's show and that what he says goes and that's it, no questions asked."

Chad, who could play guitar, bass, and violin, was also a songwriter and wanted to start contributing material to the band. But even though he was into a lot of the same music that Chris and Kurt were—the Young Marble Giants, the Beatles, Scratch Acid, and the Butthole Surfers—his songwriting style defined the Bainbridge Island sound (which he helped to create before joining Nirvana)—ultra-quirky, pastoral, vaguely prog-rock. "Elfin music," says Kurt. "You just kind of shudder because it's so stupid and dorky." Kurt says they were open to other material, but Chad's music didn't fit the band. "It just wasn't good," says Kurt, "and there was nothing else to be said about it. It was really sad because he felt like he wasn't part of the band because he couldn't really create." And so Chad wound up living out a time-honored rock-biz joke. "Q: What was the last thing the drummer said before he was fired? A: 'Hey, guys, I wrote some songs I want us to play!'"

By late May, after the U.S. tour had ended, Nirvana had started to attract the attention of major labels. Bootlegs of the demo circulated around the music industry, and even though they were hardly as polished as the finished *Nevermind* recordings would be, the buzz was loud. Ironically, Sub Pop had probably helped spread the buzz about Nirvana by touting the band as a valuable property to the labels they wanted to do a distribution agreement with.

(© Michael Lavine)

And that's when Kurt and Chris chose to fire Chad Channing. Nervous and sad, they took the thirty-five-minute ferry ride from Seattle to Chad's house on Bainbridge Island to give him the news. They told him—Chris did most of the talking—gave him a hug good-bye, and then they left. "I felt like I'd just killed somebody," says Kurt.

Chad's take on the meeting is that he wasn't fired—he quit. "We talked for a while and I just told them this was how I felt and they knew that," he says. "It wasn't like we weren't getting along—we always got along as human beings. It was strictly along the musical line that it just wasn't working anymore. That's where it ended, right there. I never felt like I was totally in the band. I felt like I was just a drummer. I was thinking, why don't they get a drum machine—get it over with. Then they could program it and do anything they damn well wanted."

"Sometimes I just felt sorry for Chad," says Bruce Pavitt. "You could tell that... I didn't feel that they treated him with a lot of respect."

Even though Kurt thought Chad was a really nice guy, he never got along with him. Kurt suspects Chad didn't get along with him for some of the same reasons that Jason didn't. Kurt was still prone to being "volatile"—getting drunk and turning into a negative creep. "I was just trying to be 'punk rock' or something," Kurt admits. "I had this terrible Johnny Rotten complex." Chad, used to the mellow, quasi-hippie Bainbridge Island scene, couldn't relate to such a sarcastic pessimist.

Kurt was still openly judgmental, quick to point out people's faults, something Chad frowned upon. Kurt knew he had a problem and tried hard to contain it, but couldn't always, especially when talking about their *bête noire*, crude Seattle sludge-rockers Blood Circus, whose early success baffled Kurt and Chris. "It was almost impossible for me to get along on any level with Chad because I basically couldn't say anything without offending him," says Kurt. "I thought he was judging me for judging other people." Their mutual animosity grew, although they would never say it was. "What an asshole," Chad would think to himself. "What a hippie," Kurt thought.

Kurt had played drums for years, so he was very picky about drumming. He didn't think much of Chad's playing, and that further fueled his animosity. "He really had bad timing and he wasn't a very powerful drummer," says Kurt. Kurt liked Chad much better than any other drummer they'd had, so he encouraged him to take lessons so he could improve. Kurt also says that Chad would tire quickly and start to make more and more mistakes as the set wore on; often, there would be interminable delays while Chad retuned his drums, although Kurt insists he was really resting.

"Sometimes there would be weird things," says Chris. "He'd go off in space—there wouldn't even be a drum beat any more. I remember looking over at Kurt and Kurt looking over at me like, 'What the fuck was *that*?'"

"That really is how the instrument smashing came about," says Kurt. "I got so pissed off at Chad that I'd jump into the drum set, then smash my guitar." Early video tapes of the band show that sets often ended with someone hurling a guitar or a guitar case at Chad, soon followed by Kurt and/or Chris sailing into the drum kit.

Chris is still slightly evasive when explaining why Chad got the sack. At first, he chalks it up to good old musical differences. "He kind of wanted to do his own thing," he says, adding that Chad was a "light, jazzy" drummer by nature and had to alter his style in order to play in Nirvana. We needed a real thumper." But on the Vig demo, Chad hit very hard and truth be told, Dave Grohl virtually duplicated all his parts for *Nevermind*.

"We've been through a lot with this whole success thing, with all the pressure and stuff," Chris continues. "I'm just glad [Chad] didn't have to go through all that, because..." and he trails off. "It was always kind of awkward with Chad. It was weird. I don't regret it at all, though. He just wanted to do his own thing. He had a different perspective than us. A lot of times he had a way better perspective. Way more objective and way more innocent and really good. We were going to make this big step—sign to a major label—and he wasn't right for us. It just wasn't right."

"Even when I look at it now," says Chad. "I don't regret anything. I'd probably be pretty damn wealthy, but would I be happy? That's the question mark there.

"It's kind of weird," he continues. "I mean, I could be there—but I'm not. But at the same time, I'm happy for them. I would have been bummed if it just petered out and the band broke up. I hope they're enjoying themselves and that the pressures aren't too much."

The bad feelings seem to be few. "Overall, I have massive love for that guy," says Kurt. "I kind of admire him because he's really satisfied with the way that he is. He seems like a really happy person and he always has been."

Chad now plays in a fine band called Fire Ants and made a tidy sum from the royalties of *Bleach* and *Incesticide*.

Without a drummer, they canceled a proposed March 1990, U.K. tour and asked Dale Crover to fill in on a seven-date West Coast tour with Sonic Youth in mid-August. Crover agreed to play, but on one condition. "I told them—whatever you do, do not jump into my drum set. *Do not.*" Not only did they comply with that request, but they also did not smash one guitar on the tour. "I'm glad they didn't do that stuff," says Crover. "I'd seen them do it before and I just thought it was anticlimactic. Kurt trying to break a guitar—it takes him fifteen minutes. By the time it's over, it's like, big deal. I think that's guitar murder. I think guitars have souls. I don't think any of that stuff's cool at all. Instruments have souls—why would you want to murder a guitar? I think it's pointless. Haven't you ever seen the Who, guys?"

***

Kurt and Tracy continued living together for over a month until Tracy could get enough money to get an apartment in Tacoma, which was closer to work. But Kurt wasn't at the apartment much. Usually, he was staying over at the home of Tobi Vail, one of only a handful of girlfriends Kurt ever had.

Kurt says he slept with a total of two women on all of Nirvana's tours. Perhaps he had learned a lesson from an incident that occurred on the band's second U.S. tour. After realizing that their audience at a sleazy dive in Iowa was mostly "frat jock people," Kurt downed a big jug of Long Island Iced Tea during a particularly shambolic set. Afterward, they all stumbled over to someone's house and spent the night. Kurt met a girl. "We had sex in the van in front of the house and I woke up in the morning to the sound of breaking glass," Kurt says. "It turned out to be her boyfriend with a hammer, smashing out the windows of the van. We were stark naked, covered in glass, wondering what we should do. He was walking around the van screaming 'Bitch, bitch! I'm going to kill you!'

"But then he took off."

Kurt had been looking for a dynamic and artistic girlfriend like Tobi. She had her own fanzine and was busy helping to start the Riot Grrl movement, a group of young women dedicated to promoting female empowerment through music, fanzines, and eventually, the national media, with her friend Kathleen Hanna. Through Tobi, Kurt began to investigate feminism and other social and political causes. "I thought I was in love again," says Kurt, "and it was just wishful thinking."

A couple of months after the Smart sessions, Chris called up Butch Vig and asked him if he'd be interested in producing a major label record with them at some point. Vig said sure.

Meanwhile, back at Sub Pop, Jonathan Poneman wanted another Nirvana single. "Dive," the B-side, was culled from the Vig sessions. "Dive" reprised the best elements of *Bleach*—the grinding guitar sound, the high, desperate growling vocals, the deliciously leaden riff. It was pop music, but it was very, very heavy pop music. "Dive in me!" Kurt wailed. For the A-side, Kurt wanted to take advantage of the fact that Tad was in the studio with Jack Endino and record a song while Tad was on dinner break. Tad Doyle vehemently disliked the idea, but Endino managed to talk him into it. In one hour on July 11, 1990, they did the basics for "Sliver," using Tad's drums, bass, and guitar.

"Sliver" featured drummer Dan Peters of Mudhoney, who were on hiatus while guitarist Steve Turner decided whether he wanted to

Anarchy reigned at the Motor Sports show. (© Charles Peterson)

pursue a graduate degree. The band auditioned a couple of drum-mers before Peters, already a veteran of many Seattle bands, an affa-ble fellow known for his fleet and powerful stickwork. He'd heard that Nirvana was looking for a drummer and bumped into Shelli at a bar and asked if she'd mention he was available.

They started playing with Peters soon after. "It definitely felt good to play with someone who was rhythmically competent," says Kurt. "But it wasn't quite perfect."

For practice, Kurt came up to Seattle from Olympia and Chris came from Tacoma and they practiced in Peters's truly grungy rehearsal room in an industrial building in south Seattle (First Avenue South and Spokane Street) known as the Dutchman, the very room where countless bands have rehearsed before and since, among them early bands such as Bundle of Hiss, Feast and Room Nine, as well as Screaming Trees, TAD, Love Battery, and Seven Year Bitch. If grunge had a birthplace, this was it. Rehearsals were brief and to the point, and little was said.

As far as drums went, Kurt and Chris were of the "bigger is bet-ter" school, while Peters had a great-sounding but small drum kit

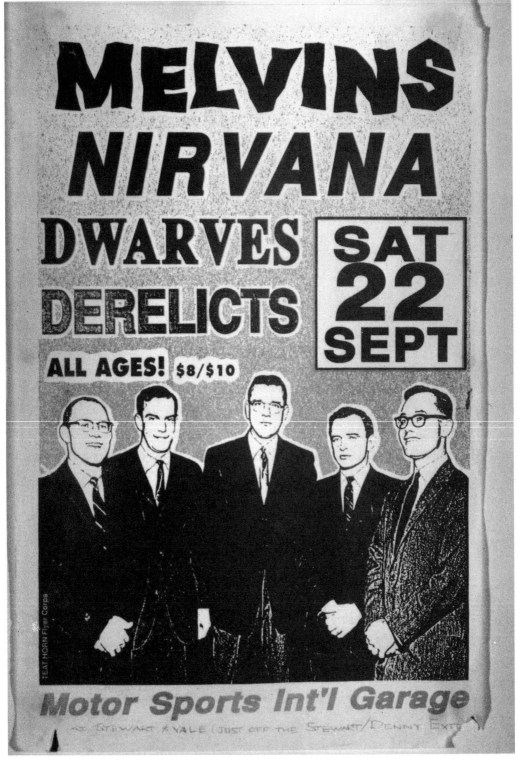

Poster for the fateful Motor Sports show.

that couldn't keep up with the sonic onslaught. "I'd be in the practice space with them and the amplifier was turned up to ten," says Peters. "They'd always be going, 'I can't hear that bass drum.' Yeah, well, no shit you can't hear the bass drum—*I* can't even hear the bass drum!"

One day Kurt and Chris brought Peters a huge but dilapidated drum set to play. Particular about what he played, Peters would take only the bass drum. "If I knew that they were really that serious, I would have pursued another drum kit somehow," says Peters. "But I wouldn't play this big hunk of shit they wanted me to play."

Peters began to see the writing on the wall.

Still, he did play on "Sliver," a key track in the Nirvana repertoire. Like many of Kurt's songs, "Sliver" seems to be autobiographical. It's about a boy who is left with his grandparents for the evening while his mother goes out. He can't eat, he doesn't want to play, he just wants to go home. He falls asleep and wakes up in his mother's arms. Even the cover of the single is a picture of a transparent man, as if to say that the song within enabled the listener to see right through Kurt.

They had written it with Peters one day at practice. It came together within a matter of minutes, with Kurt coming up with the lyrics—in typical fashion—just before they recorded it. "The chemistry was definitely there with Danny, Chris, and I," says Kurt. "We could have ended up writing some really good songs together."

It was a bit of an experiment. "I decided I wanted to write the most ridiculous pop song that I had ever written," says Kurt. "It was like a statement in a way. I had to write a real pop song and release it on a single to prepare people for the next record. I wanted to write more songs like that."

Kurt was listening to a lot of pop-oriented music at that point, including the legendary Seattle garage band the Sonics and the Smithereens; he was also delving deep into the R.E.M. catalogue.

It's the most literal lyric Kurt has ever written. "For some reason, it's one of the easiest songs for people to comprehend because it's that way," he says, implying that he doesn't understand why people don't grasp his more abstract songs just as easily. "That's why I choose not to write that way. I don't like things that are so obvious."

The only elusive aspect of the song is the title, which Kurt says he picked because "I had a feeling that if I called it 'Sliver,' most people would call it 'Silver.'" Kurt is still very pleased with everything about the track. "It has a massive naïveté to it," he says. "It was done so fast and raw and perfect that I don't think we could capture that again if we decided to rerecord it. It's just one of those recordings

Nirvana at the Motor Sports show. Barely visible is Danny Peters on drums. Note the undersized drum set. (© Charles Peterson)

that happened and you can't try to reproduce it." It had that childlike quality that Kurt loved in the bands he heard on K Records, like Beat Happening and Young Marble Giants.

Many, including Wendy, believe the song is autobiographical, but Kurt says he doesn't recall being afraid of going to his grandparents' house. He may be disingenuous here, because the real point of the song is the anguished cry as the child is reunited with his mother.

The song also pointed toward a new songwriting direction. The song was grungy enough, but it was also very tightly composed, a very "pop" song, as opposed to the "rock" riff-oriented music the band had played thus far.

(Tacked onto the end of the seven-inch version of "Sliver" is a hilarious snippet of conversation between Jonathan Poneman and a freshly awoken and very hung over Chris Novoselic. Chris recorded the exchange by accident on his answering machine one afternoon.)

Peters played one gig with Nirvana, a September 22 show at the Motor Sports International and Garage, a former parking garage (now demolished) at Minor and Howell streets. Nirvana headlined over the Dwarves and their one-time mentors, the Melvins. With fifteen hundred customers, it was their biggest show in Seattle at that point. The band debuted several songs from the Vig demos, including "Pay to Play," "Imodium," and "In Bloom." There was no stage security at all, so people would climb up and dive off, but not before accidentally marring almost every song by knocking over a mike or bumping into a musician. It was just nuts.

In the audience was Dave Grohl.

CHAPTER SEVEN

David Eric Grohl was born on January 14, 1969, in Warren, Ohio, to James and Virginia Grohl. His father was then a journalist for the Scripps-Howard newspaper chain, his mother a high school English teacher. Dave has a sister, Lisa, three years older than he is. The Grohls left Columbus, Ohio, and moved to Springfield, Virginia, when Dave was three. When he was six, they divorced. "My mother and father were pretty much at other ends of the spectrum—he's a real conservative, neat, Washington, D.C., kind of man and my mother's more of a liberal, free-thinking, creative sort of person," says Dave. He says the divorce didn't affect him much, perhaps because he was so young at the time.

Dave was raised by his mom, whom he adores. "She's the most incredible woman in the world," he says, obviously filled with pride. "She's so great. She's strong, independent, sweet, intelligent, funny, and she's just the best."

Raising two kids on alimony payments and a schoolteacher's modest income was hard. "There were tough times when we'd eat peanut butter and pickle sandwiches for dinner," Dave recalls.

As a kid, Dave appeared professionally in a Washington theater company, but his main love was music. He formed a little duo with his buddy Larry called the H. G. Hancock Band when he was ten. They'd write songs and Dave would play a one-stringed guitar while Larry banged on pots and pans.

Dave started playing guitar when he was twelve and took lessons for a couple of years. He'd write songs about his friends or his dog and play them into a boom box, then play the tape back over the stereo while he recorded the drum parts back onto the boom box.

Eventually, he got sick of lessons and just played in neighborhood bands doing the typical Rolling Stones and Beatles covers. Dave hadn't yet discovered punk rock, although he'd already gotten a taste of new wave from the same B-52's appearance on "Saturday Night Live" that Kurt had seen. He had gone out and bought the requisite checkered Vans as well as records by the B-52's and Devo, but nothing prepared him for the time he visited his cousin Tracy, who lived in Evanston, Illinois, in the summer of 1982, when Dave was thirteen.

When Dave and his sister Lisa came to the door, Dave's aunt called Tracy downstairs. "And Tracy starts coming down the stairs and she was *totally punk*," says Dave. "Bondage pants and chains and crew cut and we were like 'Wow! Tracy's punk now!'" Tracy took Dave and Lisa to punk shows all that summer, seeing shows by bands like Naked Raygun, Rights of the Accused, Channel Three, and Violent Apathy. "From then on we were totally punk," says Dave. "We went home and bought *Maximumrocknroll* and tried to figure it all out."

Punk agreed with Dave. He liked "just being a little punk shit running around town and being a little derelict," he says. "I suppose that was half the attraction—being a slacker." The other half was the extreme energy of the music. "I was super-hyperactive," Dave says (although not hyper enough to get put on Ritalin).

The solidly middle-class people of Springfield were more tolerant of punk rock than the folks in Aberdeen. Dave always had "good, cool" friends. He was popular enough to get elected vice president of his freshman class at Thomas Jefferson High School in Alexandria, Virginia. Before he did the morning announcements every morning over the school intercom, he'd treat the whole school to a little blast of the Circle Jerks or Bad Brains.

Like Chris and Kurt, Dave was a stoner in high school. "I smoked too much pot," says Dave sadly. "That's the only thing that I really kick myself for doing because it seriously burned me out—bad. From the time I was fifteen to twenty, I smoked four or five times a day and a lot. Every day of my life. You just get so burned out. You don't feel burned out when you're smoking it but once you stop you realize, 'Oh, I lost something here.'"

Pot began affecting his grades, so he and his mother decided that he would attend Bishop Ireton, a Catholic school. Meanwhile, he had decided that the drummer in his "bad punk" band, Freak Baby, was so lousy that he could play better. He'd sit down at the drums and bang around a little after practice, but most of his self-education on the drums came the classic way. In his bedroom, Dave would pull up a chair for a high-hat, a book for a snare, and his bed for tom-toms and play along to music by hardcore bands like Minor Threat, DRI, and Bad Brains.

When they kicked out the bass player in Freak Baby, the drummer switched to bass and Dave switched to drums. They changed their name to Mission Impossible and played fast hardcore punk, so fast that they eventually changed their name to Fast, which broke up around 1986.

Being a suburban stoner, it was only natural for Dave to get into Led Zeppelin. It was even more natural for him to start copping the classic licks of Led Zep drummer John Bonham. "I used to rip him off like crazy and then I figured out the weird stuttered kick drum in 'Kashmir' and that opened up a million new doors," says Dave. "You take pieces from other drummers and like the drummer from the Bad Brains to John Bonham to the drummer from Devo and it eventually becomes this big mush and that's me—just one big rip-off!"

After Fast, Dave was in a band called Dain Bramage that mixed hardcore punk with the sounds of adventurous pre- and post-punk bands like Television and Mission of Burma. "Everybody just hated us," says Dave. The dogmatic hardcore scene didn't take too well to outside influences (except for reggae) and Dain Bramage couldn't get many gigs because they weren't on the DC-based indie Dischord label, which was cofounded by Ian MacKaye of Minor Threat (and later, Fugazi) and was then the only game in town for hardcore bands.

As a joke, Dave originally put Bonham's three-circle logo on the front of his bass drum; later on, he got the logo tattooed on his arm, then variations of it on his wrist and then his other arm. He's also got a homemade tattoo of the Black Flag logo on his forearm that he made when he was thirteen.

Dave had long admired a local D.C. hardcore band called Scream, who had already put out several records on Dischord, and then he saw an ad in the local music paper saying that Scream was looking for a drummer. "I thought I'd try out just to tell my friends that I jammed with Scream," Dave says. He called, but the band never called him back because he was too young—and he had told them he was nineteen even though he was really sixteen. Finally, Dave wangled an audition, and after jamming a few times, Scream asked Dave to join the band. Dave said he was committed to Dain Bramage but a couple of months later he got back in touch with them and convinced them to take him on.

Dave dropped out of high school late in his junior year. "I was seventeen and extremely anxious to see the world and play, so I did," Dave says. "I'm totally glad I did it." Dave plans to go to college some day, though.

Much later, when Wendy Cobain met Virginia Grohl in New York for Nirvana's "Saturday Night Live" appearance, they compared notes on their sons. "We were just amazed at how much these two kids are alike," says Wendy. "They're like twins that got separated somehow."

"I don't see that at all," Dave says at first, then he adds, "In some ways I can, because I remember the first time I went into the house where Kurt grew up and we went upstairs where his room was and there was stuff written on the walls—the brain with a little question mark—and I remember being stoned and drawing a little brain with a question mark in it in like seventh or eighth grade. When I saw that I thought it was kind of strange. And we're both total slobs."

Dave was supposed to go to night school, but he spent the tuition money on pot instead. He rehearsed with Scream for six months and then the band went on a two-month U.S. tour in October of 1987.

"Touring with Scream was so much fun—it was a lesson in life," says Dave. "Learning to budget yourself on seven dollars a day. You had three meals—or two—and you have to somehow save up money or ask for the next three days' per diem if you want to buy pot. You can't buy cigarettes more than three times a week. If you do, you have to buy bargain brand. I'd never seen the country before and everything was just so fucking *punk*."

Dave became a big Melvins fan after seeing them open for hardcore bands in D.C. When he read in *Maximumrocknroll* that they had re-formed after a brief breakup, Scream was on tour in Memphis. Dave had bought an Elvis postcard and happened to get Elvis's uncle Vester Presley to sign it. He sent it to the Melvins in San Francisco and asked if they'd come to Scream's show there. The night before the gig, Dave found out that Scream and the Melvins were on the same bill. Dave befriended the Melvins and they swapped addresses and have corresponded ever since.

Back in San Francisco for another tour, Dave went backstage after a Melvins gig, where Kurt and Chris were hanging out. They were in town to rehearse with Dale Crover for the 1990 West Coast tour with Sonic Youth. "I remember [Kurt] sitting in this chair looking pissed," Dave recalls, while Chris was being exceptionally loud and boisterous. "Who *is* that guy?" Dave asked Osborne. He didn't wind up speaking to either of them.

During one of their forays down to L.A. to meet the labels, Kurt and Chris stopped in San Francisco to hang out with the Melvins, who told them there was a great hardcore band playing at the I-Beam called Scream. They went and were promptly knocked out by their drummer. "God, what a great drummer," Chris thought. "Wish he'd be in our band."

Dave recorded one studio and two live albums with Scream, who blossomed into one of America's most explosive hardcore bands, and toured the U.S. and Europe until the middle of September 1990, when "girlfriend trouble" compelled bass player Skeeter to leave the tour suddenly. Stranded in Los Angeles with no money, Dave called his friend Buzz Osborne.

Osborne knew Kurt and Chris loved Dave's drumming and called Chris to tell him he'd given Dave his number. When Dave called, Chris was ecstatic, but he felt obligated to at least ask Dave a few questions before going any further. He was into the right bands and Chris invited him up to Seattle.

Dave had heard Nirvana for the first time during one of Scream's frequent European tours. "You look at the cover of *Bleach*," he says, "and you just think they're these big burly unshaven logger, drinking guys. They look kind of nasty on the front, almost like a metal band, but with this retarded weirdness about them." He thought they sounded a bit like the Melvins, which was okay by him.

Dave took apart his drums, fit all the pieces into one big cardboard box, and flew up to Seattle with only a bag of clothes. Kurt and Chris picked him up at Sea-Tac Airport and began the drive to Tacoma. To break the ice, Dave offered Kurt an apple. "No thanks," Kurt replied. "It'll make my teeth bleed."

That wasn't the first awkward moment they had had. On the

This guitar has seconds to live. Kurt at the Motor Sports show.
(© Ian T. Tilton)

phone with Kurt before he headed up to Seattle, Dave mentioned a
party he had gone to after a Scream show in Olympia. The band had
bought a bunch of beer and the great disco music spilling out onto the
street augured well for a happening bash. They arrived at the apartment to find about twenty people, with all the guys on one side of the
room and all the girls on another. "They were total Olympia hot
chocolate party Hello Kitty people," says Dave. The band stood
around drinking beer and feeling awkward until suddenly someone
turned off the stereo. "This girl comes in and sits down and plugs in
this guitar and starts playing this total bad teen suicide awful music,
'Boys, boys/ Bad/ Die,'" Dave says. "And after every song everyone
would clap and we were like, 'Let's get out here!'" Dave had just

begun insulting the "sad little girl with the bad fucking songs" when Kurt said, "Oh yeah, that's my girlfriend, Tobi."

Kurt was actually at the party and remembers that the members of Scream were making fun of everybody there. "They were real rocker dudes," says Kurt. "I hated them, I thought they were assholes." Kurt remembers Dave in particular. "He brought up this Primus tape from their car and tried to play it and everyone got mad at him."

The Motor Sports gig happened to be the night after Dave arrived. He was stunned by the size and enthusiasm of the crowd—the only other local show he'd seen that big was Fugazi in D.C. In Seattle, punk rock had become big business. "It seemed like a local punk scene gone bad, in a way," says Dave. "I saw the Nirvana T-shirt stand—every fucking kid and their brother buying the 'crack smokin', fudge packin' T-shirt. They must have sold two hundred T-shirts that night—that's *insane* for a local punk rock show."

"I didn't know what I was getting myself into at all."

Dave was not terribly impressed by Nirvana. "I thought they were all right," he says. "They didn't completely blow me away. The Melvins played before them and I was so into the Melvins that I was spent by the time Nirvana went on."

Also from the **Sounds** shoot: Kurt smiles! Future Nirvana drummer Dave Grohl is at left. The can of sausage would reappear in the "Sliver" video two years later. No one knows why. (© Ian T. Tilton)

Still, the material seemed fun to play and besides, although Dave thought Danny Peters was "a fucking incredible drummer," he didn't think Nirvana sounded quite right with Peters. He was probably right—Peters is an excellent, hard-hitting drummer, but doesn't play in the heavy, Bonhamesque style that Nirvana requires. Peters played well at the Motor Sports show, but he didn't quite fit—it was like a man wearing a very nice hat that nevertheless didn't go with his suit.

Danny Peters, Kurt, and Chris pose for a **Sounds** magazine photo shoot at Chris and Shelli's house the day after the Motor Sports show. (© Ian T. Tilton)

Dave stayed with Chris and Shelli at first. The day after the Motor Sports show, Chris and Shelli threw a barbecue, during which Chris, Kurt, and Danny Peters did an interview for a cover story in the now defunct English music weekly *Sounds*. No one was to know they were auditioning a new drummer.

A few days later, Kurt and Chris auditioned Dave at the Dutchman. "We knew in two minutes that he was the right drummer," says Chris. "He was a hard hitter. He was really dynamic. He was so bright, so hot, so vital. He rocked." Dave was steady, solid, tasteful, and definitely a hard hitter. When he played a roll on his snare, it sounded like the powerful chop of spinning helicopter blades; when he pounded on his gigantic tom-toms, they didn't make a tone so much as they exploded like rifle shots; his outsized cymbals fluttered like punching bags under his attack. Dave could also sing, giving the band the potential for live harmonies for the first time.

Then there was the delicate matter of telling Danny Peters that he was out of the band after only a few weeks.

During an acoustic appearance on Calvin Johnson's KAOS radio show a few days later, Kurt revealed that they had a new drummer and that he hadn't even broken the news to Peters yet. "Who *is* the new drummer?" Johnson asked. "His name is Dave and he's a baby Dale Crover," Kurt answered. "He plays almost as good as Dale. And within a few years' practice, he may even give him a run for his money."

Kurt acknowledged the awkward situation with Peters. "Dan's such a beautiful guy and such a beautiful drummer," he said, "but you can't pass up an opportunity to play with the drummer of our dreams, which is Dave. He's been the drummer of our dreams for like two years. It's a bummer, a big bummer."

A tour of England had been planned. "Kurt called me up," says Peters, "and he said he thought they were going to go with Geffen and I'm like 'Cool.' Then I go, 'So what about this tour?' And he goes, 'Ahhh. Ummm. Well, ah, well... We got another drummer.' And I wasn't bummed at all. I kind of half-assed expected it and I was like, 'Oh, that's cool.' I wasn't sure how they were feeling because their communication skills at that time were kind of not happening. I wasn't bummed at all. I'm still not bummed."

And as Chris points out, "If he was going to join our band, that would be the end of Mudhoney. And we loved Mudhoney so much, we didn't want to be responsible for that."

"Dave suits them way better than I did," Peters admits. "He really does. To me, that's more important, too. He's got the heavy shit right there. He beats the fuck out of those drums. They definitely got the person that suited them better."

Peters went on to a short stint with Screaming Trees, then Mudhoney re-formed and eventually signed with Warners in 1992. Peters says he's having a great time with Mudhoney, one of America's greatest rock and roll bands. "The only thing is," he says, "[Nirvana] put out one fuckin' killer record and I sure would have liked to play on it."

Meanwhile, Scream dissolved and the guitarist and the singer, brothers Franz and Pete Stahl, later formed Wool. In the summer of

1993, Dave joined Skeeter and the Stahls for a triumphant Scream reunion tour.

Kurt and Chris had found a rehearsal space in Tacoma, a converted barn—it had brown shag carpet and a massive P.A. that made a loud hissing sound. They shared it with a slick bar band—students from the Guitar Institute of Technology, by Chris's guess.

Dave stayed with Chris and Shelli for a month, then moved in with Kurt in Olympia. The Cobain/Grohl house was knee-deep in corn dog sticks. "It was the most filthy pigsty I'd ever lived in," says Kurt (and that's saying a lot). They passed the time by shooting a BB gun, occasionally scoring a direct hit on the windows of the State Lottery Building across the street.

Dave describes the apartment as "small, cluttered, dirty, smelly." Six-foot-tall Dave slept on a five-foot couch. He slept in the same room as Kurt's tank and the clicking of the turtles' shells against the glass as they tried to escape would keep him up at night. "It just felt so weird," says Dave. "The last two and a half *years* have been pretty weird.

"There wasn't a lot to do," Dave continues. "There was a lot of time just spent sitting in the room totally silent reading or just totally silent doing nothing, staring at walls or going downtown and seeing a ninety-nine-cent movie or shooting BB guns in the backyard." Kurt and Dave began going to sleep at six in the morning as the sun was coming up and waking as the sun was going down, never seeing sunlight.

The two barely spoke. The conversation rarely got past "Are you hungry?" "Yes."

Still, Kurt became more social after Dave moved in. "Kurt sort of came out of his shell," says Slim Moon. "He was around more, he seemed happier with his life. He was hanging out with actual Olympians." Being around so many artistic people seemed to have an energizing, inspiring effect on Kurt; in Olympia, he could express himself without inhibition or fear of rejection. As a highly creative person, Kurt yearned to be around other creative people. In Olympia, he appreciated that he was appreciated.

Kurt had been going out with Tobi Vail since before Dave moved in. She was a couple of years younger than Kurt and had no intention of settling into a long-term relationship. "I was definitely looking for somebody I could spend quite a few years with," Kurt says, even though he was only twenty-three at the time. "I wanted that security and I knew that it wasn't with her. So I was just wasting my time and I just felt bad about it." By late 1990, that fact was becoming painfully apparent, and that's when Kurt says he broke up with Tobi.

"He was just a wreck," says Dave, "just a mess." But Kurt insists that it wasn't strictly because of Tobi. "It was just that I was tired of my life, basically," he says. "I was tired of living in Olympia with nothing to do. All during the time that Tracy and I were breaking up, I wanted to move to Seattle. I knew that I was long overdue for a change. I didn't have any extreme thing I could do to just get out of it right away. It wasn't like all the other times where I could have a fight with somebody and get kicked out of their house and have no choice but to do something else.

"I was just tired of not finding the right mate," Kurt says. "I'd been looking all my life. I just got tired of trying to have a girlfriend that I knew that I wouldn't eventually spend more than a couple of months with. I've always been old-fashioned in that respect. I've always wanted a girlfriend that I could have a good relationship with for a long time. I wish I was capable of just playing the field, but I always wanted more than that."

The rides in the van to Tacoma for practice had already been quiet enough, but then Kurt stopped talking completely. Finally, after weeks and weeks of this, they were driving home from practice one night when Kurt broke the silence by saying "You know, I'm not always like this," adding that he would eventually recover from the breakup. "I just kind of said, 'Oh, that's cool,'" Dave says. "But I was thinking to myself, 'Oh, thank *God!*'"

They practiced from ten o'clock to one in the morning almost every night over a four- or five-month period. The band's chemistry was quickly falling into place. "We felt like we could do whatever we wanted to do," Dave says. "There weren't any restrictions and it got weird and jammy and we'd do these noisy new wave noise experimental jam things. We'd always start off the practice just jamming. We'd set up and plug in and jam for twenty minutes on nothing at all." Out of the jams sprang countless songs, but they'd soon forget them or lose the tapes they recorded them on. "There were probably thirty or forty songs we had written that are just gone," Dave says.

After a few weeks, Dave played his first show with Nirvana at the North Shore Surf Club in Olympia. The show had sold out on one day's notice and Dave was so amazed that he called his mother and sister about it. They opened with a cover of the Vaselines' "Son of a Gun." Or at least they tried to—they blew a circuit twice before someone realized all the amps were on one line. It was a frenzied show—Dave played with such force that he broke his snare drum. "I picked it up and held it in front of the audience to show them that we have a new drummer who's very good," says Kurt.

"Kurt and Chris knew—and everybody else knew who saw them play—that they were only a hint of what they could be until Dave joined the band," says Slim Moon. "He just knew how to play drums and he understood their music. Chad just never got it and the guys before Chad never really got it. Danny was a great drummer but he just wasn't right."

Then they went over to Europe for a tour with L.A. rockers L7, ostensibly to promote the "Sliver"/"Dive" single, which didn't actually come out until a month after they left. At London's Heathrow Airport, they met tour manager Alex Macleod. Macleod and Dave had met on a Scream tour and they hadn't exactly hit it off. The working papers for the tour listed Danny Peters as Nirvana's drummer, so Macleod was surprised to see Dave coming through Customs at the airport. "Oh, fuck," thought Dave. "Oh, fuck," thought Macleod.

But they quickly made amends, partly out of necessity and partly because they shared an appreciation for what Macleod calls "inane, senseless humor."

Along for the ride were soundman Craig Montgomery, monitor man Ian Beveridge, and a lot of equipment. They also had a VCR and two tapes—a Monty Python episode and *Spinal Tap*, which had long since become standard equipment on any tour bus.

They played to packed houses of about a thousand people a night, winning rave reviews from the all-important U.K. music weeklies. Kurt only half-sarcastically told Keith Cameron in the October 27 *Sounds*, "I don't wanna have any other kind of job, I can't work among people. I may as well try and make a career out of this. All my life my dream has been to be a big rock star—just may as well abuse it while you can." He added that the band was exploring a more pop style of songwriting—"We figured we may as well get on the radio and try and make a little bit of money at it."

Nirvana's U.K. publicist Anton Brookes recalls that Kurt was very confident that he would soon realize his dream. "I remember Kurt saying that the album was going to go Top Ten and there were these tracks that were going to be massive as singles," Brookes says. "You could see in his face that he totally believed that. He *knew* it."

Meanwhile, John Silva at Gold Mountain Management in L.A. had recently begun calling up the band and offering his expertise;

Chris began consulting him informally on business matters. Gold Mountain, founded by industry veteran Danny Goldberg, counted decided nonpunks such as Bonnie Raitt and Belinda Carlisle as clients, but they also had Sonic Youth. And since whatever Sonic Youth did was by its very nature cool, Gold Mountain was cool by Nirvana. And since Thurston Moore was raving about Nirvana to Gold Mountain, the feeling was mutual. Goldberg was still kicking himself for passing on Dinosaur Jr even after Moore raved about them and he wasn't going to make the same mistake twice.

In November, Gold Mountain flew the band down to L.A., and met with Goldberg and Silva, a hip, bright, and aggressive young manager who had worked with several alternative acts including Redd Kross and House of Freaks. Silva was in touch with the underground enough to have amassed a gigantic seven-inch indie-rock singles collection; he'd even shared an apartment with the Dead Kennedys' Jello Biafra. Chris liked the fact that Goldberg was also the head of the Southern California chapter of the ACLU; Dave dug that Goldberg had been a publicist for Led Zeppelin in the mid-seventies. After a meeting with Goldberg and Silva, Kurt and Chris left and called Silva from the lobby of the building to say they were going with Gold Mountain. They would have told him in person, they said, but they were late for another major label schmooze.

Sleep had become Kurt's favorite pastime—he often claimed to be a narcoleptic and to this day, he usually wears pajamas, probably to make sure he's properly dressed just in case Mr. Sandman should come knocking. "I'd sleep just to get away from the pain," Kurt explains. "While I was asleep, my stomach wouldn't hurt. Then I'd wake up and curse myself that I was still alive."

One day, Kurt was up at the Gold Mountain offices, moping around. "What the fuck are you moping about?" asked John Silva.

Kurt replied, "I'm *awake*, aren't I?"

"I just like to sleep," Kurt says. "I find myself falling asleep at times when I'm fed up with people or bored. If I don't want to socialize and I'm stuck in a social situation, like backstage or being on tour in general, I just sleep throughout the day. I would prefer to be in a coma and just be woken up and wheeled out onto the stage and play and then put back in my own little world rather than deal with... For so many years, I've felt like most of my conversation has been exhausted, there's not much I can look forward to. Everyday simple pleasures that people might have in having conversations or talking about inane things I just find really boring, so I'd rather just be asleep."

With lawyer Alan Mintz shopping around the band to all the major labels, Gold Mountain on their side, and a colossal buzz that just kept growing, Nirvana became the object of every major label A&R person's desire from coast to coast. The band was very wary of the slick, big-city corporate label types. At the fancy restaurants they'd get taken to, Kurt would just eat the expensive food and not say a word, while Chris would usually get quite drunk. It was essentially a milder version of their first meeting with Jonathan Poneman. But this time, they made sure they were nice enough to he labels so that they would get asked back to dinner a few more times, which, after all, was the point. "We felt like snotty little hotshit kids," Dave says. "We felt like we were getting away with something."

At first, the band was confused. Why was everyone so interested in a punk rock band from Aberdeen? For one thing, bands such as U2, R.E.M., and Jane's Addiction were beginning to score gold and platinum records. "Alternative rock" was the new industry buzzword. The canned, lightweight pop then dominating the charts—Paula Abdul, Milli Vanilli, etc.—was making the major labels some quick money, but the labels knew they had neglected to cultivate artists with long-term potential. Alternative bands fit the bill nicely and the best of them had an important thing going for them—a large and loyal fan base. Just like Nirvana.

Other indie bands were being courted, too, like Dinosaur Jr, fIREHOSE, and Teenage Fanclub.

After a while, Kurt, Chris, and Dave began to understand all this and started thinking that they might actually be in a position to be a moderate commercial success—enough to make a living at it, anyway.

The band flew to New York to check out Charisma Records and Columbia Records. Dave was homesick, so he flew to New York on a record label's tab and then caught a shuttle down to D.C. At Columbia, they met label president Donny Ienner, who told them, "Listen, men, I'm not going to dick you around. We want to turn you into stars." Actually, that's precisely what they wanted to hear—Kurt and Chris were afraid that they were going to be treated as a fringe band that no one at a major label would pay any attention to. But Columbia seemed "too Mafiaesque, a little too corporate," Kurt says. They liked Charisma, even though the label saw fit to make a special "Welcome Nirvana" video that was playing as they walked into the conference room.

Later on in the week, Dave rejoined the band in New York as they continued their whirlwind tour of the various labels. Kurt was so quiet and Chris was so talkative that many label execs assumed that

Chris was the frontman of the band. This turned out to be an excellent way of separating the wheat from the chaff.

Dave thought the whole thing was pretty silly. "Basically, all I did was try to figure out how you become an A&R person," he says. "Each one of them, I would ask, 'So what did you do before you became an A&R person?' Every one of them had worked at Tower Records."

The band visited one major label where a loudmouth exec bellowed across his vast desk, "What do you guys want?"

"We want to be the biggest fucking band in the world," Kurt deadpanned.

"Now that's what I like to hear!" boomed the suit. "None of this dickin' around! None of this building from building blocks, brick by brick! Fuck it! That's great!"

"The best thing about the major label hunt was the collection of A&R people's business cards that you got," says Dave. "So when you went into shitty little lounges or taverns, you kind of drop it to the person that's performing there and give them the impression that you're an A&R person from a major label and you're interested in their act. You kind of slide it to them and say 'Give me a call.' So all those A&R men we dealt with are probably still getting calls from lounge bands all over Tacoma."

With Alan Mintz as their legal seeing-eye dog, they visited several other labels, where their music would mysteriously be playing in nearly every office. At Capitol in L.A., they met a promotion man. "He's this good old boy from Texas, looks like he would like to beat my mom up," says Kurt. "I just wanted to dance on top of his desk with a dress on and piss all over the place."

"He asked me, 'So on that song "Polly," are you *beatin'* that bitch?' I said, 'Yes, I am.' Then two other big jock radio programmers walked into his office and said, 'Hey, we got two tickets to the Lakers game!' And they all stood up and started cheering. We knew this wasn't the label for us."

Still, they went out to dinner with another Capitol label exec that night. "Just bring us some food, just bring us all the food you have," he ordered the waitress impatiently. "Put it on this table. I don't care what it is." He began talking about spending a million dollars to get Nirvana out of the Sub Pop contract.

A million dollars. For a week, Kurt was seriously thinking of pulling the Great Rock and Roll Swindle—sign the contract, take the million dollars, *and then break up*. The Sex Pistols had achieved a similar feat not once but twice. Kurt would rant about the idea to Chris. "We've *got* to—it would be such a cool thing to do," he'd say.

"It would be so rock and roll." Unsure whether this was even possible, Kurt broached the subject with Mintz, who just thought he was kidding.

The way Gold Mountain saw it, it had come down to two labels: Geffen and Charisma. The way Nirvana saw it, it came down to two labels, too: Geffen and K. "We were really close to signing with K Records," Kurt reveals. "Those were the two we were choosing." The idea was, they'd pull the swindle, break up, change their name, and go to K. "I thought a million dollars was more money than anyone could ever have," says Kurt. "I thought a million dollars would support us and the record label for the rest of our lives, which isn't the case at all, now that I made a million dollars and spent a million dollars in a year."

Eventually, the Great Rock and Roll Swindle fantasy subsided. Because so many labels were interested in Nirvana, they were in a good bargaining position when it came to negotiating a contract. Geffen wasn't offering the most money of any of the band's suitors, but Geffen already had Sonic Youth, and Kim Gordon was urging them to sign with Geffen. And all along, Gold Mountain had been steering the band toward Geffen because they knew the label would work hard at the surely long, hard task of breaking Nirvana—the label had already done well with Sonic Youth, selling 250,000 copies of their major label debut, *Goo*. Geffen also had two key players: director of alternative music promotion Mark Kates and marketing exec Ray Farrell, both of whom had spent years in the indie world before moving to a major label.

So they went to Geffen. "We just figured it was all just a crap shoot anyway," says Chris. Sonic Youth's A&R man, Gary Gersh, signed the band. Gersh had first seen the band with Kim Gordon and Thurston Moore at the April 1990 Pyramid show in New York. He had been sufficiently impressed to give them a call later. After talking with them and hearing the Smart sessions tape Gersh was even more impressed. In Nirvana, he heard "the energy and the simplicity and the aggressiveness of the Who." In Kurt, he saw a gifted songwriter with impeccable instincts about the direction he wanted his band to go. Gersh was savvy enough to be able to explain the band to the label, and just as importantly, hip enough to explain the label to the band.

The band got a $287,000 advance, which was swiftly decimated by taxes, legal fees, the management's cut, and debts. Instead of the big dough, they had gone for the strong contract, including full mechanical royalties if and after the album hit gold. No one could have guessed it at the time, but in retrospect, abandoning a higher advance in favor of an elevated royalty rate was a brilliant move, making the band millions of dollars they wouldn't have gotten otherwise.

Then there was the matter of that darned Sub Pop contract. The then-struggling indie label received an initial $75,000 buyout fee (half of which came out of Nirvana's advance), a reported two points (2 percent of sales) on the next two records, and even got the Sub Pop logo on the back cover of every copy of *Nevermind*. The arrangement took a bite out of the band's income, but it also almost single-handedly resuscitated Sub Pop. "I don't necessarily regret it now because I enjoy knowing that I'm helping Sub Pop put out some really good music," says Kurt.

"I don't doubt that for a minute," says Poneman, "had we not had that agreement, Bruce and I would probably be washing dishes at this moment."

Sub Pop released one last Nirvana record, a split single featuring Nirvana and the Fluid. Kurt felt Nirvana's version of the Vaseline's "Molly's Lips" was ragged and called up Jonathan Poneman and asked him not to release it, but it was part of the buyout deal. Etched into the run-out groove of the record was a single word—"Later."

While the band members waited for their advance money to come through, Gold Mountain doled out a thousand dollars a month for each band member, barely minimum wage. Still they had to pawn instruments just to keep themselves fed. Sometimes they'd go down to the Positively 4th Street record store in Olympia and sell T-shirts. "You get thirty-five bucks and you're so happy," says Dave, "because you don't have to eat corn dogs that night—*you can have a Hungry Man Dinner!*" The band didn't formally sign a contract until just before recording *Nevermind*.

In November 1990, Dave was down in Los Angeles sitting in with L7 at a Rock for Choice benefit. He called Chris to ask him to wire some money and they were just about to hang up when Chris suddenly said, "Wait a minute. I gotta tell you something. Kurt's been doing heroin."

"What?" said Dave, shocked. "How did you find out?"

"He told me," Chris said. "Don't tell him that I told you."

When Dave came back home, Kurt mentioned he'd done heroin and Dave tried to stay cool about it and just asked what it was like. "It sucked, it's stupid," Kurt replied. "It makes you feel gross and bad. I just wanted to try it."

"Kurt said he wouldn't do it again and I believed him," Dave says. "It seemed so innocent. It seemed like a kid sticking a fire-cracker in a cat's butt and lighting it off for the hell of it. It didn't seem like anything at all."

"The whole winter that Dave and I spent together in that little apartment was the most depressing time I'd had in years," Kurt recalls. "It was so fucking small and dirty and cold and gray every fucking day. I almost went insane at one point. I just couldn't handle it. I was so bored and so poor. We were signed to Geffen for months and we didn't have any money. We ended up having to pawn our amps and our TV, all kinds of stuff, just to get money to eat corn dogs. It just felt really weird to be signed to this multimillion-dollar corporation and be totally dirt poor. All we did was practice. It was the only thing that saved us. Even that got repetitious after a while."

And so Kurt had sought refuge in heroin. He had been wanting to do it again and finally found a dealer in Olympia. He did it about once a week, not often enough to get a habit. Not even Dave knew he was doing it. "It's weird, because with someone like Kurt, who's a sloth anyway, how are you to know?" he says.

No one in the band knew until the night that Kurt called Chris. Chris had gotten extremely worried and hung up. A little while later, he and Shelli called back and told Kurt that they loved him and they didn't want him to do drugs. "It was nice," Kurt says, the tone of his voice implying that he appreciated the gesture, but it wasn't enough to get him to stop.

"I told him he was playing with dynamite," says Chris. "It bummed me out. It was shocking. I didn't like it at all. I just don't see anything in that shit. I just told him that's the way I feel." After that, Kurt tried to hide his drug use, but Chris always knew. "I knew he'd hang around these certain people and it was 'Oh, Kurt's getting high,'" Chris says.

By that time, Kurt and Tracy had gotten back in touch and they went together to see Tobi Vail's Riot Grrl band Bikini Kill at a party in Olympia. "He kept nodding off and whatnot in the car on the way there," says Tracy. "He used to fall asleep, but he'd never fall asleep *that* fast." On the way to another party that night, Kurt asked if they could stop at his house so he could go to the bathroom. After a while Tracy went up so she could go, too. After fifteen minutes she heard a big crash in the bathroom. "So I go in the bathroom and he's kind of passed out on the toilet with one sleeve rolled up and I pick him up and he starts laughing and then he nods off instantly and then he laughs again. I said, 'Kurt, what the hell are you doing?'"

"How did you know I did it?"

"Look at you, Kurt," Tracy said. "You've got one sleeve rolled up, there's a spoon in the sink, you're passed out on the toilet, and there's a bottle of bleach on the floor. You never clean *anything*—why else would you have a bottle of bleach if it wasn't for your needle?"

"At that time," says Tracy, "I didn't know it was going to go as far as it did. I don't think he did it when we were going out, as far as I know." Kurt told Tracy that heroin made him really social. "He felt like he could go out and have a good time and talk to people and not feel uncomfortable," she says.

"The funny thing is, when he was getting all these tests for his stomach, he actually came home one time from the hospital and he said, 'They tried to give me another blood test and they already gave me four tests.' He walked out of there because he said he would almost faint when they tried to draw blood because he couldn't stand the needle in his arm."

On New Year's Day of 1991, the band went back to the Music Source, where they had done the *Blew* EP sessions and recorded several tracks with soundman Craig Montgomery, completing two, "Aneurysm" and "Even in His Youth," both of which later appeared as B-sides and on *Incesticide*.

Gersh thought the band should rerecord the seven songs from the Smart sessions and suggested several relatively fancy producers, including Scott Litt, who had worked on R.E.M.'s breakthrough records, long-time Neil Young producer David Briggs, and Don

Chris at the Commodore Ballroom in Vancouver, April 1991.
(© Charles Peterson)

Chris and Kurt demonstrate their onstage chemistry at the Commodore Ballroom. (© Charles Peterson)

Dixon, who had produced R.E.M., the Reivers, the Smithereens, and many others.

At one point, Kurt told the Seattle music paper *Backlash* that Vig would be the main producer, but they'd use other producers for the songs the band deemed "commercial."

Briggs and Dixon actually flew up to Seattle to meet the band. Dixon made the final cut, and tentative plans were made for him to produce and Vig to engineer. But then something fell through. Some say that rumors that the band had received an astronomical advance had fooled some producers into pricing themselves out of the job, but the band was really holding out for Vig all along. Vig, a supremely nice guy, simply knew where they were coming from, musically and philosophically, better than anyone else.

Vig had never done a major label project and Gersh initially bridled, but came around to the idea after figuring that even if Vig didn't get the right sounds during recording, they could do the time-honored thing and fix it in the mix. So Nirvana got their way—this time. Vig got the call just a couple of weeks before recording was to begin.

The band sent him some rehearsal tapes they made on a boom

NIRVANA

FITS OF DEPRESSION
BIKINI KILL
WED APRIL 17
OK HOTEL
212 ALASKAN WY. PH.621-7903

The April 17th show when Nirvana debuted
"Smells Like Teen Spirit." Says Nils Bernstein,
"Everybody went crazy." (Poster by Mark Bendix)

box. The band played so loud that the sound was wildly distorted, but Vig could make out some great tunes. Vig already knew most of the songs from the Smart sessions, but there were a few new ones, too, like "Come as You Are" and "Smells Like Teen Spirit" that sounded like they had a lot of promise.

"We knew that the stuff we were coming up with was catchy and cool and just good strong songs," Dave says. "We kind of could tell that they were really great. We didn't expect what happened to happen, but we knew it was going to be a really good record."

CHAPTER EIGHT

The band formally signed with Geffen on April 30, 1991. Soon after, Kurt called his father out of the blue and told him the big news. He said he was going to go down to Los Angeles to record in a few days, and that he was very excited about everything that was happening. They talked for over an hour, just catching up. Finally, Don told Kurt to stay in touch, they said good-bye, and hung up the phone. And then Don Cobain cried.

Chris and Shelli drove their Volkswagen van with all the band's equipment in it down to L.A. Kurt and Dave had decided they were going to drive down, too, in order to experience the romance of the open road. They took off a few days early in a beat-up old Datsun, looking forward to the adventures ahead. But the car overheated every fifteen minutes or so and it took them three hours to go a hundred miles. So they limped back to Tacoma, parked the car in a quarry, and pelted it with rocks for half an hour before driving it to Chris's house, where they picked up their trusty white Dodge tour van. They stopped in San Francisco and stayed at Dale Crover's house for a few days before setting off for L.A., going straight to the Universal Studios tour as soon as they arrived.

In the days before the sessions began, Vig and the band fine-tuned some of the arrangements at a rehearsal studio. All the new material was very promising, but the first time they played "Teen Spirit," the normally low-key Vig began pacing around the room with excitement. One night, Chris got a little plastered and commandeered the studio-wide intercom system and broadcast heartfelt words of encouragement to his fellow musicians throughout the rehearsal complex, including people like Lenny Kravitz and Belinda Carlisle. "Okay, you motherfuckers!" Chris hollered. "Get your ass in *gear!*"

Next, they went to a drum rental place and selected a brass snare for Dave. It was the loudest one they had. The employees had nicknamed it "the Terminator."

They stayed in furnished apartments in a nearby building called the Oakwood—"It was so gross with this mauve and powder blue," sniffs Chris. Naturally, they trashed the place, breaking a coffee table and a framed painting of flowers. "We were just in L.A. and for lack of anything to do," Chris explains. "It's fun having a party—there doesn't have to be any reason or any kind of anxiety or anything. It's just fun to go crazy."

Soon, a woman with the improbable name of Courtney Love began stopping by the Oakwood to see Kurt.

Courtney had seen Nirvana open for the Dharma Bums at the Satyricon club in Portland, Oregon, in 1989. Watching Kurt on stage, she thought to herself, "He's got Dave Pirner damage, but he's way cuter." She thought he was "hot in a Sub Pop rock god sort of way." After the set, as was his custom, Kurt wandered away from the stage area in order to get out of packing up gear. He walked by Courtney's table, sat down, poured himself a beer from her pitcher, and glared at her. She glared back.

"I thought she looked like Nancy Spungen," Kurt says, chuckling. "She looked like a classic punk rock chick. I did feel kind of attracted to her. Probably wanted to fuck her that night, but she left." They talked for a little bit and he gave her a few stickers he had made that had Chim-Chim and the Nirvana logo. "I put them all on my suitcase," says Courtney, "and I didn't even like his band."

Courtney had had a crush on Kurt ever since. Asked to describe her attraction to Kurt, something rare happens—Courtney Love is at

Courtney Love. (© Charles Peterson)

a loss for words. "I don't know," she says, suddenly girlish, almost blushing. "I feel embarrassed. I just thought he was really beautiful. He was really cool and he had really beautiful hands. He was really beautiful. I can't explain it."

A couple of years older than Kurt, Courtney was also the product of a broken home, and like Kurt had an itinerant childhood, although while Kurt had bounced around tiny Grays Harbor County, Courtney's travels had spanned several continents. Her mother took her from L.A. to New Zealand to work on a farm, then they moved to Australia and back to the States, where Courtney eventually wound up in an Oregon reform school. She supported herself as a stripper during her teens, traveling from Portland to Japan to Ireland; by 1981, she was hanging out in the then-explosive Liverpool scene with post-punk luminaries like Julian Cope of the Teardrop Explodes and members of Echo and the Bunnymen.

NIRVANA

The Chim-Chim sticker that Kurt gave to Courtney at the Satyricon.

She sang in an early incarnation of Faith No More in San Francisco and later moved to Minneapolis and formed a short-lived band with Jennifer Finch and Kat Bjelland called Sugar Baby Doll (Finch went on to form L7, Bjelland now leads Babes in Toyland). She landed a bit part in *Sid And Nancy* and later co-starred in the abysmal 1987 post-punk spaghetti western *Straight to Hell*, which featured the Pogues, Joe Strummer, and Elvis Costello. She founded the band Hole in March of 1990. She was already well known—some would say notorious—on the indie circuit.

Around December of 1990, Courtney and Dave became friendly through Dave's former girlfriend, Jennifer Finch. "She was fun to talk to because if you were bored, you could spend three hours on the phone," Dave says of Courtney. "It was funny because I'd never talked to anyone who was so entertainment business-wise or L.A.-wise as Courtney. It was kind of neat to have a conversation with someone who you could picture being behind a desk at *US* magazine or something."

After Courtney revealed to Dave that she had a crush on Kurt, Dave told Courtney that Kurt liked her, too, but she didn't quite believe it. Still, she gave Dave a package to give to Kurt—little sea shells and pine cones and miniature teacups and a tiny doll, all packed into a small heart-shaped box. Courtney swears that if she hadn't forgotten that he never replied, she wouldn't have bothered chasing him anymore.

Kurt and Courtney met again at a Butthole Surfers/Redd Kross/L7 show at the Palladium in Los Angeles in May of 1991, shortly before the band began recording *Nevermind*. They were instantly attracted to each other. Courtney chose to express her attraction by punching Kurt in the stomach. He punched her back, then he leaped on her and they began wrestling. After a little while, Courtney got up, kicked Kurt, and walked away. "It was a mating ritual for dysfunctional people," Courtney cracks.

In three months, Hole would release its debut album, *Pretty on the Inside*. A harrowing, confrontational, and fearless dissection of childhood damage and feminine self-hatred, the record began with Courtney snarling, "When I was a teenage whore…" and went on from there. The English music press were already raving about the band and Courtney in particular; journalists fell all over themselves for an interview with this brash, outspoken, and devastatingly witty American. The album was a longtime U.K. indie chart entry after its debut in August of 1991.

Although many would soon come to believe—and still do—that Courtney was a gold-digger, she insists she didn't think Kurt would ever be anything more than a revered cult figure when she began chasing him. "I thought I was going to be more famous than him," says Courtney. "That was pretty obvious to me." The way she looks at it now, marrying Kurt Cobain was a bad career move.

There is no doubt that Courtney likes attention. But much of her grandstanding can be seen as an effort to assert herself, to avoid getting outshone by Kurt's brilliant star. Imagine the situation where the spouse who wants to be famous is overtaken by the spouse who never wanted to be. Of course, Courtney would eventually achieve her own kind of fame—or infamy—her name becoming a household synonym for a delinquent mother.

Courtney happened to live only a block away from the Oakwood and she stopped by a few times. Chris didn't pay her much mind. "She was some loud girl," he says. "I'd never heard of her before."

But Kurt was interested. "We bonded over pharmaceuticals," Courtney says. "I had Vicodin extra-strength, which was pills, and he had Hycomine cough syrup. I said 'You're a pussy, you shouldn't drink that syrup because it's bad for your stomach.'"

Kurt called her up at five in the morning on the pretense of asking if she had any drugs. Courtney said no and made a date with Kurt for the next day. He stood her up and then kept his phone off the hook so she couldn't call. "I couldn't decide if I actually wanted to consummate our relationship," he explains, smiling.

"She seemed like poison because I'd just gotten out of the last relationship that I didn't even want to be in," says Kurt. "I was determined to be a bachelor for a few months. I just had to be. But I knew that I liked Courtney so much right away that it was a really hard struggle to stay away from her for so many months. It was harder than shit. During that time that I attempted to be a bachelor and sow my oats and live the bachelor rock and roll lifestyle, I didn't end up fucking anybody or having a good time at all." He decided to concentrate on making the album.

They recorded in May and June of 1991 at Sound City Studios in suburban Van Nuys, California. The studio had seen better days in the seventies, when Fleetwood Mac had recorded *Rumours* there. Other previous clients included Ronnie James Dio, Tom Petty, Foreigner, the Jackson 5, Rick Springfield, Crazy Horse, Ratt, and even Kurt's childhood hero, Evel Knievel. It had a big drum room, a great old Neve mixing board, and the rates were reasonable. The original budget was about sixty-five thousand dollars including Butch Vig's services—a mere pittance in major label terms. For that amount of money, they could afford to scrap the whole thing if it didn't work out and start all over again.

Kurt gives part of the credit for the quality of the album to the fact that they were back in sunny L.A. "It was really nice to all of a sudden find yourself in a totally warm, tropical climate," he says. "I don't think it would have turned out nearly as well if we did it in Washington."

Vig would make them comfortable by just hanging with them in the studio and not pushing them into the recording booth as soon as they walked through the door. And he tried to keep them out of the control room.

They'd work eight to ten hours a day, sometimes blowing off steam by playing covers of old seventies favorites such as Alice Cooper, Black Sabbath, and Aerosmith—the musical equivalent of comfort food.

Dave hit the drums so hard that they had to change the heads every other song. Although they're played with vastly more power and precision, Dave's drum parts on songs that appeared on the Smart sessions are very close to what Chad had played. "Chad wasn't the most solid drummer and he wasn't the most consistent drummer but he came up with really really cool stuff," Dave says. "I like the way he plays—the stuff on *Bleach*, it's almost drunken."

Kurt's punk ethic was even stronger than Vig's, apparently, because Kurt would often refuse to do a second take. Vig had to fig-

Producer Butch Vig tuning Dave's drums during the **Nevermind** sessions.

ure out how to get him to do a second take and often would roll tape even when Kurt was warming up, just in case he got something usable.

Kurt had worked out his vocals so well that they barely varied in phrasing and intensity from one take to the next, so Vig would often take advantage of this consistency and mix the two takes together, especially on choruses for that extra sing-along effect. (That's Dave singing the high harmonies on "In Bloom," however. He had trouble hitting those stratospheric notes, but if he'd blow a take, he'd just take a drag on his cigarette and try again. Many takes later, Vig got what he wanted.)

With instrumental takes, if they didn't get something right away, they'd just move onto something else—after two or three tries, it was often a matter of diminishing returns. "I wanted him to double his guitars on some of the songs, especially on choruses," says Vig, "and he didn't really want to do that. My logic was, 'When you guys play live, it's just so incredibly loud and intense—it's larger than life and I'm trying to use some of these things I know in the studio to make you guys come across that way on record.' A lot of times, he'd go, 'I don't feel like doing that right now,' but for the most part, when I asked him to do stuff, he'd eventually do it. There weren't any major arguments or anything, but I could tell when I was pushing him a little far and he didn't want to do something. A couple of times, he just put his guitar down or walked away from the mike and said, 'I don't want to do it anymore.' And I knew I wasn't going to get anything else out of him."

On "Territorial Pissings," Kurt ignored Vig's protests and plugged his guitar directly into the mixing board—no amplifier—in the style of countless low-budget punk records of the late seventies and early eighties. The song was recorded in one take. In the intro, Chris sang a bit of the chorus to the Youngbloods' altruistic late sixties hippie hit, "Get Together." "They just said 'Sing something,'" says Chris, "so I did it in one take. It just kind of happened. I wanted to put some kind of corny hippie idealism in it. But it wasn't really that thought into. I *like* that Youngbloods song.

"Maybe it was about lost ideals," Chris says. "Like, what happened to those ideals? 'Everybody get together, try to love one another.' And then there's 'Territorial Pissings.' Maybe some baby boomer will hear that and wonder, 'Hey, what happened to those ideals?'"

Vig says that "Something in the Way"—written just a week before it was recorded—was probably the most difficult song on the album to record. They tried it a few times with the rest of the band playing along, but it didn't work. Finally, Vig called Kurt into the control room and asked how *he* thought the song should go. Kurt sat down on the couch with his nylon-string acoustic guitar and sang the song in a barely audible whisper. "Stay *right* there," Vig said as he dashed out to the office and told them to turn off every phone and every fan and every other machine in the whole place. Vig recorded the song that way, with the levels cranked up as high as they could go to catch Kurt's voice—it's so quiet that you can practically hear Kurt's tongue sliding over his teeth as he sings. Later, they added bass, more vocals, and drums. "We had to keep yelling at Dave to play wimpy," says Vig. "He'd start playing the song lightly and halfway through the first verse he'd be playing pretty hard. His natural inclination is to attack the drum kit. He finally got it, but I think it almost killed him to just tap his way through."

Some of the lyrics were completely finished, but many others weren't, and Kurt would ask the others which line they liked best— sometimes, the lines would give the song widely different meanings, like when "Pay to Play" became "Stay Away." He'd also try different melodies.

Just a few weeks before recording was to start, Kurt showed a riff to the band and they jammed on it for the better part of an hour, playing with dynamics and different arrangements until it became a song, which Kurt titled "Smells Like Teen Spirit." Chris didn't especially like the song at first. "It was just one of the songs we did for the record," Chris says. "I remember when we first did it, it was nothing special. But after it was recorded, I thought, 'Hey, this is really good. It really rocks.'" Right away, both Chris and Kurt heard one of their influences in the song. "The Pixies," says Chris. "We saw it right away. Both of us said, 'This really sounds like the Pixies. People are really going to nail us for it.'"

Although they almost threw away the song, no one ever did nail them for sounding like the Pixies, although much comment was later made that the song bore more than a passing resemblance to Boston's 1976 hit "More Than a Feeling."

Once Chris and Dave had finished their basic tracks—which was a matter of days—they were done. Kurt was kept busy doing vocals, playing guitar overdubs, and writing lyrics, sometimes delaying production for precious hours until he found the right words. Kurt wrote most of the words for "On a Plain" minutes before he sang them. The "Don't quote me on that" line came from a dumb little running joke they had that week. "Someone would say something like 'Where's the mayonnaise?'" Dave recalls, "and someone else would answer, 'It's in the fridge, but don't quote me on that.'"

It was more important to Vig that Kurt sing the songs with conviction rather than good diction. That wasn't a problem, however—once Kurt decided on finished lyrics, he sang so hard that he could often do only one or two vocals before his voice gave out and he'd be done for the day. His voice audibly goes to pieces on "Territorial Pissings."

Kurt didn't know any dealers in L.A., so instead of doing heroin, he drank codeine cough syrup constantly during the sessions, not to mention a half of a fifth of Jack Daniel's every day. He wanted the cough syrup for the opiate, but it also helped preserve his voice. Unfortunately, he ran out of it by the time he was to start doing vocal tracks. There were a few days when he could do only one or two takes before his throat gave out entirely, which upset Kurt a lot. (He still takes cough syrup on tour for his chronic bronchitis. "It's the only thing that saves me," Kurt claims.)

Ten minutes and three seconds after the last chord of "Something in the Way" faded away came a surprise track. Although it never had an official name other than perhaps "The Noise Jam," the track has come to be known as "Endless, Nameless." They'd been playing variations on "Endless, Nameless" for months before the *Nevermind* ses-

The guitar Kurt smashed during "Endless, Nameless."

sions. At the end of practice, Kurt would tune his guitar way down and they'd just bang away, making caterwauling feedback noise and occasionally drifting into the song's main riff.

When the session for "Lithium" began going awry, Kurt asked Vig to keep the tape rolling while the band tried an experiment. He went out into the studio and began flailing his guitar and screaming into a microphone as the band followed suit. Even Kurt isn't sure what's he's screaming, but he believes it's along the lines of "I think I can, I know I can." Audible on the track (right around 19:32 on the CD) is the sound of Kurt smashing his guitar. Afterward, they realized that was the only left-handed guitar he had that fit the track, so the sessions were over for the day. They did a quick mix of the song and figured they'd find a place for it. Due to a technical error, "Endless, Nameless" didn't make the initial pressing of *Nevermind*.

The ten minutes of silence after "Something in the Way" was the band's way of playing with the new CD format, just like the Beatles put inscrutable messages in the run-out groove of *Sgt. Pepper* or put "Her Majesty" at the end of *Abbey Road*. Kurt had done something similar before. When he and his buddy Jesse Reed shared their studio apartment back in Aberdeen, Kurt took a ninety-minute blank cassette tape, wound it forward to nearly the end and recorded himself saying in a scary voice, "Jesse... Jesse... I'm coming to get yoooooo..." As they were getting ready to go to bed he popped the tape into the stereo, hit "play" and turned the volume down low. Forty minutes later, a voice said "Jesse..." and Reed sat up startled. "Hey, did you hear that?"

"Hear *what*?" Kurt replied, smirking to himself in the dark.

One night during the sessions, Chris got picked up on a driving while intoxicated charge in Los Angeles. He guzzled the last bit of liquor just as the cop was walking toward his car. With no money in their pockets, Kurt and Dave walked several miles back home, while the police took Chris to the city jail and then the county jail. When he was put in the holding tank, he tried to look as tough as he could so no one would hassle him. "There was fifty guys crammed in this cell," Chris says. "You open the cell door and boom—the heat hits you from all the people in there."

Immediately, a small, dapper black man with a withered arm and an unlit cigarette strode up to Chris and rasped, "Heymanyougotanymatches?"

"What?"

"Yougotanymatches?"

"No," Chris replied.

"There's like fifty guys in there with these cigarettes and nobody has a fuckin' match!" Chris chuckles. "It was totally quiet, except when somebody would walk in and that little guy would say, 'Yougotanymatches?' Finally this guy walked in with matches and they all just lit up like crazy, smoke is filling the room."

After sixteen hours in stir, Chris was bailed out by John Silva. Chris eventually got off with a fine and had to attend a series of seminars where victims of drunk drivers told their horrific stories.

Vig had started to sense something was going to happen with the record. All sorts of people had somehow gotten wind of the project and were asking him for tapes.

Kurt had three or four untitled songs and song fragments that were very melodic and not as heavy as most of the other material. A&R executive Gary Gersh remembers a conversation he had with Kurt where "We thought, let's not put it on this record because we don't want to make this record look like—they weren't finished, first of all—but the jump from an independent label to a major was like some big huge commercial sell-out or something," Gersh says. "Let's make the artistic jump as gradual as you feel comfortable with." Which is A&R-speak for "It's going to look like you're selling out if you put these pop songs on the record." So, once again, as he had on *Bleach*, Kurt had to adjust his recordings to the tastes of the market-place.

Although Gersh says he "always" stopped by the studio and was "a little bit therapist, a little bit referee," both Chris and Kurt say he barely showed up at all. In fact, Dave got so worried that Gersh wasn't around that he thought Gersh had lost his enthusiasm for the project. He even went so far as to place a worried phone call to John Silva, who assured him that most bands would kill for such a hands-off A&R person.

By everyone else's account, Gersh would often stop by the studio after the band had gone home, and Vig would play him rough mixes. Astutely, Gersh had chosen not to meddle, and by doing so, he had built up enough credibility with the band that when he had to step in and take charge at a certain very delicate moment in the recording, the band respected his ideas.

Vig was going to mix the record, too, but because the recording had gone behind schedule, the four or five days that were supposed to elapse between recording and mixing so that Vig and the band could rest their ears had evaporated. Vig finished recording and went straight into mixing, but the mixes didn't turn out well—they were flat and lacked power, especially in the drums.

Gersh noticed Vig was tired and took the opportunity to call in veteran mixer Andy Wallace, who had done terrific work on Slayer's *Seasons in the Abyss*. Although the band was skeptical, they "just went along with the game," as Chris puts it.

This was also Vig's major label debut and he may have overcompensated slightly. "That record is pretty hacked up," Chris says. "Some songs were pretty straight ahead but a couple of songs were electronic sleight of hand. It's a really produced record." Occasionally, Vig would have to stitch together several different parts to get a complete performance, but the lion's share of slickness came from Andy Wallace. Vig's mixes sound positively naked in comparison to the final result. Wallace sweetened the sound, filtering the raw tracks through various special effects boxes, cranking out about one mix a day.

Between extra lodging, extra studio time and Wallace's fee, calling in Wallace doubled the budget of the record, which was still comparatively modest.

The band wasn't wild about Wallace's presence. "We'd get in and he'd play us his mix and he wasn't too kind to suggestions," Dave recalls. "He did a lot of tweaking of the drums, making them more digital-sounding. Everything had a produced weirdness. All we wanted to do was record these songs and get a record out because it had been so long since *Bleach* and we'd been playing these songs and they were great and we were excited and we wanted to record them before we got totally sick of them, which we already were. So it was just like, 'Let's get it over with.'"

Part of the reason the album sounds so slick is the fact that the room miking of the drums didn't work out well, and so Wallace used digital reverb to fix the sound and further pumped up the drums with equalization and some samples that he blended in behind the kick drum and the snare. "He gave some real wide stereo separation using some doubling and delays on guitars and things," says Vig. "He put a little bit of gloss on the voice but I don't think he went too far with it. If anything, we wanted to make sure the mixes still sounded fairly organic." For all the studio tricks, Wallace didn't use as much as most pop albums.

Listening to the album now, it sounds as if the music were a jagged stone encased in Lucite. "That's Andy Wallace," Kurt says, adding that Geffen loved it that way because they were used to records like that. It was all for the best anyway, according to Kurt, "because it sold eight million records and now we're allowed to do whatever we want. It was part of the plan that we had to try to get on the radio and get our foot in the door and be able to do whatever we want for the rest of the time we're a band."

"We tried to have a fine line between being commercial and sounding alternative," says Chris.

"Looking back on the production of *Nevermind*, I'm embarrassed by it now," Kurt says. "It's closer to a Motley Crue record than it is a punk rock record."

During the recording, Kurt and Dave had seen a documentary on underwater birth, and Kurt mentioned it as a cover idea to Robert Fisher, an art director at Geffen. Fisher found some pictures of babies being born underwater but they were too graphic, so they settled for a stock photo of a swimming baby. Kurt joked they should add a fish hook with a dollar bill on it, and the idea stuck. Then it transpired that the stock house which controlled the photograph wanted $7,500 a year for as long as the album was in print, so Fisher got underwater photographer Kirk Weddle to go down to a pool for babies and take some more shots.

The band chose one of five different photographs, with a shot of

What's missing from from this picture? The alternate artwork for the **Nevermind** cover. (photo by Kirk Weddle, courtesy Geffen Records)

five-month-old Spencer Elden emerging as the winner. The only thing was, the baby's penis was quite visible. "If there's a problem with his dick," Fisher said, "we can cut it off." Some people in the Geffen/DGC sales department did worry that the traditionally conservative chain stores might object to the penis and Fisher even went so far as to begin preparing a cover with the penis airbrushed out. Kurt had anticipated some outcry as well, and had already composed some copy to put on a sticker over the problematic member. It read, "If you're offended by this, you must be a closet pedophile."

Spencer Elden's penis stayed on.

There was only slight umbrage taken at the naked infant. In April of 1992, a city code enforcement officer allegedly advised the Wild Planet record store in Ventura, California, to cover the baby's penis on a poster they had in the window. They used a pink Post-It note. "It's just weird that anybody should have a problem with a baby," says Chris.

There were many different interpretations of the cover. Some thought the baby represented the band, and that swimming toward the dollar bill represented their sell-out. But the image probably appealed to Kurt because it echoed his ideas about recapturing his innocent childhood bliss; like many of his paintings, the cover sym-

bolized the very moment when that bliss would begin to disappear. More overtly, the image also signaled a departure from the acquisitive, yuppie eighties, a rejection of the materialism which backfired into junk bond scandals, corrupt savings and loan institutions, and a whole lot of repossessed BMWs. When the book of the nineties is written, the cover of *Nevermind* should be on the first page.

Then there was a photo shoot with Michael Lavine, who had flown out from New York. During the shoot, the band passed a bottle of whiskey around until they were all quite stewed. "Hurry up, take the photo before I pass out," Kurt begged Lavine.

Outtakes from the infamous underwater photo session.
(© Kirk Weddle)

Later on, the group did an underwater photo session in a pool with Kirk Weddle to play off the cover concept. The shoot turned into a Spinal Tap–style fiasco. "It was really stormy the weekend before and the pool got really clouded up," says Fisher, "and the pump broke two days before so the water was really cold and Kurt was really sick and they were hating being in the water. It was kind of a nightmare. Kurt had a hard time—it seemed like he had a real buoyancy problem—he'd kick and thrash and he'd still be on top of the water. He just couldn't submerge himself." Fisher eventually had to make a composite of three different shots to get something usable. The photo appeared in an ad campaign.

The photo on the back of the album is from when Kurt was in a "bohemian photography stage" and features the ubiquitous Chim-Chim. Behind Chim-Chim is the meat-and-diseased-vagina collage that Kurt put on his refrigerator back in Olympia. Close inspection of the photo reveals a picture of Kiss a little bit above Chim-Chim's head.

The band's bio contained some hilarious whoppers. "Cobain, a sawblade painter specializing in wildlife and landscapes, met Novoselic at the Grays Harbor Institute of Northwest Crafts," the

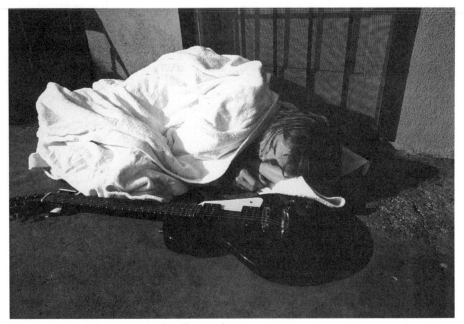

Kurt catching forty winks by the pool. (© Kirk Weddle)

bio said. "Novoselic had a passion for gluing seashells and driftwood on burlap and, he remembers, 'I liked what Kurt was doing. I asked him what his thoughts were on a macaroni mobile I was working on. He suggested I glue glitter on it. That really made it!' The incident formed the basis of Nirvana's magic."

Later in the bio, Dave explains his first encounter with Kurt and Chris. "They wore berets, sunglasses, sandals and had goatees. Chris walked around with these poetry books by Rod McKuen and Kurt would do interpretive dances while Chris recited."

"Our songs have the standard pop format: verse, chorus, verse, chorus, solo, bad solo," Kurt said. "All in all, we sound like the Knack and the Bay City Rollers being molested by Black Flag and Black Sabbath."

From the Michael Lavine session done shortly after
completing **Nevermind**. (© Michael Lavine)

In mid-June, right after the record was finished, they landed an opening slot on a quickie eight-date West Coast tour with Dinosaur Jr. Shelli worked at the T-shirt stand. As the tour wound through Denver, L.A., and Santa Cruz, it began to seem like people were more excited about Nirvana than the headliner.

In August, Nirvana opened for their heroes, Sonic Youth, on a European festival tour. "That was a wild tour," Chris says. "We got in a lot of trouble. Busting stuff up. Drunk, getting kicked out of clubs." Chris would know. He missed Shelli and he was homesick, and he'd get very drunk and disorderly on the tour. Eventually, John Silva called Shelli and asked her to talk to Chris. It worked a little bit, but finally, Shelli simply flew to Europe and kept Chris company, earning her keep by working at the T-shirt stand again.

Sonic Youth had made sure that their new favorite band was on the tour, smoothing the way for Nirvana with promoters and generally making sure they were well taken care of. They were by the side of the stage at every show, checking them out. If Kurt jumped off the stage, Sonic Youth's Thurston Moore would often be the one to haul him back up again.

Mostly, it was an idyllic time. Various members of Nirvana, Sonic Youth, and Dinosaur Jr all hung out together and laughed and drank and gossiped and talked about music and no one was a global superstar yet. Nirvana was playing festivals for the first time. They were curious and enthusiastic about what lay before them. "The most exciting time for a band is right before they become really popular," Kurt says. "I'd love to be in bands that just do that every two years. Every time I look back at the best times in this band it was right before *Nevermind* came out. It was awesome. That's when the band is at its best—they're really trying hard and there's so much excitement in the air you can just taste it."

The band drank a lot. Part of their contract specified one bottle of vodka and one bottle of Glenfiddich at every show. Dave didn't actually drink much at first, but Chris would drain the Glenfiddich and Kurt and his buddy Ian Dickson, whom he brought along for the ride, would split the vodka. Eventually, even Dave broke down and would swig on a bottle of red wine during the drumless "Polly." "You stick all this free alcohol in front of people night after night and you get bored waiting around and you think, 'Oh, maybe I'll have a drink,'" says tour manager Alex Macleod. "And things go downhill from there."

Early in the tour at England's mammoth Reading Festival, Courtney, Kat Bjelland, and Kim Gordon were sitting in one of the trailers backstage, drinking whiskey and talking about Kurt. Filmmaker Dave Markey, shooting footage for what would become the documentary film *1991: The Year That Punk Broke*, stuck a camera in the door and Courtney stared straight into the lens and said "Kurt Cobain makes my heart stop. But he's a shit," and walked away.

Later, Courtney, Kurt, Mudhoney's Mark Arm and Dan Peters, and *Melody Maker* writer Everett True were indulging in some innocent backstage vandalism. Peters flung a big bottle of oil and it leaked, dousing Courtney's face and hair. Embarrassed, she ran away in tears—it reminded her of the humiliation she used to feel in school. That night, they were all watching Iggy Pop's set by the side of the stage and Kurt whispered in Courtney's ear, "I would never have picked on you in high school." "It was like he had ESP or something," says Courtney.

Kurt admits to plenty of bruises for his efforts, but he says he never really hurt himself by hurling his body into the drum set until he slightly dislocated his shoulder at Reading that year. "I have this protective shield around me that stops me from getting hurt," he half jokes.

By the time of the 1992 Reading Festival, they had gotten it down to a science, piling up the equipment with special care, then knocking it all down with gleeful malice for a good fifteen minutes after every show.

"It got to the point where it was like, people see the 'Lithium' video and that's three minutes of the ultimate Nirvana experience—we're rocking out, the crowd's going nuts, shit's getting broken—this is what it's like to see Nirvana play," says Dave. "From then on, everywhere we go, we walk offstage and we haven't smashed anything and people are like, 'What's your problem? Where's *Nirvana?*' So then it got to the point where it became a parody where everybody expects us to do this, so you might as well make fun of it. So you set things up and you set this on top of this and set this over there and do everything methodically."

Later on the summer '91 festival tour, Kurt, Chris, Dave, Courtney, her then-boyfriend Billy Corgan of Smashing Pumpkins, and a few others went out to a club in London. Kurt boasted to Courtney, "*I'm* going to be a rock star soon."

"You are *not.*"

"Yes I am. I'm going to be a big rock star. I'm going to buy antiques—really *expensive* antiques for my *wife.*"

That night, Kurt went home with two English girls, very out of character. "I hope you get *fucked!*" Courtney called out to him as he left. As it happens, he didn't.

Nirvana played a Belgian festival called Pukkelpop, which translates as "Zit-pop." Nirvana's set began at eleven in the morning, but that wasn't too early for the band to get drunk before the show. "And," as Alex Macleod says, "things went downhill from there."

The band switched around all the name tags on the dinner tables backstage, so that the Ramones and their entourage of twelve were seated at a table for two which was meant for then-Pixies leader Black Francis and his girlfriend. Even John Silva got into the act and started a food fight.

Kurt was walking around with a Black Francis name tag stuck to his chest all day and by seven o'clock in the evening had built up quite a head of steam. While Black Francis played his solo set, Kurt spied a fire extinguisher by the side of the stage and started hosing down Black Francis. A horde of security men dashed toward Kurt as he dropped the hose and ran for his life.

One country where Nirvana didn't do as well as it could have is Germany. During the European summer festival tour with Sonic Youth, they played a show in Bremen. A woman from the German branch of MCA, Geffen's parent company, stopped by and and presented the band with a garbage can with a talking basketball hoop on it that made a crowd noise after every basket. It was filled with candy and American magazines and had a cheerful little card that read "Welcome to Germany and MCA!"

By this point, the band was fully dedicated to completely destroying their dressing room every night of the tour. The German MCA rep walked in after Nirvana's set to witness the band, falling-down drunk, trashing their dressing room and throwing all her gifts all over the place. Meanwhile, sometime during the show, Sonic Youth's Kim Gordon had found the note on the garbage can and written "Fuck you!" on it. The MCA rep saw this and assumed the band had written it to her; then Chris shot off a fire extinguisher. As Alex Macleod puts it, "It all went downhill from there."

Later that evening, while sitting in the tour bus doing interviews, Kurt was playing with a lighter and managed to set the curtains on fire. They quickly doused them with some water, but seconds later, the same MCA rep knocked on the door and was greeted by Kurt, who was enveloped in a cloud of putrid smoke from the curtains; she walked off·in a huff (somehow the English music press reported that the band had burned down their bus).

That night they got an apoplectic phone call from John Silva. "You guys have *got* to take it easy! What did you *do*?'"

"We thought we were dropped," Dave says. "We were going 'All right, we got our advance and we've already been dropped! *Wooooo!*'"

Kurt's Great Rock and Roll Swindle fantasy had almost come true without anybody even trying.

The band got drunk before their set at the final show of the tour in Rotterdam. Chris climbed up the P.A. stack at the end of the set, with his trousers around his ankles and a bottle in his hand. Security ran onstage and hauled him down while Kurt trashed everything in sight. One of the security men took a swing at Chris and a brawl broke out right on stage. Chris eventually got thrown out of the venue and came back and started a fight with the promoter.

***

The band went home for a while, then went down to L.A. to shoot the "Teen Spirit" video. Kurt worked up a treatment for the video, which originally included vignettes resembling something out of the Ramones movie *Rock and Roll High School*, or perhaps more like *Over the Edge*, an excellent 1979 movie about a band of crazed juvenile delinquents who smoke pot, drink, and vandalize a Southern California suburb. In the finale, their parents hold a meeting at the high school, but soon the local kids lock them inside, smash their cars, and set the building on fire. "That [movie] pretty much defined my whole personality," says Kurt. "It was really cool. Total anarchy."

The video was shot for a modest thirty-three thousand dollars on a Culver City, California, sound stage made up to look like a high school gym, or what Dave fondly calls a "pep rally from hell." The janitor was played by Rudy Larosa, who was actually the janitor in director Sam Bayer's apartment building. Kurt had envisioned another type of gym—"it looked too contemporary," he says—and the backdrop bugged him, too. It reminded him of those bland backdrops used in aspirin commercials or Time-Life infomercials.

Kurt had other ideas for the clip—he wanted all the kids to run outside and start smashing things up and ruining cars. He wanted to have everyone in the audience come down and empty out their wallets into a big bonfire. He wanted to have a bonfire inside the gymnasium and burn some effigies. The last shot of the video, in which the janitor walks by a bound and gagged principal, was originally part of a larger scenario, but it got axed early on in the editing process.

The cheerleaders were Kurt's idea. "But I wanted really ugly overweight cheerleaders," he says, "and a couple of guys, too, just because I'm sickened by the stereotypical prom queen."

Bayer vetoed the ideas. The band nicknamed him "Jethro Napoleon." "He's got a little Napoleon complex," Kurt says of the diminutive Bayer. "He was just so hyper, such a rocker guy. I just couldn't believe it. I couldn't believe we actually submitted to that."

At one point during the shoot Bayer shouted, "All right, I'm going to lose my audience right now if everybody doesn't shut up!" And everybody in the audience went, "Oooooo," openly laughing at Bayer and heckling him. "It was just like we were in school," says Kurt, smiling. "He was the mean teacher."

"But by the end of the day," Kurt says, a mischievous sparkle in his eye, "we were having fun."

Kurt wanted everyone to come down from the bleachers and mosh. Bayer didn't like the idea but Kurt eventually talked him into it. And anarchy did eventually reign on the set. "Nobody knock anything over until I tell you because I want to get good close-up shots of it," Bayer told the assembled crowd, which had gathered after the band had announced just the day before on KXLU, a local college radio station, that they needed an audience for their video shoot. But after hours and hours of sitting around just watching the tedious goings-on, the audience was ready to explode. When they finally got to come down out of the bleachers, everybody started flipping out and knocking things over and running amok. People were mobbing Kurt and stealing Chris's guitar and Dave's cymbals. "Once the kids came out dancing they just said 'Fuck you,' because they were so tired of his shit throughout the day," Kurt says. The video's sense of joyous rebellion was for real.

Chris was having fun the whole time. He had brought a liter of Jim Beam to the set and had that and some pot with his friends during the lengthy waits between takes. Halfway through the shoot he passed out, then woke up just in time for the next take.

Kurt didn't like the edit Bayer had done, so he personally oversaw a new cut of the video. Over Bayer's protests, he added the next-to-last shot, a close-up of Kurt's face. It was a brilliant move— throughout the video, Kurt had come off as an intense but shy character, hiding behind his hair. It amounted to a tease, and the close-up was the payoff—he was not bad-looking (if he would only wash his hair).

For all its "alternative" overtones, "Teen Spirit" has all the classic elements of video: pretty girls in revealing clothes, kids dancing the latest dance and flaunting the latest fashions, the requisite dry-ice fog, guys with long hair playing guitars—kids getting off on kids' music. The point was that for the first time, the trappings were updated for a new generation—the flannel shirts, the moshing, the tattoos and anarchy symbols. The correlation with Nirvana's music —not stylistically trailblazing yet powerful and classic—is clear.

Then came the infamous *Nevermind* release party, September 13, 1991, at Seattle's trendy Re-bar club. The band was told it would be a low-key affair and that they could invite their friends. They arrived to find the walls of the club plastered with Nirvana posters. They had to schmooze with all kinds of dull music biz types and endure hearing their album played twice in a row. Kurt especially found all the attention embarrassing, especially in front of his Olympia friends.

Nevermind Triskaidekaphobia, Here's Nirvana

On Friday the 13th, join Nirvana and DGC Records for a release party in honor of Nirvana's DGC debut album <u>Nevermind</u>.

Friday, September 13
Re-bar
1114 Howell
Seattle, WA
(206) 233-9873
6:00 PM to 8:00 PM

Edible food, drinks, prizes you might want to take home, a few surprises, people to meet, the band to greet....But nevermind all that, the important part is the music. Hear <u>Nevermind</u> in its entirety and loud.

This invitation admits you and a guest only, and must be presented at the door. Space is limited. 21 & over with I.D.

Because of Washington state's harsh alcohol laws, there wasn't any hard liquor available, so someone smuggled in a half gallon bottle of whiskey and hid it in the photo booth, where those in the know retired for a quick snort of Jim Beam. Soon everyone was quite plowed. They got DJ Bruce Pavitt to ditch *Nevermind* and play the trashiest new wave and disco music they could find. After the band finished ripping all the posters off the walls, Chris heaved a tamale at Kurt and Dylan Carlson. Kurt remembers retaliating with a salvo of guacamole. ("Actually, it was a Green Goddess herb dip," corrects Nirvana fan club president Nils Bernstein, who catered the party.)

Soon, food was flying everywhere, with no regard for the industry geeks whose suits were getting splattered with food. And that was when Nirvana got kicked out of their own record release party.

They all piled into a Cadillac that Geffen/DGC Northwest promo woman Susie Tennant had rented for the occasion and the party raged on into the wee hours of the morning at her house. As everyone was leaving, Bruce Pavitt was down on the street, sitting on the curb and puking into the gutter as he waited for a cab. Kurt took this opportunity to lean out the window and pelt him with eggs.

Everyone knew they had a good album, but the plan was that if the management worked really, really hard and the label worked really, really hard and the band worked really, really hard, then maybe—just maybe—they could have a gold record by September of 1992.

The band got an inkling of things to come at an in-store appearance at Beehive Records in Seattle's University District. The band played a set to a packed house and afterward were besieged by autograph seekers. "There were all these weird, fawning people," recalls Dylan Carlson, who happened to work there. "These three guys from the Green River Community College radio station, Kurt was talking to them and telling them about Bikini Kill and how they should listen to them. These three guys didn't want to hear that. They just wanted to talk to Kurt and to touch Kurt and get an autograph." Then a couple of geeks Kurt remembered from Montesano showed up. "I realized that if people you went to high school with—especially in Montesano—were aware that I was a rock star in Seattle, then it was getting kind of big," Kurt says. Afterward, Chris, Kurt, Dave, and a small group of friends retreated to a bar and got promptly and thoroughly trashed.

Then it was off to Toronto to begin a headlining tour, which kicked off September 20, four days before *Nevermind* was released. Along for the ride on different legs of the tour were opening bands the Melvins on the East Coast and Canada, Das Damen and Urge Overkill in the south and Midwest and Sister Double Happiness on the West Coast. For the occasion, Kurt put a sticker on his guitar that read "VANDALISM: BEAUTIFUL AS A ROCK IN A COP'S FACE" ("Corn on the cops! Corn on the cops!").

As he watched Kurt get off the plane, tour manager Monty Lee Wilkes remembers thinking to himself, "There's something not right about this guy."

And it's very likely that Kurt thought the same. Right off the bat, Wilkes's "rock dude" poodle haircut marked him as something of an outsider. "I don't fit into that whole scene," Wilkes says. "I'm orga-

Chris rocking the Beehive record store. Looking on are Susie Tennant (white shorts) and Dylan Carlson (to her left). (© Charles Peterson)

nized, I'm clean, I wear clean clothes every day, I take a bath once a day. They don't like me."

There seems to be little doubt that the guys in the band delighted in giving Wilkes a hard time. "Everything you fix," says Wilkes, "a guy like Kurt goes and deliberately unfixes it because he's a cutie pie, you know?" The running joke among the crew was to see whether Wilkes was wearing the same shirt he was the previous day, because that meant he'd been up all night taking care of all the screw-ups the band had created. Furthermore, the beleaguered Wilkes was not only the tour manager of an extremely chaotic tour, he was also the tour accountant and production manager, besides being the sound-man for the first half of the tour and the lighting designer for the second. "Toward the end of that tour," he says, "I was throwing up blood from being stressed out."

Wilkes carried around a road case which unfolded into a portable office, complete with Macintosh desktop and laptop computers, fax, modem, printer ("always loaded with paper," he boasts), office supplies, books, forms, and a telephone. Wilkes denies claims of color-coded paper clips. "Funny joke," he sneers. "That's completely untrue." He does, however, cop to the color-coded pens. "I'm a very organized person," he explains.

One of the things that had made Kurt and Chris unhappy with Sub Pop was the fact they did only a handful of interviews the whole time they were on the label. They mentioned this to the Geffen/DGC publicity department, who proceeded to arrange up to a half-dozen interviews a day for each member of the band while they were on tour. After two months of journalists asking things like "Why did you sign to a major?" or "Why did you put a baby on the cover of the record?" it became a grind.

"We did so many interviews blindly, just walking into radio stations and doing unnecessary interviews with metal magazines, anything," says Kurt. "It was a nice education to make us realize we have to know what magazine we're doing an interview for before we just blindly do it." Two months later, all those magazines came out at once, producing a gigantic Nirvana media blitz. "We thought that most of these interviews would just die off into obscurity," Kurt says. "We thought we needed to do all these interviews to maybe sell a hundred thousand records."

They'd ferret out which interviewers were on the ball by seeing who fell for the bogus stories about Kurt and Chris meeting in arts and crafts class. Once they found a sucker, they'd go to town.

Kurt and Dave roomed together during the tour and one night, Dave was in bed watching TV when he heard Kurt giggling and giggling in the bathroom. Finally, Dave asked, "What are you *doing*?" Kurt had shaved off all of his goatee except for the mustache. When he walked out of the bathroom to show Dave, he was still giggling, but he stopped long enough to share the joke. "I look like my father!"

Early in the tour, an MTV News crew showed up to do a shoot on the band before soundcheck in a bar adjacent to the Axis club in Boston. To help things along, someone had provided a Twister game and a can of Crisco vegetable shortening. Chris got into it the most, stripping down to his jockey shorts (dark blue) and slathering himself with the Crisco before starting the game. They had just started when Chris suddenly pulled up the Twister board and threw it away, then wiped the grease off his body with an American flag that happened to be hanging on a nearby wall—some of the gook had found its way down the crack of his butt and so he wiped it from there, too. An ex-Marine and his beefy buddies who happened to be looking on

Kurt and Chris at City Gardens in Trenton, New Jersey. (© Stephan Apicella-Hitchcock)

took exception to Chris's taste in toilet paper and began screaming at him and Chris had to be escorted out of the club.

On that day, September 24, 1991, *Nevermind* was released and 46,251 copies were shipped to stores around the country.

After a Pittsburgh show, there was a dispute about T-shirt sales with the promoter. The band trashed their dressing room—nothing new—and left. Later, in the wee hours of the morning, two agents of the city arson squad banged on Monty Lee Wilkes's door and began questioning him. It seems someone had set a couch on fire backstage at the club and they seemed to think a member of Nirvana had done it. After a long conversation, Wilkes convinced the agents that the band had left the club by the time the fire was set. "It gave me a whole new outlook on the whole goddamn thing and it made me wonder just what the fuck I'd gotten myself into," says Wilkes.

After a show at the 40 Watt Club in Athens, Georgia, the band staged a little mutiny. They were supposed to drive to Atlanta so they could do a press day, but instead refused Wilkes's pleas and partied at R.E.M. guitarist Peter Buck's house all night. Of course, it was Wilkes who got the brunt of John Silva's wrath.

By this time, the tour had picked up opening band Urge Overkill, a much beloved indie band from Chicago. The guys in Urge Overkill were blown away by the force of Nirvana's music, but also by their unstated yet clear message. "It was fuck the government, fuck the status quo and the stupid people," says the band's Ed "King" Roeser. "And you can extend the whole philosophy to antiracism, antisexism, antifascism, anticensorship, etc. Somehow that message got across to the people at these shows."

Courtney heard from the manager of the 40 Watt Club that Kurt couldn't stop talking about her. This was too good to believe. So she began calling Dave on tour. When they finished talking, she'd ask to speak to Kurt. After a couple of days, they began to really hit it off and eventually, Courtney wouldn't even bother talking to Dave first.

Monitor man and drum tech Miles

Kurt audience-surfing at the Marquee in New York. (© Kristin Callahan/London Features)

197

Dave at the Marquee. (© Kristin Callahan/London Features)

Kennedy was astounded by the force of Dave's playing. "Just by playing so hard, he'd break drum thrones," he says. "There were just piles of sawdust on the drum riser from his drumsticks. He was just an animal." Dave's drum set lasted about halfway through the tour, until an October 12 gig at the Cabaret Metro in Chicago when the band destroyed it after a particularly good set. "There was nothing left any bigger than a six-inch circle of wood from the kick drum," says Wilkes.

"That's just what happened when they got so much energy and emotion worked up playing their set that it was the only way they could come to a good close," says Miles Kennedy.

It also happened to be the day that *Nevermind* debuted on the Billboard album charts at a respectable #144.

That night, Courtney showed up at a party after the gig. Legend has it that she and Kurt had sex up against the bar. "God," Kurt says with a laugh, "that's so disgusting. Right—everyone was around in a circle, watching us fuck. You've *got* to put it in the book that we didn't fuck." They did kiss for the first time and Courtney ran out to a pay phone to tell a friend in L.A. The rest of the night, they wrestled on the floor and threw glasses at each other. Courtney had a bag of lingerie with her for some reason and Kurt ended up modeling the contents. They got kicked out of the place twice.

Dave was asleep by the time Kurt and Courtney shambled drunkenly into Kurt and Dave's hotel room and started making loud and passionate love on the bed next to Dave's. "I tried to ignore it but I couldn't," Dave says. "I had. To leave. The room." He wound up knocking on soundman Craig Montgomery's door and sleeping there for the night.

Nevermind had begun blowing out of the stores immediately, but out on the road, no one in the band really realized what was going on. Weeks went by before someone told Kurt that the album was selling and MTV was playing "Teen Spirit" constantly. Kurt remembers an almost out of body experience when he first saw himself on television. "Jeez, do I really belong there?" he thought to himself. "I just looked so familiar to myself," he says.

As the tour wound through places like Providence and Memphis and St. Louis, gradually, the promo people who would show up backstage at shows changed from the alternative marketing people to AOR (Album Oriented Rock) and even CHR (Contemporary Hit Radio, or Top 40). Radio was picking up in a big way and MTV was playing "Teen Spirit" during the day—not just on the channel's alternative ghetto, *120 Minutes*. The channel had even begun running the words to "Teen Spirit" across the screen as the video played.

Meanwhile, a Christian-oriented L.A. band that had been called Nirvana since 1983 had issued cease-and-desist orders to radio and TV stations who were playing Nirvana's music and videos. Both bands can use the name. When Nirvana sued the local band for two million dollars for issuing the order, the matter came before a federal court in L.A. in mid-October. The L.A. Nirvana agreed to sell its trademark to Nirvana for fifty thousand dollars and to retract the cease-and-desist order.

With each copy of *Nevermind* sold, the band began to have less of an idea of who their audience was. With the college/indie crowd, they had a pretty good clue—people who were fairly intelligent, politically progressive, nonsexist, non-macho, and very much musically discerning. Now their shows were filling with jock numbskulls, frat boys, and metal kids. Their skyrocketing sales meant only one thing to Kurt, Chris, and Dave—they were losing their community.

The band was less then thrilled with their newfound audience, and they weren't shy about letting anyone know. As Chris told *Rolling Stone*, "When we went to make this record, I had *such* a feeling of us versus them. All those people waving the flag and being brainwashed. I really hated them. And all of a sudden, they're all buying our record, and I just think, 'You don't get it at all.'"

"I found myself being overly obnoxious during the *Nevermind* tour because I noticed that there were more average people coming into our shows and I didn't want them there," Kurt says. "They started to get on my nerves."

Accordingly, instrument-smashing reached an all-time high, and not just because they could finally afford it. "We were feeling so weird because we were being treated like kings," says Kurt, "so we had to destroy everything.

"I was obnoxious and showing my weenie and acting like a fag and dancing around and wearing dresses and just being drunk," Kurt continues. "I would say things like 'All right! Frat rock! Look at all these frat geeks out here!' I'm usually not very vocal on stage, but during that tour, I was a jerk. We were out of control."

Kurt's particular high point came at an October 19 show at the Trees club in Dallas. His bronchitis has been acting up for the past week and he was quite ill. That day, a doctor visited the hotel and gave Kurt some potent antibiotic shots, but neglected to warn him not to drink that night. "I started drinking and I just felt *insane*," he says, "like I did a whole bunch of speed or something. I just wasn't very rational at all."

Kurt had been complaining all along the tour that he couldn't hear himself in the monitors, but no one seemed to be doing anything about it. He was losing his voice and it made performing miserable. "That night I just decided to do something about it," Kurt says. "I decided to throw a star fit."

The club was alarmingly overcrowded; people could barely breathe, let alone move. In the middle of a song, Kurt suddenly took off his guitar and started tomahawking the monitor board by the side of the stage. He broke his favorite Mustang guitar, but he also broke the monitor board. After a long delay as the crowd chanted "bullSHIT! bullSHIT!" they got the monitor to work again through one speaker and the band resumed the set.

Unfortunately, the monitor system belonged to the best friend of one of the bouncers at the show, a heavily tattooed, mohawked gentleman with the regulation butt-crack peering above the back of his jeans. During "Love Buzz" Kurt jumped into the audience and although the bouncer made it seem as if he was trying to pull Kurt out of the audience he was actually holding him by the hair and hitting him. "I decided to get one good blow in before he beat me up after the show," Kurt says. "So I smacked him in the face with my guitar. He got a big gash on his forehead." The bouncer punched Kurt in the back of the head while his back was turned and Kurt crumpled; then he kicked him while he was down. In a flash, Dave vaulted over the front of his drum set; two roadies held the bouncer, rivulets of blood streaming down his face, while Chris stood between him and Kurt and told him to cool out.

Eventually, the band came back and played another half-hour. Someone had placed a wooden loading palette over the monitor board in case Kurt got any more wild ideas.

After the show, the bouncer was waiting outside for the band with a couple of his friends. "They all happened to be wearing Carcass and S.O.D. T-shirts," Kurt says, "like speed metal meatheads." "He was totally violent and macho," Kurt continues. "He was screaming, beet red with blood all over himself. 'I'm gonna kill you!'" The band took off in a cab, only to get caught in a traffic jam right in front of the club, like some nightmare version of *A Hard Day's Night*. The bouncer and his friends began thumping on the cab and eventually one of them kicked in a window and tried to grab Kurt just as the cab pulled away.

A little later, the cabdriver pulled over, took a joint down from his sun visor, and they all took a few tokes to calm down.

In the meantime, *Nevermind* had jumped thirty-five places to #109.

Courtney had been popping up sporadically along the way. She seemed to have a positive influence on Kurt's mood. Even the crew noticed it. "I think that helped him deal with it a lot," says Miles Kennedy. "I think it gave him someone to talk to and someone to deal with it with—someone who wasn't in the band or the crew."

As the tour wore on, the van became more and more crammed with all manner of broken equipment and accumulated garbage. After a while, there was barely any room for people. During one drive, Wilkes remembers being forced to sit on the edge of a seat for hours on end. "I look in the back and there's Courtney and Kurt," says Wilkes, "curled up amid empty bags of chips and spilled beers and everything else."

"It was pathetic."

On the morning of October 25, Kurt and Chris taped an interview for MTV's heavy metal show, "Headbanger's Ball," where "Teen Spirit" was the "#5 Skullcrusher of the Week." Kurt wasn't feeling too chipper—he hadn't had much sleep the night before and he was hung over as well. "I was sleeping just seconds before we aired," he explains. "Courtney and I had just stayed up all night drinking and fucking, so I had about two hours of sleep. It was during our romantic period."

Chris wore his usual duds—including nerdy deck sneakers—but Kurt donned a striking yellow organza dress and dark sunglasses. Although Chris did most of the talking, it was hard to take one's eyes off Kurt. "It's 'Headbanger's Ball' so I thought I'd wear a gown," Kurt explained. "Chris wouldn't wear his tux. He didn't give me a corsage, either."

"At least I asked you out," Chris replied just a tad too effeminately, enough to prompt a nervous little laugh from metalhead host Riki Rachtman. "This thing has gotten pretty wild," Rachtman said, recovering nicely. "Everywhere you go, in all different types of the music scene, people really seem to be getting into Nirvana."

"Everyone wants to be hip," Kurt cracked softly.

"Maybe they like the record," Chris offered.

By the time they got to the October 29 show in Portland, Susie Tennant took the band aside and told them, "Congratulations! Your record went gold today!" No one in the band cared all that much. "I didn't give a shit, really," Chris says. "Yeah, I was happy about it. It was pretty cool. It was kind of neat. But I don't give a shit about some kind of achievement like that. It's cool—I guess."

Monty Lee Wilkes says he had turned down a lucrative tour with another band after Nirvana invited him to go on their upcoming European tour. "We really want you to go, man," Wilkes says Chris told him. "You're the *best* road manager we've ever had and we want to keep you *forever*." Then, the night of the Portland show, three days before they were to leave for Europe, Wilkes was told he wouldn't be going.

There was no love lost there. "Chris is basically a drunken hippie," says Wilkes. "Kurt, he just doesn't say much—never *did* say much unless he wanted something." Wilkes feels a lot kindlier toward Dave, though. "Dave is the greatest," he says. "I just totally dig Dave. Great fuckin' guy, great guy."

A legendary homecoming show on Halloween at the Paramount in Seattle was filmed by DGC. Parts of it can be seen in the "Lithium" video and it may one day be edited into a full-length film. Opening were Mudhoney and Tobi Vail's band, Bikini Kill, who hit the stage draped in lingerie, with words like "slut" and "whore" written all over their bodies.

The band got one day's rest before setting off for a European tour on November 2, the day that *Nevermind* first entered the Top 40 at #35. The record was now selling at an amazing rate, certainly far exceeding the expectations of anyone at Geffen/DGC or Gold Mountain.

They played their first date of the European leg of the *Nevermind* tour at the Bierkeller in Bristol, England.

Every time they'd check into a hotel room, they'd switch on the TV and see the "Teen Spirit" video. The radio seemingly played nothing but "Teen Spirit." The press had gotten out of hand—they were doing between ten and fifteen interviews a day and every show was sold out. In Italy, a thousand kids who couldn't get a ticket simply rushed the doors and barged their way in.

At every step of the way, the shows were dangerously oversold, the stage cluttered with TV crews pointing cameras in Kurt's face as he tried to sing. "We resented it, so we turned into assholes," says Kurt. "We got drunk a lot and wrecked more equipment than we needed to. We just decided to be real abusive pricks and give interviewers a hard time. We weren't taking it seriously. We felt we needed to start averting the whole thing before it got out of hand. We wanted to make life miserable for people."

And after all, life was miserable for *them*, too. To begin with, the tour bus wasn't a sleeper; it was a sightseeing bus. There were no bunks, just seats, and the oversized windows let in light and noise. Their driver only made matters worse. In Europe, bus drivers must take breaks after a certain amount of time or distance, as measured by a device called a tachograph. The driver was very strict about this, earning him the nickname Tacho Bill. Tacho Bill would also get lost a lot, and soundman Craig Montgomery often wound up doing the navigating. Meanwhile, Bill would tap the accelerator instead of just cruising, so the bus lurched nauseatingly throughout the month-long tour.

For comic relief on the bus, they'd play a legendary prank phone call tape in which a man with a piercing New York accent verbally abuses everyone from florists to auto mechanics. After a while, it became the constant in joke of the tour, and guests would be shocked as the members of the tour entourage would call each other "jerky" and "fuckface" for no apparent reason.

Touring in Europe is always more exhausting because of the disorienting and rapid-fire changes in time zones, food, and language, not to mention the fact that bands have to deal with a different record company in every country. And there's more media—with every new country came a whole new set of TV stations, newspapers, and magazines. Often, the band couldn't refuse to do press because that would mean that, for instance, the entire nation of Denmark wouldn't have a television interview with Nirvana.

And sometimes it was just a matter of temperament. "This was a *punk rock* band," Danny Goldberg of Gold Mountain observes. "This was not a band of choirboys. Their moodiness got covered by the press this time, but it was nothing new."

Back in the States, Nirvanamania was rampant. The album was ascending the Billboard chart by leaps and bounds, going from #35 to #17 to #9 (Top 10!) to #4 and hovering around the Top 10 throughout most of November and December. People were flocking to the stores to buy it, critics debated the ambiguities and profundities of Kurt's lyrics, the underground scene began to talk of an indie revolution, you couldn't switch on MTV without seeing the "Teen Spirit" video, you couldn't go anywhere in Seattle without overhearing a conversation about the band's success, and everywhere, anyone who cared a whit about rock and roll was pondering what it all meant.

Kurt couldn't bring himself to acknowledge to himself what the hubbub was all about. "Obviously, I wouldn't want to allow my ego to admit that we're that great of a band, that we deserve that much attention, but I knew that it was better than 99 percent of anything else on a commercial level," he says. "I knew we were a hundred times better than fucking Guns n' Roses or Whitesnake or any of that shit. It just made me feel stupid because there are so many other bands in the underground that are as good or better than we are and we're the only ones getting any attention. It just made me feel sorry for everybody that was freaking out about it because it just seemed sad that we're one of the only bands like us that are being exposed to the mainstream."

Then they hit on the idea of using their fame to promote bands that they thought were just as deserving. "We were pretty excited about it at first—we actually thought we could make a dent," says Kurt. "But the only thing that's happened since we became popular is the Lemonheads, a fucking alternative cover band, are now one of David Letterman's favorite groups."

Actually, many bands who have appeared in Nirvana's T-shirt collection have at least landed major label contracts: Flipper, Daniel Johnston, Eugenius, the Melvins, Wool, and Shonen Knife, among others. "But it's not so the bands can get signed," Kurt says. "It's so some idiot out in suburbia will try to look for their album."

In Mezzago, near Milan, Shelli and Urge Overkill's Ed "King" Roeser had figured out a way to break into the hotel wine cellar by taking the service elevator. "They came up with a case of all these different kinds of wine and we drank just about every bottle," Urge's Nash Kato recalls. "The hotel, the next morning, it was like a vomitorium. You could hear it up and down the hall. I went into Chris and Shelli's room and they were hurling *together*, like as man and wife."

A couple of days later, *Nevermind* went platinum in the United States. Says Chris, "It goes platinum and we're all over MTV and it's like weird, like, now what? Where do we go from here? Are we going to be Led Zeppelin and the big band of the nineties or are we just going to fall apart or what?"

Since both were on tour in Europe at the same time, Kurt and Courtney renewed their telephone romance. "That's when we started really falling in love—on the phone," says Kurt. "We called each other almost every night and faxed each other every other day. I had like a three thousand dollar phone bill." Courtney skipped out on a Hole show just to hang out with Kurt in Amsterdam.

Despite the riot of excitement going on in Nirvana's honor, Kurt still felt he led a humdrum existence and that Courtney was a way out. "Initially, I just wanted to add some excitement in my life," says Kurt. "I'd never met anyone so outspoken and charismatic. It seems like she is a magnet for exciting things to happen. If I just happened to walk down the street with her, someone might attack us with a knife for no reason, just because she seems like the kind of person that attracts things like that. And I just wanted to piss people off, basically."

Kurt would often get bored on tour. "The highlight of the tour usually ends up with Chris being really drunk and obnoxious and standing on a table and taking his clothes off," Kurt says. "Or we'll shoot off a fire extinguisher or something like that. I just wanted to do something that was really exciting. I wanted to try to start having an exciting life. I figured Courtney was the best option. I knew that there wouldn't be a single person in the Nirvana camp that would approve of it. Because they're all so fucking boring. Their lives are so normal. I hate to say it, but that's just the way I feel. Everyone that I know that we work with, there's not much punk rock going on. There's no one willing to take risks, like 'let's just take off.' It's always such a strict regimen—'Let's get to the show, let's play, let's eat dinner and go to sleep.' I just got tired of it."

Courtney suited Kurt's image of himself as the "black sheep" of the band. "I was going off with Courtney and we were scoring drugs and we were fucking up against a wall outside and stuff and causing scenes just to do it," he says. "It was fun to be with someone who would stand up all of a sudden and smash a glass on the table and scream at me and throw me down. It was just really fun."

A powerful personality such as Courtney had an equally powerful effect on the entourage. "I think everyone was taken aback a bit at first," says tour manager Alex Macleod, chuckling. "She would appear and it was like a tornado coming. Everyone was tired and laid back and she would arrive and she would talk your ears off—she had so much energy, God knows how she did it. But she was good fun. She was amusing."

Dave, who is not a "morning person," began rooming with Macleod. But as the tour went on, Macleod acted more and more annoyed at Dave. Finally Dave couldn't stand it anymore and confronted him.

"What's your problem? What's wrong?" Dave asked.

"Fuck *you*!" Macleod shot back.

Apparently, whenever Macleod would try to wake Dave up in the morning, Dave would yell in his sleep, "FUCK YOU! LEAVE ME THE FUCK *ALONE*! THIS IS BULLSHIT!" then settle peacefully back into his pillow. Later, he'd go down to breakfast and wonder why Macleod was scowling at him.

The stress of the tour began taking its toll and by Thanksgiving, the band was starting to send S.O.S. calls to John Silva at Gold Mountain. "We were all tired," Chris says. "I'd be drunk. I got on this kick where I'd drink about three bottles of wine a night. I was all sick and coughing. I was pale, I had blue lips. Smoke hash, cigarettes, and fuckin' drink Bordeaux. 'Where's my Bordeaux?' I drank like three bottles a night. First bottle, that would be a primer. A few shows I barely remember playing."

Chris has a one-word explanation for his drinking. "Stress," he says. "I was stressed out. That was the only way I could cope with it."

"It felt as if we couldn't be stopped—or we didn't know where it was taking us and we were just sort of along for the ride," Dave says.

Kurt's stomach had started acting up on the American tour. A chronic flu that lasted throughout the European tour brought on bronchitis and Kurt couldn't stop smoking his hand-rolled cigarettes. "I just remember being real miserable and starving and sick all the time," says Kurt. "I was constantly drinking cough syrup and drinking. My bronchitis acted up so bad that I was vomiting while I was coughing before shows a few times. I remember in Edinburgh, we called this doctor. I was vomiting and coughing into this garbage can and he couldn't do shit for me."

Even steady Dave was starting to crack. "I started getting afraid of flying, really bad," he says. "Weird things started freaking me out, like all of a sudden I became claustrophobic and I'd never been claustrophobic before.

"I was insane," Dave says. "I was out of my fucking mind. I was sick of playing, sick of it. I would get so freaked out during shows— and I still do. While we're playing, I will just get freaked out that I'm going to freak out and go insane and puke and vomit and faint and then a hundred thousand people will have to go home and I'll be personally responsible. That happens to me every time we play. I can't explain it—it's this weird thing that's been with me all my life—a bad, bad anxiety thing all my life. One time, somebody told me you could hypnotize yourself if you stare in the mirror for hours on end and I did and I did kind of hypnotize myself and it freaked me out for the rest of my life really bad, and it still does. I was like thirteen or fourteen.

"I don't know how to explain it and it's not as insane as it sounds," he continues. "All it is is an impending fear of going insane every minute of the day. It's not something you get scared of for five minutes and then it goes away. You're constantly thinking about how do you know when you've gone insane? Where is the point where you just snap and you're completely out of your mind? So on that tour, everything was so completely insane, everything was just going at a hundred miles an hour and it was intensified tenfold."

On December 5, the night before Nirvana played the Trans-Musicale Festival in Rennes, France, Kurt and Courtney were lying in bed and they decided to get married.

The next day in Rennes, while Kurt stayed in his hotel room,

Chris downed an entire bottle of wine at a press conference. Dave couldn't get a word in edgewise.

Needless to say, it came as a huge relief when the band decided to cancel the rest of the tour before they hit the stage at the Trans-Musicale. "We were going to go to Scandinavia and it was going to be below zero and every flight was at six in the morning," says Chris. "It would have been a disaster, it would have been a fucking disaster. We would have fell apart, we would have freaked out. There would have been freak outs. It was better to go home and rest."

Before the nine-thousand-person capacity crowd, they opened with a silly, over-the-top version of the Who's "Baba O'Riley" with Dave on lead vocals. "I walked out there blitzed out of my fuckin' mind," Chris says. "And then I went home and had feverish delusions all night long. Laying in bed, thinking there was a ghost in the room or something. I just sweated all night long."

After the tour, Kurt, Chris, and Dave went their separate ways. Chris and Shelli went house shopping and found a place. At first they were going to put down a modest down payment. Then the royalty checks started to come in and they decided they could put up half the money. Then the royalty checks really started coming and they simply bought their $265,000 home outright.

"Three days after it was over, you were in withdrawal from not playing and then you start wanting to play again," Dave says.

CHAPTER NINE

Nevermind came without a lyric sheet. "I guess I wasn't confident enough," Kurt says. At first, he wanted to print some of his poems, then some "revolutionary debris," then nothing at all—no pictures or anything. At the last minute, he picked some lines out of the songs (and a couple that aren't in any of the songs) and ran them together into a poem.

Kurt says "revolutionary debris" meant "all kinds of anarchistic, revolutionary essays and diagrams about how to make your own bomb." "And I just thought we better hold off on that," he says. "If we ever really want to do that, we'd be more effective if we gained popularity first. Then people might actually think twice about it, rather than us alienating everybody right off the bat. But once we started to get really popular, it was really hard to hold back. We played the game as long as we could."

IT IS NOW TIME TO MAKE IT UNCLEAR

Part of playing the game is going out to dinner with powerful music magazine editors and pretending to be friendly with them so they'll give the band an article or a favorable review. On one of these junkets, the band went out to lunch at a swank Beverly Hills eatery with *Rip* magazine editor Lonn Friend.

Before lunch, Kurt, Chris, and Dave visited Friend's office. "I looked up on his wall and I noticed that Lonn has a fetish," says Kurt. "A rock and roll butt fetish. He has to have all these pictures taken with him and up-and-coming bands where either he's naked or the bands have to drop their pants. He's pinching their butts. There are all these pictures of him with naked rock stars that have been in this magazine. He's in the bathtub naked and they're standing around him and it started to scare me."

"It was a disgusting scene because we were basically pimping our personalities to this person to see if he liked us before he decided to promote us," Kurt continues. "It was the most sickening thing I ever experienced. I just decided to not say a word and sit there and be pissed off and act really insane. The only words he said to me after he got up to leave were, 'Kurt, you shouldn't talk so much.' He was really offended, totally pissed off."

Sure enough, *Rip* didn't support Nirvana until it practically had to, at the height of Nirvanamania. When the band refused to cooperate any more with *Rip* after the magazine ran a special edition on the band without their permission, the letters page just happened to feature more and more anti-Nirvana screeds. "If we were smart," says Kurt, "we would have played the game a little bit longer to get the acceptance of the *Rip* readers, to where they liked us so much that no matter what we said, it wouldn't matter. But we blew our wad too soon. But at the same time, I feel sorry for those kids, I was one of them. You can't blame a fourteen-year-old kid for calling someone a fag if he's grown up in an environment where his stepdad has been saying that for years and it's an accepted thing that you're practically forced into."

While oldsters called Kurt's lyrics incoherent, his Whitman's Samplers of images, ideas, and emotions fitted the short attention spans of channel-hopping kids everywhere. "I very rarely write about one theme or one subject," Kurt once told the *Seattle Times*. "I end up getting bored with that theme and write something else halfway through the rest of the song, and finish the song with a different idea."

Like the Pixies' Black Francis, Kurt didn't necessarily write his lyrics for linear sense. They're at their most successful when words and music collide to produce a powerful and distinct third sensation —"A denial, a denial" ("Teen Spirit"); "And I don't have a gun" ("Come as You Are"); "she said" ("Breed") or even a good old "yeah," repeated thirteen times for emphasis in "Lithium." Most of the lyrics come from lines of poetry that Kurt writes in spiral-bound notebooks every night before going to sleep, so the impressionistic quality comes mostly from the juxtaposition of seemingly unrelated lines, rather than a stream-of-consciousness approach from word to word.

The effect is like a musical Rorschach test, but more importantly, they added up to very coherent ideas and emotions that you can comprehend conceptually. Of course, sometimes even Kurt got a little confused. "What the hell am I trying to say?" he sang on "On a Plain."

In his songwriting, Kurt deals in extremes and opposites that animate the songs. One of the most famously obscure couplets in "Smells Like Teen Spirit" was "A mulatto, an albino/ A mosquito, my libido." It is really nothing more than two pairs of opposites, a funny way of saying the narrator is very horny. The lyrics often loft an idea and then shoot it down with one little burst of cynicism. Even the music echoes the dynamic contrasts of the imagery. Many of the songs— "Smells Like Teen Spirit" and "Lithium" foremost—alternate between subdued, rippling sections and all-out screaming blitzkriegs, while the album itself encompasses songs like the acoustic "Polly" and the majestic "Something in the Way" as well as primal scream workouts like "Territorial Pissings" and "Stay Away."

Kurt is smart enough to recognize that the dualities are a reflection of himself and perhaps his audience. "I'm such a nihilistic jerk half the time and other times I'm so vulnerable and sincere," he says. "That's pretty much how every song comes out. It's like a mixture of both of them. That's how most people my age are. They're sarcastic one minute and then caring the next. It's a hard line to follow." Few songs on *Nevermind* combine that mixture better than "Teen Spirit."

"It was basically a scam," Kurt says of the song. "It was just an idea that I had. I felt a duty to describe what I felt about my surroundings and my generation and people my age."

One night, Kurt and Kathleen Hanna from Bikini Kill had gone out drinking and then went on a graffiti spree, spray painting Olympia with "revolutionary" and feminist slogans (including the ever-popular "GOD IS GAY"). When they got back to Kurt's apart-

spirit flight
11811 West Olympic Blvd
Los Angeles
CA 90064   smells like teen spirit   feel

Come out and play make up the rules so stupid
I know I hope to buy the truth

216
758+ Take off your clothes I'll see you in court
2250

we know we'll lose we wont be bored
Come out and play, make up the rules

Dyslexic idiot savant with bad hearing
load up on guns & bring your friends
The secret hand shakes pretend

Neurotically Lathargic   Tribe   variety   Undeserving

our little group has always been, and always will
until the end
We cut our hands & made a pact   swore   we'er never going back

Tribe
territory
Pissings
Leaving / Spraying
Your mark

A mulato an Albino
A mousquito my Libido
YAY   A deposit
for A bottle
stink inside it No Role model
A Denial

The same percent has always
been And always will until the end
say anything
just to have an
opinion

Who will be the King & Queen
of the Outcasted teens
I hate to use percentages It's nice to know there is
A choice

Early lyric sheet for "Smells Like Teen Spirit." "Who will be the King &
Queen/of the outcasted teens."

ment, they continued talking about teen revolution and writing graffitti on Kurt's walls. Hanna wrote the words "Kurt smells like Teen Spirit." "I took that as a compliment," says Kurt. "I thought that was a reaction to the conversation we were having but it really meant that I smelled like the deodorant. I didn't know that the deodorant spray existed until months after the single came out. I've never worn any cologne or underarm deodorant."

Virtually ever since he arrived, Kurt had been inundated with the Calvinists' discussions of "teen revolution" in Olympia coffee shops; after all, that's what bohemian people in their early twenties do—it's in the rule book. "I knew there was some kind of revolution," he says. "Whether it was a positive thing or not, I didn't really care or know."

The Calvinists would bridle at the comparison, but in many respects, teen revolution resembled the aims of the Woodstock Nation. It meant that young people were creating and controlling their own culture as well as their political situation, rescuing them from a cynical and corrupt older generation. The idea was to make youth culture honest, accessible, and fair in all respects—on the artistic side, on the business side, and even in the audience—making it the diametrical opposite of what corporate America had turned it into. After that, political change would be inevitable.

Kurt didn't doubt that the Calvinists were earnest and he liked their ideas, but he also was dubious about their prospects. He found their altruism naive—they didn't seem to realize it was all a pipe dream. "Everyone seems to be striving for Utopia in the underground scene but there are so many different factions and they're so segregated that it's impossible," Kurt says. "If you can't get a fucking underground movement to band together and to stop bickering about unnecessary little things, then how the fuck do you expect to have an effect on a mass level?"

Kurt even felt that pressure was being put on Nirvana to help with the revolutionary effort. "I just felt that my band was in a situation where it was expected to fight in a revolutionary sense toward the major corporate machine," says Kurt. "It was expected by a lot of people. A lot of people just flat out told me that 'You can really use this as a tool. You can use this as something that will really change the world.' I just thought, 'How dare you put that kind of fucking pressure on me. It's stupid. And I feel stupid and contagious.'"

So "Teen Spirit" is alternately a sarcastic reaction to the idea of actually having a revolution, yet it also embraces the idea. But the point that emerges isn't just the conflict of two opposing ideas, but the confusion and anger that that conflict produces in the narrator —he's angry that he's confused. "It's fun to lose and to pretend" acknowledges the thrill of altruism, even while implying that it's plainly futile. "The entire song is made up of contradictory ideas," Kurt says. "It's just making fun of the thought of having a revolution. But it's a nice thought."

Part of embracing the revolution is blasting the apathetic types who aren't part of it. Even Kurt admits that his generation is more blighted by apathy than most. "Oh, absolutely," he says. "Especially people in rock bands who aren't educated. That's also an attack on us. We were expected to shed a minimal amount of light on our ideals, where we come from, but we're not even capable of that, really. We've done a pretty good job of it, but that was never our goal in the first place. We wanted to be in a fucking band."

"Teen Spirit" sounds violent—the drums clearly take a vicious pounding, the guitars are a swarming mass of barely contained brutality, the vocals are more screamed than sung. "I don't think of the song like that," Kurt says. "It's really not that abrasive of a song at all, really. It only really screams at the end. It's so clean and it's such a perfect mixture of cleanliness and nice candy-ass production and there were soft spots in it and there was a hook that just drilled in your head throughout the entire song. It may be extreme to some people who aren't used to it, but I think it's kind of lame, myself."

Kurt's family turmoil may have had a lot to do with why Nirvana's music sounds so angry. "I'm sure it did," Kurt says, "but I have enough anger in me just toward society that I would definitely have looked for this kind of music anyhow."

Dave Grohl has a slightly different take on the song's message. "I don't think there was one, to tell you the truth," he says. "Most of it has to do with the title of the song, and that was just something that a friend had written on the wall. It was funny and clever. That, paired with the video of us at the pep rally from hell, I think that had a lot to do with it. Just seeing Kurt write the lyrics to a song five minutes before he first sings them, you just kind of find it a little bit hard to believe that the song has a lot to say about something. You need syllables to fill up this space or you need something that rhymes."

Impromptu scribblings aside, one remarkable aspect of "Teen Spirit" was that unlike many previous songs of its type, it didn't blame the older generation for anything—it laid the blame at the feet of its own audience. That implies a sense of responsibility that didn't quite fit the slacker stereotype. Although "Teen Spirit" was a bold and provocative dare, Kurt feels he crossed the line into condemnation. "I got caught up in pointing the finger at this generation," says Kurt. "The results of that aren't very positive at all. All it does is alienate people and make them feel the same feeling you get from an evil stepdad. It's like, 'You'd better do it right' or 'You'd better be more effective or I'm not going to like you anymore.' I don't mean to do that because I know that throughout the eighties, my generation was fucking helpless. There was so much right wing power that there was almost nothing we could do."

"I know that I've probably conveyed this feeling of 'Kurt Cobain hates his audience because they're apathetic,' which isn't the case at all. Within the last two years, I've noticed a consciousness that's way more positive, way more intelligent in the younger generation and the proof is in stupid things like *Sassy* magazine and MTV in general. Whether you want to admit that or not, there is a positive consciousness and people are becoming more human. I've always been optimistic, but it's the little Johnny Rotten inside me that has to be a sarcastic asshole."

"Introducing that song, in the position that we were in, I couldn't possibly say that I was making fun or being sarcastic or being judgmental toward the youth-rock movement because I would have come across as instantly negative. I wanted to fool people at first. I wanted people to think that we were no different than Guns n' Roses. Because that way they would listen to the music first, accept us, and then maybe start listening to a few things that we had to say, after the fact, after we had the recognition. It was easier to operate that way."

"In Bloom" was originally aimed at the dilettantes of the underground scene, the jocks and shallow mainstream types who had begun to blunder into Nirvana shows after *Bleach*. But remarkably, it translated even better to the kind of mass popularity the band enjoyed. The song mixes images of fertility and decay with a chorus about a gun-toting guy who likes to sing along to Nirvana's music, "but he knows not what it means." The brilliant irony is that the tune is so catchy that millions of people actually do sing along to it. It's also a good description of former band members like Jason Everman, Dave Foster, and Aaron Burckhard, who were honestly attracted to the band's music but didn't quite go along with Kurt and Chris's punk rock ethos.

"Come as You Are" sounds unlike anything else on the record—with its mysterious murky, watery feeling, it shows Kurt's metamorphosis from misanthrope to a more open-minded person. "I'm tired of people passing judgments on one another and expecting people to live up to their expectations," says Kurt. "I've done that all my life. I'm a Pisces and it's a natural thing for Pisces to be upset with people and expect them to be a certain way and then they aren't, so you're just mad at them all the time. I just got tired of it." The narrator admits that he's unsure how the other person will be, but is ready to

Knows not what it means
Sell the kids for food
~~weather changes~~ the mood
Spring is here again
Re-productive glands
. ~~her~~ AHHH

Hes the one - who likes All the
pretty Songs - And He likes
to sing Along - And He likes
to shoot his gun

But he knows not what it means
knows not what it means And I SAY AHH

~~NOSE~~ Holes Are flared
little Boys Are scared
~~territory~~ claim
~~Not So HArd to TAMe~~

Territory
claim
TAMe

Early lyric sheet for "In Bloom."

accept the other person, contradictions and all. Furthermore, he
adds that he won't be judgmental when the meeting occurs—"And I
swear that I don't have a gun." It's a remarkably beautiful sentiment.

More dualities emerge as Kurt beckons someone to "Take your
time, hurry up" and to "Come dowsed in mud, soaked in bleach."
Kurt is full of opposites, too: masculine/feminine, violent/nonviolent,
pop/punk. He's decided to accept it all, to come as he is. Perhaps

Early lyric sheet for "Lithium."

instead of resolving the contradictions, he'll let them live together under one roof, sometimes warring, sometimes joining to produce a powerful third entity.

Once "Breed" builds up its hurtling momentum, Kurt wails "I don't care" half a dozen times, then "I don't mind" and finally "I'm afraid," saying about as much about the straight line between apathy, ignorance, and fear as needs to be said. "I don't mind if I don't have a mind" is merely icing on the cake.

The title of "Lithium" is an update on Marx's description of religion as the "opiate of the masses." Kurt says that the song may well have been inspired by Jesse Reed's family, the only born-agains he had ever had direct contact with. Kurt says he isn't necessarily antireligion. "I've always felt that some people should have religion in their lives," he says. "That's fine. If it's going to save someone, it's okay. And the person in that song needed it." The song is not strictly autobiographical, but it's easy to see a resemblance between Kurt's despair and loneliness in Olympia and the sorry state that the character is in. Kurt didn't find religion that winter of 1990, but he did find another kind of nirvana.

"Polly" is based on an actual incident which occurred in Tacoma in June of 1987. A fourteen-year-old girl returning from a punk show at the Community World Theater was kidnapped by a man named Gerald Friend (no relation to Lonn), who hung the girl upside down from a pulley attached to the ceiling of his mobile home and raped and tortured her with a leather whip, a razor, hot wax, and a blowtorch. She later escaped from his car when he stopped for gas. Friend was later arrested and eventually convicted and will likely spend the rest of his life in jail. Kurt's only embellishment to the story was the hint that the woman got away by fooling the rapist into thinking she enjoyed what he was doing to her.

Rape is a continuing theme in both Kurt's interviews and his songs. It's almost as if he's apologizing for his entire gender. "I don't feel bad about being a man at all," Kurt says. "There are all kinds of men that are on the side of the woman and support them and help influence other men. In fact, a man using himself as an example toward other men can probably make more impact than a woman can."

Although the title of "Territorial Pissings" blasts macho posturing, the song is frequently the occasion of the band's end-of-set instrument-smashing orgies. The lyrics are basically a handful of disconnected ideas which appealed to Kurt. He explains the opening words of the song ("When I was an alien...") by revealing that he always wanted to believe he was really from outer space. The fantasy, which he only recently stopped playing with in his mind, was that he was actually an alien foundling. "I wanted to be from another planet really bad," says Kurt. "Every night I used to talk to my real parents and my real family in the skies. I knew that there were thousands of other alien babies dropped off and they were all over the place and that I'd met quite a few of them." For Kurt, the fantasy supported the idea that "there's some special reason for me to be here."

(Coincidentally, the creatures in Kurt's paintings look remarkably like artist's rendering of aliens which have appeared in everything from the *Weekly World News* to the cover of *Communion*, Whitley Strieber's allegedly nonfiction book about close encounters with beings from outer space.)

The song also proves that Kurt wasn't above penning a few lyrical clinkers—"Just because you're paranoid doesn't mean they're not after you" is a pretty hoary coffee mug adage.

"Never met a wise man, if so it's a woman." "The biggest piece of proof that I have is that there are hardly any women who have been in charge of starting a war," Kurt says. "They're actually less violent." By this time, one begins to wonder how Kurt rationalizes being a man at all. His first response is revealing. "I don't know," he says. "Castration." Later on in "On a Plain," he is "neutered and spayed"; in "Come as You Are," he doesn't "have a gun."

It's been pointed out many times that the first three songs on the album mention guns. "Dave Grohl's father tried to make an analogy about that," Kurt says. "Something about how I tie guns with my penis. I don't know why. I wasn't conscious of the fact that I mentioned guns three times. I've tried to figure out an explanation for it myself and I can't. I really can't." To paraphrase Dr. Freud, sometimes a gun is just a gun. But not this time.

"Drain You" is a love song, or rather a song about love. In Kurt's universe, the two babies of the song represent two people reduced to a state of perfect innocence by their love. "I always thought of two brat kids who are in the same hospital bed," he says. The lyrics mix the utter dependence of infants with their narcissism—"I don't care what you think/ Unless it is about me," one of them says. Although there is an obvious sexual connotation, the image of draining off an infection mainly has to do with relieving the other of bad feelings, like sucking out the venom from a snake bite. The medical theme—the song is rife with fluids, infection, and vitamins—would dominate the next album.

The title of "Lounge Act" came from the fact that "We just thought that song sounded like such a lounge song," says Kurt, "like some bar band would play." But the lyrics are nothing of the kind. "That song is mostly about... having a certain vision and being smothered by a relationship and not being able to finish what you wanted to do artistically because the other person gets in your way," Kurt says.

The line that goes "I've got this friend you see who makes me feel..." refers to some of Kurt's Olympia friends and the Riot Grrl movement who inspired Kurt to surrender his misanthropy and break out of what he calls the "nihilistic monk world" that he had made for himself in his little shoe box of an apartment.

"Stay Away" undoubtedly began as an indictment of the Calvinist scene in Olympia, but in a broader sense, it could apply to any conformist clique—"Monkey see monkey do/ I don't know why I'd rather be dead than cool."

The title of "On a Plain" could be read as a pun, as in "airplane." Although he was otherwise miserable, Kurt had realized his dreams by the time he had written that song. He was getting flown to L.A. and New York because big record companies desperately wanted to sign his band. "I suppose it's some way of me saying I'm still complaining and bitching about things but I really have it better off than I had ever expected to be," Kurt admits.

Part of the lyrical motif of "On a Plain" is the construction of the song itself. "I'll start this off without any words," Kurt begins. He explains the line "Somewhere I have heard this before/ In a dream my memory has stored" by saying that "I'd heard that bridge in some other song, I don't know what it is," Kurt says. "I'll find out some day," he adds, with enough sarcasm in his voice to imply that he means that the original author will slap him with a copyright suit. When he wrote "One more special message to go, then I'm done and I can go home," he meant that "On a Plain" was the last song that he had to write lyrics for.

"It is now time to make it unclear/ To write off lines that don't make any sense." "That was my way of saying the first couple of lines seem like statements but they don't have any meaning," says Kurt. "I'm just making it obvious that there's really no meaning in it, so don't take it too seriously."

But perhaps he's protesting too much. "My mother died every night" and "the black sheep got blackmailed again" are loaded with personal resonance for Kurt. The former line sounds like a reference to Wendy's traumatic experience with her abusive boyfriend; Kurt often refers to himself as a black sheep. Make these points to him and he shrugs, laughs quietly, and mumbles "I don't know…" After such revealing lines, "It is now time to make it unclear" seems like an attempt by Kurt to cover his tracks, as if he's given too much away.

For all his disavowal of most of the other songs on the record, Kurt does acknowledge that "Something in the Way" is about his experiences living under the bridge in Aberdeen. It's exaggerated for effect, though. "That was like if I was living under the bridge and I was dying of AIDS, if I was sick and I couldn't move and I was a total street person," he says. "That was kind of the fantasy of it."

* * *

Although Kurt roundly rejected the "spokesperson for a generation" tag, he will admit that the album did crystallize something about his peers. "Oh definitely," he says. "We're a perfect example of the average uneducated twentysomething in America in the nineties, definitely."

And the twentysomethings are the generation that's been led to believe that they missed out on all the best times. "That's pretty much the definition of what we are, is punk rockers who weren't into punk rock when it was thriving," Kurt says. "All my life, that's been the case, because when I got into the Beatles, the Beatles had been broken up for years and I didn't know it. I was real excited about going to see the Beatles and I found out they had broken up. Same thing with Led Zeppelin. They'd been broken up for years already."

But there's more to it than that. "I think there's a universal display of psychological damage that everyone my age has acquired," Kurt says. "I notice a lot of people a lot like me who are neurotic in certain social situations. I just notice that everyone in their early twenties have been damaged by their parents equally." Kurt describes a scenario in which his generation's parents grew up in the bland, conformist fifties and early sixties, then had kids just as the late sixties began. The onslaught of new ideas threw their old values into a tailspin and they reacted by drinking and doing drugs. And getting divorces.

"Every parent made the same mistake," Kurt says. "I don't know exactly what it is, but my story is exactly the same as 90 percent of everyone my age. Everyone's parents got divorced, their kids smoked pot all through high school, they grew up during the era when there was a massive Communist threat and everyone thought we were going to die from nuclear war, and more and more violence started to infuse into our society, and everyone's reaction is the same. And everyone's personalities are practically the same. There's just a handful of people my age, there's maybe five different personalities and they're all kind of intertwined with one another.

"I don't think our musical version of that is any different than any of the other bands that have come out at the same time we have," Kurt says. "I don't think we're more special as far as having that same kind of damage that our parents or our society gave us. It's the same. We got more attention because our songs have hooks and they kind of stick in people's minds. The majority of any bands you interview would have divorced parents. All these kids my age found themselves asking the same question at the same time—why the fuck are my parents getting divorced? What's going on? Something's not right. Something about the way our parents were brought up isn't the way it's supposed to be. They fucked up somewhere. They're living in a fantasy world. They must have done something wrong." Those are some tough thoughts to have, especially if, like Kurt, you were eight years old.

Analyzing his own songs at length reminded Kurt of something. "I'm just starting to realize why I had such a hard time with interviews when this record came out," he said. "People were going through the songs and trying to get me to explain them and I just don't even have any opinions on them. They are all basically saying the same thing: I have this conflict between good and evil and man and woman and that's about it."

CHAPTER TEN

The massive success of *Nevermind* was a complete surprise, but in retrospect, there were plenty of warning signs. Copies of the Smart sessions tracks had been circulating throughout the industry and on bootlegs for well over a year before *Nevermind* came out, so industry tastemakers and music aficionados were already spreading the word about the band; the line for the *Nevermind* release party wound around the block. Nirvana's "CRACK SMOKIN', KITTY PETTIN'" T-shirts were very popular, providing massive amounts of free advertising. The band had done three U.S. tours and visited Europe twice; they'd gotten the enthusiastic blessing of the influential U.K. music weeklies, not to mention the all-important Sonic Youth seal of approval.

Sub Pop succeeded because Pavitt and Poneman had studied the successes and failures of other labels and cannily exploited the infrastructure they had already built. In the same way, the infrastructure was already set up for Nirvana to succeed as well. Promoters and booking agents now knew how to deal with this new breed of bands and several even specialized exclusively in them. Nirvana retained top lawyer Alan Mintz, who had built up expertise and contacts by winning excellent deals for Jane's Addiction, Toad the Wet Sprocket, and a host of other new bands; Nirvana saw Sonic Youth's satisfaction with Gold Mountain, Geffen, and even video director Kevin Kerslake, and eventually followed them to all three. R.E.M. opened up the doors at radio for the band; these days, Kurt even uses R.E.M.'s accountant.

By September 24, 1991, Sub Pop and grunge rock had begun to bubble their way into mass consciousness, but most consumers didn't know how to find the records, and the music wasn't being written up in the mainstream music press or played on big radio stations or MTV, so no one knew what grunge to buy even if they did find it. The miracle of major label distribution gave *Nevermind* a major leg up by making it one of the first grunge records—and that little Sub Pop logo made it official—to get distributed to the major record store chains, where anyone could (and did) buy a copy. Also, the album came out at the beginning of the academic year, when college radio programmers are energetically looking for material to beef up their play lists.

The music itself was a refinement and amplification of what bands such as Hüsker Dü and the Replacements had done, although at root it plugged into a collective consciousness of both Black Sabbath and the Beatles. And then there was that smooth production.

Nevermind was one of the first "alternative" records to sound good on the radio. Highly compressed—meaning the extremes of high and low volume were electronically limited—Andy Wallace's mixes were custom-tailored for mainstream radio, which is, after all, still where sales campaigns are won or lost. Compared to the usual raw alternative recordings, *Nevermind* sounded like a Bon Jovi record—the production sugar-coated the band's bitter punk pill.

Steve Fisk, who produced the *Blew* sessions, feels that the record, with its heavily flanged bass and guitars and big reverberant drums, sounds very much like an early eighties British new wave record, hence what he calls "The Janet Theory."

"When Janet was fifteen, she was really into the Smiths," Fisk begins. "They made her feel special about herself and she spent long hours in her room with her Walkman on and her parents couldn't bug her and those morbid lyrics really reinforced all that. When they broke up it was very hard for her. Then Morrissey went solo but all her friends got into it and it was very hackneyed."

"At maybe sixteen or seventeen she went into her British death gloom phase for real," Fisk continues. "Then she dyed her hair black and looked like Siouxsie, not understanding that it was a whole played-out cliché by that point. This is like 1986. It pissed off her parents and none of her friends were doing something that radical with their looks so it really made her feel good. Of course, that look came to the malls. And it got played out.

"Somewhere along the line she got onto the Sub Pop Singles Club. And she found some music that would really piss people off and she became Grunge Girl. Collectively, that demographic was spring-loaded for a New Wave punk record like *Nevermind*."

"The lyrics are happy songs with sad lyrics—it's the Cure, it's Joy Division," says Fisk. "So poor Janet, she couldn't help but like it."

Kurt Cobain enjoys this theory very much. "It's probably true," he says, laughing.

The media made much of the fact that Bill Clinton was America's first baby boomer president, but they largely ignored the fact that boomers had already been dominating U.S. culture for years—especially the music biz. Baby boomers control virtually every aspect of the mainstream music industry, guiding the signing of acts, radio airplay, press coverage.

So baby boomer totems such as the Rolling Stones, the Beatles, and Bob Dylan remain benchmarks; everything else is just a pale shadow. The boomers bombard the airwaves with classic rock. And when people get sick of hearing "Brown Sugar" for the 3,298th time, they slot in a "new" artist like the Black Crowes or the Spin Doctors who gladly caters to the same boomer standards, even as they claim to be "rebels."

But by the time *Nevermind* was released, a large new demographic had emerged. The twentysomethings hadn't been raised on *Let It Bleed*, the White Album, and *Blonde on Blonde*—those were oldies. Some called them the Baby Busters, but they actually outnumber the Boomers. And they wanted some music they could call their own.

Nevermind came along at exactly the right time. This was music by, for, and about a whole new group of young people who had been overlooked, ignored, or condescended to. As the twentysomething band Sloan sang in "Left of Centre," "I really can't remember the last time I was the center of the target of pop culture... I'm slightly left of centre/ of the bullseye you've created/ It's sad to know that if you hit me/ it's because you were not careful."

Ultimately, it wasn't so much that Nirvana was saying anything new about growing up in America; it was the way they said it. It represented, as *Los Angeles Times* pop critic Robert Hilburn said, "the awakening voice of a new generation." This had all sorts of implications, from consumer marketing to political demographics. It also marked the definitive end of the baby boomers, who prided themselves on their youth, as the sole arbiters of youth culture. A backlash was clearly in the cards.

As if there was any doubt, *Nevermind* proved once and for all that indie rock had completely turned in on itself and become far from the unifying force that rock began as. Just as Kurt took the gutsy step of exploring his pop gift, *Nevermind* forced the denizens of the indie world to consider whether they could like music that *everyone* could like and to consider the possibility that one of their own could make popular music that withstood an unspoken indie loyalty test. Some felt Nirvana's mere popularity disqualified them.

It was also "alternative" music that mainstream people could like, too. Suddenly, alternative rock wasn't just the province of jaded college kids—it began to reflect the social realities of a struggling, changing nation. *Nevermind* and the funk and roll phenomenon (the Red Hot Chili Peppers, Fishbone, Faith No More, etc.) then enjoying its first flowering renewed the inclusive power of rock. As Kurt came from working-class stock, the success of *Nevermind* was the ultimate expression of Sub Pop's populist ideals—it figures that the band came from an unlikely place such as Aberdeen, rather than Seattle.

Not only was the music compelling and catchy, but it captured the spirit of the age. In one of countless articles on the emerging twentysomething phenomenon, the *Atlantic* magazine commented in a December, 1992, cover story that "This generation—more accurately this generation's reputation—has become a Boomer metaphor for America's loss of purpose, disappointment with institutions, despair over the culture and fear for the future." In that environment, it's no wonder that a song featuring a young man screaming with rage and pain could hit number one.

Kurt screams in a code that millions can understand. He communicates in the same scattershot, intuitive way that his generation has been trained to assimilate and to express information, thanks to the usual litany of tens of thousands of hours of television advertising before they were even able to read, lousy schools, the glut of the information age, video games, etc. Kurt's lyrics make unusual sense of chaos. When he screams "a denial, a denial" over and over again at the end of "Teen Spirit," it's something that is understood on a deep level. And either you get it or you don't. It clearly draws the lines, even as it deals in universals. And it's one of the most transcendent moments in rock music.

The "Teen Spirit" single went out to radio on August 27, then it went on sale two weeks later on September 10. The single sold well but didn't immediately explode, but meanwhile, MTV accepted the video and a buzz was growing—the song was all over college and alternative radio.

"Teen Spirit" was not supposed to be the hit. The second single, "Come as You Are," was supposed to be the track that would cross over to other radio formats; "Teen Spirit" was the base-building alternative cut. "None of us heard it as a crossover song," says Gold Mountain's Danny Goldberg, "but the public heard it and it was instantaneous. Right away, the then-emerging format of alternative radio began playing "Teen Spirit." "They heard it on alternative radio," says Goldberg, "and then they rushed out like lemmings to buy it."

It's hard to believe that a song can become a hit simply because it's very good, but this appears to be the case. "Every once in a while, a song *is* that powerful," says Goldberg. "And in their instance, they not only had a song that was that powerful—it combined with an image that was very attractive to a certain subculture."

MTV did not begin pumping the "Teen Spirit" video immediately. The video did receive a prestigious world premiere (making Nirvana the first debut act since Bart Simpson to be so honored) on *120 Minutes*, but only after Amy Finnerty, then a junior member of the programming department and a longtime supporter of new music at the channel, went into her boss's office and threw "a little tantrum." Thereafter, the clip languished in graveyard rotation until entering the Buzz Bin, where the video channel hypes new artists, on October 14, three weeks after the album was released. It stayed in the Buzz Bin for nine weeks, getting, as they say in the broadcast business, heavy phones. MTV market research revealed that "Teen Spirit" appealed to viewers across the demographic board.

Goldberg says the album was virtually gold before MTV started playing the "Teen Spirit" video with any frequency. MTV, he says was just a "multiplier." "It was really obvious that it was just the music—the song and the desire on the part of the audience for a band to emerge did it," says Goldberg. "R.E.M. maybe created that yearning, Jane's Addiction maybe created that yearning, but whatever it was, Nirvana was definitely in the right place at the right time."

Nevermind grossed $50 million for Geffen, not bad for an initial investment of $550,000. Still, no one rushes forward to take the credit. As Geffen president Ed Rosenblatt said to the *New York Times*, "We didn't do anything. It was just one of those 'get out of the way and duck' records." The phrase "Get out of the way and duck" is repeated over and over again like a mantra by Geffen execs. What they mean is that as records hit certain sales plateaus, different marketing approaches kick in; for the first million or so sales, *Nevermind* sold too fast for the marketing force to implement any approach. "It was almost disappointing how fast it was going," says Goldberg. "We were just trying to experience it because we knew it was a very rare occurrence."

The success of *Nevermind* was reminiscent of the massive word of mouth campaign that had launched Bruce Springsteen a decade and a half earlier. What happened to Nirvana has certainly happened before in less glamorous instances—no one anticipated that Peter Frampton would sell over ten million copies of 1975's *Frampton Comes Alive!*, while Vanilla Ice's ten-times-platinum major label debut also came out of nowhere, garnering very little initial radio or MTV exposure and exploding largely through word of mouth.

Nevermind did eventually get some goosing, however. DGC added the record to cooperative advertising programs with record store chains, stepped up distribution of promo items like posters and mobiles, gave certain retailers a discount on the wholesale price of the album, and then gave them more time to pay for the ones they bought. Sales kept exploding.

Soundscan, a new system for charting records, was another factor. Based strictly on sales instead of an easily manipulated system of reporting, Soundscan revealed what people were actually buying, instead of what the major labels wanted people to buy. The *New York Times* reported that Geffen/DGC used Soundscan as a marketing tool for *Nevermind*. Soundscan revealed that in certain markets, Nirvana was outselling Metallica four to one, information Geffen/DGC used to get Nirvana onto radio stations that were playing Metallica.

"Between September 24 and Christmas, it just had a life of its own," says Gary Gersh. By January, newsstands were packed with Nirvana stories and the January 11 "Saturday Night Live" appearance further pushed sales. By this point, *Nevermind* was selling over 300,000 copies a week—including 373,250 in the last week of December, as kids went out and spent their Christmas cash and gift certificates on the album all their friends were talking about. That was when Nirvana unseated Michael Jackson at the number-one spot on *Billboard*'s Top 200 Albums chart. The band was selling better than Garth Brooks, Metallica, U2, Guns n' Roses and Hammer.

Billboard magazine called *Nevermind* "a cross-format phenomenon," appearing on hard rock, modern rock, college, and AOR stations, and eventually CHR.

The fact that the album went to number one was something of a freak, however. As luck would have it, U2 had decided to release its version of an art-rock record, Michael Jackson continued his artistic slide and Guns n' Roses saw fit to release two albums at once. "They went up against some bad competition, so it wasn't hard for them to do great," says Steve Fisk. "Whenever music gets bad enough, that creates a window of opportunity and shit happens."

As Nirvana went out on a U.S. tour of venues that were far too small for their skyrocketing sales, it created an effect not unlike the one created by putting out their first single as a limited edition of one thousand. It made the ticket that much hotter, ratcheting up curiosity about the group and boosting sales.

The *Nevermind* phenomenon symbolized a sea-change in rock music. The so-called "hair farmer" bands—Poison, Warrant, Winger, etc.—that the Hollywood music establishment cranked out were perceived as mere entertainers, corporate employees, poseurs, fakes. And their substandard music and the pervasive sexism and machismo that invariably went hand-in-hand with it were getting very played out. And although they may have made a catchy song here and there, they didn't have any resonance.

Part of the excitement was the excitement itself—it had been a long time since a rock band *mattered*, when an album seemed to define such a large and imminent cultural moment. There was something in the air and Nirvana turned it into music.

Buying a Nirvana album was something of a consumer insurrection. People were rejecting the old guard and going with what they felt instead of what a large and well-oiled hype machine was telling them to buy. People were choosing substance over image. It was a somewhat tenuous connection, but there was a feeling in the bones that something surprising was going to happen in the election that November.

The success of the album coincided with a general yen for "reality," encompassing things like MTV's "Unplugged" show, renewed interest in additive-free foods, the advent of network news segments that punctured the artifice of political advertising. "We weren't doing any posing and we weren't trying to be something that we weren't," Dave Grohl says. "It was sort of a package deal—you've got good music, you've got normal-looking people, just like Bruce Springsteen can sell out the Enormodome in New Jersey because he's 'a fuckin' average Joe.' I think it had a lot to do with something like that, maybe—people seeing normal people and appreciating that."

"Nirvana embodied the yearning for a moral universe that was more real and more sincere than what was going on in the conventional rock world at the time," says Goldberg, "and I think that resonates with a yearning in the culture for the post-Reagan set of values. There is a connection between their desire for authenticity and sincerity and ethics—it's a real commitment to an attitude that is very attractive. They convey a set of values that's egalitarian and ethics-driven and less macho, power-driven. All that stuff, combined with the musical genius, is what they are."

Although Dave denies he is "Mr. Analysis," he has an excellent grasp of the circumstances which gave rise to *Nevermind*'s success. "There was a weird lull, a void in rock," he says. "If you looked at the Top 10 in the year before *Nevermind*, there was rarely any rock music in it except for bad heavy metal shit that no one could relate to. When our music came out, I think it was a combination of stoners, skaters, of derelict kids who saw a group of derelict kids playing music that sounded like we were pissed. And I think a lot of people related to that. And the songs were good songs. Kurt has a great voice. The songs were catchy and they were simple, just like an ABC song when you were a kid."

An unstated goal of rock music is to bug one's parents. But twentysomethings' parents were raised on rock and roll themselves, so the job had become a lot tougher than it was in the sixties. With its ravaged screaming, pervasive distortion, and bludgeoning attack, *Nevermind* fulfilled that goal admirably.

But beneath all that, there was no denying that the music was simply extraordinary. It captured all the energy and excitement of punk and applied it to songs that people could hum long after the album was finished playing. Unlike so many albums that consist of one or two singles and a bunch of filler, *Nevermind* is a really good album from front to back. You can put the CD on and listen to the whole thing and not skip over anything. "The key to Nirvana is the songs are great, truly great," says the fiftysomething Ed Rosenblatt. "I'm talking on a level with R.E.M., on a level with Paul Simon."

Strangely, the press and the public don't think of him as such, but Kurt Cobain is a songwriter's songwriter. In one fell swoop, Kurt reclaimed pop songwriting from the convoluted, inbred freak it had become. This wasn't songwriting for its own sake, as practiced by the likes of Elvis Costello, Marshall Crenshaw, and Michael Penn, who lately seemed to take special pleasure in obscuring the very emotions they so very artfully claimed to convey. Kurt's music went simply and directly to the soul. His lyrics weren't tortured wordplay aimed at tickling the fancy of some jaded rock critic, the chord progressions weren't designed to impress a Juilliard student; instead, the words heightened the total sensation of the music. Like a cool guitar sound or a riff, they made it rock. The music was ingenious in its economy, the melodies were indelible.

Butch Vig chalks a lot of it up to Kurt's voice. "If you took all his songs and had someone else sing them, it wouldn't be the same," he says. "There's something in Kurt's persona that takes them to another level. There's mystery and passion and intensity and something that's almost otherworldly in his voice. You hear his voice and it conjures up some kind of image in your mind."

It's a phenomenon that *Rolling Stone* critic Ralph J. Gleason once identified as the "yarrrrragh," a Gaelic word that refers to that rare quality that some voices have, an edge, an ability to say something about the human condition that goes far beyond merely singing the right lyrics and hitting the right notes. Semiologist Roland Bartles called it "the grain of the voice." Either you have it or you don't. Robert Johnson had it, Hank Williams had it; these days, it's people like the Screaming Trees' Mark Lanegan and Kurt Cobain.

But each member brought something to the band. While Kurt's contributions are perhaps more obvious, Chris was for a long time the sole liaison between the band and the press, his business sense is indispensable and early on, his outspoken political sensibility helped to lend the band critical weight. Chris's onstage chemistry with Kurt is indefinable but clear. And not to be overlooked is his steadfast support of Kurt over the years in pursuing his musical vision.

Dave's contribution to the band has largely been unsung. His powerful drumming propelled the band to a whole new plane, visually as well as musically. Try to imagine "Come as You Are" without the inspired cymbal bashing near the end that simply sends the track through the roof, the mighty snare rolls that machine-gun the band into the chorus of "In Bloom." Although Dave is a merciless basher, his parts are also distinctly musical—it wouldn't be difficult to figure out what song he was playing even without the rest of the music. His personal contribution is also essential. "Pretty much under every circumstance, David's the one who's rock-solid the whole time," says Alex Macleod. "He's a good influence on both of them."

"They've got it all, basically—great drummer, great singer, great image, great songs, great sense of the media, great live band," says Danny Goldberg. "It all kind of worked. They excelled in a half-dozen areas."

The album's impact was such that nowadays, industry pundits talk about the "post-Nirvana music business." One impact, as Matt Lukin puts it, is that after Nirvana, "The underground isn't as underground as it used to be."

Nirvana's success also demonstrated to the music business the snowballing power of the indie network. Nirvana could not have broken without all the years of hard work by labels like SST, Twin/Tone, and Touch & Go, as well as bands like Sonic Youth, Black Flag, the Minutemen, the Replacements, and R.E.M., all of whom built a system by which kids could catch the indie buzz—outside of the influence of the major labels.

Consequently, labels began paying more attention to bands with a following—i.e., bands that people actually *liked*—rather than creating one out of promotional dollars. They ceded some—though hardly all—of the control of what gets signed and promoted to a grass-roots level. As regional music scenes gained power, they began to decentralize the music business.

It shifted a fair amount of power from the corporate rock factions at the major labels to the people who had been following the indie rock scene. "There's no question that there's fifteen or twenty A&R people who can sign acts now who couldn't do that two years ago," says Goldberg. Those people began catching the next plane to Seattle and pretty soon any musician from the area with long hair and a flannel shirt could get signed for $350,000. At one point in early 1992, Northwest bands were getting signed at the incredible rate of one a week. The industry will be working all the bands that the new wave of A&R people is signing for years to come.

Post-Nirvana, some hotly pursued alternative bands commanded a much higher advance than before. And since the labels didn't quite understand their music or their milieu, the bands were granted complete creative control.

As boomers get older, they buy fewer records. *Nevermind* heralded this changing of the music consumer guard. The major labels knew they had to begin addressing this emerging market. And that market suddenly became polarized between the people who would buy Def Leppard records, for instance, and those who wouldn't.

Mainstream radio got taught a lesson because a record caught on without it. And everyone knew it wasn't a fluke because *Nevermind* was an undeniably great record. And there was an army of like-minded bands right behind Nirvana.

By making a great album within the confines of a major label superstructure, keeping their integrity while acknowledging mainstream sonic tastes, Nirvana made a point. Perhaps the ultimate message of the success of *Nevermind* was that even one little band (or person) can make big changes in a large and seemingly immovable institution.

CHAPTER ELEVEN

Kurt and Courtney had done heroin together in Amsterdam for two days around Thanksgiving of 1991. "It was *my* idea," says Kurt. "*I* was the one that instigated it. But I didn't really know how to get it, so Courtney was the one who would be able to somehow get it. She would be the one who would take me to the place where we might have a chance of being able to find it. We only did it twice on the whole tour." They found a guy on the street who took them to the city's infamous red light district, where they scored. Later, they did some more in London.

Kurt's stomach pain had been driving him insane on the European tour, making him chronically irritable and antisocial. "A lot of the hatred would surface because I was in such a fucked-up mental state," he says. "I was so angry with my body that I couldn't deal with anyone socially. I was just totally neurotic because I was in pain all the time. People had no idea I was in pain and I couldn't complain about it twenty-four hours a day."

He says the pain made him suicidal, so he simply chose his poison. "I just decided I wanted to have a life," he says. "If I'm going to kill myself, I'm going to kill myself for a reason instead of some stupid stomach problem. So I decided to take everything in excess all at once."

In early December, when Kurt returned to Seattle after the tour and Courtney was still in Europe with Hole, he began hanging out with a recovering addict. He soon sweet-talked her into getting him heroin. At first, she'd cop for him only when she felt like it, but soon she was getting heroin for him every day.

Soon, Kurt and his supplier got a scare. "I *didn't* OD," he maintains. "She *thought* that I was OD'ing and so she started giving me mouth to mouth but I had just stood up too fast and fell down. She was giving me mouth to mouth and said I was turning blue but I wasn't out for very long at all—maybe half a minute. It was just kind of scary to her. She overexaggerated on it."

Kurt eventually met the dealer and scored on his own. "I was determined to get a habit," he says. "I *wanted* to. It was *my* choice. I said, 'This is the only thing that's saving me from blowing my head off right now. I've been to ten doctors and nothing they can do about it. I've got to do something to stop this pain.'" He also admits there was the simple pleasure of getting high, but that wasn't the point.

"It started with three days in a row of doing heroin and I don't have a stomach pain," he says. "That was such a relief. I decided, 'Fuck, I'm going to do this for a whole year. I'll eventually stop. I can't do it forever because I'll fucking die.' I don't regret it at all because it was such a relief from not having stomach pain every day. My mental state just went totally up. I healed myself." Except for a long and profound relapse when he detoxed, the mysterious stomach pain has largely disappeared.

It was probably two weeks or so, but Kurt has little idea how long he was in Seattle or where he stayed before going down to L.A. "God, I don't even know," he says. "I wasn't there for very long. Jesus, where did I sleep?"

When Courtney came home to Los Angeles from her tour with Hole later in December, Kurt called and said, "Let's live together."

They briefly lived in an apartment Courtney shared with Hole guitarist Eric Erlandson and another friend until it was made apparent that they weren't welcome because of their drug use.

They bounced from hotel to hotel, doing what Courtney calls "bad Mexican L.A. heroin." Kurt would do the lion's share of the drugs. Courtney never quite got the hang of injecting drugs, so Kurt would often shoot her up "whenever she'd beg me hard enough." She already had a dark little scar on the inside of her elbow from when other people had botched injections.

What were those weeks like? "I don't really remember," Kurt replies, even though it's only a little over a year later. "I just remember us both being total slobs."

Heroin is a very seductive drug. It feels very relaxing, very comfortable. At low doses, it can make even the shyest user very social; high doses produce the phenomenon of "nodding out," when the user seems to fall asleep, even in mid-sentence. The high can last for ten hours, but the more you do, the less it lasts. It's a very insidious drug—it takes a while to become addicted, but once that happens, it suddenly becomes very *un*comfortable to stop doing it. And then the cravings start. After a while, it becomes very hard to think clearly and to monitor and control the emotions, and often, the user isn't even aware that this is happening.

Just after Christmas, the band set off on a brief tour with Pearl Jam and the Red Hot Chili Peppers, who headlined. No one was happy about Nirvana playing second fiddle to the Peppers, but they had already committed to it during the chaos of the American tour. At any rate, Nirvana stole the show. For one thing, their album was number six with a bullet. And they had outstanding material—songs like "Lithium," "Teen Spirit" and "In Bloom." The best the Chili Peppers could muster was a cover of Stevie Wonder's "Higher Ground." Pearl Jam was just getting its act together.

The Chili Peppers tour is when Chris finally admitted to himself that Kurt was heavily into heroin. "He looked like shit," Chris says. "He looked like a ghoul." Chris knew he couldn't do anything about it. "I just figured it's his fucking trip, it's his life, he can do whatever he wants," he says. "You can't change anybody or preach some kind of morals or anything. What am I going to do? Nothing. So I just do my own thing."

Everyone assumed that Courtney had gotten Kurt to do heroin. "Everybody was blaming *her*," says Shelli. "She was the big scapegoat. If he wouldn't have hooked up with her, he would have hooked up with somebody else and done heroin. That's just the fact of the matter. It was easy to blame her at first—and looking back, that's what everybody did. They still do it. Just because she's loud and out-spoken and has her own point of view..."

Blaming Courtney fit into the convenient stereotype of the domineering bitch and the henpecked wimp. For one thing, it's nearly inconceivable that someone could simply talk someone else into doing heroin—people who do heroin *want* to do it. And the fact is, Kurt had been doing heroin off and on for years by then; Courtney hadn't done it in three years. "[It's] such a fucking typical sexist stupid thing to say, so classic," Kurt says. "Man, when I got off the European tour, I went out of my *way* to get drugs every fucking day. On my own."

Chris was also struggling with his own demons. After a New Year's Eve show at the Cow Palace in San Francisco, he drunkenly hit his head on a low-slung heater element in a backstage passageway. He resolved to go on the wagon for as long as he could.

The first press to acknowledge the heroin rumors was a January profile in *BAM* magazine which claimed that Kurt was "nodding off in mid-sentence," adding that "the pinned pupils, sunken cheeks, and scabbed, sallow skin suggest something more serious than fatigue." Soon, an item in the industry tip sheet *Hits* was hinting that Kurt was "slam-dancing with Mr. Brownstone," Guns n' Roses slang for doing heroin. The tidbit ran in a column written by Lonn Friend, the *Rip* magazine editor that Kurt had snubbed not so long before.

"By the end, it started to really suck because I started to get really paranoid because there were things being written about me being a heroin addict," Kurt says. "I just started getting paranoid that cops were going to bust into our house or I'd get pulled over and they'd recognize me, find my track marks and take me to jail. The biggest fear was detoxing cold turkey. I knew I'd probably die if that happened, because the cops wouldn't give a fuck—they wouldn't put me in a hospital, they'd just let me go cold turkey and I'd die in jail. So that was kind of scary. In the morning, I'd drive real cautiously to the drug dealer's house."

A lot of people around them struggled to understand why Kurt and Courtney were doing this to themselves. "It's like this," says Courtney. "'Hey, you know what? I just sold a million fuckin' records and I got a million bucks and I'm going to share it with you and let's get high!'"

Heroin still held an allure as a staple of rock culture. "That's the drug that makes you sleepy and happy," says Courtney. "That's the drug you do if you're in a fuckin' four-star hotel and you can order all the goddamn room service that you want and you can just lay in bed and drool all over yourself because you've got a million bucks in the bank. That's the drug you want to do if you want to be a kid forever."

The seductive combination of being head over heels in love and basking in the warm, embryonic comfort of heroin—away from the strains and responsibilities of being an internationally recognized rock star—must have been overpowering. "It was a love thing," Courtney says. "It was a drug/love thing. I met this person that's perfect for me, I'm in love. Even though it's not my million bucks, so what. Whatever. He's saying you can have it, so whatever, I'll just have his million bucks and let's just do some drugs. That's what it was about." If one of the reasons Kurt did heroin was in a misguided attempt to cope with his fame, perhaps Courtney used heroin to deal with Kurt's fame as well.

So there *was* an element of just wanting to get high. "There might have been in *her* eyes," Kurt says, who still maintains that he basically did heroin for its analgesic properties.

They went up to Seattle for a while, then spent a week in San Francisco, oblivious to the fact that Kurt's band was the hottest, most talked-about group on the planet.

In the midst of all this, the unthinkable happened. *Nevermind* hit #1 on the Billboard album charts the week of January 11, 1992, topping U2, Guns n' Roses and Garth Brooks, and even pushing Michael Jackson off the top spot. Besides hitting #1 in the United States, *Nevermind* also topped the charts in Belgium, France, Ireland, Israel, Spain, Sweden, and Canada, and went Top 3 in virtually every other major market in the world except for Italy, Japan, and oddly enough, the U.K.(although it did stay in the British Top 25 for months).

Meanwhile, the band was being wooed by Guns n' Roses and Metallica to appear on their joint U.S. tour that summer. Despite some very high-level pressure, Kurt and the band refused. They'd never be caught dead playing with Guns n' Roses.

Then the band went to New York to tape a live set for MTV and to play "Saturday Night Live" on January 11. When the car that had turned up at their hotel in Seattle turned out to be a limousine, Kurt and Courtney sent it back and asked for a more modest car. There were no smaller cars available, so the livery company sent another

The MTV taping, January 10, 1992. (Mark Kates)

limousine. When all was said and done, Kurt and Courtney missed their flight.

By then, Kurt and Courtney had been doing heroin long enough to begin to get addicted.

"I remember walking into their hotel room and for the first time, really realizing that these two are fucked *up*," says Dave. "They were just nodding out in bed, just wasted. It was disgusting and gross. It doesn't make me angry at *them*, it makes me angry that they would be so pathetic as to do something like that. I think it's pathetic for anyone to do something to make themselves that functionless and a drooling fucking baby. It's like 'Hey, let's do a drug that knocks us out and makes us look stupid.' It's stupid and gross and pathetic for anyone to take it to that point."

("I went up to his room and Kurt came to the door in his underwear and Courtney, all I saw was a little piece of hair sticking out from underneath the covers," says Wendy. "There was like five deli trays, room carts with old food. And I said, 'Kurt, why don't you get a maid in here?' And Courtney says, 'He can't. They steal his underwear.'")

Although Kurt had been doing heroin for over a month, even his closest associates hadn't noticed until now. "I didn't realize that he was getting fucked up until "Saturday Night Live" just because I'm stupid and I just couldn't pick out something like that," Dave admits. "I'm naive and didn't want to believe it."

There was at least one thing to be grateful about. "Thank God those two didn't do cocaine," says Dave, "because they'd be the biggest fucking assholes in the world."

It wasn't as if they were violent or irrational or any sloppier than they usually were. "Kurt was mostly just sleepy," says soundman Craig Montgomery. "They just seemed to be in a fog. They seemed not to care about much of anything, including their friends. That's the way it felt sometimes. They were in their own little world. And I'm sure they felt like the whole world was against them, too."

The day of their "Saturday Night Live" appearance, the band did a now infamous shoot with photographer Michael Lavine. Exhausted and having tanked up just beforehand, Kurt nodded out a couple of times in front of the camera. "I just blocked it out," says Chris. "I didn't give a shit."

Of the shoot, Kurt remembers "Dead silence. Dirty looks and dead silence. [Chris and Dave] weren't the type to confront anyone about anything. They were so passive-aggressive that they would rather give off bad vibes than talk about anything. I mean, what are they supposed to do? They're not going to be able to tell me to stop. So I didn't really care. Obviously to them it was like practicing witchcraft or something. They didn't know anything about it so they thought that any second I was going to die."

Lavine was terribly worried, too. "I asked him, 'Why are you doing this?' He said, 'It's the only thing that helps my stomach pain,'" says Lavine. "I didn't have enough guts to say 'Kurt, that's a bunch of shit.'"

That night, the band played "Teen Spirit" and later, "Territorial Pissings," with the band trashing their instruments for a finale. Kurt took the opportunity to give some national exposure to an old favorite and wore a Flipper T-shirt he'd made at the Lavine shoot. During the closing credits, Chris kissed both Kurt and Dave flat on the mouth, just to annoy the homophobic rednecks back home, and all the other homophobes in their vast new audience. With twenty-five million people looking on, there was a lot of *bourgeoisie* to shock.

The next day, Kurt and Courtney did another shoot with Michael Lavine for a cover story in *Sassy* magazine, *the* monthly bible of hip teen girls (and certain vampiric adults). "They were totally in love," says Lavine. "You couldn't separate them. They *are* in love—it's not

Kurt nodding out at the Lavine session. (© Michael Lavine)

like this fake thing. They have a genuine chemistry toward each other."

The April issue of *Sassy* put a kissing Kurt and Courtney on the cover. "Ain't Love Grand?" read the cover line. Without seeming to know quite what she was saying, writer Christina Kelly observed, "It's looking very *Sid and Nancy*."

Kurt brought a friend along on their trip to New York who would go out and score for them and then bring the heroin back to the hotel. Kurt gradually realized that the friend was a junkie, too, and was ripping them off. So once, he went down to Manhattan's notorious Alphabet City himself and bought some heroin on the street while Courtney waited in a nearby Indian restaurant. "People just wait in a line," Kurt says. "Lawyers, business people in three-piece suits, junkies, low-lifes, all different kinds of people."

Meanwhile, his hopes raised, Don Cobain had been trying to contact Kurt again ever since Kurt called him just before recording *Nevermind*. "I don't know how many million times I tried to get ahold of him," says Don. "I called Geffen Records and Gold Mountain Management in Los Angeles, I called Sub Pop Records, I sent telegrams to "Saturday Night Live," I sent letters to him and all the places where he'd been, tried to a get ahold through his mom..." But he never heard back.

The rock and roll trail is littered with heroin fatalities: Sid Vicious, Tim Buckley, Janis Joplin, Andrew Wood of Mother Love Bone, the Red Hot Chili Peppers' Hillel Slovak, and more recently, Stefanie Sargent of the Seattle band Seven Year Bitch, who OD'd in 1992. "Those people did every drug in the book all at once," Kurt scoffs. "They get drunk and then they get high and then they die. I never drank—I learned that from junkies. You just don't mix alcohol and heroin at all or you'll die. It cuts down on respiratory twice as much. You pass out when you're drunk and you wake up and get high and there's no way you're going to survive that. Everyone I know of who's OD'd has gotten drunk. And it's been late at night, too."

Returning from New York, Kurt and Courtney moved into a modest apartment on Spaulding Avenue in the Fairfax district of Los Angeles. Their day-to-day existence was fairly routine. "I just got up and got drugs and listened to music and painted and played guitar," Kurt says. "That's about it. Watched TV. It was recuperation. I'd been on tour for seven months. I needed to do that."

"We went through a lot of blankets because you keep dropping your cigarette—it's pretty gross," Courtney says. "I threw all those blankets out."

Every morning, Kurt would drive to the home of one of their two drug dealers. To them, Kurt was just another customer. "They didn't care if I was a rock star or not," says Kurt. "They'd dealt to rock stars before." Kurt doesn't know how much he was doing in grams, but he knows he had a hundred-dollar-a-day habit.

Courtney had a very mild habit. "When I gave her drugs, I would do this much," Kurt says, indicating a large amount," and I would give her that much," indicating a very small amount. "I was real selfish," he admits. "She probably had a twenty-dollar habit, if that. It was more psychological than it was physical."

Kurt says he never OD'd, although he did once get a case of "cotton fever," which happens when a stray strand of cotton gets into the needle and is then injected into the vein, producing an extremely high fever and an excruciating headache. Kurt went to the hospital and was given Benadryl, an over-the-counter antihistamine, which cured him. The rumor was that he had overdosed.

They grew paranoid. In the middle of the night, Courtney would think she heard an intruder and Kurt would take out the handgun that Dylan Carlson had given him and check it out. No one was ever there.

"I'm not against guns at all," Kurt says. "I own one. I believe in them for protection. I'm not as much of a hippie as some people would want me to be. I could blow somebody away easily, no problem, if I had to protect myself or my family. I actually kind of like them now. I'm thinking about buying another one."

Still, most people wouldn't have figured Kurt "And I swear that I don't have a gun" Cobain to be the proud owner of a firearm. "I wouldn't, either," Kurt says. "They're absolute evil things. I shot a gun with Dylan about a year ago. We went down to Aberdeen and went out in the woods and shot this gun and it was just such a reminder of how brutal they are, how much damage they can do to a person. It's a necessary thing—it's a defense weapon."

Looming ahead was a tour that went from California to Oregon to Australia, New Zealand, Japan, and Hawaii that was scheduled to kick off on January 24.

Courtney found out she was pregnant sometime around "Saturday Night Live"—whether before or after is unclear. Kurt and Courtney hadn't been using birth control, even though Courtney was mainlining heroin. Courtney calls that "a morality issue" and insists that she knew she'd quit if she discovered she was pregnant. "I was an idiot —what can I say?" she says now. "But I'm not immoral."

They had wanted to have a baby, but sometime in 1993, and certainly after they had finished with their dalliance with heroin. In the meantime, they thought maybe they'd get a little capuchin monkey. When they found out Courtney was pregnant, Kurt was ready to insist on an abortion because he assumed, like everyone else, that the baby would be born retarded or deformed. Courtney never even considered it. "We should breed," she thought. "It's better than buying a monkey."

They consulted a teratogenic (birth defects) specialist who informed them that heroin use, especially if confined to the first trimester, was virtually harmless to the fetus if the mother's withdrawal wasn't too traumatic (there is a slight chance that the child may experience mild learning disabilities later on in life, however).

Amazing but true. "But tell that to a middle American housewife," says Kurt. "You can't expect anyone to believe it."

"We knew it really wasn't the best of times to have a child," Kurt says, "but we were just determined to have one. We figured we may as well do it now. It definitely would have been better on Courtney's part if she would have waited and put out her record a little while ago but, I don't know, I don't regret it now. Frances wouldn't be Frances if we had her later."

"I thought [having the baby] would probably be a good thing," says Danny Goldberg, "but I was also worried about the roller coaster that it puts you on, and when you combine *that* roller coaster with the roller coaster of massive success, you're dealing with one of the most complicated, stressful things that a human being can go through."

Kurt began to see the light at the end of his addiction. "I'm sure the awareness the baby was coming was a major factor," says Goldberg. "Having a kid is a big deal—it's one of the biggest things that happens to you. It's corny, but all different kinds of people, including punk rockers, do react that way."

"I didn't have a baby to stop doing drugs," says Courtney, "but I knew that I would continue to do drugs and my career would go to fucking hell and I wouldn't give a shit and I'd be one of those junkies that I've seen at N.A. meetings with track marks on their hands and neck."

"If I've ever seen Satan, that's it, because it's so insidious," says Courtney. "It breaks you down morally. It's very insidious. You have this angel that's really beautiful, it's not like this guy with horns, it's this beautiful angel who's promising you another heaven."

They entered the strange world of chemical dependency medicine. Various doctors competed for their business, as if they were another celebrity trophy to put on their wall. It was just like a bidding war.

Kurt knew he had to detox for the tour, so he and Courtney decided to detox together. A doctor checked them into a Holiday Inn and prescribed them various drugs to tide them through the three-day withdrawal period. Periodically, trusty Alex Macleod would stop by and make sure they were all right.

Kurt says detoxing was easy. "It wasn't a heavy drug addiction at all," Kurt says. "I'd only been doing it for a month straight and I'd just started to get addicted, probably that week that I got off of them. Withdrawals were nothing. I just slept for three days and woke up."

"I thought, 'Gee, if this is what detoxing is like, I could do this the rest of my life.' But once I got into a four-hundred-dollar habit and I detoxed off of that, it was a different story. A very different story."

But Courtney has a different take. "That was a sick scene because you get diarrhea and lots of sleeping pills and it was just vomiting," she says. "That was gross. That was a sick scene if ever there was a sick scene." As Kurt admits, "The bathroom didn't smell very good."

By the time of the "Come as You Are" video shoot, Chris and Dave hadn't seen Kurt since "Saturday Night Live." They had heard secondhand that Kurt was going through detox. In Dave's words, "It was not something to be talked about." It was just two days before they were to leave for Australia.

According to Dave, Kurt looked "Bad. Gray. He just looked sad." And Kurt wasn't even using by that time. "That's why he looked so sad," says Dave. "Because he wasn't."

"I couldn't understand," Dave says. "If something like that is destroying somebody... I guess I don't understand addiction. Along with addiction comes denial or lies or deceit or paranoia, things that I just didn't understand. I understand them now a little better, but at the time, I didn't understand addiction and so I just thought, 'What the fuck are you thinking? Why are you doing this?'"

After the unpleasant experience with "Teen Spirit" video director Sam Bayer, Kurt had gone hunting for a new director and discovered Kevin Kerslake, who had done clips for Iggy Pop, Mazzy Star, Soul Asylum, and Sonic Youth. Kerslake's impressionistic, ethereal style didn't always suit the major labels, but Kurt now had the clout to choose any director within reason. So Kerslake it was.

Unable to come up with few visual ideas beyond playing off the album cover and including "a lot of purples and reds," Kurt let Kerslake conceptualize the clip. "I didn't care at that point," Kurt says.

The follow-up to the "Teen Spirit" video was crucial—would they go with a similar approach or would they try to redefine themselves?

Besides the color scheme, the only other thing Kurt wanted was for the band's faces to be obscured. That breaks an unspoken cardinal rule of video, but once again Kurt had the clout to get away with it. With Kurt's, Chris's, and Dave's faces obscured by running water, video effects, or shadows, the "Come as You Are" video pulled off the tricky feat of promoting a song without contributing to the overexposure of the band; Nirvana was seen and not seen. And the clip cemented their fame by exploiting the fact that everyone knew who it was anyway.

It was the beginning of a long series of collaborations with

Kerslake. "It turned out fine, it turned out great," Kurt says. "We finally found someone that shared the same vision as we do."

Kerslake came up with the idea of using projections of the band members in the background of many of the shots. They shot most of that footage in a park in the Hollywood Hills a few days before the main shoot. Kerslake encouraged the guys to "abuse the camera" and Kurt in particular was more than willing to comply.

The shoot went smoothly, but Kurt was clearly having a bad time of it. "It was strange because here's Chris and I running around this field having a great time, it's a sunny day," says Dave, "and Kurt just wasn't feeling too good." "I was on detox pills," Kurt explains, "so I wasn't very animated." Still, Kurt was able to swing on a chandelier for an hour, taking rests on a ladder between takes.

When Kerslake came back to the band with his rough cut, Kurt, Chris, and Dave had surprisingly good suggestions. "They were all valid comments—artistically, they've all got really good taste, which is pretty rare for musicians," Kerslake says. "A lot of musicians hole themselves up in their room with their guitar and they don't have any feelers out to all the other aesthetic aspects of what is asked of them in this day and age. All the references that they talked about were revered artists, painters, filmmakers, stuff like that, so it was grounded in some artistic savvy."

One of their suggestions was to cut out the more goofy footage shot for the projections, in favor of more ethereal stuff. "That was the recoil from 'Teen Spirit,'" Kerslake says. The video aired in March and was a huge success, if not quite as successful as "Teen Spirit."

People in the band's inner circle began wondering if going on tour at that point was the right thing to do. "Everybody knew that it wasn't," says Dave. "Kurt knew that it wasn't, I knew that it wasn't, Chris knew that it wasn't. Maybe we didn't know within the first two days of the tour, but after a week and a half, sure, everybody knew it wasn't. Shows were all right, we got through the set every night. But if Kurt wants something, he'll do anything to get it."

"It took a lot of courage for him to do that tour," Dave adds. "He felt like shit, looked like shit, but he got over it. He worked it out."

During the Australian tour, Kurt's stomach problem flared up worse than it had in years. The first few days, Kurt felt fine. Then suddenly, he was in intense pain. He was vomiting constantly and couldn't eat. He would call up Courtney, crying from the pain. At one point, he very nearly took the next plane home.

One day, Kurt says he was sitting on the steps of a hotel, wincing with pain, and Shelli walked up to him and said, "Kurt, I just hate to

Kurt during the Australian tour. (© Neil Wallace)

see you doing this to yourself. I can't stand to see you hurting your body like this."

"I just wanted to fucking punch her in the face because, just like everyone else, she just assumed that I was doing drugs," he says. "I was thinking, 'You fucking people have no clue how much pain I'm in all the time. It's from a natural thing that's in my body.' I couldn't believe it. I'll never forget those words because it just defined everyone's attitude toward me. Every time that I wasn't even doing drugs, they suspected that I was. They still do."

Tour manager Alex Macleod worried about Kurt, too. "I didn't like what I was seeing in someone I had so much respect and love for," says Macleod. "I was really scared, more than anything else, constantly. Scared of what he was going to do, who he was going to hook up with. It was kind of strange."

When Kurt suffered a particularly severe stomach pain attack, Macleod took him to a hospital emergency room, but not before mistakenly informing the doctors that Kurt was still detoxing from heroin. While he was on the examination table, Kurt says he heard one doctor snicker and say to another, "Oh, he's just a junkie, he's still coming off of drugs." Disgusted, Kurt walked out of the hospital and simply toughed out the pain.

He finally went to a "rock doctor" who had a picture of himself with the Rolling Stones on his office wall. Kurt told the doctor his stomach history and the doctor replied, "I know what your problem is," having been filled in by Macleod beforehand. "I think I'm going to get some kind of stomach medicine and the doctor just assumes that I'd just recently gotten off of heroin and I'm going through detox and I'm on tour," says Kurt, "so I'd better do what Keith Richards would have done and take methadone. It's called Physeptone in Australia, so I thought they were just stomach pills."

The Physeptone miraculously took away the stomach pain completely. Kurt couldn't wait to tell his doctor about these great new pills.

On February 1, after dipping to #4 for a couple of weeks, *Nevermind* again hit #1.

Kurt giving it some attitude during Mark Seliger's **Rolling Stone** photo shoot in Australia. P.S.—wrong finger. (© Mark Seliger)

Kurt onstage in Australia. (© Mark Seliger)

They finished the tour, then played a show in Auckland, New Zealand, then off to Singapore for a day of press. When they arrived at the Singapore airport, there was a waiting mob of about two hundred and fifty teenaged fans who waved "Welcome to Singapore" banners and chased after the band and grabbed at their hair. It turned out that this was standard practice in Singapore. The label had even printed an announcement of their arrival—including flight number and arrival time—in the newspaper and handed out the banners.

Then it was on to Japan, where Courtney joined the tour, and then Hawaii. By that time, Kurt was hooked on opiates again—without, he claims, even realizing it until he called his doctor and discovered what he was taking.

Kurt and Courtney got married in Waikiki, Hawaii, on February 24, 1992. At Courtney's insistence, the couple had already worked out a prenuptial agreement. "I didn't want Kurt running away with all my money," Courtney jokes (presumably).

Dave and his friend and drum tech Barrett Jones had both brought girlfriends to Hawaii, but Kurt and Courtney didn't want them there. "They all came from Seattle and they were all going to come back and say 'We were at Kurt and Courtney's wedding!' and lie about things," says Courtney. Besides, Kurt thought he might cry at the ceremony and wanted it to be as private and small as possible.

"Shelli and Chris were being really shitty to us and they thought I was doing all these drugs and I'm in Japan—how could I be doing any drugs?" says Courtney (then again, Kurt did have some Physeptone). Kurt had a crew member summon Chris up to his hotel room, where Kurt informed Chris that he didn't want anyone at the wedding who didn't want them to get married—meaning Shelli. Chris said if his wife wasn't going, he wasn't going either. "I don't regret it, I don't take it back one bit," says Courtney. "I can't see it happening with Shelli there at that point in time."

"It was *our* choice," Shelli insists. "It was weird because I knew what was going on and I knew that she was pregnant and I had a real objection to her doing drugs while she was pregnant," she says, then catches herself and adds, "Maybe at that point, maybe she was, maybe she wasn't. I don't know, but we all *assumed*. I didn't want to go because I knew if she was pregnant and doing drugs, I didn't agree with it and I didn't agree with Kurt being so fucked up all the time and I just decided I wasn't going to go." She says somebody talked her into going for the sake of band harmony. "Then we ended up not going because they didn't want me to go, which hurt my feelings," Shelli says. "Although things had gotten to a really bad point, I was still thinking that Kurt and I were still friends and that things could be worked out."

By the time they got to Hawaii, Kurt had run out of Physeptone and convinced a friend to bring him some heroin so he wouldn't start detoxing while he was there. Kurt was even high on heroin at his own wedding. "I wasn't *very* high, though," he explains. "I just did a little teeny bit just so I didn't get sick."

Present at the ceremony, on a cliff overlooking a beach, were Dave, Alex Macleod, soundman Ian Beveridge, Dylan Carlson and his girlfriend, and Nirvana guitar tech Nick Close. The bride wore an antique lace dress that once belonged to Frances Farmer and the groom wore green flannel pajamas. Everyone wore leis. A nondenominational female minister that Courtney found through the Hawaiian wedding bureau performed the brief ceremony. Kurt did cry, Courtney didn't. "It was very transcendent," says Courtney. "It was like being on acid. It was great. It was very much different than just being boyfriend and girlfriend. It's a good thing, I'm glad we did it."

Afterward, they got very depressed over the Chris and Shelli thing.

And Shelli and Chris got depressed over the Kurt and Courtney thing. "Kurt alienated us, but we alienated him, too," Shelli says, "just by not being up front. Everybody was talking behind their backs. It was getting nasty and it wasn't fair. It's easy to gossip and it's easy when you have to spend every day with people and she was pregnant, I think, at that point and she wasn't being nice anymore and Kurt was not being nice anymore. The lines were being drawn and it was really stupid and there was no reason why it should have been like that. Everybody was just, 'You're just a bunch of drug addicts.' You alienate people by doing that."

Later, when the band was playing in Argentina in October of 1992, Courtney and Shelli finally talked it over. "I told her, 'Look, I never hated you,'" says Shelli. "She *thought* I hated her, so she treated me like 'you hate me, so I don't like you, either.' Then I started not liking her. It was a big misunderstanding."

Kurt was back on methadone for the *Rolling Stone* interview with this writer a day after he returned to the Spaulding apartment. He looked terrible and spoke even more quietly than usual. For most of the interview, he stayed under the bed covers in his pajamas, even though it was a particularly balmy L.A. evening. His complexion was bad, he could barely sit up in bed, and he said he'd been throwing up all day. His pupils weren't pinned, but it was pretty obvious that the guy had a monkey on his back.

We talked about the heroin rumors and he flatly denied they were true. "I had a responsibility," Kurt says now. "I had a responsibility to the kids to not let on that I did drugs."

Even though he was bedridden, Kurt was ecstatic about his life. He was very much in love. "It's like Evian water and battery acid," Kurt said of his relationship with Courtney in the *Rolling Stone* story. And when you mix the two, according to Kurt, "You get love."

Rolling Stone had asked for an interview for a cover story and Kurt agreed, even though he's no fan of the magazine. "Every time I've ever picked up a *Rolling Stone*," he says, "I've gotten so disgusted and filled with so much rage that I ended up ripping it up. It's the epitome of yuppiedom. It's the perfect example of everything I hate. It's disgusting." Later, he got annoyed that the magazine

The cover shot **Rolling Stone** didn't use. (© Mark Seliger)

pinched the "Smells Like Teen Spirit" tag for a cover piece on the execrable television series, "Beverly Hills 90210."

Kurt claims he later forgot that he agreed to the story (plausible, considering his chemical state at the time). One morning during the Australian tour, he was awakened and told it was time for the *Rolling Stone* shoot. At first, Kurt refused, but then everyone from band members to the road crew urged him to go through with it. Then he began to try to think of something clever to put on a T-shirt that would keep the photo from being used. He hastily came up with "Corporate magazines still suck," a paraphrase of SST Records' slogan "Corporate rock still sucks." "It was a stupid little statement to *Rolling Stone*," Kurt says, "saying that you're not a hip magazine now just because you have a supposedly hip band on your cover.

"It wasn't necessarily to whatever his name is [*Rolling Stone* publisher Jann Wenner], like 'okay, let's see if you can put *this* on your cover.' I wasn't trying to make any kind of bold statement—it was just a joke. I didn't even really think about it. It was a decision made ten minutes before we did the photo shoot. It wasn't like I sat up all night and thought 'What should I write?' The funniest reaction to that is people taking it so literally—like I hate anything corporate, yet I'm on a corporate label. No shit. Obviously, I would wish that people would give me the benefit of the doubt to realize that I'm smart enough to understand that."

Actually, rock's magazine of record might have taken far more offense at another T-shirt Kurt had prepared just for the occasion. It portrayed a punk rock duck with the inscription "Kill the Grateful Dead."

For all his iconoclasm, Kurt was well on his way to becoming the cliché of the wasted rocker. The success of *Nevermind* presented several difficult situations for Kurt. For one thing, a guy who loathed mainstream rock was now de facto *making* mainstream rock.

And a shy and reclusive man had gone from total obscurity to unwanted worldwide fame in three years. "Famous is the last thing I wanted to be," Kurt says. As the figurehead of the band, the brunt of the media spotlight shone on Kurt—his personal life and even his psyche were being relentlessly dissected in the media. The cover line on the *Rolling Stone* cover story read "Inside the heart and mind of Kurt Cobain."

Kurt openly resented his fame and most of his audience took that as a slap in the face. In turn, Kurt began to resent the prying of the press and his audience even more. "The classic reaction to someone who complains they're in the limelight is 'You made your bed, now you have to sleep in it. You're public domain now and everyone has a right to know everything about you,'" he says. "No one has any right to know anything about my personal life. If they want to know about the music and how I try to write it, then that's fine. Of course, it ties in with my personal life, but not as much as everyone thinks. I just always felt violated and I don't agree with people who say they have a right to know. I have a right to try to change that perception. I have a right to try to change people's way of thinking about celebrities. It *should* be changed. It *should* be different. They should be treated as human beings and their privacy should be respected."

Meanwhile, *Nevermind* was in the Top 3, and it remained there until mid-April.

At the apartment on North Spaulding, Kurt did his best to avoid tempting Courtney by shooting in a locked closet in an extra room down the hallway where he kept his heroin and his needles and his spoons and his rubbing alcohol. "I knew I was tempting her all the time," says Kurt. "I was high all the time. I just had to keep doing it. I didn't have it out of my system. I knew if I quit then, I'd end up doing it again for at least the next couple of years all the time. I figured I'd just burn myself out of it because I hadn't experienced the full junkie feeling yet. I was still healthy."

"I didn't find myself just sitting in the house and nodding off and sleeping," Kurt says. "I was always doing something artistic. I got a lot of paintings done and wrote a lot of songs.

"It was a lot less turbulent than everyone thinks," says Kurt. "It was pretty boring."

Artistically, it was a fertile time for Kurt—he painted a lot and wrote many of the songs which appeared on *In Utero*. "I did all my best songs on heroin this year," he says. But he was falling out of touch with the band and Gold Mountain and he and Courtney were quickly falling into sweet oblivion. "Those guys went off into their own world and they were kind of thought of as vampires because they'd be gone and sleep all day," says Chris.

They barely spoke for five months, even at rehearsals.

But Chris was very upset about what was happening to his old friend. He would rant at Dave or Shelli, "Kurt's a fucking junkie asshole and I hate him!" Chris was angry with Kurt, he says, "Probably because I felt like he left me. I was really concerned and worried about him and there was nothing I could do about it. I was just taking my anger out on him.

"It was hard to understand," says Chris. "I couldn't get over the whole hurdle of heroin."

Part of the problem was that as usual, Chris didn't confront the problem with Kurt directly. "We've never really communicated very well when there's been a problem between us," Kurt says. "We never talk about it, we just let it pass. We've never confronted one another about things that piss each other off. During the time that I was doing drugs, I did notice that people weren't calling as much but I also made it clear to everyone that I wanted to take a break. I remember Dave called up one day real hostile and asking me if I wanted to even be in the band anymore because we were getting pressure from everyone to go on tour and I decided I didn't want to be on tour this year because I needed a break."

"I don't know how much heroin Kurt was doing because I never saw him," Chris says. "I never saw Kurt fucked up on heroin. I never went to his house. I saw him high a few times, but never really a fuckin' mess. I never saw that. That's just what I heard or what I assumed. He was down in L.A. I'd never go down to L.A., I'd never go to his house. I didn't want to go. Because I was afraid of what I might see. A lot of my perspective was secondhand."

Dave wasn't as affected as Chris was by it all. "We do depend on each other for certain things, but for the most part, we're really removed from each other—far removed," Dave says. "As close as we may seem sometimes, it's not like bosom buddies. It's not like a business thing where we talk to each other because we're in the same band—we're friends but we're not best friends or even great friends. So I don't know if it let me down or not because I didn't feel like I'd invested so much in the relationship anyway that I was being robbed.

"As far as us getting together and playing music, it never really affected the band," Dave says. "When it started affecting the band's reputation, I got a little more upset."

Because he didn't feel close enough to Kurt, Dave didn't feel it was his place to step in. "With something as touchy as that, if you see someone doing something like that to themselves, the first thing you want to do is tell them, 'Look—stop.' But how do you go to someone you're friends with but at the same time, you don't feel as close to. You don't feel like it's your place."

Dave, even more than Chris, managed to stay out of the fray. "It's weird, because there are so many people that work with the band that don't really have anything to do with me," Dave says. "Basically, all I do is I walk up on stage and I play drums. And then afterward, I go home. There's just so much that goes on that I don't even know about. In a lot of ways that can be a blessing, but on the other hand it makes you wonder about your importance."

Kurt didn't want to go out on tour again and have his stomach act up again, and besides, he wanted to be with Courtney throughout her pregnancy. Career-wise, it couldn't have come at a worse time. If Nirvana had toured the United States that spring—and an extensive U.S. arena tour was planned for April and May—*Nevermind* would have stayed at the top of the charts for even longer than it did.

Chris, for one, didn't care. "We toured for three years," he says. "The tour just seemed like a lot more pressure, anyway. Before, we were just vagabonds in a van, doing our thing. Now you've got a tour manager and a crew and it's a production. You've got schedules and shit. It used to be, 'Stage time's at six o'clock.' And we could say, 'Fuck it, we're going to buy records.' We'd be on an adventure. And now it's a circus."

Gradually, the ice broke between Kurt and Chris. "Kurt and I would have these cool talks," says Chris. "Every once in a while we'd call and talk about things and I'd really feel better about a lot of things, just through talking. You don't talk for a while and you just sit around and all these ideas pop into your head and you start believing them."

Later, a video sonogram revealed a normally developing baby (a picture of Frances in utero graces the insert of the "Lithium" single). "Oh God, it was incredible," Kurt says, suddenly aglow. "It was one of the most amazing things. It wasn't just a picture—it was a video, so you could see her moving around. It was the first time we realized she was a living thing. You could see her heart beating." While he was watching the footage, Kurt swears he saw Frances give heavy metal's familiar forefinger-and-pinky Satan salute.

In March, pretentious pop thrush Tori Amos released a piano version of "Teen Spirit" on an EP. "Every morning when [Courtney and I] woke up we'd turn it up as loud as we could and dance around like a *Solid Gold* dancer," says Kurt, wearing his best poker face. "It felt really weird because the neighbors were listening. Maybe they thought I was an egomaniac, but I was really just miming the song and dancing around. It's a great breakfast cereal version."

Then came a bitter dispute over publishing royalties that came the closest to breaking up the band as anything ever has. Like everyone else, Kurt didn't expect that the band would sell millions of records. To avoid a potentially divisive situation in which he would have gotten an overwhelming slice of a very small pie, leaving the other two rather poor, he agreed to split royalties for music writing equally with Chris and Dave, even though he writes, by his estimate, 90 percent of the music.

"I write the songs, I come up with the basic idea, and then we work on it as a band," says Kurt. "Most of the time that I'm asking Chris and Dave their opinion, it's just to make them feel a part of the band. I always have the ultimate decision."

But once the album took off so phenomenally, Kurt changed his mind and asked for a more representative publishing split—not, he says, because of the money, which is relatively negligible (Kurt says the difference comes to about $150,000). "I realized how much more pressures are on me and how I deserve a little bit more because I'm the lead singer, all these perspectives are being written about me, I have to take all that pressure," says Kurt. "And I have to deal with the pressure of writing the songs. I don't care if someone else gets the credit for it but I should at least be financially compensated for it."

Dave and Chris had no qualms with that, and it does seem reasonable—Chris and Dave would still make plenty of money. But when Kurt asked for the new arrangement to be retroactive to the release of *Nevermind*, they erupted. Kurt, they argued, was virtually taking money out of their pockets. The uproar lasted only one week in March, but it nearly split the band.

"Chris and I were just like, 'If this is any indication of how much of a dick Kurt is going to be, then I don't want to be in a band with someone like that,'" Dave says. Meanwhile, everyone with a vested interest in the band was urging Chris and Dave to back down. "Everybody was saying 'Let him have this one because the band will break up. You guys could make fifteen million dollars next year. Just let him have this one,'" Dave says.

On the phone one day, Kurt said to Dave, "I can't believe you guys are being so greedy."

"Whatever," Dave replied disgustedly, and Kurt hung up on him.

"At the time, I was ready to fucking quit the band over it," says Kurt. "I couldn't believe that [they were] giving me so much shit about this." Kurt eventually got his retroactive split—75 percent of the music writing royalties. The bad feelings still simmer.

Kurt checked into Exodus, a rehab program favored by rock stars. "It was disgusting," says Kurt. "Right away, these forty-year-old hippie long-term-junkie-type counselors would come in and try to talk to me on a rock and roll level, like, 'I know where you're at, man. Drugs are real prevalent in rock and roll and I've seen it all in the seventies. Would you mind if David Crosby came in and said hello? Or Steven Tyler?' Rattling off these rock stars' names. I was like, 'Fuck that. I don't have any respect for these people at all.'"

Kurt stayed for four days in his tacky, hospital-like room, reading in his uncomfortable bed. Then he abruptly left before his treatment was completed. "I was feeling all right," he says. "I thought it was over and then I ended up trying to detox at home because it wasn't quite over like I thought it was." He sweated it out for a few more days. Then he and Courtney went up to Seattle and Kurt got high. By the time they returned to L.A., he had a habit again.

Courtney spent more time with her guitarist Eric Erlandson in order to stay away from Kurt. She would occasionally go to the nursery at Cedars-Sinai and look at the babies to strengthen her resolve to stay clean.

In July, the "Lithium" single was released, with the B-side containing a live version of "Been A Son" and a previously unreleased track called "Curmudgeon." It also contained, at long last, all the lyrics to *Nevermind*. Soon after, the "Lithium" video aired. A fairly routine collage of footage from the big homecoming concert at the Paramount the previous Halloween and footage from the film *1991: The Year That Punk Broke* (the shot of Kurt taking a running leap at the drum set is from the 1991 Reading Festival; he dislocated his arm). Although it was enlivened by Kerslake's neat trick of using the more violent footage during the quiet parts of the songs and vice versa, it was something of a disappointment from a band and a song that promised so much. Some of the problem might have been that due to his drug habit, Kurt was simply not up to the job of helping to conceptualize a video, but he and Kerslake had actually been brainstorming for a much more ambitious project.

Kerslake says it was to be an animated film about a girl named Prego who lives in a house in a forest. One day, she finds a big pile of eggs in her closet and puts them in a train of three wagons that she wheels through the forest until she comes to a king's castle. By that time, all the eggs but one have cracked and she takes that egg and carries it up to the king's throne and places it on a large book that's on his lap. He's asleep, but when he awakes, he opens his legs and the book slides between them and closes on the egg. When Kurt and Kerslake discovered that the animation would take four months to do, they went with the easily produced live collage.

Meanwhile, the band had set out on a two-week tour to make up the dates they had canceled the previous December in Ireland, Northern Ireland, and Scandinavia, as well visit France and Spain. "It was pretty insane," says Dave of the tour, "and there was a lot of crazy shit going on and it was bad and it was not fun."

Part of the problem was the fact that the band had grown to dislike outdoor festivals, where they would often play in daylight, with the open air eating up the sound from the monitors and the wind blowing the P.A. sound all over the place. "I think the whole band realized we weren't having a good time anymore," Kurt says. Dave remarked to *NME* writer Keith Cameron that for the first time, he didn't even know the names of the crew members. The major label shit was hitting the punk rock fan.

But that was the least of it. Kurt was still using and worse still, his stomach was erupting again. To make it through the tour, Kurt skirted miles of red tape by getting some methadone pills from a "quack doctor" and then got some more from an AIDS patient that another doctor hooked him up with.

The morning after a June 22 Belfast show, Kurt collapsed in convulsions over breakfast. "I forgot to take my methadone pills that night before I went to bed," Kurt says. "I woke up with withdrawals. My stomach was so bad that I decided if I took methadone then I would just puke it up so I had them take me to a hospital so I could get some morphine." Allegedly the ambulance driver had phoned all the tabloids and the rumor started that Kurt had OD'd, despite the fact that, as Kurt points out, it's pretty tough to get heroin in Belfast. The official word from the Nirvana camp was that Kurt had a bleeding ulcer brought on by "junk food."

After that, Kurt got the hairy eyeball from nearly everybody on the tour. "I didn't do anything but forget to take my methadone pills the night before and had to be rushed to the hospital—big deal," Kurt says. "Dave could have hurt himself in a fucking jock accident. Chris could have fallen off the stage drunk that night." The specter of the incident hung over the rest of the tour. The band had been stonewalling on the heroin issue for months; now, it was obvious that word was going to get out sooner or later.

Bad vibes rattled around the entourage. For one thing, Courtney was six months pregnant and in full hormonal swing. For another, "Everybody was tired of me doing drugs," Kurt says, "even though I wasn't doing drugs, I was on methadone. I couldn't do anything but ignore it. All I could do was say fuck you to everyone. It's my problem and they shouldn't be so concerned with it. I could point fingers at everybody else and tell them that they're drunks. They've bought the same drug hysteria propaganda that has been going on in the United States since the Reagan years. They don't understand it, they've never done it, and so they're afraid and it creates bad vibes."

It wasn't like Kurt and Courtney didn't have a sense of humor about it all—they would check into hotels as "Mr. and Mrs. Simon Ritchie," the real name of Sid Vicious.

Gold Mountain hired a couple of professional "minders" to keep an eye on Kurt and Courtney. The day after the incident in Belfast, the band was in Paris for a show at Le Zenith. Kurt walked out of his hotel room to get some food and noticed one of the minders sitting in the room right next to his, facing his open door, just waiting for Kurt to try to leave. "I was being monitored by two goons," Kurt says, "and I was going out to have some *fish*. I wasn't looking for drugs at all. I had methadone, I was fine. I had absolutely no desire to do drugs but I was being treated like a fucking baby. They were turning this band into everything it wasn't supposed to be."

Indignant, Kurt and Courtney packed up their belongings, sneaked out of the hotel, and checked into another without telling anyone where they were until the next day. "They were eating their shit, they were so afraid of what was going to happen," Kurt says.

Food was also a problem, although Kurt had long ago learned to bring his own cereal and canned goods. "There's never any good food in Europe," he claims, raising eyebrows all the way from Paris to Rome.

"During the time that everyone thought we were on massive drugs and Courtney was injecting turkey basters full of heroin straight into her stomach," Kurt says, "the whole thing was no one knew anything and they were so spineless and afraid to ask us anything."

Seeing as "Dave at least listens and he's not very judgmental," Kurt opened up to him about what was really going on. "Dave's practically the only person I've ever really talked to about any of this shit," Kurt says. "Chris was massively judgmental—all he did was give me bad vibes all the time and dirty looks."

Fans like to think that their favorite bands are like the Monkees—living together, sharing good times and bad, and generally knowing everything about each other. But the fact of the matter was that Nirvana wasn't such an intimate, tight-knit group anymore. Granted, it may have been for his own good, but once Shelli began going on tour, Chris didn't hang out with the band as much anymore, then Courtney came along with Kurt. "We weren't doing things together anymore," Kurt says. "Before, we were going out and hanging around every night because we were best friends and we didn't know anybody else. Slowly, everybody started getting a mate and we wouldn't be in the same hotel rooms and everything like that. Before, we stayed in the same hotel room."

Because no one directly asked Kurt what was going on, even the inner circle thrived on rumor, infuriating Kurt and alienating everyone else even further. "I can't stand people who don't confront anyone," Kurt says, seemingly oblivious to the fact that he himself is a prime offender in this regard. "If you have a problem with somebody, you should just flat out ask them. They would never do that.

They would just get on the bus and it was bad vibes—you could just see it radiating off of them. It just festered in my mind how spineless these people are, how they don't know what the fuck is going on at all but they're all *assuming* and they're in my *own fucking band*."

Chris feels it was a vicious cycle fed by both sides. "When he isolated himself, people would react to it, but he isolated himself to react to people's reactions," says Chris. "It just degenerates into bullshit."

"I was way more miserable during all the tours that I was vomiting every night and not eating and being totally straight," Kurt says. "I was way more of a bastard and a negative person. They couldn't be around me half the time. I was just looking straight ahead and concentrating on not puking all the time that it was hard for anyone to communicate with me. But when I started doing drugs, I was feeling fine—and happy for the first time in a long time. I was hoping that everything would be fine with them, but simply because I was doing drugs, it created more problems even though I was finally relieved."

In Spain, Courtney experienced some mild contractions and became terrified that she might give birth prematurely. "Of course," says Kurt, "she had them right before we had to play a show so I had to play a show wondering if Courtney's going to die or if she's going to have a baby." After the concert, Kurt raced to the hospital. "It was the most groaty, disgusting hospital I've ever seen—dirt on the walls, the nurses were screaming in Spanish at Courtney, telling her to stay down," Kurt says. They moved her to a clinic, where they called their obstetrician, who believed there was no serious problem, but advised them to take the next plane home, just in case. "We had to buy two seats in first class so Courtney could lay down," Kurt says. "Of course, it got reported as two *rows*."

In early July, Kurt and Courtney came back from the tour to discover a major disaster. With the idea that a burglar wouldn't think of looking there, Kurt had put his favorite guitar and more importantly, several tapes and notebooks full of poetry and song ideas in the bathtub. But while they were gone, a plumbing problem had filled the bathroom with sludge, ruining everything—the guitar, the tapes, and the notebooks.

They soon found a new apartment, a comfortable two-bedroom in a relatively low-rent ("Right down the hill was a crack street," says Kurt) neighborhood in the Hollywood Hills, near the Hollywood Bowl, with a sweeping view of the hills. Kurt simply started writing all over again.

Meanwhile, yet another band named Nirvana—a British group that had enjoyed one minor hit in the sixties—filed suit for sole rights to the name in the U.K. But when it was pointed out that Nirvana had been popular in Britain for over two years and they had done nothing about it, the case was dropped.

Also in July, Hole signed to DGC for a reported million dollars in a deal even richer and more favorable than the one Nirvana got. A *Newsweek* article on the onslaught of so-called "alternative" band signings in the wake of Nirvana quoted one industry maven as saying that "Sleeping with Kurt Cobain is worth a million dollars." DGC denies this had anything at all to do with the signing. Off in the distance is heard incredulous laughter.

Except for the methadone he took on the summer tour, Kurt did heroin for months, for almost the entire pregnancy. Meanwhile, he was having to do more and more just to get the same kick, eventually working up to a four-hundred-dollar-a-day habit. He couldn't get up any higher because that was the maximum his bank's cash machine would dispense in one day.

"I ended up doing a hundred-dollar shot in one shot and not even feeling it, hardly," he says. "I was just filling up the syringe as far as it could go without pulling the end off. At that point, it was like, why do it?" The next step would have been to start doing speedballs, the mix of cocaine and heroin which had killed John Belushi. With the baby imminent, Kurt checked into Cedars-Sinai on August 4 to detox, spending a total of twenty-five days there.

"He looked at killing himself on the one hand or living on the other," says Danny Goldberg. "He decided to live."

Hole guitarist Eric Erlandson visited Courtney and Kurt throughout the ordeal. "He totally saved our lives during that whole time," says Kurt. "He was the only piece of reality, the only calm person who was there as an example of what life could be like afterward, once this crazy shit was over with." In gratitude, they put Erlandson in their will.

Except for Erlandson, no one visited Kurt in the early stages of his rehabilitation. "I was in a really vulnerable emotional state, which is the first ten days of detox when you're really fucked up and crying all the time," Kurt says. "It messes with your mind so much— it's like a never-ending acid trip. That's exactly what detox is like. It's like being on the heaviest dose of acid and not coming off of it for ten days, never sleeping. Time just stands still and anything will affect you emotionally—anything you read or see on television will make you cry. So it actually wouldn't have been a good time because I would have burst out crying in front of them, anyhow.

"I didn't get any support from anybody the first two times I tried, either," he continues. "No one came to visit me or call me or anything. This time I demanded that someone come and visit me so I felt like I had some friends. So eventually [Chris and Dave] came down."

"It was good to see him but it kind of bummed me out to see him in such bad shape," says Chris. "He was on some kind of medication, lying in bed, and I was thinking, 'Fuck, so this is where all this got you.'"

One day, Dave and Chris stopped by to discuss whether they were going to play a benefit to fight Oregon's infamously homophobic Proposition 9, play a homecoming concert in Seattle to benefit the anticensorship Washington Music Industry Coalition, or appear on the MTV Video Music Awards. They decided to do all three.

While Kurt was detoxing and Courtney was waiting for the baby to be born, a profile of Courtney appeared in *Vanity Fair*.

CHAPTER TWELVE

Courtney originally did the *Vanity Fair* story believing that it would be a mostly flattering piece on her and her music. She was overlooking the fact that her band had only released one extremely modest-selling independent label album a year before, a point of little import to *Vanity Fair*'s upscale readership. This bit of hubris blinded her to the fact that the article was being done by Lynn Hirschberg, well known for her unflattering celebrity profiles. Courtney thought the article would put her on the map.

It did.

She was used to an adoring U.K. music press that understood her sardonic, sarcastic sense of humor, didn't ask hard questions, didn't do much investigation, and kept secrets in exchange for the favor of a hip musician. Lynn Hirschberg had no such allegiances.

Courtney says the story was arranged when she was still using. "Had I not done drugs, I would have been lucid enough to see that *Vanity Fair* was going to stitch me up—what *else* were they going to do with me?" she says, adding that she thought that a hostile article in the "conservative" *Vanity Fair* would probably translate into a study in outlaw cool to the rock community.

The article appeared in the September 1992 issue. One of the many controversial aspects of the piece was a photo of a quite pregnant Courtney naked from the waist down in a bit of see-through lingerie. No big deal, but it turned out she had been smoking a cigarette in the photograph, and that editor Tina Brown had ordered it airbrushed out.

Courtney says they had done a marathon photo session for the piece, going through dozens of rolls of film and several costume and set changes. At one point, in the middle of changing costumes, she says she just happened to have a puff on a cigarette, and photographer Michel Comte just happened to be right there to capture it. She is, however, smoking in at least one other picture in the session. After the article appeared, magazines all over the world were clamoring for the unairbrushed photo. Courtney claims she and Kurt bought the pictures back for fifty thousand dollars, a price she calls "blackmail."

But that was the least of it. The piece described Courtney as a "train-wreck personality" who "isn't particularly interested in the consequences of her actions." It strongly hinted that she had introduced Kurt to heroin, although that was not the case. Hirshberg quoted various unnamed "industry insiders" who "fear for the health of the child," without mentioning whether these industry insiders had done any studies in teratogenic medicine.

But far more damaging was one quote in the piece. After a description of how she and Kurt went to Alphabet City to score during the "Saturday Night Live" visit, Courtney added, "After that, I did heroin for a couple of months," which meant that she had done heroin long after she knew she was pregnant. Courtney vigorously protested that she had been misquoted; Hirschberg maintained that she had the tapes.

Although the article seems to conclusively paint Courtney as a conniver, various factual errors throughout the piece would seem to compromise Hirschberg's accuracy. For instance, she wrote that Danny Goldberg was a vice president at Polygram Records, when in fact he was a vice president of Atlantic; the piece also claimed that Goldberg was Nirvana's manager, but he actually had few managerial chores at Gold Mountain, where he is now merely a consultant— John Silva is Nirvana's manager. Hirschberg maintained that Kurt and Courtney first met "eight or so years ago," which would have put Kurt in high school. The piece perpetuated the gold-digger theory by saying that the next time Courtney met Kurt after their first meeting in Portland, "Kurt was a star," which was not true. Hirschberg also misreported an easily verified story about the bidding war over Hole.

Most unfortunately, the piece also seemed to completely miss Courtney's sardonic sense of humor. This is a woman who, in the course of a delicate conversation about the whole "was she or wasn't she" controversy, can come out with a deliberately sarcastic line like "If there is ever a time that a person *should* be on drugs, it's when they're pregnant, because it sucks" without considering how it would look in print. Spend even a little quality time with Courtney and it's clear that an exchange she had with Kurt about firing Dave was purely facetious.

If *Nevermind* was a success because the band was in the right place at the right time, the *Vanity Fair* piece found the Cobains at the wrong place at the wrong time. Besides the nation's continuing drug hysteria and a misguided Republican crusade for "family values," the story also tapped into America's sudden guilt about what it had done to its children over the past decade. Suddenly, the U.S. media became fixated on child abuse stories, from the kids who were left "home alone" while their parents vacationed in Mexico to the poor little Long Island girl who was shackled for days in an underground bunker. A mom who had allegedly done heroin (not to mention smoked cigarettes) while pregnant pressed some powerful buttons.

"I wouldn't have thought that I could be dwarfed or squashed or raped or incredibly hurt by a story in that magazine," Courtney says. "But the power of it was so intense. It was unbelievable. I read a fax of it and my bones shook. I knew that my world was over. I was dead. That was it. The rest of my life. Not only was I going to walk around with a big black mark but any happiness that I had known, I was going to have to fight for, for the rest of my life. It shouldn't be that way, but I exposed myself to it. Had I not taken drugs in the first place, I would have been lucid enough to know what she was about, I wouldn't have been candid, I would have figured out where I fit in the scheme of the *Vanity Fair* world."

Courtney likes to think the story was some kind of set-up—perhaps commandeered by *Vanity Fair* darling Madonna, whose new record label, Maverick, she had recently spurned, and loudly.

But a simpler explanation is that Courtney made for good copy—she was an outspoken woman with a checkered past who happened to be married to the rock star of the moment. While they maintain it is a pack of lies, even the Cobains acknowledge that Hirschberg's piece was at least an entertaining read—and the worst thing that ever happened to them.

Courtney checked herself into a hospital, she says, "because I was going to go crazy. I was going to take drugs. I've never been a person to take drugs in a crisis. I usually take drugs when I'm happy. I felt really like killing myself. I was eight and a half months pregnant. I couldn't kill myself so I checked into a hospital for two weeks before the baby was born."

Meanwhile, Kurt was detoxing and, once again, in enormous pain. Unable to eat, he was placed on an IV and got weaker and weaker for a time, then rallied. His rehabilitation was slowed by the fact that he was occasionally given morphine to kill the stomach pain. He saw a battalion of gastrointestinal specialists who took X-rays, upper GI's, lower GI's, CAT scans, etc. He was weak. He was ready to snap. "He'd been crying for weeks," says Courtney. "It was nothing *but* crying. All we *did* was cry. It was horrible."

At first, Kurt didn't understand the implications of the *Vanity Fair* story. "It was obviously upsetting," he says, "but I was in such a vulnerable state of mind and my mind was so clouded from getting off of drugs that I would have rather just let it pass for a while, but Courtney was so upset about it. She was about to have a baby—she wasn't in a clouded state of mind at all."

Gradually, it dawned on Kurt what the story was doing to his and Courtney's reputation. "One day I snapped out of it and realized how awful it was," he says. "It was definitely affecting our livelihood and our image and everything to a real extreme." And since the *Vanity Fair* piece was based largely on unnamed "inside sources," they had to deal with the profound disappointment and paranoia that arose from the fact that some of their most trusted friends and associates had betrayed them.

"We'd already been turned into cartoon characters by then and it justified everything—all the lies and rumors that had been going around," says Kurt. "I just found it amazing that someone could get away with something like that, that she couldn't go to jail for it or get busted somehow or sued. I thought we'd be able to sue her, but it's a matter of having the millions of dollars to fight in court with [*Vanity Fair* publisher] Condé Nast, who would support her."

"I just decided, 'Fuck this, I don't want to be in a band anymore. It just isn't worth it. I want to kill [Hirschberg],'" Kurt says. "As soon as I get out of this fucking hospital, I'm going to kill this woman with my bare hands. I'm going to stab her to death. First I'm going to take her dog and slit its guts out in front of her and then shit all over her and stab her to death.'" He was too weak to do that so he says he considered hiring a hit man, then calmed down a bit and thought about asking David Geffen to pull some strings to get Hirschberg fired or else he'd quit the band. None of this ever happened.

Kurt still gets scarily angry when the subject of Lynn Hirschberg's story comes up. "She'd better hope to God that some-day I don't find myself destitute without a wife and a baby," he says. "Because I'll fucking get revenge on her. Before I leave this earth, she's going out with me."

On the morning of August 18, 1992, Courtney began to go into labor. She stunned her doctors by picking up her IV and slamming out of the room. She marched over to Kurt's room, clear across the hospital, and screamed, "You get out of this bed and you come down now! You are not leaving me to do this by myself, fuck you!" She came back to find that the hospital security force had "gone apeshit." Kurt was still groggy from a dose of sleeping pills and in extreme pain, but managed to get himself down to the delivery room a little later.

At seven forty-eight in the morning, Frances Bean Cobain was born. She weighed seven pounds, one ounce, and according to the Cobains she was perfectly healthy.

Kurt didn't witness his own daughter's birth. He had passed out. "I'm having the baby, it's coming out, he's puking, he's passing out, and I'm holding his hand and rubbing his stomach while the baby's coming out of me," says Courtney. "It was pretty weird," she says, laughing darkly.

"I was so fucking scared—it was probably a classic case of what the typical father goes through," says Kurt, who was still hooked up to an IV and in the midst of rehab. "I was just so weak and sick and afraid that something was going to happen to Courtney or the baby."

A press release from Gold Mountain a few days later aimed to refute all the speculation about Frances. "The infant is in good con-dition, is feeding well and growing at the normal rate expected for a newborn," the statement said, adding, "The vicious rumors that Frances was suffering any withdrawals at the time of birth are completely false, and in fact, she has not suffered any discomfort since delivery."

If their baby was a boy, they were going to name it Eugene, after Eugene Kelly of the Vaselines. When they found out that they were to have a girl, they thought of Kelly's partner in the Vaselines, Frances McKee. At the time, they weren't thinking of Frances Farmer, the Hollywood actress who was blacklisted and hounded into insanity in the fifties, but Kurt now wishes that was the reason. He adds that the word "bean" has cropped up in both his and Courtney's lives many times, but mostly they came up with the name after noticing that Frances actually looked like a kidney bean in her early sonograms.

Tarnished reputations turned out to be only the beginning of the *Vanity Fair* controversy.

Even Kurt and Courtney's lawyer, Rosemary Carroll, believes that the *Vanity Fair* article prompted the Los Angeles County Department of Children's Services to begin taking action against them. The agency must have seen the *Vanity Fair* piece—(both Carroll and the Cobains claim it was stapled to the top of the report on them). The story was so well publicized that the agency could not ignore it, even though Courtney had allegedly detoxed almost immediately after learning she was pregnant. Whether anticipating pressure from higher-ups or even public outcry, it's not outside the realm of possibility that the agency was virtually obligated to hassle this rock star couple.

Late in Courtney's pregnancy, Children's Services threatened to relieve Kurt and Courtney of custody of Frances. At a hearing in Family Court, where rules of evidence are relaxed, Children's Services used the *Vanity Fair* article and what later proved to be a spurious urine test to argue that both Kurt and Courtney were multiple substance abusers and therefore did not deserve to have custody of their child. The judge agreed and ordered Kurt to go to yet another detox center for another thirty days, even though he was completely clean after his stay at Cedars.

But that was the least of it. Two weeks after their daughter was born, Kurt and Courtney were forced to surrender custody of Frances to Courtney's sister Jamie. For a month after that, Kurt and Courtney were not allowed to be alone with their own daughter.

Kurt genuinely believes it was a conspiracy. "It was all a total scam," he says. "It was an attempt to use us as an example because we stand for everything that goes against the grain of conformist American entertainment. It was a witch hunt. It was an outright Frances Farmer case where we were being mistreated beyond belief. Social Services literally took the *Vanity Fair* article and Xeroxed it and then took that pee test that Courtney took in the first trimester of her pregnancy and used that as an excuse to take our baby away."

No one knew this was happening except for a very close inner circle of the Nirvana organization. Given that the couple was fighting for the custody of their own baby—and that a magazine article was virtually being used as evidence—their extreme reactions to subsequent bad press start to become more understandable.

Courtney still becomes distraught when telling the tale. Toward the end of her account of the *Vanity Fair* fiasco, this tough, seemingly indomitable woman begins to cry openly. "It's one thing to ruin your credibility or to be publicly humiliated but they took our *baby* away and there was nothing wrong with her," she says, sobbing. "I did *not* do drugs during my pregnancy after I knew I was pregnant. I went and got all the help I could fucking get. I went to every doctor in town. I have medical records to prove it and they just fucking tortured us."

It seemed hopeless—doctors, government agencies, the press all were against them. At one dark moment, they took out Kurt's handgun and considered taking their own lives.

"It was just so humiliating and it just felt like so many powerful people were out to get us that it just seemed hopeless," says Kurt. "It didn't seem like we'd ever win. It was amazing. We were totally suicidal. It's not the right time for a woman trying to get rid of the hormonal problems of just having a baby and me just getting off of drugs and just being bombarded with this. It was just too much." But in the end, they put down the gun.

The next day, the band flew to England to headline the closing night of the 1992 Reading Festival. The English press was running with rumors that the band was breaking up because of Kurt's health. Kurt says the rumors were completely unfounded. "No, it was classic, typical English journalism," he says wearily. "Sensationalism. I have absolutely no respect for the English people. They make me sick. I thought I'd never say anything racist in my life, but those people are the most snooty, cocksure, anal people and they have absolutely no regard for people's emotions. They don't think of other people as humans at all. They're the coldest people I've ever met."

Kurt had personally programmed the bill for that day, purposely leaving out "lame-ass limey bands." The festival organizers originally balked at including the Melvins and Screaming Trees, but Kurt

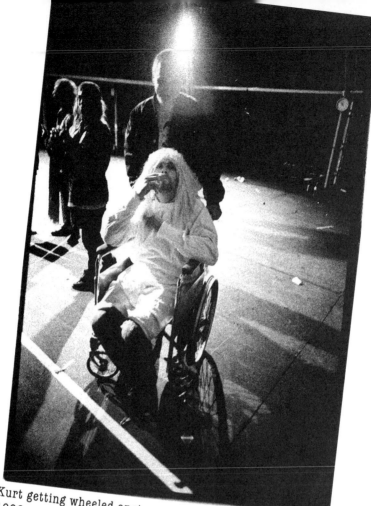

Kurt getting wheeled onstage at the Reading Festival, 1992. (© Charles Peterson)

threatened to pull out of the festival if they weren't included. Also on the all-day bill were old friends like L7, Mudhoney and Eugenius, as well as Pavement, Nick Cave, and the Bad Seeds, and the uproarious Abba tribute band Bjorn Again.

It rained all day and festival goers wallowed in the traditional Reading mud bath. At last, it was Nirvana's turn to play. Kurt rolled out on stage in a wheelchair and wearing a hospital gown, as a poke at all the rumors about his bad health. Yet less than a week before, he had vomited and then passed out onto a cot as his daughter was being born; the day before, he had contemplated killing himself. At any rate, Nirvana played a glorious show—an eight on a scale of ten,

Kurt at Reading '92.
(© Charles Peterson)

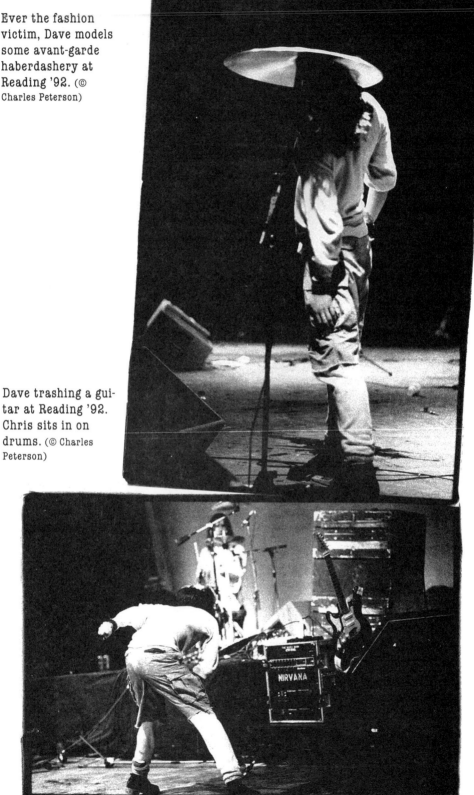

Ever the fashion victim, Dave models some avant-garde haberdashery at Reading '92. (© Charles Peterson)

Dave trashing a guitar at Reading '92. Chris sits in on drums. (© Charles Peterson)

The stage after Nirvana's triumphant set at Reading '92. (© Charles Peterson)

by Kurt's reckoning. Tens of thousands of English voices turned virtually every song of the hour and a half set into a gigantic sing-along. The band played with staggering power. Rumors of Nirvana's demise had been greatly exaggerated.

Still, the controversy surrounding the band would not go away. The two main U.K. music weeklies arranged for cover stories on the band at the time of the European make-up tour earlier that summer. *Melody Maker* agreed to run their piece, by the band's longtime friend and supporter Everett True, just after the interviews took place, while the *NME* agreed to run their piece to coincide with Reading six weeks later. Nirvana also required that the piece be written by Keith Cameron, who had developed a good relationship with the band through doing profiles on them ever since the *Sounds* cover story back in the summer of 1990. While True had glibly skirted around the controversies, in the *NME*, Cameron confronted the myriad of rumors with the wounded tone of a disillusioned fan, which is precisely what he was.

After interviewing the band at a show in Valencia, Spain, Cameron wrote that the band, or at least Kurt, had begun to behave like the self-indulgent dinosaurs they had disdained and displaced, missing soundcheck for unexplained reasons, making themselves difficult to be interviewed and photographed, and very likely, doing hard drugs. The piece ran through the litany of drug-related rumors, many of which, as it turns out, were not far off the mark. "They've begun to blow it all via smack, the biggest sucker punch of the lot," Cameron wrote. "From nobodies to superstars to fuckups in the space of six months! That had to be a record." Cameron wrote that when he asked about the heroin rumors, Kurt made him check his arms for needle marks. Of course, there were none because he was on methadone by that time.

But the real target of the piece, with its "LOVE WILL TEAR US APART" headline, was Courtney. The piece quotes one crew member who referred to Courtney as "The Wicked Witch of the West," while someone else on the tour recalled Kurt as being a nice guy, "BC— 'Before Courtney.'"

Cameron even laid into Janet Billig, who had recently joined Gold Mountain to work with Nirvana and Hole. "Her role on this tour is like a cross between wet nurse and human sponge," wrote Cameron, "indulging whims and soaking up all of Courtney's excess bullshit." Courtney, Cameron concluded, is a "Grade A pain in the arse." The band was on the verge of breaking up, and it was all her fault (Cameron now admits he was influenced by the *Vanity Fair* article).

Cameron bumped into Kurt and Eric Erlandson at the traditional post-show wingding at the Ramada hotel in Reading. Kurt scolded him for the piece, then Erlandson poured a glass of vodka and lime juice on his head. They walked away, leaving Cameron literally to cry on the shoulder of *NME* photographer Steve Double. "I wrote what I thought was a sensitive piece," he says. Cameron remains *persona non grata* with the Nirvana camp.

"If there's any sense of me feeling betrayed in any way by Nirvana, which there really probably isn't, it's that reality as I discovered it on that day in Spain," says Cameron. "This was a band that totally inspired me. They'd been the most meaningful musical event in my life, ever. And they became this cliché that your favorite bands just don't do, at least not mine. I was shocked at that reality."

Days later, Nirvana played the 1992 MTV Video Music Awards show.

The band was told they could play whatever song they wanted during their performance, which would kick off the ceremonies. At soundcheck the day before the show, the band played a then-unrecorded song called "Rape Me" and another new song provisionally entitled "New Poopy." The next day, perhaps because of the title of "Rape Me," perhaps because it wasn't a hit, perhaps because the show's organizers thought they had made a deal with Gold Mountain, MTV insisted that Nirvana play "Teen Spirit."

Hours before show time, Nirvana decided they weren't going to play.

Then the band began to ponder the repercussions of the move—MTV could fire their best friend and ally at the channel, programmer Amy Finnerty, if she didn't manage to convince them to appear, and could blackball other Gold Mountain acts including Sonic Youth and the Beastie Boys, and perhaps even other acts on Geffen/DGC. Suddenly, Nirvana found themselves forced into the world of high-stakes corporate rock—and they had to deal with the situation in a matter of hours.

Then MTV said it was "Teen Spirit." Or "Lithium." Or else.

"We didn't want to fuck everything up for everyone so we decided to play 'Lithium,'" Kurt says. "Instead of bowing out and keeping our dignity, we decided to get fucked in the ass. It would have hurt us worse than it would have hurt them if we actually had gone through with it."

Once they got on stage for the live telecast, Kurt sang and played the first few bars of "Rape Me," "just to give them a little heart palpitation." He succeeded. As soon as Kurt started playing the offending song, MTV VP Judy McGrath let out a startled little scream and dashed toward the control room. Just as they were about to cut to a commercial, the band launched into "Lithium."

As the song ended, Chris threw his bass high in the air and missed catching it. The butt end hit him square on the forehead. He writhed on the floor for a moment then ran off stage somewhere. For several tense minutes, no one could find Chris. Was he staggering deliriously around the Universal lot? Was he lying unconscious somewhere? Eventually Alex Macleod found him. He was lounging in the ready room with an ice pack on his head and a champagne bottle in his hand, chatting with former Queen guitarist Brian May.

The band didn't want to go onstage to accept the award for Best Alternative Music Video, so it was Kurt's idea to have a Michael Jackson impersonator come up and accept for them. Except for Kurt's suggestion that he introduce himself as "the King of Grunge," the impersonator improvised a speech, which was greeted by a confused silence out in the audience. No one got the concept. "I wanted it to be used as a reminder that I'm dealing with the same thing," says Kurt. "All rock stars have to deal with it. It's the fault of the fans and the media."

The band didn't have any other celebrity impersonators prepared when they won their second award, for Best New Artist, and Kurt initially refused to go up to the podium, but friends and associates convinced him that if he didn't go up, people would talk. "I was just kind of nervous up there," Kurt says. "When we played, I didn't look out in the audience and realize how big it was. And once I got up there, I realized millions of people are watching and it's a really big place and these lights are really bright and I don't want to be here, this is really stupid. I just wanted to leave right away."

Kurt managed to thank his family, his label, and the band's "true fans." Then he paused a moment, fixed the camera with a soulful gaze, smiled, and said, 'You know, it's really hard to believe everything you read." Chris spoiled the moment by bellowing into the microphone, "Remember Joseph Goebbels!" but Kurt had made his point, even though most people in the audience had no idea how much it meant to him.

But with that one little smile, Kurt struck a major blow for his tarnished image. In terms of PR value, the MTV appearance was the equivalent of eight months of touring. Before an audience of millions of people, the band reminded people of why they liked Nirvana in the first place.

But the day was far from over. Also on the bill was Pearl Jam, whom Kurt had been skewering in the press for months, although he jokingly denies there had been a full-blown feud. "No, I just happened to express my feelings toward their music, that's all," he says with a little smirk.

But it wasn't just their music—Kurt felt that the band was a bunch of hypocritical sellouts. Two members of Pearl Jam—Stone Gossard and Jeff Ament—had been in Green River, the first band to put out a record on Sub Pop. Kurt's friend Mark Arm had quit the band and formed Mudhoney because he felt that it was going in an overtly commercial direction, largely because of Ament, who was among the first of the early Sub Poppers to openly declare he wanted to be a professional musician.

"I know for a fact that at the very least, if not Stoney, then Jeff is a definite careerist—a person who will kiss ass to make sure his band gets popular so he can become rich," Kurt claims.

And Jeff Ament was also a jock, an all-state basketball player in his native Montana. "Jocks have completely taken over music," carps Kurt. "That's all there is nowadays is muscular bicep Marky Mark clones. It's pretty scary. And just to get back at them, I'm going to start playing basketball."

Pearl Jam had assumed the look and some of the sound of "grunge rock," or just enough to ride the commercial wave. It was a calculated—and highly successful—attempt to dress up the same old corporate rock in tattered flannel shirts and Doc Martens boots. Also, the band's label spent enormous amounts of money in promoting a band with no indie-style grass-roots following—it was another case of major labels burying the indie rock revolution with money. All this annoyed Kurt to no end. He began sniping at Pearl Jam in the press.

In the January 1992 issue of *Musician* magazine, Kurt had declared that the members of Pearl Jam were going to be "the ones responsible for this corporate, alternative and cock-rock fusion." "I would love to be erased from my association with that band," Kurt said of the band in the April 16 *Rolling Stone* cover story. "I do feel a duty to warn the kids about false music that's claiming to be underground or alternative. They're just jumping on the alternative bandwagon."

But by that time, he had decided to at least forgive Pearl Jam's fey but immensely likable singer, Eddie Vedder. "I later found out that Eddie basically found himself in this position," says Kurt. "He never claimed to be anybody who supports any kind of punk ideals in the first place."

Vedder was standing around the backstage area at the MTV Awards show when out of the blue, Courtney walked up to him and slow-danced with him as Eric Clapton played the elegaic "Tears in Heaven." Kurt walked over and butted in. "I stared into his eyes and told him that I thought he was a respectable human," Kurt says. "And I did tell him straight out that I still think his band sucks. I said, 'After watching you perform, I realized that you are a person that does have some passion.' It's not a fully contrived thing. There are plenty of other more evil people out in the world than him and he doesn't deserve to be scapegoated like that."

Which is where Axl Rose comes in.

Backstage, Courtney spotted Rose and called him over to where they were sitting with Frances. "Axl, Axl!" she said. "Will you be the godfather of our child?" With several bodyguards looming behind him, Rose leaned over, his face reddening beneath a thick layer of makeup, and pointed his finger in Kurt's face. "You shut your bitch up or I'm taking you down to the pavement!" he screeched. The Nirvana entourage exploded in laughter, except for Kurt, who made as if he was about to hand Frances to Courtney so he could stand up to Rose. But instead he glared at Courtney and said "Shut up, bitch!" and they all exploded some more.

Rose's then-girlfriend Stephanie Seymour then broke an awkward silence by innocently asking Courtney, "Are you a model?"

"No," replied Courtney. "Are you a brain surgeon?"

When the band returned to their trailer, waiting for them was the formidable Guns n' Roses entourage, veritable sides of beef. Kurt dashed into the trailer to make sure Frances was all right while Chris was surrounded. They started pushing him around. Guns bassist Duff McKagan wanted to personally beat Chris up, but a crowd began to gather and the confrontation dissolved (Guns n' Roses refuses comment on the incident).

Rose may have been angry at Nirvana for spurning his offer to open on the Guns n' Roses/Metallica tour that summer. They'd even turned down his request to play at Rose's thirtieth birthday party. There may be an unspoken jealousy at work, too. The two bands had often been pitted against each other—early on, the English music weekly *NME* had pronounced Nirvana "the Guns n' Roses it's OK to like."

Rose was such a fan that he had even put a Nirvana baseball hat in Guns n' Roses' "Don't Cry" video, but he just didn't get it. Before a Guns n' Roses show at Madison Square Garden in December 1991, the band's cameramen zoomed in on women in the audience until they lifted their shirts up, broadcasting the signal to giant video screens around the arena. The mostly male crowd stomped and hooted its approval while the other women in the audience looked embarrassed, disgusted, or giggled nervously. And what was playing during this loutish video rape? "Smells Like Teen Spirit."

Perhaps the enmity comes from the fact that the two bands are competing for roughly the same vast audience of frustrated, damaged kids. "I don't feel like I'm competing at all," Kurt says. "I've said in public enough times that I don't give a fuck about his audience." But Kurt and Rose hate each other with an almost brotherly intensity, as if they're flip sides of the same coin. "We do come from the same kind of background," Kurt says. "We come from small towns and we've been surrounded by a lot of sexism and racism most of our lives. But our internal struggles are pretty different. I feel like I've allowed myself to open my mind to a lot more things than he has.

"His role has been played for years," says Kurt. "Ever since the beginning of rock and roll, there's been an Axl Rose. And it's just boring, it's totally boring to me. Why it's such a fresh and new thing in his eyes is obviously because it's happening to *him* personally and he's such an egotistical person that he thinks that the whole world owes him something."

Still, Kurt admits Nirvana could learn a thing or two from Guns n' Roses. "They fuck things up and then they sit back and look at

Nirvana at the Seattle Center Arena. (© Charles Peterson)

what they fucked up and then try to figure out how they can fix it," he says, "whereas we fuck things up and just dwell on it and make it even worse."

Don Cobain showed up uninvited at the September 11 show at the Seattle Coliseum, a benefit for a local anticensorship organization called the Washington Music Industry Coalition. Along with his son Chad, Kurt's half brother, Don got past the ticket-takers by showing his driver's license with his name on it. He asked to get backstage, but nobody ever got back to him, so he stood around and waited. Finally, he discovered the room where the after-show gathering was. "Somebody opened the door and there he was so I just walked right in." Kurt introduced his dad to Courtney, Frances, and Chris. Don had already found out that he was a grandfather from an item in the newspaper.

Don surveyed the typical backstage scene—the bleak cinder-block walls, the sycophantic hangers-on, the depressed and dissipated post-concert vibe. "I felt sorry for him," says Don. "What a life. Didn't look that glamorous to me."

"Well, it's been a long time," said Don. It had been seven years.

"Jeez, you look old," Kurt replied.

"It was really hard," says Don of the meeting. "Really, really hard.

"I asked him if he was happy and stuff," Don says, "and he said he was happy and he said he didn't have much money and I said 'Well, are you having fun?' He said he was and I said 'Well, okay then.' I didn't know what to say because it was real hard. We hugged a couple of times and I said to just keep in contact." Don hasn't heard from Kurt since. "I guess he's been busy and stuff."

Some say Don just came out of the woodwork because his son suddenly became rich. "That's the feeling I got from his mom and different people," he says, "but I don't give a shit. I haven't got any money, I don't give a shit about money. I wish *I* could do something for *him*, because really, I don't think I ever have. I just want to wish him well. If he can make something of himself, then go for it. I just keep waiting and waiting for him to come around."

Kurt officially ended all the speculation about his drug use by admitting in a September 21 profile by veteran Los Angeles *Times* pop critic Robert Hilburn that yes, he had done heroin for "three weeks" earlier that year. After the Physeptone episode, he went into detox again, took a month to straighten himself out, "and that was it." Of course, that wasn't quite it, but it was still a major admission which went oddly unnoticed in the mainstream music press, perhaps because everybody was already sure it was true.

Kurt told Hilburn, "The biggest thing that affected me was all the insane rumors, the heroin rumors... all this speculation going on. I felt totally violated. I never realized that my private life would be such an issue."

The raft of hostile press had only begun with the *Vanity Fair* article—it continued with things like a horrendous article in the *Globe*, a

They've got money & fame but no damn heart

ROCK STAR'S BABY IS BORN A JUNKIE

Nirvana singer's pregnant wife boasted they took heroin — now tiny tot pays the shocking price!

Singer Kurt Cobain has also battled drug problems, says an insider

Tragic Francis Bean Cobain is going through agonizing withdrawal. She will suffer shivering, cramps and muscle spasms — just like this drug baby

Rocker mom Courtney Love was totally incoherent at the hospital, the source says. "She was spaced out"

By ROBIN JAMES

THE drug addict rocker wife of Nirvana singer Kurt Cobain has given birth to a tragic baby junkie, a source close to the couple reveals.

Little Francis Bean Cobain was born three weeks premature fighting for her life, with mom Courtney Love's $100-a-day heroin habit eating away inside her, the insider says. Doctors at Cedars Sinai Hospital in Los Angeles immediately put the tiny tot on a special rehab program.

"The baby had to go cold turkey, helped along by sedatives. She will go through withdrawal like anybody else coming off a powerful drug," says the insider.

"At the moment, she is high on methadone, a heroin substitute. Slowly, the doses will get less and less. She will suffer cold sweats, shivering, cramps and muscle spasms, but she should live.

"She's lucky she is in Cedars Sinai, which is one of the best hospitals in the world for treating babies like this. In many other hospitals her chances of survival would be slim indeed."

Platinum-blonde Courtney

— whose hubby Kurt has also battled drug problems — outraged America when she boasted she was still taking heroin even though she was pregnant.

But just two weeks before her child was born, she checked into the hospital to try and kick her drug habit, says the insider. Courtney was so rowdy, she had to be moved to a special area.

"For an expectant mother, she was not acting responsibly," the source says.

'Confused and disruptive'

"She was on a $100-a-day heroin habit, and was even doubling up on the prescription methadone she was buying on the black market.

"She was confused and disruptive. Both the drug treatment and the gynecology units refused to take her, saying she was too tough to handle.

"Eventually, she was taken to six south-west, an area specializing in kidney failures,

where her baby could not be monitored fully. Courtney was a real handful. She was so spaced out she had no idea what she was doing.

"It seemed so weird to see a heavily pregnant woman behaving that way. Normally, they are so cautious.

"But Courtney was totally incoherent. You couldn't make out what she was saying and she

couldn't understand what you were saying. Her room was a complete pigsty with clothes strewn everywhere and food all over the walls and floor.

"She would demand food, eat some and then throw the rest against the wall.

"She didn't know what was happening. She would even leave tips for the nurses on her food trays, thinking they were

waitresses. She was still smoking, but compared to the other ways she was abusing her body, the smoking was minor.

"When her rock and roll friends came around, they would sit around cross-legged and chant.

"A few times, there was a frantic alert after she wandered off barefoot in her nightgown."

Quantum Leap's Scott Bakula

Lee Harvey Oswald

QUANTUM LEAPS INTO KENNEDY KILLER'S SHOES!

QUANTUM LEAP star Scott Bakula will be gunning for John F. Kennedy in the shocking season opener when the time machine puts him in Lee Harvey Oswald's body.

The astounding story line was developed by producer Don Bellisario while they were both in the Marines.

The **Globe** article.

---

supermarket tabloid, which ran a story with the headline "ROCK STAR'S BABY BORN A JUNKIE," along with a disturbing picture of a crack baby. "THEY'VE GOT MONEY & FAME BUT NO DAMN HEART," the subheadline added. After a few more articles like that, Chris, Shelli, and Dave dropped their resentments and fears and supported Kurt, Courtney, and their newborn baby. "We all rallied together and it was cool," says Chris. "That's when things really turned around. Things hit rock bottom and they rebounded."

"I think they appreciated that people came to their side," Chris adds, his voice breaking with emotion.

Kurt is anxious not to appear to endorse heroin. "At the end of the last couple of months when I was doing four hundred dollars' worth every day, I was definitely noticing things about my memory and I knew that eventually my health would start getting a lot worse," he says. "It sounds like I don't regret it and I don't, but that's because I used it as a tool. I used it as a medication to get rid of a pain. And that's the biggest reason why I did it. In that sense, I don't regret it, but anybody else who's going to get addicted to drugs are obviously going to fuck up their lives eventually. If it doesn't take a year, it will be next year. I've seen it happen with every person that gets strung out. Drugs are bad for you. They *will* fuck you up.

"I just knew that I would eventually stop doing them and being married and having a baby is a really good incentive but most people don't even have that and also I'm a rich, millionaire rock star and I have a lot of things to keep right now. I have a lot of reasons to not do drugs. But try telling that to a person that feels like they don't have anything. When you're on a poverty level and you're addicted to drugs, you'll start turning tricks and you'll start ripping people off and find yourself in jail—those are all the negative things that go along with drug addiction.

"When you have more than four hundred dollars to spend a day, and you're pretty much pampered by living in this place that you know you don't have to worry about rent, you have a car that runs well and all that stuff, it's really easy to be a successful drug addict," he says. "But most people who are going to be influenced by the fact that I did drugs are going to be average people who have a job and can barely make ends meet."

Kurt realizes how all this sounds—that it was okay for him to do drugs, but nobody else. "But I'm saying that eventually, if I would have kept doing drugs, I would have lost everything, just like anyone else would have," he says. "I was able to be a successful junkie for a year, but if I kept going, I would eventually completely fuck my body up and ruin every relationship that I had and lose everything. I'd lose my friends and my family and all my money, everything—if I kept doing it. And I always knew that, too."

Courtney is also penitent. "I lived out my little rock and roll fantasy," she says. "I just wish I hadn't gotten into so much trouble for it."

CHAPTER THIRTEEN

The rest of 1992 found Kurt and Courtney still jousting with their detractors while the band tried to resume business as usual.

In October, Courtney's old Liverpool friend Julian Cope took out an ad in the music press, ostensibly to promote his new single. At one point in a lengthy rant, he declared, "Free Us (The Rock 'n' Roll Fans) From Nancy Spungen-Fixated Heroin A-Holes Who Cling To Our Greatest Rock Groups And Suck Out Their Brains..." Cope, like everyone else, had assumed he knew exactly what the story was; it was also a rather sexist attack from the otherwise self-righteously feminist Cope, who later said of Courtney in Britain's *Select* magazine, "She needs shooting and I'll shoot her."

The Cobains also felt under fire from a planned Nirvana biography by two British writers, Victoria Clarke and Britt Collins. Kurt and Courtney allege that Clarke and Collins allowed interview subjects to believe they were working with the band's approval, claimed to have slept with Dave or Kurt, and even interviewed James Moreland, Courtney's first husband (the marriage lasted a matter of days); the way they see it, the book was shaping up as an excuse for a tawdry hatchet job on Courtney. Gold

Kurt smiles **again!** (© Charles Peterson)

Mountain tried to put the kibosh on the book by sending out a letter to prospective interviewees asking them not to talk to Clarke or Collins. According to Gold Mountain, the pair apparently did not succeed in formally interviewing anyone even remotely connected with the band.

Clarke did get some media mileage from some threatening messages that she said Kurt and Courtney had left on her answering machine in late October. Clarke said the first calls came late one night from Courtney, but they were comparatively civil compared to Kurt's. The next night, he began a message, then hit the machine's two-minute limit and called back—nine times. "If anything comes out in this book which hurts my wife, I'll fucking hurt you," Kurt said, sounding, as *Select* euphemistically put it, "tired, confused, very upset." "I love to be fucked, I love to be blackmailed, I'll give you anything you want, I'm begging you. I'm on my knees and my mouth is wide open. You have absolutely no fucking idea what you are doing..."

Kurt went on to call the two writers "parasitic little cunts," adding, "At this point I don't give a flying fuck if I have this recorded that I'm threatening you. I suppose I could throw out a few hundred thousand dollars to have you snuffed out, but maybe I'll try it the legal way first."

The *New York Times* quoted Gold Mountain's Danny Goldberg as saying, "Kurt absolutely denies the notion that he or any other member of the band made any such phone calls."

"In my opinion, either this is a prank that someone has played on these women," Goldberg added, "or this is something fabricated to publicize an unauthorized biography."

Kurt, however, doesn't deny that it was his voice on the tapes. He sounded homicidal, he says, "Because I want to kill them." By the truly terrifying look on his face— jaw muscles visibly knotted, eyes darkened—one gets the idea that he really means it. "Obviously, I have a lot to lose right now so I won't be able to do it," he says. "But I have all the rest of my life. If I ever find myself destitute and I've lost my family, I won't hesitate to get revenge on people who have fucked with me. I've always been capable of that. I've tried killing people before in a fit

Kurt at an early October show at the University of Washington at Bellingham, opening for Mudhoney. (© Charles Peterson)

Chris at the Bellingham
show. (© Charles Peterson)

of rage when I've gotten in fights with people. It's definitely a charac-ter flaw, to say the least, but I feel so strongly about people unneces-sarily causing negative things to happen to people for no reason.

"I don't enjoy people fucking with my family and carrying on the tradition of lies and slander," he continues. "I don't deserve it. No one deserves it. We've been scapegoated more than any fucking band I can think of in the history of rock, to my knowledge. People fuck with us and they want dirt and they want to lie about us and I just don't understand it. I've never really tried to do anything scandalous in my life. When people unnecessarily fuck with me, I just can't help but want to beat them to death."

The undeniable creepiness of the answering machine tapes reveals that despite the great happiness he's gained with his wife and baby, Kurt still harbors a dark and seemingly bottomless well of anger and alienation. It's not as if Kurt is a complete pacificist. He says that when he was living with the Shillingers, he got in a fight with a guy who was picking on him at a party. "I picked up a stick and started beating him with it and I couldn't stop," he says. "It was disgusting. It was a really scary reminder of how violent I can be when I really want to hurt somebody. It actually felt good, I was actually laughing about it." His victim got a concussion and lapsed into a brief coma. "I was really upset about it afterward, for a long time," Kurt says. "Especially after I saw him when he got out of the hospital."

The hypocrisy of the phone calls—the sexism, even misogyny—is profoundly disillusioning. When Kurt rails against sexism and rape, it now begins to seem like a desperate attempt to stifle something ugly within himself, rather than merely standing up for what's right. It looks very, very bad. "I don't care," Kurt says. "I'm a firm believer in revenge."

When it's revealed that at the time, Kurt and Courtney were still fighting for custody of Frances and that any unflattering press that came out about them might jeopardize the proceedings, the phone calls do begin to make a little more sense. But only a *little* more. On the whole, the answering machine tapes—along with Kurt's defense of them—present a very disturbing side of Kurt. "Fine," he says. "I don't care. I guess I *am* unbalanced in that part of my psyche. I wouldn't hesitate and if I ever do see [Collins or Clarke] in public, I'm going to beat the fucking shit out of either one of them. If they can get away with doing that much damage to me and my family, then I can sit in jail for a few months for battery. I don't really care at this point."

A few weeks later, Kurt had simmered down. "I don't ever talk like that," he maintained. "That's the first time I've ever been so vicious and so sexist and weird. I just wanted to seem as extreme and irrational as possible to scare them. For all I care, they are exactly those things. I don't feel bad about saying any of that stuff because they *are* cunts. Men can be cunts, too."

Kurt believes their scare tactics worked by scaring Collins and Clarke into toning down their book. Ironically, though, publishing industry scuttlebutt has it that discreet legal pressure from Gold Mountain could have gotten publisher Hyperion Books to shelve the project quietly—but after Collins and Clarke made the answering machine tapes public, Hyperion could not be seen as having backed down under pressure. Ironically, as of this writing, the book had not reached the stores in the U.S.

On October 30, four years to the day after Kurt first smashed a guitar at a modest dorm party at Evergreen State College, the band played a nearly sold-out show at the fifty-thousand-seat Velez Sarsfield Stadium in Buenos Aires, Argentina. They had hardly practiced, their enthusiasm was low, and they played badly. They had done it for the money and it showed. They vowed never to make the same mistake again.

Part of the agreement was that Nirvana could choose their opening act. They went with Calamity Jane, a virtually unknown all-female band from Portland, Oregon. The overwhelmingly male crowd hated them. From a seat in the highest tier at the far end of the stadium, Kurt watched in disgust as within a minute's time, virtually the entire crowd was chanting *"Puta madre!"* at the band and throwing lighters, beer cans, dirt clods, coins and whatever else they could find onto the stage. "It was the largest display of sexism I've ever seen at once," Kurt says.

Chris knew what Kurt was going to do and tried to calm him down. But Kurt was determined to sabotage the show. The first thing they played was an improvised jam, which deteriorated into a fifteen-minute feedback fest from Kurt, with brief breaks when he would stop to glare at the crowd. Between songs, Kurt would tease the crowd by beginning to play "Teen Spirit" and then stopping. After a perfunctory set, they played a definitive version of "Endless, Nameless." "It was so intense," Kurt says. "There was so much emotion in it and feedback was coming out of my guitar just perfectly. I was manipulating it better than I ever had. It was really a great experience. It was really fun." They never did play "Teen Spirit."

Kurt jams with Mudhoney at an early October show at the Crocodile Cafe in Seattle. Singer Mark Arm does the swim. (© Charles Peterson)

***

The "In Bloom" video reached MTV in late November, about a month after it was shot. At first, Kurt had an idea for another film, this time a surrealistic fable about a little girl who is born into a Ku Klux Klan family and one day realizes how evil her parents are. Like the aborted "Lithium" concept, it was too ambitious, so Kurt came up with the idea of parodying an appearance on an early sixties TV variety program à la the "Ed Sullivan Show," which was essentially the dawn of rock video. He asked Kevin Kerslake to find authentic cameras from the period. Kerslake dug up some old Kinescopes to shoot the video with.

Spontaneity was key, and there was no script. Kurt aimed to keep it simple. "That's how things should happen," Kurt says. "Just do whatever you can instead of some long, drawn-out script, acting and

Dave at the Crocodile. (© Charles Peterson)

practicing your moves." The philosophy would carry over into the making of the band's next album. Unlike most video shoots, even the most low-budget, they ran through the song only five times. Despite the feeling that they are performing in front of a huge television studio audience, there were only a handful of people on the modest soundstage.

That's Doug Llewelyn, the "People's Court" post-trial interviewer, as the host (coincidentally, Llewelyn's first job was on "The Ed Sullivan Show").

They dressed up in ridiculous Beach Boys-style suits, although Kurt thoughtfully brought along some dresses for himself and the band, just in case. Chris cut his hair for the occasion and he liked it so much he kept it that way. The glasses Kurt wore made him dizzy. They also made him look very much like his father did at his age.

The cuts to the amped-up kids in the audience make them look like conformist freaks—they're so "normal" they're weird. The great mainstream masses look weird to the band, instead of vice versa. It's quite a leap from the "Teen Spirit" video, where the audience members were the band's peers and even went so far as to dance and mingle with the band. In "In Bloom," the audience is separated from the band not only by space but also time.

Of course, the kids in those early sixties audiences would become the baby boomers of today. The "audience as freaks" idea, says Kurt, "was kind of an attack on what those kids turned into. I'm sure the majority of them turned into yuppies. It was kind of a dis on their generation, the whole *Rolling Stone* generation. There was nothing wrong with those kids at the time—they were totally innocent and into rock and roll. Now they're in control of the media and the corporations and they're cranking out the very same shit that they used to despise. There are still Fabians and the Monkees, but at least the Monkees had good songs, instead of New Kids on the Block."

The video lampooned the idea of manufactured pop idols like Fabian and the Monkees; it was also an ironic comment on the fact that Nirvana had attained similar status. "These three fine young men from Seattle," the announcer declares, "are thoroughly all right and decent fellas." The slicked-back hair, the nerdy suits, and the band's stiff, repressed movements highlighted the absurdity of the notion of squeaky-clean pop idols and the uncompromising moral standard they were expected to live up to. By wearing dresses and destroying the set, they are literally trashing that idea. "Let's hear it for these three nice, decent, clean-cut young men!" Lewellyn says to the audience at the end of the clip. "I really can't say enough nice things about them!"

The humor of the clip was also quite strategic. With all the rumors about the band over the previous year, a few laughs were simply good PR. "I'd just been so tired for the last year of people taking us so seriously and being so concerned with what we do and what we say that I wanted to fuck off and show them that we have a humorous side to us," Kurt says. "It's always been there, but a lot of people have misread it, not understood it."

The original plan was to first send MTV a cut of the video with the sixties pop idol motif all the way through. The highlight came when the camera came in for a close-up for Kurt's guitar solo—instead of the guitar, the shot shows the top of Kurt's bobbing head the whole time, only to cut to the guitar just as the solo ends. After that version ran awhile, they planned to release the version where the band changes into dresses halfway through, which would have made for a neat surprise.

Unfortunately, the MTV "alternative" show "120 Minutes" insisted on debuting the video, and Kurt doubted they'd get the humor of the all-pop idol version, so they went with a third version, which was all dresses and destruction, thereby killing the gag (the planned first version never did air).

On December 15, *Incesticide* was released. Ever since the *Nevermind* sessions, the band had planned to issue an "odds and sods" album of live tracks, B-sides, and selections from the Crover demo, basically to beat the bootleggers and to give fans good sound quality for less money than a bootlegger would charge. Then Sub Pop announced that *they* were planning a Nirvana rarities album, too. With typical Sub Pop candor, it was tentatively titled *Cash Cow*. Having two Nirvana rarities albums was a bit much, and pooling the material would produce a definitive collection, so Gary Gersh made a deal with Sub Pop. This way, the band would have more control over the final product—from music to artwork—and distribution would be far superior to what Sub Pop could muster.

The album shows off the extremes the band has been through; from the grinding, nearly tuneless chain of riffs called "Aero Zeppelin" to the fully realized pop of "Sliver," from the Gang of Four-ish sounds of "Hairspray Queen" to the cover of Devo's "Turnaround," the collection contains all the elements of the Nirvana sound. It's all there—Nirvana synthesized seventies hard rock, punk-pop, new wave like Devo and the Knack, and what Kurt calls "new wave" (Butthole Surfers, Saccharine Trust, Big Black), etc., into a unique voice. "It does explain what kind of a band we were when we first started—obviously a Gang of Four and Scratch Acid rip-off," Kurt says.

The final track, the mighty "Aneurysm," demonstrates how Dave's juggernautic beats helped turn Nirvana from an interesting indie group into a world-class rock and roll band. The track also points the way toward the more experimental elements of the next album.

"Turnaround" and the Vaselines covers "Son of a Gun" and "Molly's Lips" had all been broadcast on John Peel's BBC-1 radio show in October of 1990. All three had been included on *Hormoaning*, a much sought-after Japan and Australia–only EP released to coincide with the early 1992 tour there. "Stain" hailed from the *Blew* EP and "Been a Son," "(New Wave) Polly" and "Aneurysm" from a 1991 session for Mark Goodier's show on BBC (a better version of "Aneurysm," recorded by Nirvana soundman Craig Montgomery, appeared on *Hormoaning* and as an extra track on the "Teen Spirit" CD single).

The cover, a painting by Kurt, is incredibly revealing. In it, a damaged baby clings to a skeletal parental figure which seems to be ignoring the baby. It looks longingly at some flowers. They are poppies. Typically, Kurt denies the tableaux has any significance. "It's just the image I came up with," he says. The poppies, he says, came from a postcard that just happened to be lying on his floor.

The painting well fits Kurt's friend Dylan Carlson's learned assessment of the major theme of Kurt's paintings: "Innocence and authentic vision beset upon by a cruel and uncaring universe. Artists continuously attempting to extract beauty from the world and being unable to because of being denied a beatific relationship with the world." A bit academic, but right on the mark.

Kurt's original liner notes included a strongly worded broadside directed at Lynn Hirschberg, but the brass at Geffen/DGC deemed them "pretty harsh" and asked him to tone them down. "I just went into the *Vanity Fair* and media scam," Kurt explains. "It was really negative, although it was very truthful. It came straight from my heart and I really felt that and I still do. Anyone looking back on it would see complaining. No one has enough empathy for me or Courtney to look beyond that and realize that it should be a legitimate complaint."

The notes are typical of Kurt's two-fold nature. They begin in a celebratory mode, plugging favorite bands like the Raincoats in an extended anecdote, then Shonen Knife, the Vaselines, Sonic Youth, Mudhoney, the Breeders, Jad Fair, Fits of Depression, etc. The tone shifts as Kurt launches a brief defense of Courtney, "the supreme example of dignity, ethics and honesty." Soon, he is sending "a big 'fuck you' to those of you who have the audacity to claim that I'm so naive and stupid that I would allow myself to be taken advantage of and manipulated" and telling the homophobes, racists, and sexists in their audience to "leave us the fuck alone!"

Added to the broadsides against his generation in "Smells Like Teen Spirit" and remarks made in virtually every interview he'd done, the missive seemed to cement Kurt's reputation as man who held a nearly bottomless disdain for his own audience. "He needs a PR makeover," Courtney says of Kurt. "It's like he's a snob and he's too good for everybody. If I was a kid, I'd spend my twenty dollars on Alice in Chains and the Chili Peppers because they *like* me—I'm not good enough for Kurt."

Of course, *Incesticide* is not a complete anthology of Nirvana's non-LP output. Left off the album were the excellent "Token Eastern Song," an outtake from the *Blew* sessions, a staggering cover of the Wipers' "D-7," which rounded out *Hormoaning*, "Even in His Youth," a cover of the Velvet Underground's "Here She Comes Now" done for the Community label, the remaining two tracks from the Crover demo, "Pen Cap Chew" and "If You Must" and the "Lithium" B-side "Curmudgeon," not to mention any number of live tracks recorded at the Halloween 1991 show at the Paramount in Seattle.

With the "In Bloom" video still on MTV and the possibility of Nirvana burnout quite real—*Nevermind* had been out for fifteen months by that point—Geffen/DGC elected not to push *Incesticide*, merely letting fans discover it for themselves. Vague plans for a single and video of "Sliver" were lofted and shot down. The album went gold the following February.

Meanwhile, Gold Mountain's Nirvana hype machine managed to get a story in *Spin* magazine, a fluffy interview with Kurt and Courtney by Sub Pop's Jonathan Poneman which neglected to reveal that Poneman had a substantial financial stake in his subject's latest release (as the last remnant of the buyout deal, Sub Pop got a cut of *Incesticide*). Of course, the real point of the story was the cover shot. Although the headline trumpeted "Nirvana: Artist of the Year," the cover featured a heavily airbrushed Cobain family portrait with Mom and Dad proudly cradling a perfectly normal-looking baby. It was aimed directly at Children's Services.

The popularity of the lighthearted "In Bloom" video couldn't have been better timed to take the edge off the controversies swirling around Kurt and Courtney. Newspapers all over the country reported that on December 29, Courtney had filed a suit regarding the leak of her medical records to *L.A. Weekly*. Many papers reported that she was merely suing Cedars-Sinai hospital for releasing the records, but according to a published report in the *L.A. Times*, the suit also named Courtney's physician and alleged medical fraud and negligence, invasion of privacy, wrongful disclosure of medical information, and negligent and intentional infliction of emotional distress. The suit was settled out of court in April of 1993.

The public didn't know it, but the battle to have free and clear custody of Frances still raged on. Frances now lived with Kurt and Courtney, but the couple had to submit to regular urine tests and a social worker had to check up on them periodically to make sure they were raising their child in an acceptable manner.

Kurt says he and Courtney spent a million dollars in 1992—
$80,000 went to personal expenses, $380,000 went to the taxman;
they also bought a relatively modest house for $300,000. "The rest of
it was because of Lynn Hirschberg," he says, referring to the legal
bills they piled up in their efforts to keep Frances and defend their
name. "That bitch owes me something."

Kurt onstage at the Seattle Center Arena. (© Charles Peterson)

After all that's happened, it's not surprising to hear that Kurt has found that being a professional rock musician is not quite what he imagined back when he was banging out his raunchy punk rock songs all alone in his bedroom in Aberdeen. "It's become a job, whether I like it or not," he says. "It's something that I love doing and would always want to do, but I have to be honest—I don't enjoy it nearly as much as I used to when I was practicing every night, imagining what it would be like. It's nothing like what it was like the first couple of years of actually playing in front of a few people, loading up the van and going to a rock show to actually *play*. The privilege of that just can't be reproduced after doing it for ten years. The same feeling is not there."

"I'm surprised to get as excited about it as I do still," he continues. "Sometimes I'm just blown away that I can enjoy it as much

IT'S ANGER, IT'S DEATH, AND ABSOLUTE TOTAL BLISS

as I do when we have a really good show. I'm feeling really good and loose, it really doesn't matter if the crowd is into it or not. I don't judge it by that at all because usually the crowd is the same wherever we go. It has to do with my mood usually—if I feel relaxed and I really want to play, it just happens to be that time of day when I would have wanted to play if I didn't have to play a show, then it usually goes really well and I appreciate it a lot."

What goes through Kurt's mind as he performs on stage? "It's just a mixture of every emotion that I've ever experienced," he says. "It's anger, it's death, and absolute total bliss, as happy as I've ever been when I was a carefree child running around throwing rocks at cops. It's just everything. Every song feels different."

So all the wailing and flailing and intense, distorted volume are not quite what they seem. "People see energy like that and screaming, people see it as a negative release, like we've got to get it out of us or we're going to kill somebody," Dave says. "But I'm happy when I play this music. It makes me really happy. Maybe when I was thirteen or fourteen I was mad at Springfield, Virginia, and things just rubbed me the wrong way. It's just fun to make noise and the bigger the noise, the funner it is. So the more noise you've got going, the better you feel."

The only times Kurt feels real anger on stage is when the monitors aren't working well, which often precipitates instrument smashing or abrupt stage exits. "If I can't hear myself, I cannot have a good show," he says. "I can't fake it. I feel like a fool. The audience doesn't deserve to be witnessing this when I can't hear myself because I'm not giving it 100 percent. I can't stand there and pretend I'm having a good time when I'm not. So I feel like I'm cheating the audience when that happens." Nowadays, the band can demand and receive whatever they want in terms of sound equipment.

Despite what he said before, Kurt is very aware of the vibe from the audience. "A lot of times I'll be going through the motions and I'll look up at the audience and realize that they're really enjoying themselves and that makes me happy," he says. "It's quite a sight to see that many people pogoing at once. Definitely one of the only things that our band has introduced to rock and roll is gathering that many people in one place to pogo."

There's a reason the band has lasted through all the trials and tribulations, and at the very core of it is the solid relationship between Kurt and Chris. Just as it's tempting to fit Kurt and Courtney's relationship into a stereotypical framework, the same could be said for Kurt and Chris. To be sure, there are elements of Mutt and Jeff—the short, high-strung one and the big, steady sidekick. Chris usually is more level-headed about business decisions. It's Chris who calms Kurt down when he gets flustered by anything from a belligerent bouncer to a lousy monitor mix.

But they complement each other perfectly. "Sometimes Kurt will be quiet and Chris will be loud, other times Kurt will be loud and Chris will be the one trying to keep things in control," says Tracy Marander. "It's almost yin and yang in a way."

"We've always had enough respect for each other to figure out what irks one another beforehand, what little personality defects that bother each other, and try to stop them before it turns into a fight," Kurt says. "We've never spoken mean words to each other. It's really weird. It's not because we love each other so much—we both think of each other as hypocrites and there are things about each other that I'm sure we despise—but there's no point. We just have this common knowledge that there's no point in fighting with one another because for the sake of the band, it's an irrelevant thing."

The one complaint Kurt has about Chris is that Chris's sense of humor drowns his out. "He's really a funny person," Kurt allows. "He's real clever in an almost inane way—the things that he says are just so asinine at times that they're hilarious. They make me laugh. But I feel like he restrains me from joining in on this sense of humor and actually contributing to it. I'm allowed to laugh at things that he says, but for some reason, I'm not allowed to be funny on the same level as he is."

Then again, with Kurt getting so much of the attention, it's only fair that Chris grab some of the limelight with his easy sense of humor. "Yeah," Kurt says, "but it sucks to have to be around somebody where you can't be yourself 100 percent. When me and Dave are together and Chris isn't around, it's totally hilarious. We're just playing off one another and it's really fun and I enjoy it. But when all three of us get together, Chris is in the middle and Dave and I are on the side. I take all the serious questions and Chris makes all the smarmy comments and funny things. And Dave is in the middle of both of us. You don't know *where* he stands."

But of course Kurt is usually too shy to be funny around large groups of people. "Everybody knows if Kurt smiles, it lights up the fucking room, because he usually doesn't," says Dave. "I don't know if he's really unhappy or if he's always been unhappy or if he just doesn't know how to be happy. When we'd shoot BB guns in the backyard or throw rocks at cars from the roof of the house or shoot out the windows at the lottery building with a BB gun when we were trying to quit smoking and we had nothing better to do, you'd see the laughing, funny, ha-ha-ha Kurt come into play, which a lot of people don't see."

Most people have never seen that side of Kurt, except the "In Bloom" video or perhaps a few choice scenes in *1991: The Year That Punk Broke*. "A lot of people think he's always the quiet-bitter-angry-confused little pixie, but he's not," Dave says. "I don't even know him that well and I know that much."

Kurt isn't the only one who's felt overwhelmed. "For the first year of me being in the band, there was just no reason at all for me to be at interviews," Dave says. "Chris is really politically motivated and really bright. He has a lot to say even though he sometimes gets spasms of the brain and can't spit out what he means to say. He really was the king of the interview and Kurt always had the beyond-clever snaps of wit. And I was like a paperweight."

Although Dave is much more socially integral to the band than any other drummer has ever been, Nirvana is still not exactly the Three Musketeers, all for one and one for all. "Chris and Kurt are unlike any people I've ever met before," Dave says. "They're hard to understand and they're hard to really feel like you're getting along with them, like you can really sit down and talk to them. Some people you can hit it off with immediately and you can talk about anything. With Chris and Kurt, I always felt so different from them. They'd known each other for a long time and sort of had the same sense of humor. Only recently—and this is just barely—did I feel like I really know them more and really felt like I was in the band."

"I don't feel like the new guy anymore, but I don't really know if I feel *vital* to the band," Dave continues. "You're joining a band that's had five drummers before—you might as well be on an hourly wage."

"It was kind of strange—and it still is, too," he says. "It's weird because I've always felt expendable. If they were tired of me being in the band they could always find another drummer, so I've always had that in the back of my mind. It's understandable—I don't think that drums in the band are of such importance that one person's style would really make a difference. A drummer like Dale Crover, you can tell when Dale is playing in Nirvana because he's the best drummer in the world. I've always thought if things didn't work out, they could always get Dale.

"It's not an apocalyptic thing, but I've never had a feeling of real security.

"Playing with Chris and Kurt is really great and we really do have something that nobody else has and I realize that," Dave says.

"When I say that they could get any other drummer, it's true, but there is a chemistry between the three of us. I hate flattering myself by saying that the band wouldn't be the same without me, but deep down I know it's true—it would be different. Sure, someone else could play the stuff that I'm playing and someone could play as hard as I play. Anybody could do what I do—it's no big deal, but there is a chemistry that clicks sometimes.

"With Chris and Kurt, there's never really any reassurance," Dave says. "It's never like, 'Wow, that was great!' It's like, you just do it." On the other hand, he feels that part of the magic of their collaboration lies precisely in the fact that they don't communicate with each other very well. "No one really says anything," he says, "so when we write a song, the arrangement just falls together—it's not so conscious. We don't decide 'We need a bridge *here*.' It just sort of happens."

Success has driven the three apart to a certain extent. "We get along well, the three of us, and at times it was sort of palsy-walsy, but never too much," Dave says. "Kurt and I used to spend every minute of the day with each other. We became really close, as close as we could get, I suppose, when we lived in Olympia. Then after that, we kind of got distant again. Things get crazy and you kind of want to get away from it all."

What's it like to be famous? "The only thing I can think of is paranoia—it makes you feel like someone's watching you," Kurt says. "It really isn't as hard as I thought it would be—or as hard as it seemed like it was at first. I used to resent people for recognizing me. I'd blame *them*. 'Don't fuckin' look at me. What the hell are you looking at?' You can't blame them for looking. But it *is* annoying."

Yet for all his outspoken abhorrence of fame, Kurt now wants to have another crack at it. "It's not that I like it any more, it's just that I'm getting familiar with it," he says. "I know how to react when people stare at me. I don't feel quite as paranoid as I did. I could probably learn to live with being famous. It doesn't mean that I've given in and I actually enjoy it, I just have a better attitude toward it than I did before."

Although Chris and Dave do it all the time, going out in public is a somewhat different proposition for Kurt. Because he is the frontman, because he is reclusive, because of the drugs, and because of the formidable mystique around his music, a Kurt spotting, even in Seattle, is the talk of the town. He's learning how to deal with getting ogled.

"Most of the time I'll smile and let them know that I understand

that they recognize me, because I'd do the same thing if I recognized
a star," he says. "If they keep staring and they're being obnoxious or
if they snicker or something like that, I give them a dirty look or ask
them what their problem is or confront them about it. Lots of times,
people have just laughed in my face when they recognize me. I
couldn't believe it. I can understand it now. Like a sarcastic thing—
'Look at that fucking idiot!' 'It's *him*! Ha-ha!' Those are the people
that I really like to deal with because I'll walk right up to them and
start drilling them with questions, like what's their problem. They
are just amazed because they think of me as someone who wouldn't
confront them and when I do, they clam up and turn beet red and
run away sometimes."

People expect celebrities to brim with a constant supply of good
cheer, something that Kurt rarely seems to do. It can make for some
awkward situations. "Most people think if I look at them and I don't
smile, that I'm pissed off, so I go out of my way to make it look like
I'm enjoying myself," Kurt says. "I usually *am* enjoying myself. I'm
hardly ever depressed any more, so it's a lot easier to be able to do
that."

Kurt also has to fight another perception. Rock stars just aren't
supposed to have chronic health problems. Many believed that
Kurt's stomach problem was merely a "stomach problem"—a
euphemism for a heroin habit (and occasionally it was). But he really
does have intense, chronic stomach pain. "I've seen it, I've been
there," says Chris. "I've been there when he's had his major episodes
and it's terrible because there's nothing you can do."

Kurt has seen countless specialists for his stomach—nine in the first part of 1993 alone—who remain baffled as to what his problem might be. Ulcers have been ruled out. The latest theory is that a kink in Kurt's spine due to his scoliosis is pinching a nerve which leads to his stomach. Besides opiate-derived analgesics, the only effective cure Kurt has found is performing on stage, when a massive endorphin rush kills the pain.

Ironically, Kurt's condition may have something to do with his agonized wail. Or vice versa. Asked to pinpoint the source of the pain, he indicates a spot just below his breastbone—it also happens to be exactly where he says his scream originates.

"There's been so many times when I'll be sitting there eating and having massive pain and no one even realizes it," Kurt says. "I'm so tired of complaining about it. It hurts on tour so often, I have no choice but to go about my business. After a show, I have to try to force myself to eat. I'm sitting in my hotel room, forcing myself to eat, taking a bite, and drinking water and doubling up and puking. Halfway through the European tour, I remember saying I'll never go on tour again until I have this fixed because I wanted to kill myself. I wanted to fucking blow my head off, I was so tired of it. There's no way I'm going to live like that. It turned me into a neurotic freak. I was psychologically fucked up. I was having a lot of mental problems because I was having chronic pain every single day."

Heroin was one way of killing the pain, although Kurt subsequently found a legal and relatively safe remedy for his condition—Buprenex, a mild synthetic opiate which he injected directly into his stomach during an attack. Often he would go a week without resorting to the drug, but when he did something stressful, like playing a show or shooting a video, he'd do it several times a day. Recently, a doctor diagnosed his stomach pain as a result of a pinched nerve in his spine, brought on by his scoliosis. The physical therapy he's getting for his back seems to be working and Kurt says he's glad that he isn't dependent on a chemical for his well-being anymore. Nowadays, he eats better food and even does push-ups and sit-ups before going to bed. He actually looks forward to touring again.

Another stumbling block for Kurt is the public's perception that he is a frail, passive person who has little idea what he is doing. "In addition to everything else, he is a literal genius about what it is to be a rock artist," says Gold Mountain's Danny Goldberg. "It's not something that he has not thought about." Goldberg tells a story about Kurt at the MTV taping back in January 1992, while he and Courtney were binging on heroin.

"Kurt's just wiped out and he looks terrible and he says, 'I want to see it back,'" he recalls. "So they play back about fifteen different takes of four or five different songs. He just sat there and said, 'That's no good.' 'That one's no good.' 'That one you can put in "The Year in Rock" but I don't want it on regularly.' 'That one is the one you put on *120 Minutes*. 'After a week I only want this one repeated.' He could barely walk across the room, but they were all exactly the right decisions and it was not like anyone else's opinion mattered. When it comes to the professional product of what Nirvana is, he makes all of those decisions and he makes them from a place of tremendous consciousness."

Kurt is also savvy about publicity. Everybody who was anybody was backstage at the 1991 Rock for Choice benefit in L.A.; Perry Farrell was there, even Axl Rose was there. In a crowded hallway, Kurt mentioned to Danny Goldberg that journalists had been asking the band a lot of political questions and missing the band's sense of humor. Kurt had figured out that they were being prompted by a specific paragraph in the band's bio and asked Goldberg if it could be removed. Goldberg was very impressed. "I've *never* had an artist— or a manager or a publicist—pick up within a month the effect of a bio on the types of questions being asked and *then* figure out how to edit it to skew it slightly differently," he says, marveling.

Goldberg likens Kurt's savvy to John Lennon's, recalling a celebrated 1970 *Rolling Stone* interview with Lennon in which he revealed things like the fact that the Beatles always took care not to release a record at the same time as the Stones. At the time, fans were shocked by such conscious manipulation, but, as Goldberg says, "You don't become the Beatles by accident. And you don't become Nirvana by accident, either."

The John Lennon comparisons trouble the Cobains, if only because of what that makes Courtney. She once greeted a visitor to the Cobains' hotel room by saying, "Okay, you want to see Yoko Ono? Here goes." Whereupon she proceeded to pick up the phone, call Gold Mountain on Nirvana business, and positively excoriate whatever hapless person was on the other end of the line.

"Sometimes Kurt just doesn't feel like saying stuff, so he has her say it for him," says Goldberg. "When Courtney does that, it's because he has asked her to do it. It's a terrible mistake if anyone ever thinks that she does things on her own. Sometimes, he just would rather not talk, so he'll have her call. But the idea that she could make him do anything that he doesn't want to do is just so absurd. You can't get this guy to drink a glass of water or walk across a room to turn over a cassette or do *anything* he doesn't want to do. He is one of the most willful people I've ever met in my life. Sometimes I think he'll just ask her to be the bad guy."

Many wonder why Courtney should be involved in her husband's business affairs at all. "Because I'm too lazy to deal with it," Kurt replies. "I'll just bend over and help them slip it in my ass. I forget about things all the time and everyone takes advantage of that. If it wasn't for Courtney going out of her way to just take care of things without even asking me sometimes—obviously I would allow her to do it anyway—it's mainly for the benefit of our baby so we can make sure we have some money in the next ten years. I'm just too lazy. I decided a couple of years ago that I wasn't going to deal with the business side of it. Now I have to. I'm getting better at it. I'm learning from her."

Goldberg cites his experience as a publicist with Led Zeppelin. Although Jimmy Page was a quiet man, he ran Led Zeppelin with an iron fist—it just wasn't *his* fist. When he didn't like something that was going on, he'd just mention it to manager Peter Grant and Grant would do whatever yelling was necessary. "I'm not saying that Courtney has got the same relationship that Peter had to Jimmy," Goldberg says, "I'm just saying that people who are quiet are not necessarily passive."

Often, Courtney is simply looking out for the man who is her husband.."If they're on tour and he's got a terrible stomach and there's a certain kind of food that doesn't give him stomachaches and they go into a dressing room somewhere and that food's not there and he's going to be doubled over in pain, she does make a big scene," Goldberg says. "But she has nothing to do with things like who's producing the record or what the songs are or whether they tour or don't tour."

"Honestly, she's not very involved," Goldberg continues. "She's just very visible—you can't miss her when she's in a room. She's loud and she's forceful and she's flamboyant."

Even Kurt admits his wife can sometimes be a social liability. "She'll confront people even when there's no point in confronting them," Kurt says. "There'll be someone who's obviously a sexist jerk but you have to be around this person because you're working with them at this time and there's really no penetrating this person, you know they're a lost cause, but she'll go out of her way to confront him and make a bad scene in front of all these people just to let him know, 'Don't fuckin' bullshit me at all.' She didn't make a dent in this person at all. But still, it's her duty to do things like that. Even though it doesn't make anything better, it still needs to be done. I'll just leave the person alone. That's the difference between her and me—she's definitely a fighter."

Naturally, Courtney makes for a formidable business adversary.

"I will ask my management to do something for me twenty times," Kurt says, "and finally Courtney calls up and screams at them and it finally sticks in their brain. They get off the phone and they go, 'What a cunt!' But the thing gets done." Of course, the question is, at what cost?

Courtney is extremely intelligent and does not suffer fools gladly. The slightest misstep, even in the most casual of conversations, is often rewarded with a withering comment—or worse. But Kurt is no fool, either. He readily acknowledges that his wife's brusque personal style hurts far more often than it helps. "She's totally abusive to people and she doesn't even realize it, she's so used to talking that way," Kurt says. "And a lot of times she unnecessarily jumps to conclusions. And that's her downfall. That's why she doesn't get taken seriously." Even he admits they fight nearly every day.

It's been said that if Courtney were a man, her extreme forwardness and caustic manner wouldn't earn her any flak at all. But even Kurt agrees she'd get it no matter what sex she was. "I remind her of that almost every day," he says with a sly chuckle, their latest spat probably still fresh in his mind. "She admits it and she tries really hard but there's this chemical in her mind that just won't allow her to think before she freaks out on people. A lot of times, someone deserves it, though."

It's an interesting situation for such a sensitive person as Kurt. "Well, I'm not as sensitive as most people probably think," he says, defensively. "There are so many positive qualities about her that it doesn't even matter. She's already getting a lot better at it. It just takes people a long time to change their ways. It's the only character flaw she has is that she jumps the gun too fast."

Although tension still flares between Courtney and the other members of the band, things are definitely looking up. Many say Courtney has been changing for the better, especially after Frances was born. "She has definitely become a person who admits she's wrong," Kurt says. "It usually takes two or three examples before she will admit it, but she does. She isn't *that* pigheaded."

The Courtney factor still dogs the band. The idea persists that Courtney controls Kurt, that she is sapping his talent, that she will break up the band. Call it the Delilah Complex. But she simply is not the monster that much of her recent press has painted her to be. It wasn't for nothing that Kurt said "Don't believe everything you read." But thanks to the ripple effect of the *Vanity Fair* profile, it has become increasingly difficult to portray Courtney Love as anything but a horror without seeming to be a stooge or a liar. And while

Courtney isn't above reproach, it's obvious that there's a considerable sexist force behind the attacks on her character.

Kurt is hardly optimistic about the future. "No matter what we do or how clean we live our lives, we're not going to survive this because there are too many enemies and we threaten too many people," he says. "Everyone wants to see us die. We might just keep going just to spite those fuckheads. They've already treaded past the most offensive part, which is attacking my family, and that could go on for years, but there's going to be a time when I'm not going to be able to deal with it anymore, when my daughter is old enough to realize what's going on. She's already going to be twelve years old and start reading all this old press and ask, 'Hey, did you really take drugs when I was a baby?' It's going to be a hard thing to convince her of all the things that aren't true."

"There are some amazing things that have happened that I'm so blessed with, but there are so many damaging things at the same time," Kurt says. "I should be completely rehabilitated as far as my bad attitude—at this point, if everything had gone fine, I would be so much of a happier person, my humor would have started to come out more.

"I used to be a pretty funny person, always going out of my way to look on the funnier side of life, but I've withdrawn back into a bad attitude. I'm sure it will just be a matter of time because the positive things—the baby and the wife—are so great, they're so etched in my life as being positive things that I'm blessed with and grateful for that if people just keep their fucking mouths shut and stop the accusations, in a couple of years, I'll probably be okay. But I just don't see it ending. Just yesterday, another fucking article came out..."

Dave is more than happy to be the least visible member of Nirvana. He doesn't even want to do interviews anymore. "One," he says, "because I'm too lazy and two, because why does everyone want to know what I have to say? What's the big deal? It's like one-two-three-four, I play drums and that's about it. I'll put my face on the record and go home at night and clean the house. I just want to lead a normal life. I don't want to be the drummer of Nirvana for the rest of my life, so I lay low.

"It's such a blessing to play in the band and see and do everything that we've done, and not pay the price that a lot of people have to pay," says Dave. "I take pride in leading the most simple life of anybody in the band because I don't do much, other than be happy. There's so much that goes on with Kurt and Courtney that I can't keep up with."

Kurt and close personal friend Ren Hoek at the **Advocate** shoot.
(© Charles Peterson)

CHAPTER FOURTEEN

In 1993, Nirvana began to return to business as usual.

In January, the band played two huge shows with their old friends L7 in Brazil early in the year, the first on the sixteenth at Morumbi Stadium in São Paulo and another show a week later at the seventy-thousand-seat Apoetose Stadium in Rio de Janeiro.

The band was in peak form. The São Paulo show, according to Alex Macleod, was "punk rock heaven, baby." Just for the occasion, they played "Rio" by Duran Duran, with Dave on bass and vocals, Chris playing guitar, and Kurt behind the drums. Later, they played a seemingly endless version of Terry Jacks's insipid 1974 bubblegum hit "Seasons in the Sun." Flea from the Red Hot Chili Peppers played the "Teen Spirit" solo on trumpet.

Back home, Kurt became his own publicist and personally arranged for interviews with the *Advocate*, a national gay magazine, and *Monk*, a roving magazine written by two guys in a Winnebago who travel around America and focus on a different city in each issue.

The *Advocate* piece was a master stroke. It encouraged Nirvana fans to buy a gay-oriented magazine. And it exposed the band to an audience that doesn't tend to go for rock bands like Nirvana.

In the interview, Kurt mentioned that he had thought he was gay for a brief time in high school, and added "I'm definitely gay in spirit, and I probably could be bisexual." Somehow that got translated by several major newspapers, as well as the entire Gannett newspaper chain, into a statement that he was a "practicing bisexual" and that "this was just fine with his wife."

In February, Kurt designed a custom guitar for Fender—a cross between a Jaguar and a Mustang. A limited run for his use only was planned, but in the spring of 1993, a consumer edition was being considered.

At the start of the third week in February, the band traveled to Minnesota to record their new album with producer Steve Albini.

Kurt had the basic ideas for most of the songs by the time he and Courtney had left the Spaulding apartment in the summer of 1992. They just needed structure, which was worked out in rehearsals with Chris and Dave. Early versions of three of the songs—"Rape Me," "Dumb," and "Pennyroyal Tea"—had been kicking around on bootlegs since just after *Nevermind*. Kurt had wanted to begin recording the album that summer, but all three members lived in different cities and they weren't in close touch; besides, Kurt and Courtney were about to have a baby.

Kurt had always wanted to record with Albini, ever since he first heard Big Black, an incendiary, tremendously influential Chicago trio on Touch & Go Records that combined nasty guitar textures, bilious, nasal vocals, and the incessant pounding of a drum machine to induce visions of urban rage and paranoia. Albini went on to a thriving, even legendary, career recording (like Jack Endino, never *producing*) various bands like Helmet, Superchunk, PJ Harvey, and even EMF, as well as countless underground heroes, such as the Jesus Lizard and Tar.

But Kurt was particularly after the drum sound he had heard on two Albini projects—the Pixies' epochal 1988 album *Surfer Rosa* and the Breeders' excellent 1990 album *Pod*. It's a natural, powerful sound produced with canny microphone placement rather than phony sounding effects boxes. It reminded Kurt of the drum sound on Aerosmith's 1976 *Rocks* album.

After Big Black, Albini fronted the unfortunately named thrash band Rapeman. Within indie-rock circles, a reputation as a misogynist seems to dog Albini, which would make him an odd choice for Kurt. "That's what I've heard from people, but I just thought until I meet him, I don't really care, because if he turns out to be an asshole, I'll at least use him for his recording abilities," Kurt says. "Definitely a few sexist things leaked out of him, but that's just the scene he's in. There's a few misogynists that I admire like William Burroughs. Brion Gysin is a total misogynist and I like his writing. I hate people for being misogynists and I would choose not to be associated with them but sometimes they produce some good work. They just have a flaw that they need to work on.

"I learned a long time ago that if you're too strict about things and you cut yourself off from people who have those tendencies, you're limiting yourself," Kurt says. "There are things that can be learned from people like that. And why not try to persuade them into thinking differently rather than just banning them, putting a veto on them, and not having anything to do with them. All it does is make them resentful and they won't even think about the things that they do wrong."

So, misogynist or not, Kurt was eager to get Albini, or more specifically, the Albini sound. "That sound is as close to the sound that I hear in my head that I've ever found," he says, "so I just had to do it."

For months before the band contacted him, rumors had been circulating that Albini was to produce the next Nirvana album. At last he sent a disclaimer to the U.K. music press stating that "the appearance in the press of this mistake fosters the impression that I only work with bands who've been on television. This is not the case!" Days later, Gold Mountain contacted Albini.

This was the man who once told a friend that he thought Nirvana was just "R.E.M. with a fuzzbox." "I thought they were an unremarkable version of the Seattle sound," Albini admits. "I thought they were typical of the bands of this era and of that locale."

It's an opinion he still holds, so one wonders why Albini would take the assignment. The way he puts it, it was a mission of mercy. "This is going to sound kind of stupid," he says, "but in a way, I felt sorry for them. The position they were in, there was a bunch of bigwig music industry scum whose fortunes depended on Nirvana making hit records. It seemed obvious to me that fundamentally they were the same sort of people as all the small-fry bands I deal with. They were basically punk rock fans, they're people that were in a band that came up from an independent scene and it was sort of a fluke that they got famous."

"It seemed that they understood doing things the way I usually do them and they would appreciate making a record like that," Albini continues. "But if I didn't do it, they weren't going to be allowed to make a record like that by the record company or by anyone else who worked with them. Any other producer that would work with Nirvana, for a start, would rob them, would want to get a lot of money out of them. And they'd probably be banking on making a hit record, in which case he would be making a record that he thought fit the mold of the hit singles record, not a powerful, personal punk rock record, which is the sort of record I got the impression they wanted to make."

In addition to a $24,000 studio bill, Albini's fee was $100,000, but unlike virtually any other producer, Albini refused to take points (a percentage of sales) on the album. "I just think that taking points on an album is an immoral position—I cannot do it, I think it's almost criminal," says Albini. "Anyone who takes a royalty off a band's record—other than someone who actually writes music or plays on the record—is a thief."

Albini didn't want the album to sound anything like *Nevermind*. "It sounds like that not because that's the way the band sounds," he says, "but because that's the way the producer and the remix guy and the record company *wanted* it to sound."

Once again, Kurt finished writing most of the lyrics within days of recording his vocals, culling most of them from notebooks full of poetry.

Booking themselves in as "The Simon Ritchie Group," the band recorded and mixed the entire album in two weeks at Pachyderm Studios, located about fifty miles south of Minneapolis in the middle of the Minnesota tundra. It's a favorite haunt of Albini's, where he has produced the Wedding Present, PJ Harvey, Killing Joke, Failure, and others. Clients stay at a large house which Chris described as "Mike Brady meets Frank Lloyd Wright." The studio is a separate building about a hundred yards through the woods. The spacious wood-paneled main room where they set up the drums had a large window that looked out onto the snowy Minnesotan winter. The Neve mixing board had been used to make AC/DC's *Back In Black*.

The band had made it abundantly clear to DGC and Gold Mountain that they didn't want any interference with the recording—they'd learned at least one lesson from *Nevermind*. They didn't even play any work tapes for their A&R man Gary Gersh, a pretty cheeky maneuver, to say the least. But Nirvana now had enough clout that Geffen wouldn't dare reject the album—or would they? "If they do, they know we'll break up," says Kurt. "Fuck, we made them fifty million dollars last year."

For most of the two weeks it took to make the album, it was just Albini, Kurt, Chris, Dave, and assistant engineer Robert "Bob" S. Weston IV.

Although it was ostensibly a low-budget project, Albini says the band was not above typical indulged rock star behavior. The band didn't actually show up with their equipment and instead had it shipped, then wasted the better part of three days waiting for it to arrive. Albini says the band wanted someone to Fed Ex a boom box to them instead of just going out and buying one; when Kurt began having trouble tuning his guitar, they wanted to fly in their guitar tech Ernie Bailey. "When you've got millions of dollars, maybe you go a little crazy and start doing stuff like that," says Albini.

But once they actually started recording, it went very quickly and they completed all the recording—basic drum, bass, and guitar tracks, guitar solos, and vocals—in about six days. Kurt says they could have done the whole album in a week if they had really wanted to.

They recorded live—meaning bass, drums, and guitar all at once—and kept virtually everything they laid down. Kurt added another guitar track to about half of the songs, then added guitar solos, then vocals. This time, he didn't run out of cough syrup before it was time to sing.

"It was the easiest recording we've ever done, hands down," says Kurt, who had anticipated at least some disagreements with Albini. "I thought we would eventually get on each other's nerves and end up screaming at each other. I was prepared to have to live with this person who was supposedly a sexist jerk, but he was surprisingly helpful and friendly and easy to get along with."

Personally, Albini was pleasantly surprised by all three band members. "Kurt is actually quite normal," Albini says. "He's been through a lot and you can tell that it's beaten up on him. He's kind of sallow and a little bit somber and melancholy but I think he's melancholy because he's in a situation that he thinks is not as pleasant as it should be, considering all the attributes—he's got a lot of money, he's famous, he's in a successful, popular rock band, so things should be going fairly easily for him and they're not. That's a dichotomy that he's uncomfortable with and I think he's coming to accept it.

"He is an intelligent guy—he doesn't come off that way," Albini continues. "He plays dumb occasionally to try to get people to trip themselves up. Also I think he thinks it cool to be naive and dumb. But I think he's an intelligent guy and he's handled it better than most people. He still has a healthy suspicion of the other big shots in the music industry. A lot of people in his position would have completely converted and gone to the position where 'They're people just like us and I give them all the credit I would give you.' I think he recognizes that most of the players and movers and shakers in the music scene are real pieces of shit."

"Probably the easiest guy to deal with of them all was Dave Grohl," Albini says. "For one, he's an excellent drummer, so there's never any worry whether he's going to be able to play. His playing was rock solid and probably the highlight of my appreciation of the band was watching Dave play the drums. He's also a very pleasant, very goofy guy to be around."

Albini respected Chris as well. "If he listens to something and he doesn't like it," he says, "he will say that he doesn't like it but he's adult enough that he can say 'Well, this is the sort of thing that might grow on me. I'll let it sit there for a while before I veto it.'" Albini also feels that Chris has to do a fair amount of "mopping up." "Like if Kurt doesn't know how to plug in his guitar and tune it, for example, and Chris does, he doesn't make a big deal about it," Albini says. "Chris will just run in there and take care of it."

As Albini himself insists, he's more of an engineer than a producer—he gets sounds rather than arrangements. So although he had his own opinions, Albini encouraged the band to decide what was a good take and what wasn't. "If he would have had his way, the record would have turned out way raunchier than it did," Kurt says. "He wanted to mix the vocals at an unnecessarily low level. That's not the way we sound good."

Albini was confident that Kurt knew what he was doing.

"Generally speaking, he knows what he thinks is acceptable and what isn't acceptable," says Albini. "He can make concrete steps to improve things that he doesn't think are acceptable. After the fact, when he's in a vacuum, when he's back at home, occasionally he gets a little too overcritical and introspective about things. But while he's actually doing it, he's very efficient."

The idea was to go for a natural sound. "The last Nirvana album, to my ears, is sort of a standard hack recording that has then been turned into a very, very controlled, compressed radio-friendly mix," says Albini. "That is not, in my opinion, very flattering to a rock band."

The all-important drum sound was achieved with virtually no electronic chicanery—just a lot of microphones placed around the room to pick up the room's natural reverberance. If you've got a good drummer, a good drum set, and a good-sounding room, you're home free. "Dave Grohl's an amazing drummer," says Albini. "If you take a good drummer and put him in front of a drum kit that sounds good acoustically and just record it, you've done the job."

Kurt's vocals also had few effects. Instead of electronically doctoring the vocal tracks to make it seem like they were done in a nice, resonant room, Albini simply recorded the sound of someone singing in a nice, resonant room. "On the last album, there was a lot of double-tracked vocals and stuff, which is a hack production technique to make vocals sound 'special,'" Albini says. "It's been done so much over the last ten years that to me, that now sounds ordinary. That's now a standard production trick. To hear just the sound of a guy singing in a room—which is on the new album, it's just one take of Kurt singing in a room—that sounds so different from what else is out there that it sounds like a special effect."

In Utero is the equivalent of an acoustic album—but it gets back to basics in a way that isn't as forced and obvious as the "unplugged" trend. This is Nirvana's version of the stereotypical indulgent follow-up album—they're doing exactly what they've always dreamed of doing. Usually, that means two double-length CD's full of filler and overinflated wankery, the budget ballooning with university marching bands, legions of chanting Gyuto monks and months and months of time wasted in the studio. Instead, Nirvana recorded the follow-up to a quadruple platinum album in two weeks on a vintage twenty-four-track analog board.

Of course, some would say they made a low-budget album out of some sort of indie-rock guilt complex. "We didn't make a raw record to make a statement at all, to prove that we can do whatever we want," Kurt insists. "That's exactly what we've always wanted to sound like." Many have contemplated such a move, but no one has ever actually done what Nirvana did. Kurt covers himself, though, because even the most "new wave" songs have hooks—the spiraling ascending riff on "Scentless Apprentice," the wrenching, Zeppelinesque breaks in "Milk It."

And as far as modest recording strategies go, Nirvana was not the only one. A low-tech, low-profile approach had already begun sweeping—or rather, resweeping—underground rock in the early nineties. As a reaction against the cold, digital CD and the cynical, greedy way it was foisted on the public—and as a cost-cutting measure—Nirvana favorites such as Pavement and Sebadoh became proponents of "chimp rock," or "no-fi," as this crude approach to recording became known. Ever with their eyes on the horizon, Sonic Youth purposely recorded their *Dirty* album (1991) with plenty of distortion and at a lower than usual tape speed for even lower fi.

The approach isn't confined to cheap equipment or primitive recording techniques—a first-take, best-take philosophy is part and parcel. Besides making the music more spontaneous—when you think you're only going to get one take, you try harder—it's also a dare: Can the music stand without layers of studio gloss? As they began to get into the no fi ethos, *Nevermind* became even more repugnant to Kurt, Chris, and Dave than it already was. Rock history will probably record *In Utero* as a giant step back to the future.

A little over a week into the recording, Courtney flew in, basically because she missed Kurt. Albini says she tried to butt in on the proceedings, but he won't say exactly what the problem was. "I don't feel like embarrassing Kurt by talking about what a psycho hosebeast his wife is," says Albini, "especially because he knows it already."

"The only way Steve Albini would think I was a perfect girlfriend," Courtney replies, "would be if I was from the East Coast, played the cello, had big tits and small hoop earrings, wore black turtlenecks, had all matching luggage, and never said a *word*."

Eventually, Courtney and Dave got into a huge spat, but no one will talk about it.

The mixing was done in under a week—quick by the band's standards, but not for Albini, who was used to mixing an entire album in a day or two. If a mix wasn't working out, they'd all goof off the rest of the day and do things like watch the complete series of David Attenborough nature videos or go in for a little pyromania. "Steve

was really into lighting his ass on fire," says Kurt. "He'd pour rubbing alcohol on his ass and light it on fire. He likes to do that." Chris spent most of his spare time working on a magazine article about his latest visit to Croatia.

At one point during the recording, Kurt drew a simple but evocative caricature of the band on a drum head. "When you see Kurt do something like that, you think about the way Kurt writes songs," Dave says. "They're so simple and so to the point and so right. Something that would take me an hour to explain, Kurt would sum up in two words. That's something he has that I've never seen in anyone else."

They also used their spare time to make prank phone calls and record them for later delectation. Kurt had gotten a message from Gold Mountain that Gene Simmons from Kiss wanted to talk to him. Albini "just happened" to find the number sitting by the studio phone and decided to call Simmons and pretend to be Kurt. It turned out that Simmons wanted Nirvana to play on a planned Kiss tribute album and even offered to co-write a song with Kurt. Albini also called Eddie Vedder and pretended to be legendary producer Tony Visconti (David Bowie, T. Rex, etc.). "Your voice really speaks to me," said Albini, who offered to get Vedder in with "a real band" to do some recording. Vedder bought it, but said he'd rather just make a home recording and sell it for five bucks a throw.

They called Evan Dando of the Lemonheads on tour in Australia and told him that Madonna was on the line, and to please hold. Dando bought it hook, line, and sinker, growing more and more anxious the longer he waited on hold. "I'm going to start beating off!" he says at one point on the tape. Gradually, he gets more and more impatient. Finally Albini, saying he's Madonna's assistant, tells Dando that Madonna will have to call back.

The capper was a call Dave made to John Silva to fill him in on how the project was going—"Things are going really bad," Dave says solemnly. "Chris was throwing up blood last night..."

To celebrate the completion of the record, they had a listening party and sat around and smoked cigars, except for Kurt, who stuck to his trusty Winston Lights.

So what does Albini think of *In Utero?* "I like it far more than I thought I was going to," he allows. "I like this record way more than I've ever liked a Nirvana record. I find myself listening to it of my own free will, occasionally."

"I think it's a far better record than they could have made under any other circumstances," Albini continues. "Is it one of my top ten favorite albums of all time? No. Is it in my top one hundred albums? Maybe."

Kurt admits his lyrics are hard to decipher. "I slur and run words together a lot," he says, "and I have a fake English accent sometimes." This time, Kurt might actually consent to print his lyrics. "I really like them, there's really nothing that's embarrassing about them so I might print them this time," he says. "I'd rather do it now than read reviews and have these idiots write the wrong lyrics in."

Besides the pedestrian fact that it's their third album, the classic causes of the sophomore jinx did not apply to *Verse Chorus Verse.* Often, when bands get famous quickly, they fall into the easy life, disconnected from what inspired them in the first place. This was clearly not the case for Kurt or indeed Chris and Dave, for that matter. The material for follow-up albums is typically thrown together on the run during a lengthy tour that often ends a week before recording begins. That didn't apply either—Nirvana didn't tour for most of 1992 and into 1993, so Kurt had plenty of time to develop material.

But Kurt's expressions of pain, which once tapped into the mass consciousness so perfectly, may now be less relevant. Just when the country is starting to feel optimistic again, here comes Kurt with a huge sack of woe. And the cause of his pain is no longer something that everyone can relate to. Most people are not familiar with the sensation of being publicly pilloried because of their drug use. Months before the album was released, it remained to be seen if Kurt had translated his personal experience into a universal feeling, as he has done in the past.

The lyrics aren't as impressionistic this time—they're more straightforward, which is not to say they're as literal as "Sliver" or "Polly." A medical theme runs through most lyrics, expanding the vocabulary of "Drain You." Virtually every song contains some image of sickness and disease and over the course of the album, Kurt alludes to: sunburn, acne, cancer, bad posture, open sores, growing pains, hangovers, anemia, insomnia, constipation, indigestion. He finds this litany hilarious. "I'm always the last to realize things like that, like the way I used guns in the last record," he says. "I didn't mean to turn it into a concept album."

Once again, the record is a product of Kurt's opposing sensibilities. On the one hand, as Courtney says, "He chews bubblegum in his soul." But that deeply held pop instinct has an equal and opposite reaction. "Sometimes, he may be his own worst enemy in terms of thinking something is too hooky or too poppy," says Butch Vig. "I think maybe that's one of the reasons they wanted this new record to be really intensely brutal sounding."

The music reflects some powerful opposing forces in Kurt's life; the rage, frustration, and fear caused by his and Courtney's various predicaments and the equally powerful feelings of love and optimism inspired by his wife and child. That's why *In Utero* takes the manic-depressive musical mode of *Nevermind* to a whole new extreme. The Beatlesque "Dumb" happily coexists beside the all-out frenzied punk graffiti of "Milk It," while "All Apologies" is worlds away from the apoplectic "Scentless Apprentice." It's as if Kurt has given up trying to meld his punk and pop instincts into one harmonious whole. Forget it. This is war.

Amazingly, Kurt denies it to the bitter end. "I don't think of it as any harsher or any more emotional than the other two records," Kurt says. "I'm still equally as pissed off about the things that made me pissed off a few years ago. It's people doing evil things to other people for no reason. And I just want to beat the shit out of them. That's the bottom line. And all I can do is scream into a microphone instead," he adds, laughing at the futility of it all.

Kurt had a little more time to work on the lyrics for *In Utero* than he did for *Bleach* and *Nevermind*. "I swear the lyrics I wrote on those last two albums were so rushed," Kurt says. "They were absolute last-minute, quick-fix, taken from poems. Most of the lines that I took from poems had to be rearranged to fit the song phonetically, so they don't have much personal meaning at all, really."

"There's definitely some pieces in there that reflect on my personal life," Kurt says, "but really, they aren't as personal as everyone thinks they are. I would *like* them to be more personal. The *emotions*, the songs themselves are personal. I can't do it—I've tried to write personally and it just doesn't seem to work. It would be too obvious. Some things that you could read in could fit into anyone's life that had any amount of pain at all. It's pretty cliché." Of course, it isn't cliché—it's just that once again, Kurt rightly won't reveal just how personal this album is, if only to encourage different interpretations.

But even Dave acknowledges that the lyrics are loaded with personal meaning. "I guess just knowing what has happened in the past eight months and listening to some of the lyrics and knowing what they're pertaining to is kind of strange," Dave says, "because there's a lot of spite, a lot of 'Fuck you' or 'I've been fucked over.' And a lot of lines that refer to money or legalities or babies. The hit I get off of that is very weird. It's intense but at the same time it just seems like Kurt feels like he's backed up against a wall and he's just going to scream his way out. A lot of what he has to say is related to a lot of the shit he's gone through. And it's not so much teen angst anymore. It's a whole different ball game: rock star angst. At the same time, the lyrics are similar to the first demo they'd done.

"There are a lot of lyrics to this record whereas with *Nevermind*, there was a verse and a chorus and it was usually repeated," says Dave. "But on this one, there's a lot of lyrics and with a lot of lyrics comes a lot to say. So you kind of figure that Kurt has something to say."

"I really haven't had that exciting of a life," Kurt protests none too convincingly. "There are a lot of things I wish I would have done, instead of just sitting around and complaining about having a boring life. So I pretty much like to make it up—I'd rather tell a story about somebody else."

Kurt likes to talk about his "boring life," but there's no doubt that he's merely being disingenuous. For one thing, the year before the recording of *In Utero* was hardly Dullsville. "No, it wasn't," he says, "but if I were to write some songs expressing my anger toward the media, it would really be cliché and everyone's expecting that, so I'm not going to write a single fucking song, I'm not going to give anyone the pleasure. I would be easily able to write a song and it wouldn't be so obvious that I would come out and say 'Fuck the media.'"

"Rape Me" would seem to be about just that. "I wrote that before this happened, but it could easily fit in," he concedes. "It was actually about rape. That was what it initially was supposed to be about, but now I could definitely use it as an example of my life for the past six months or year, easily."

Kurt had written "Rape Me" on an acoustic guitar at the Oakwood as they were starting to mix *Nevermind*. Although the song addresses an issue that Kurt has long felt strongly about, it has certainly taken on a new cast since the savaging he and Courtney endured. It seems to be addressed to all the journalists who assailed the couple, all the fans who bothered Kurt for his autograph, all the people who wanted to squeeze whatever they could out of Kurt and the band without thinking about the personal toll it was taking. "Yeah, it could, it definitely could," he says.

The song is perhaps the ultimate statement of resignation from someone who's been beaten so badly already that it doesn't matter anymore. "Rape me, my friend" is an invitation to a public that doesn't realize its adoration is hurting its object. "I'm not the only one," Kurt wails, meaning Courtney and Frances, too. The "Teen Spirit" reference in the opening guitar strum is no accident. Like the chorus of "In Bloom," it packs a powerfully ironic musical joke— "Teen Spirit," after all, is the song that started the whole thing.

"My favorite inside source," Kurt sings on the bridge, "Appreciate your concern/ You'll always stink and burn." The lines are a not so opaque reference to the manager of a Seattle band, who patronized Kurt about his addiction and whom the Cobains believe was a key anonymous interviewee for the *Vanity Fair* article. They even sent the manager a Christmas card last year that read, "To our favorite inside source."

Kurt says that "Milk It" is a really good example of the direction the band had been moving toward in the six months before recording. "We've been trying to write new wave songs," he says, "something that's aggressive and weird and experimental but still has... It's still not going any farther out of the boundaries than we've gone before but it's *different*. It's a really good mixture of sounding like a punk rock band yet being melodic—or at least memorable."

The song contains yet another metaphor for a co-dependent relationship, this time expressed in even more chilling terms. "I have my own pet virus," Kurt sings, his voice trembling with dread, "Her milk is my shit, my shit is her milk." The song explodes into the chorus, "Doll steak, test meat," at once nonsensical and hellish, delivered in bursts of hysterical rage.

"I just tried to use a medical theme—viruses and organisms and stuff," Kurt says of the lyrics. "Just word-play, images." But surely it's not "just word-play, images"—Kurt couldn't just sing a page out of the phone book with the same passion and conviction. "Yeah, I could," he insists. "That's practically what it is. That's what those lyrics *are*. But I think they're written cleverly enough, I like them enough to where I'm not embarrassed to sing them. In general, it's about my battle with things that piss me off. And that's the theme of the whole album—with every album I do, actually."

"Scentless Apprentice" came together during the rehearsals for the album and marks a watershed for the band. First, Dave showed Kurt the guitar riff which forms the backbone of the song. "It was such a cliché grunge Tad riff that I was reluctant to even jam on it," Kurt says frankly. "But I just decided to write a song with that just to make him feel better, to tell you the truth, and it turned out really cool." Kurt brought in the ascending hook line and Chris devised the second section and then Kurt arranged it all. It was the most collaborative song the band has ever done.

"I think most of the reason that song sounds good is because of the singing style and the guitar parts that I do over the top of the basic rhythm," Kurt says. "But hell, that was great—he came up with the beginning of the song and we worked off of that and that was really different. We've never done that before." They split the music royalties evenly.

"Scentless Apprentice" was inspired by Patrick Süskind's 1986 novel *Perfume*, about a maniacal perfume maker in pre-Revolutionary France who has no scent, yet his acute sense of smell alienates him from society. Perhaps this is a character Kurt can relate to. "Yeah, more so a few years ago," he says. "I felt like that guy a lot. I just wanted to be as far away from people as I could—their smells disgust me. The scent of human."

Although it's an identical sentiment, the hysterically screamed chorus of the song—"Go away, go away"—makes the raw wails of "Stay Away" sound mighty tame in comparison.

Kurt explains "Heart Shaped Box" by saying, "Every time I see documentaries or infomercials about little kids with cancer I just freak out. It affects me on the highest emotional level, more than anything else on television. Anytime I think about it, it makes me sadder than anything than I can think of. Whenever I see these little bald kids..." He stops and pauses for half a minute as his face reddens and his eyes well up with tears. "It's just really sad," he finally manages to say.

Kurt came up with "Heart Shaped Box" at the Spaulding apartment, where Courtney had laid out her extensive collection of heart-shaped candy boxes in the front room. Kurt has always liked heart-shaped boxes, too, but he insists they don't have too much to do with the song. "Most of the lines in it are just from [different] poems any-way," he says. "I just thought they painted a good picture, every line. But the basic idea of the song is about little kids with cancer."

He forgot about the song for a while, then picked it up again at the Hollywood Hills apartment. The band tried it out several times but nothing came of it. "I was just so tired of them relying on me to come up with everything all the time," Kurt says. "During those practices, I was trying to wait for Chris and Dave to come up with something but it just turned into noise all the time." But one day, they were jamming on some ideas when Kurt decided to give the song one last try. "I just all of a sudden wrote the whole song as we were jamming on it," he says. "I came up with the vocal style instantly and it just all flowed out real fast. We finally realized that it was a good song."

Despite Kurt's emotional description, the song seems not to be about little bald-headed kids with cancer at all. It seems to be about Courtney. "Meat-eating orchids forgive no one just yet" and "I wish I could eat your cancer when you turn black" would appear to refer to his wife's storm-cloud disposition while lines like "Throw down your umbilical noose so I can climb right back" and being "locked inside your heart-shaped box" describe an almost horrific dependency. But the biting sarcasm in the chorus shows signs of an imminent psycho-logical jailbreak—"Hey, I've got a new complaint," Kurt sings, "Forever in debt to your priceless advice."

Kurt does project—and cultivate—an air of childlike vulner-ability and naïveté which can coax others to coddle him. The K Records ethos may be an inspiration for that air, but it may also be a way of rationalizing it. The members of the band, and Kurt very much in particular, have become very dependent on others to insu-late them from the realities of their career, attracting the inevitable coterie of hangers-on from the press, radio, and other media who somehow feel charged to "protect" the band, proud of their posses-sion of closely held secrets, sure they're helping Kurt by shielding him from the cold, cruel world. Then again, Kurt has always had someone who would take care of him, from Wendy to Tracy to Chris and Dave to Courtney.

"Serve the Servants" is a typical smattering of different themes. One of them is the aftermath of Nirvanamania, beginning with the opening lines, "Teenage angst has paid off well/ Now I'm bored and old." "That's obviously the state I feel right now," Kurt says. "Not really, but I may as well make some sarcastic comment on the phenomenon of Nirvana." "Self-appointed judges judge more than they have sold"—people who criticize Kurt and the band without knowing what it's like to be in their position. The "Get Courtney" movement also makes another appearance—"If she floats then she is not a witch." The line refers to a test used to see if someone was a witch—the town wise men would weigh down the hapless suspect with rocks and throw her in a well. If she sank, she wasn't a witch. Unfortunately, she was also now dead.

"Serve the Servants" also contains a very direct and personal message to Don Cobain that will be heard from Iceland to Australia, from Los Angeles to London. "I tried hard to have a father/ but instead I had a dad/ I just want you to know that I don't hate you anymore/ There is nothing I could say that I haven't thought before." The second line is a rather cruel thing to say—that Kurt won't tell his father what he really thinks of him. The lines got put in at the last minute. "They just happened to fit really well," says Kurt.

"I just want him to know that, that I don't have anything against him anymore. But I just don't want to talk to him because I don't have anything to share with him. I'm sure that would probably really upset him, but that's just the way it is.

"But that's not what the song was originally about," Kurt says. "I mean, none of the songs are about anything when I write them. That's pretty much one of the only things that would be personally tied with me."

"The legendary divorce is such a bore," he adds at the end of the chorus. Kurt is growing tired of the well-publicized idea that his parents' divorce made a traumatic impact on his life. "It's nothing that's amazing or anything new, that's for sure," he says. "I'm a product of a spoiled America. Think of how much worse my family life could be if I grew up in a depression or something. There are so many worse things than a divorce. I've just been brooding and bellyaching about something I couldn't have, which is a family, a solid family unit, for too long. I've grown out of it now. I'm glad that I could share it with kids who have had the same experiences, but overall it's sad that if two people choose to marry and have children that they can't at least get along. It amazes me that people who think they're in love with one another can't even have enough courtesy to their children to talk to one another civilly when they see each other even once in a while when they pick the kids up from the visit. That's sad, but it's not more my story than it is anyone else's."

Kurt tended toward lengthy titles for the new songs, basically as a reaction against the way so many so-called "alternative" bands use one-word titles for song and album titles. "It's a cop-out," says the guy who named his first three albums *Bleach*, *Nevermind*, and *Incesticide*. "Ooooh, just think of the irony in this word, 'cartoon,'" he mocks. "There are so many angles on it."

Hence "Frances Farmer Will Have Her Revenge on Seattle," written in honor of the Cobains' patron martyr, many of whose persecutors remain in Seattle to this day. "In her false witness/ We hope you're still with us" is a clear message to the fans about the Hirschberg piece in *Vanity Fair*, while the next line, "To see if they float or drown," repeats the witch-test imagery in "Serve the Servants." The song ends on a note close to Kurt's heart—revenge. "She'll come back as fire/To burn all the liars/And leave a blanket of ash on the ground."

"I guess that's my way of letting the world know that bureaucracy is everywhere and it can happen to anybody and it's a really evil thing," Kurt says. "The story of Frances Farmer is so sad and it can happen to anybody and it almost felt at a time that it was happening to us, so there is a little personal part but it's mainly just exposing the Frances Farmer story to people.

"Seattle is supposedly this perfect, utopic place," says Kurt. "Judges and heads of state were part of this conspiracy to put her in a mental institution, give her a lobotomy, and she was gang raped every night she was there and she had to eat her own shit and she was branded a Communist because she wrote a poem when she was fourteen entitled 'God Is Dead.' They just fucked with her all the time. From the time she was fourteen to when she was a star, they just constantly had her arrested for no reason and totally ruined her reputation by writing right wing lies in magazines and newspapers and stuff and it turned her insane, turned her into a barbiturate addict and alcoholic and she got a lobotomy and ended up being a maid at a Four Seasons and eventually died. There are a lot of very important people in Seattle involved in that conspiracy and they're still alive today, sitting in their nice fucking houses."

Although Farmer's tale is even more dire than Kurt and Courtney's, their stories are quite similar. "I expect a lot of these titles and little lines in some of the songs to be read as totally personal," Kurt says, "but there are other angles on them, too. I would rather focus on the Frances Farmer story; it just so happens that there are similar things involved in our story."

"I miss the comfort in being sad"—Kurt is not used to happiness, a condition which he turned into a whole song in "Dumb."

Kurt wrote the main outlines of the Beatlesque "Dumb" during the summer of 1990, just before the band signed with Geffen and debuted it on Calvin Johnson's KAOS radio program that fall. "I think I'm dumb or maybe just happy," Kurt sings. "I just tried to use some confusion theme," he says. It's just interesting that being happy would prove confusing.

Although it was written long before the fact, the verse which goes "My heart is broke but I have some glue/ Help me inhale and mend it with you/ We'll float around and hang out on clouds/ Then we'll come down and have a hangover" makes for a good synopsis of his and Courtney's months in the drug wilderness; distraught after breaking up with Tobi, he sought refuge in heroin with Courtney, then paid the consequences afterward.

The eagle-eared will notice that the song's chords are similar to those of "Polly."

Kurt also wrote the anthemic "Pennyroyal Tea" in the apartment on Pear Street during the bleak winter of 1990, after the band signed. "Dave and I were screwing around on a four-track and I wrote that song in about thirty seconds," says Kurt. "And I sat down for like a half an hour and wrote the lyrics and then we recorded it."

Pennyroyal is an herb known for its medicinal properties, one of which is an abortive, but only in lethal doses. "I thought that was a cool image," says Kurt. "I've known girls who tried to drink it because they thought they were pregnant. It's a cleansing theme where I'm trying to get all my bad evil spirits out of me and drinking Pennyroyal tea would cleanse that away. You have to drink gallons of it and I heard it doesn't work very well. I've never found herbs to ever work for me—anything. Ginseng and any of that other shit is all a bunch of hippie left wing fascist propaganda."

"Very Ape" used to have the working title, "Perky New Wave Number." "I really didn't have any idea what the song is about," Kurt says. "It's kind of an attack on men in a way and people that have flaws in their personality and they're real manly and macho." The "King of Illiterature" line is probably a reference to the way Courtney chides Kurt about not being well read.

On the face of it, "Tourette's" has nothing to do with anything. "I just babbled," Kurt says. "I didn't make any sentences or any words, I just screamed." An early lyric sheet for the song merely printed the words "Fuck shit piss." But the title recalls something Kurt said about all the negative press he had been getting. "All my life, I've had a bad attitude and it does me no good to become even more of a bitter person because of stuff like this," he said. "I just don't know how I can do it. I was starting to get a good attitude again and I'd been validated as a musician and a songwriter and everything and all of a sudden I'm this massive scapegoat. I have this attitude that makes me look even more like an asshole. There's a big threat of me turning into this crazy street person. Some eighty-year-old guy with Tourette's Syndrome, cursing his head off, telling the whole world they're fucked."

The title of "Radio Friendly Unit Shifter" is obviously a reference to *Nevermind*. "A blanket acned with cigarette burns" harks back to the scene at the Spaulding apartment, while "Use just once and destroy/ Invasion of our piracy" is yet another reference to harassment by both a fickle public and a hostile, invasive press. Yet even Kurt acknowledges that the song is a throwaway. "It could have been better," he says. "I know we could have had a few better songs on the album."

Surely the confessional lyrics of "All Apologies" have some personal meaning for Kurt. "It really doesn't have any relevance at all," he says, as usual. "The song isn't about anything, really." He did dedicate the song to Frances and Courtney onstage at Reading in 1992, though. "I like to think that that song is for them, but the words really don't fit in relation to us. I wrote it for them but none of the lyrics really expose anything. The feeling does, but not the lyrics." The feeling, Kurt says, is "Peaceful, happy, comfort—just happy happiness." And the way Kurt sings "Yeah, yeah, yeah, yeah" after the second chorus, it's hard not to feel the same thing.

"I always manage to write a couple of happy songs," he says, "but then there are lots of neutral songs, too, that sound angry but really aren't anything."

So an angry sound is just a starting point, a status quo. Kurt laughs when it's suggested that his natural state is one of agitation. Not unlike the music of Dinosaur Jr's J Mascis, whose laid-back vocal persona exists against a constant backdrop of angry, teeming distortion. "That's not really a character he plays—he *is* that person," says Kurt. "God, I wish I could get away with that because I've always thought I was really close to J Mascis as a person, personality-wise—just quiet and talking with a cigarette voice, but I couldn't sing like that. I have a different side to me that's really hyperactive."

Like Mascis, Kurt appears passive, yet both control virtually every aspect of their band's music and image. It galls Kurt to realize that most people aren't conscious of this. "I just can't believe that people wouldn't listen to this music and think a little bit more highly of me than they do," he says. "I come up with every idea for everything we do, practically. Everything. It's mind-boggling and it's a lot of pressure. It just pisses me off to see on the back of the *Bleach* album, 'art direction by Lisa Orth' and everyone thinks that Lisa Orth came up with that picture and the idea and the way it was all set up. I came up with the whole idea and they get credit for it. I don't need it to ·feed my ego, I just want people to know that I can do other things than just the music."

Originally, the album was going to be called *I Hate Myself and I Want to Die*. Ever since the Australian tour, the phrase had been Kurt's standard answer whenever someone asked him how he was doing. After a few weeks, the title was ruled out. "That's pushing it too much," Chris says. "Kids would commit suicide and we'd get sued." Kurt meant the title as a joke. "I'm tired of taking this band so seriously and everyone else taking it so seriously and trying to read into things," he said. "Basically that's what all our songs are about—confusion and I hate myself and I don't want to live, so I thought it was really appropriate."

Then the title was changed to *Verse Chorus Verse*, a sarcastic comment on the standard pop song framework that Kurt says he is tiring of. "I would hate to keep rewriting this formula," Kurt says. "It's a formula. I've mastered this. It's over, as far as I'm concerned, but I know I can probably write a couple more albums like this and be happy with it, but less and less happy every time we do one. Then again, I thought that before I recorded this record and now it turned out exactly how I wanted it to and I'm really proud of it."

But by late May, the album's title had changed to *In Utero*. Kurt had noticed the phrase in some poetry that Courtney had written and decided that it fit the album art perfectly. Of course, it also fit Kurt's conception of earthly bliss. He didn't care if people thought it was too close to the embryonic imagery of the cover of their previous album. The artwork, all conceptualized by Kurt and executed by *Nevermind* designer Robert Fisher, teems with feminine imagery. The front cover features a transparent woman, the female counterpart to the "Sliver" single cover, but winged like some Greek goddess (the feminine symbols sprinkled throughout can be decoded using a book called *The Woman's Dictionary of Symbols and Sacred Objects*). For the back cover, Kurt arranged an assortment of plastic fetus models and other body parts, lilies, and orchids on a rug at his house (the photograph is by Charles Peterson). "I always thought orchids, and especially lilies, look like a vagina," Kurt says. "So it's sex and woman and *In Utero* and vaginas and birth and death."

CHAPTER FIFTEEN

Once the album was completed, the band sent unmastered tapes off to Geffen president Ed Rosenblatt and Gary Gersh, as well as their lawyer and the inner circle of Gold Mountain. Kurt's description of their feedback was succinct. "The grown-ups don't like it," he said with a mixture of disappointment and disbelief. In fact, "the grown-ups"—management and senior label execs—*hated* it. Kurt says they told him the songwriting was "not up to par," the sound "unlistenable." There also seemed to be uncertainty whether mainstream radio would go for the Steve Albini sound.

"As it turns out," says Albini, "the record company would much rather they made an indulgent rock star album because then they'd have something to promote. And the band would be broke and the more broke the band is, the better it is for the record company, because then they can pull the strings more."

It turned out that few people at Gold Mountain or Geffen really wanted the band to record with Albini to begin with, although the band was free to have their way. Faced with the disapproval of virtually everyone involved in Nirvana's career, Kurt thought he was getting an unstated message: scrap the album and start all over again—there was still plenty of time and the Albini sessions hadn't cost all that much, considering they were following up a quadruple-platinum album.

"I should just rerecord this record," Kurt sneers, "and do the same thing we did last year because we sold out last year—there's no reason to try to redeem ourselves as artists at this point. I can't help myself—I'm just putting out a record that I would like to listen to at home. I never listen to *Nevermind*. I haven't listened to it since we put it out. That says something. I can't stand that kind of production and I don't listen to bands that do have that kind of production, no matter how good their songs are. It just bothers me."

Friends of the band loved the record, however. As of early April, the band was determined to release the record as it was and damn the torpedoes—DGC would put the record out. "They're going to eat my shit," Kurt says. "Of course, they want another *Nevermind*, but I'd rather die than do that. This is exactly the kind of record I would buy as a fan, that I would enjoy owning. I couldn't be truer to myself than to put this out the way it is. It's my favorite production and my favorite songs."

But even right after returning from Minnesota—and before anyone else had heard the tracks—Kurt and Chris were beginning to worry about the bass sound, which they felt was too mushy and not musical enough, and the vocals, which were too low in the mix, the latter a common complaint leveled at Albini's productions. Still, those reservations took a backseat to their resolve to release an unvarnished, straightforwardly recorded album.

In hindsight, it's obvious that *Nevermind* was a strong rightward swing of the band's artistic pendulum toward pop, while *In Utero* leans more heavily on the arty, aggressive side which was showcased on *Incesticide*. "There's always been songs like 'About a Girl' and there's always been songs like 'Paper Cuts,'" Chris says.

"*Nevermind* came out kind of 'About a Girl'-y and this one came out more 'Paper Cuts.' It's an artistic thing. The label's all freaked out about it. It's like, 'Shit, it's *art*—what are you going to do about it?'"

The record called the bluff of all the music biz pundits who hailed the triumph of "real music" over the processed pop that Nirvana had trounced. One or two of those pundits worked with Nirvana; *In Utero* forced them to put their money where their mouths were. "The thing about *Nevermind* was it just flew out the window," Chris says, "and now nobody can predict anything in the music industry anymore. They say there was a pre-Nirvana music industry and a post-Nirvana music industry, so we'll see how post-Nirvana the music industry really is."

The band was prepared not to match the gargantuan sales of *Nevermind*—although *In Utero* was really *good*, it was not necessarily really *commercial*. "I expect this record will sell maybe half as much," Kurt predicts. "We've offended too many people within the last year." Dave doesn't think the album will do as well either, not that he even wants it to. "Not at all," he says. "I kind of think of it sometimes as a test. We're testing the limits. A record like *Nevermind* came along and it blew things apart and it changed a lot of stuff. By doing this, maybe the next big hit could be on an eight-track. A band from out of nowhere could have an eight-track recording of a great song and it will be on the radio. The Beatles and the Rolling Stones did it."

In a sense, the band could afford to take a chance—since nobody knew exactly why the last album took off, how could anybody second-guess this one? Besides, Nirvana would likely take a pounding no matter what they did.

"It's the sophomore jinx—everybody's just waiting for us to fuck up," says Dave. "Everybody's waiting to tear this to shreds and say, 'The one-hit wonder.' I *know* that it's a good record. I know that people who like Nirvana will like this record. The seventy-five thousand people that were into Nirvana before *Nevermind* I think will like the record maybe even *more* than *Nevermind*."

So this isn't "career suicide." "No, although it will be thought of as that," Kurt says. "The album that brought them down to the gutter."

"These are the songs we came up with," says Chris. "If you don't make a raw album, you make another slick album and then people say, 'Oh, they just made a slick album so they can sell more records.' You can't win for losing. Let them say what they will—I did it my way.

"I told Kurt, 'If this record bombs and it doesn't do anything, there's still all those years we spent in the van and all the good times we had—we were happy back then and nobody can take that away from us,'" Chris says. "The music speaks for itself, we put out good records. So what if we have to play fifteen-hundred-seaters. So what if Pearl Jam and Stone Temple Pilots keep going to all the music awards shows—we were never into that shit in the first place."

Albini had been impressed that Kurt, Chris, and Dave wanted to try to forge new creative ground instead of making a record that was just a retread of the successful ideas of their last record. "Frankly, that's all the record company wanted or expected, and to date, that's what they *still* want," Albini claimed a month or so after the album was completed. "What they don't understand is that it represents the band more accurately and it is more faithful to the band's vision of their record than a record made any other way would be.

"You could put that band in the studio for a year and I don't think they could come up with a better record," Albini continues. "I think that's as good as they're going to be. If that doesn't suit their record company then their record company clearly has problems that go beyond this record. The record company has a problem with the band. The sooner everybody involved recognizes that, the easier it will be on everybody."

"The people at the record company are clearly geniuses, right?" says Albini. "They put out Nelson—they know what they're doing. This is the record company that sued Neil Young for not being commercial enough. Those are the people that are telling the band they don't know what they're doing. If you have to rely on people like that as your barometer of quality, then you're in a lot more trouble than just having a bad record. It means you're a fool."

"Literally, every other person involved in the enterprise that is Nirvana, besides the band itself, are pure pieces of shit," Albini rails. "Their management company, their record company, the A&R people, all the hangers-on, all the phonies that cling to that band as a bogus source of hipster credentials, everyone associated with the band—other than the band—I think are pieces of shit and I have no time for them.

"You know, after all this, I would be willing to do another Nirvana record," Albini said shortly after finishing the record. He would soon change his tune. "I enjoyed dealing with the guys, but I would not be willing to deal with their superstructure anymore— their management company or their record company."

* * *

On March 23 came good news. After months of legal battles, it was finally decided that none of the allegations made against Kurt and Courtney in Family Court were legally valid. The Cobains had already won legal custody of their daughter, but now, the Department of Children's Services would not supervise Kurt and Courtney's care of Frances any longer—no more humiliating urine tests, no more checkup visits from social workers, no more costly legal fights. The nightmare was over.

On April 9, the band raised over fifty thousand dollars at a benefit at the Cow Palace in San Francisco for the Tresnjevka Woman's Group, an organization based in the Croatian city of Zagreb that assists rape survivors. As part of the vicious campaign of "ethnic cleansing," Serbian soldiers had been systematically raping Muslim women so that they would eventually have Serbian babies. The victims are often mutilated, their children murdered right in front of them.

The benefit was Chris's idea. "I was really pissed off by everything I'd been reading and nobody was doing anything about it," he says. After some initial encouragement from Courtney, he started putting together the show, which also featured the Disposable Heroes of Hiphoprisy, the Breeders, and L7.

Chris also helped lead protests against Washington State House Bill 2554, better known as the "Erotic Music Bill," which would jail record store owners for selling music that was judged "erotic" and therefore somehow damaging to minors. Back in December of 1991, Chris led a march and petition drive at the state capitol building in Olympia. MTV News and *Rolling Stone* picked up the story and the governor's office was inundated with letters from people who opposed the bill. But Governor Booth Gardner, who only recently had boasted in his 1992 State of the State address that he was "the governor of the home state of Nirvana, the hottest new rock band in the country," signed the bill into law.

It was repealed, although its sponsor is vowing to submit a modified version of the bill.

"There's a lot of rap music and rock music for that matter, Andrew Dice Clay, that's just fuckin' bullshit, it's just sexist crap," Chris says, "but you have to tolerate it. You have to tolerate hate groups, too, because that's the price of freedom of speech—you place your ideals above your feelings. I can't make the Ku Klux Klan illegal because I don't like it—I can't do that because they have the right to believe what they want."

Even though he's known as "the political one," Chris doesn't exactly relish the tag. "I want to depoliticize myself—I just don't want to be this rock and roll pundit," he says. "I don't want Nirvana to be a political band—we're a rock band and I'm a bass player. I just happen to be politically active."

Despite the band's determination to release the record exactly as it was, blemishes and all, they began to have serious doubts about it around the time of the benefit show in San Francisco. There was even some talk of going back into the studio and recording a couple of new songs, just to see what they would sound like. By late April, Kurt's enthusiasm for the album had plummeted drastically. "I don't know what it is, but it doesn't make me as emotional as it does listening to *Nevermind*," he said of the new album. "When I listen to *Nevermind*, I hate the production, but there's something about it that almost makes me cry at times. With this record, I'm just deadpan."

The hope was that the album could be saved in the mastering process, when a last wave of the electronic wand can often subtly transform a record. After working with mastering wizard Bob Ludwig at his studio in Portland, Maine, Chris was satisfied with the results, but Kurt still wasn't sure. It wasn't *perfect*. Of course, that was part of the deal—you record *and* mix in two weeks with Steve Albini and you don't get pristine pop perfection, you get a raw, honest, warts-and-all rock record. It seemed that Kurt was in love with the *idea* of the low-budget philosophy, but not its actuality. Once again, his pop soul was at war with his rock sensibility.

Then a brief story in the *Chicago Tribune* quoted Steve Albini as predicting that Geffen/DGC was going to reject the Nirvana album. An item in the influential *Village Voice* soon picked up on the story.

The story snowballed, gaining a media momentum all its own. A full-page piece in *Newsweek* further sensationalized the issue. The piece quoted unnamed sources, one of whom claimed to have heard the album but instead had merely heard some demos the band had recorded with Craig Montgomery during the Brazil trip. Writer Jeff Giles quoted Jonathan Poneman as saying that Geffen was "guilty of a complete lack of faith and respect for Kurt, Dave [Grohl], and Chris [Novoselic] as artists," yet Poneman says Giles left out a key qualifier just before that statement, along the lines of "If what I hear is true, then..." In a letter to *Newsweek*, the band claimed Giles got quotes by saying he was merely writing a piece about Albini, not Nirvana.

"Most damaging to us is that Giles ridiculed our relationship with our label based on totally erroneous information," read the letter, which the band also reprinted in a costly full-page ad in *Billboard*. In a press release, Ed Rosenblatt vowed Geffen/DGC would release anything the band submitted, and, in a highly unusual move, David Geffen himself blew in an irate phone call to the magazine.

Stories in *Rolling Stone* and *Entertainment Weekly* soon followed as the controversy ballooned even more.

The truth of the matter was, the band had legitimately disliked some aspects of the Albini recordings from the start and had wanted to fix them; that their management and label wholeheartedly agreed made the band appear to be spineless pushovers and their associates to seem like greedy bullies (which is not to say that both Gold Mountain and Geffen/DGC weren't relieved when some changes were eventually made). The combination of Nirvana's clout with Geffen and the creative control built into their contract ensured that they could put out whatever record they wanted to, regardless of what anyone else thought.

The whole controversy, ignited by Albini's single broadside, was a by-product of sloppy, herd-mentality journalism. The one writer who got anywhere close to the truth of the matter was Jim DeRogatis of the *Chicago Sun-Times*. The headline to his story read "Flap Over Nirvana LP Smells Like Bogus Issue." In the piece, even Steve Albini conceded that he didn't *really* know what was going on with the album and that he had been speaking "largely out of ignorance."

Albini, it appeared, was also trying to have his cake and eat it, too—producing a major-label record for $100,000 and then disavowing the whole experience, thereby silencing cries of sell-out. This wasn't the first time he had done it, either. Albini had used similar tactics after doing major-label productions—or rather, *recordings*—for the Pixies and the Breeders. And no one pointed out that those avatars of indie credibility, Fugazi, had themselves rejected some recordings they made with Albini shortly before the *In Utero* sessions. Nobody had called *them* corporate stooges.

The band wanted to do some more work on a few songs, perhaps with R.E.M. producer Scott Litt, and remix at least a couple of tracks with, of all people, Andy Wallace. Albini vehemently rejected those ideas. He claimed he had a contract with the band that they could not remix or otherwise modify the album without his involvement. The fact that the band had not actually signed the agreement was immaterial, Albini claimed, since they had been proceeding with the project with that understanding. When Gold Mountain requested the master tapes, Albini at first refused to send them, then eventually changed his mind after a phone call from Chris. At the last minute, the band decided against working with Andy Wallace and instead decided to remix and augment "Heart Shaped Box" and "All Apologies" with Litt.

In early May, Litt and the band worked at Bad Animals Studios (owned by the Wilson sisters of Heart) in Seattle and remixed the two songs, with Kurt adding acoustic guitar and Lennonesque backing harmonies to "Heart Shaped Box." The rest of the album was left as is, although by remastering, they managed to sharpen up the bass and boost the vocals by some 3 dB's. So much for the Big Sellout.

Now that they all live in the same town, band morale is at an all-time high. Kurt, Chris, and Dave visit each other at home and hang out and listen to music, just like the old days. Late in March, while Courtney was on a quick English tour with Hole, they all met at Kurt's house to look at archival footage for a long-form video and to shoot a video for "Sliver" with director Kevin Kerslake.

For the "Sliver" video, Kurt dragged out several years' worth of dolls and knickknacks from a storage space that hadn't been opened since before recording *Nevermind*, then set it all up in his garage so that it looked just like his old apartment back in Olympia. The band set up and rocked out, with Frances in a chair by her father's side. Kerslake manned the Super 8 camera while standing on a chair for the adult's-eye-view effect. Later, Kurt cut some armholes in a big piece of cardboard, placed Frances in front of it and put his arms through it, holding her up so it looks like she's standing up on her own, dancing like a go-go girl.

MTV accepted the video in mid May, but, because of its rules about product placement, required that the band cut out a few frames of footage that featured a collage of the logos of *Maximumrocknroll* and *Better Homes and Gardens* magazines. Unfortunately, those frames also contained a little message Kurt had written: "INDIE PUNX STILL SUCKS."

The "Sliver" video showed the band in peak playful form, but even if spirits are high, the question remains as to whether the band will be a lasting proposition or just another flash in the pan. Internally, there are still many possible flashpoints: Kurt's desire to play with other people, the limitations he sees in Chris's and Dave's playing, Dave's alienation from the band, the Courtney factor. Break-up rumors have long dogged the band; although it's getting to be like the boy who cried wolf, Kurt is always threatening to quit.

"I know we're going to put out another record after this one," Chris says. "We'll play it by ear. I don't think we're going to go on and on. I think when the consensus is like 'yeah, this thing's pretty much reached its course,' I think we're going to know. But I know now that it's not over. And I never did during that whole pissed-off time. It's just going to come naturally. We're all going to get the hit, like yeah, this is it. Maybe we'll take a sabbatical that will never end, I don't know. We've put out four albums—four albums is a pretty good stretch for a band. How many bands put out four good albums without going on to be the Scorpions or Rolling Stones or whatever?"

It's strange to ponder the possibility of the band lasting out the decade. "I don't want it to, but it might," Kurt says. "It all depends on how the songs are. I was surprised to find us working together as such a unit lately." But Kurt isn't sure how much more the three of them can accomplish musically. "I would love to be able to play with other people and create something new," he says. "I'd rather do that than stay in Nirvana. I don't want to keep rewriting this style of music, I want to start doing something really different."

But there's the question of whether Chris and Dave can keep up with him. "I don't know," Kurt says. "I really don't know." Kurt thinks that Chris doesn't practice enough and that Dave isn't an imaginative enough player. Yet they have always come up with good touches that really complete a song—Kurt loves the bass line Chris dreamed up for "Heart Shaped Box"—but Kurt now wants the collaboration to take place earlier in the songwriting process. "I get really frustrated sometimes when we're trying to write a song because I'll sit there and play a riff for a long time and just listen for Chris and Dave to try to come up with something else to help change the song or go into another part and they've hardly ever done that," Kurt says. "They don't take the lead and they're always kind of following."

Of course, for the longest time, that's exactly what Kurt wanted, and Chris and Dave were more than willing to oblige. Now, Kurt waits for the other two to take the initiative without letting them know that's what he wants. But someone with that kind of imagination would almost have to be a songwriter himself. Dave writes fine songs on his own, but there's only so much a drummer can do. "Chris could be a songwriter if he actually wanted to," Kurt says. "If he had been working on his songwriting for the last few years, he'd probably be up to the level right now where he could help write half of a song for every riff that I come up with and it would be really great."

Then again, all the best bands are dictatorships. "Yeah, that's true," Kurt says. "But I would love to find people that could write songs and write them with them. That's why it's so easy to play songs with Courtney—every time we jam on something, we write a great song. It's weird. Because she's a person who takes command and isn't afraid to be the leader. And when you've got two leaders together, it takes a lot of pressure off both people. I've always wanted to have another person in the band that could write songs with me." Hence the occasional mutterings from Kurt's direction that he might start a band with Mudhoney's Mark Arm or Mark Lanegan from the Screaming Trees.

"I know we won't break up within this year," Kurt says. "I guess I just have to take it one year at a time."

In the *Rolling Stone* piece back in April of 1992, Kurt predicted very accurately what the next album would sound like—"It'll be more raw with some songs and more candy pop on some of the others," he said. "It won't be as one-dimensional." So what might the album after *In Utero* sound like? Kurt thinks it will be an extension of the ideas in "Milk It" and "Scentless Apprentice." "I definitely don't want to write more songs like 'Pennyroyal Tea' and 'Rape Me,'" he says. "That kind of classic rock and roll verse-chorus-verse, mid-tempo pop song is getting real boring. I want to do more new wave, avant garde stuff with a lot of dynamics—stops and breaks and maybe even some samples of weird noises and things—not samples of instruments. I want to turn into the Butthole Surfers, basically."

Of course, the Butthole Surfers have already done the Butthole Surfers quite successfully. "Yeah," Kurt says, "but it would be our version of it. We won't be able to escape the pop sensibility that we have. It's ingrained in our marrow—we'll never be able to get rid of melody and singing, so I want to try to take a pop song and extend it and have weird mood swings in the middle of the song, where it doesn't just follow this typical rock and roll formula. I'm tired of it."

Kurt doubts the band will have any lasting influence, say, twenty years from now. "Fuck no," he says. "It's sad to think what the state of rock and roll will be in twenty years. It's already so rehashed and so plagiarized that it's barely alive now. It's disgusting. I don't think it will be important any more.

"It's just mathematics, that's all rock and roll is," Kurt says. "Everything's based on ten. There's no such thing as infinity—it repeats itself after ten and it's over. It's the same thing with rock and roll—the neck is that long on a guitar, there are six strings, there's twelve notes, and then it repeats. It can only go to a certain point and it got to that point ten years ago. And there will be another band just like the Black Crowes twenty years from now, doing a version of the Black Crowes doing a version of the Faces."

"It starts getting watered down every five years," Kurt observes. "Kids don't even care about rock and roll as much as they used to, as the other generations have. It's already turned into nothing but a fashion statement and an identity for kids to use as a tool for them to fuck and have a social life. At that point, I can't really see music as having any importance to a teenager, really."

Of course, many people are quite content with the notion of rock and roll as nothing but a social and sexual soundtrack, but Kurt thinks it will eventually be superseded. "I think they'll use sounds and tones and use it in their virtual reality machine and just listen to it that way and get the same emotions from it and then go to a party —there will be a virtual reality machine there with a whole bunch of headphones and if you want to talk to people and listen to the virtual reality machine you can do that or you can go into the bedroom and fuck and drink, but actually I think virtual reality machines will get you high. Technology will be that good. And then there will virtual reality junkies and you'll find them dead on their couch from OD'ing."

By now, a lot of musicians might be pondering solo albums. Chris, who also happens to play some wicked guitar and banjo, says he'd like to do one some day, except he'd issue it on a ten-inch record only. He says he's already got some material—a surf song, some beat poetry. "It's going to be heavy humor," he says.

Dave says he'd like to play guitar and sing in a band some day. "Drums get kind of boring after a while," he admits. He's been quietly piling up material at Laundry Room Studios, playing all the instruments himself. First, he lays down the drum part without any other accompaniment, then adds bass, guitar, and vocals. One of the outtakes from *In Utero* was a touching, indelible song Dave wrote called "Marigold," and there's more where that came from.

"No," Kurt says, "I thought about recording stuff on a four-track and releasing it, but I wouldn't release it as a Kurt Cobain solo thing —I'd make up a name for it and try to be as anonymous as possible. I really like the idea of low-fi recordings and to throw out something that hasn't been worked on as feverishly as I would a Nirvana project."

Kurt says he's going to start his own label and call it Exploitation Records. "I'm just going to record street bums and retarded people and people with deformities and mental deficiencies," he says, "and I'm going to have a picture of that person on the front of the album

and it's going to be a low-fi recording and it's just going to be for nov-
elty reasons, for collector geeks to buy for twenty dollars apiece. I'm
not really exploiting the people on the records, I'm exploiting the
people who buy them, because there's going to be a twenty-dollar
price tag on all of them. There will be a limited edition of five hundred of the Singing Flipper Boy."

Every label needs a distributor and Exploitation Records will be
distributed through one Kurt Cobain. He says he'll simply take a box
of records along with him on tour and sell them to record stores at
every stop along the way.

Kurt also says he wants to rerelease all of Nirvana's releases on
vinyl, except remastered by recording the sound from boom box
speakers so it sounds just like a low-fi punk rock record or a bootleg,
with appropriate cover art. "It's just for my own punk rock fantasy
of thinking that maybe if *Nevermind* came out this way, it would
sound better," he says. "It would only be for me to have a box of
them."

The way Kurt looks at it, Exploitation Records might turn out to
be a much-needed source of income. "It's too bad because I spent
almost all the money I made off *Nevermind* fighting for my child
because of the insane rumors created by the media and now I don't
have anything to live off of for the rest of my life," Kurt says. "If this
record doesn't sell—you have to sell eight million records to make a
million dollars and the average middle American family makes more
than a million dollars in a lifetime—I'm not going to be set for life.
I'm going to have to get a job in ten years."

SUB POP

"Love Buzz" b/w "Big Cheese" single.
November 1988. SP 23
Limited edition of 1,000 hand-numbered copies.

"Spank Thru" on *Sub Pop 200* compilation
album. December 1988. SP 25

Bleach. June 1989. SP 34
First 1,000 copies on white vinyl. Next 2,000
contain special poster.
Remastered in April 1992 for CD and cassette.
CD version contains "Downer" as bonus track.

"Sliver" b/w "Dive" single. September 1990.
SP 73
First 3,000 seven-inch singles on blue vinyl.
CD single includes live versions of "About a
Girl" and "Spank Thru."

Split single "Molly's Lips" b/w "Candy" by the
Fluid. Sub Pop Singles Club #27
Limited edition of 7,500 copies. First 4,000 on
green vinyl.

TUPELO

Blew EP. December 1989. TUP 8

GEFFEN/DGC

"Smells Like Teen Spirit" b/w "Even in His
Youth" and "Aneurysm." September 10, 1991.
DGC 21673

Nevermind. September 24, 1991. DGC 24425
First 50,000 CD copies do not include untitled
bonus track.

"Come as You Are" March 3, 1992. DGC 21707
b/w "School" and "Drain You" recorded live at
the Paramount Theater, October 31, 1991.

"Lithium" b/w "Been a Son" (live) and
"Curmudgeon." July 21, 1992.
DGCDM 21815
CD single includes complete lyrics to
Nevermind.

Incesticide. December 15, 1992. DGC 24504

In Utero. September 14, 1993. DGC 24607

TOUCH AND GO

Split single "Oh, the Guilt" b/w "Puss" by the
Jesus Lizard. February 22, 1993. TG83
CD, cassette, single. Limited to 200,000 copies
worldwide.

COMMUNION RECORDS

Split single: a cover of the Velvet
Underground's "Here She Comes Now" b/w
"Venus in Furs" by the Melvins. 1991.
Communion 23. Limited edition of 1,000 seven-
inch singles.
Also available on *Heaven and Hell, Vol. I*, a
Velvet Underground tribute album. 1991.
Communion 20. Out of print. All three for-
mats.

C/Z

"Mexican Seafood" on *Teriyaki Asthma Vol. I*.
November 1989. CZ 009
Seven-inch limited edition of 1,000.
Also available on the CD compilation *Teriyaki
Asthma Vol. I-V*.
Compilation also features Babes in Toyland
and L7, among others.
November 1991. CZ037

"Do You Love Me" on Kiss tribute album *Hard
to Believe*. Features the only recorded appearance of Jason Everman with Nirvana. August
1990. CZ024

KILL ROCK STARS

"Beeswax" on *Kill Rock Stars* compilation.
August 21, 1991. KRS 201
Compilation also features Melvins, Bikini Kill,
Mecca Normal, Nation of Ulysses. Limited edi-
tion numbered set of 1,000 features hand-
screened cover signed by artist.

TIM KERR RECORDS

"Return of the Rat" on *Eight Songs for Greg
Sage and the Wipers*. June 20, 1992. T/K
917010 TRIB 2
Four seven-inch record set also features Hole.
Limited edition of 10,000 (6,000 colored vinyl).
CD release on March 15, 1993, features six
extra tracks including track by Thurston
Moore.

INDIVIDUAL NIRVANA MEMBERS ON RECORD

K RECORDS

Kurt appears on "Bikini Twilight" by the Go
Team (Calvin Johnson and Tobi Vail). July
1989. Go Team single.

SUB POP

Kurt appears on the Earth EP *Bureaucratic
Desire for Revenge*. October 1991. SP 123

Kurt and Chris appear on "Where Did You Sleep Last Night" on the Mark Lanegan solo album, *The Winding Sheet*. May 1990. SP61 First 1,000 copies on red vinyl. CD and cassette have extra track.

RAS
Dave appears on the Scream album *No More Censorship*. August 1988. RAS 4001

DISCHORD
Dave appears on the previously unreleased Scream album *Fumble*. July 1993. Dischord 83

YOUR CHOICE LIVE SERIES
Dave appears on a self-titled Scream live album. YC-LS 010
(German import only)

KONKURREL
Dave appears on the Scream album *Live at Van Hall*. 1989. K001/113

DSI
Dave appears on the Scream single "Mardi Gras" b/w "Land Torn Down." 1990. DSI 16 Both tracks also appear on *Fumble*.

BONER
Dave, as "Dale Nixon," plays bass, drums, and guitar on *King Buzzo*, a Buzz Osborne solo album.

TIM KERR RECORDS
Kurt plays noise guitar on "The Priest, They Called Him," a spoken-word piece by William S. Burroughs. Summer 1993. T/K 9210044/92CD044
Available on ten-inch vinyl EP and CD single. Chris appears on the cover in a priest's outfit.

NIRVANA U.K. DISCOGRAPHY

SUB POP
Import only.

TUPELO
"Spank Thru" on *Sub Pop 200* compilation album. December 1988. Vinyl only. Rereleased on CD 1990.

Bleach. June 1989. UK release has "Love Buzz" instead of "Big Cheese." Rereleased on CD on Geffen in April 1992 with "Big Cheese" and "Downer" as bonus tracks.

"Sliver" b/w "Dive" single. January 1991.

Blew EP. December 1989.

GEFFEN/DGC
"Smells Like Teen Spirit" b/w "Even in His Youth" and "Aneurysm." September 9, 1991. DGCS5.

Nevermind. September 23, 1991. DGC 24425.

"Come as You Are" b/w "School" and "Drain You" (live). March 2, 1992. DGCS7.

"Lithium" b/w "Been a Son" (live) and "Curmudgeon." July 20, 1992. DGCS9.

"In Bloom" b/w "Sliver" and "Polly" (live). November 30, 1992. GEF34. Picture disc and CD. Seven-inch version b/w "Polly" (live) only.

Incesticide. December 14, 1992. GEF 24504.

In Utero. September 13, 1993. GEF 24536.

TOUCH AND GO
Split single "Oh, the Guilt" b/w "Puss" by the Jesus Lizard. February 22, 1993. TG 83 CD, limited edition blue vinyl single.

COMMUNION RECORDS
Import only.

C/Z
Import only.

KILL ROCK STARS
Import only.

TIM KERR RECORDS
Import only.

INDIVIDUAL NIRVANA MEMBERS ON RECORD
All records mentioned in U.S. Discography import only.